INTERGOVERNMENTAL FISCAL TRANSFERS IN ASIA
Current Practice and Challenges for the Future

Edited by

Paul Smoke
Yun-Hwan Kim

Asian Development Bank

December 2002

First published December 2002

This publication was prepared by Asian Development Bank staff. The findings, interpretations, and conclusions expressed in it do not necessarily represent the views of ADB or those of its member governments. ADB does not guarantee the accuracy of the data included in this publication and accepts no responsibility whatsoever for any consequences of their use.

ISBN No. 971-561-452-3
Publication Stock No. 050102

Published by the Asian Development Bank
P. O. Box 789, 0980 Manila, Philippines

Foreword

In recent years, the issue of intergovernmental fiscal transfers has received increasing attention among policymakers for various reasons. These include (i) disparity in delivery of social services between regions, (ii) economic gap between growth centers and lagging areas, and (iii) progress in economic and political decentralization. While strengthening institutions, functions, and finances of state/local governments is becoming increasingly important, developing a more productive and equitable intergovernmental transfer scheme has likewise become a priority issue. The issue of allocating national resources to local communities has been a major policy agenda as subnational governments play a stronger role in carrying out socioeconomic policies.

For a long time, the governments in the Asia-Pacific region have made enormous efforts to minimize distortions and defects in the countries' fiscal transfer schemes. However, existing disparities in production growth, fiscal bases, and the extent of public services call for greater governmental interventions including a reform in central-state fiscal relations. An expeditious reform aimed at addressing the underlying fiscal and economic imbalances and ensuring equitable delivery of public services across states would place powerful impetus to the long-term socioeconomic progress.

The new focus on the greater fiscal role by local governments has been supported by international development agencies including ADB. ADB has stepped up its assistance for regional development projects in relation to increasing economic and political decentralization in its member countries. At present, fiscal strengths of subnational governments are assuming even greater importance in the operations of ADB as it places the emphasis of its operations on poverty reduction and the participation of local stakeholders, including local communities and low-level governments, in its projects and programs.

This operational shift has been strengthened by a significant increase in loans and technical assistance to address poverty, education, health, regional development, and environment. All of these require sound backup of fiscal resources, covering both capital and recurrent expenditures, from subnational governments as well as their enhanced institutional capacity.

Against this backdrop, ADB has undertaken cross-country comparative research to assess intergovernmental fiscal transfers. It included three country studies on India, Pakistan and the Philippines and a more general study on broad international experiences. The research has examined pertinent theories, international experiences, and evolution of fiscal equalization arrangements between the central governments and provincial or state governments, as well as the underlying rationale, problems and issues in those countries. A Conference on Intergovernmental Fiscal Transfers for Equitable In-Country Growth, which was held in September 2001 through the support and generosity of the National Institute of Public Finance and Policy (NIPFP) in New Delhi, India, discussed draft versions of these four reports and received many valuable comments. The book brings together all these reports that were commissioned by ADB as well as two more reports on Cambodia and Indonesia which the authors have kindly contributed.

The study is expected to reinforce ADB's ongoing efforts to formulate better country assistance programs and provide critical inputs to public sector reform programs in Asian developing countries.

Ifzal Ali
Chief Economist
Economics and Research Department
Asian Development Bank

Acknowledgement

We are deeply grateful to all paper writers including Nuzhat Ahmad, Joseph Capuno, Blane Lewis, Leonardo Romeo, Larry Schroeder, Paul Smoke, D.K. Srivastava and Syed Ashraf Wasti and to Yun-Hwan Kim who initiated and managed this study. We are likewise indebted to the valuable contributions of David Mammen of the Institute of Public Administration at the Robert F. Wagner Graduate School of Public Service at New York University. We also thank Maria Blanco of the Institute for her careful review and editing of the manuscripts. Special thanks are extended to Jungsoo Lee, Gunter Hecker, M.G. Quibria, Brahm Prakash and Jean-Pierre Verbiest of Asian Development Bank (ADB) who provided support and encouragement. We thank the National Institute of Public Finance and Policy (NIPFP) in New Delhi, India and its Director, Ashok Lahiri, for collaborating with ADB in the conference to discuss all papers included in this book. We are also grateful to all participants in the conference, including K.C. Pant, Deputy Chairman, and N.J. Kurian, Advisor, Planning Commission, Government of India; R.J. Chelliah, Amaresh Bagchi and Om Prakash Mathur, Professors, NIPFP; and J.L. Bajaj, Chairman, UPSERC, Lucknow. We likewise thank Frank Polman, former Country Director for ADB's India Resident Mission, who graced the opening of the conference. Special acknowledgement goes to the project staff, Sally Mabaquiao, Pat Baysa, Ludy Pardo and Jennifer Simon for overseeing the production of the book. We appreciate the contributions of Ma. Priscila del Rosario who proofread the entire manuscript. Lastly, we gratefully recognize all the efforts and contributions of those who, one way or another, provided assistance in making this technical assistance project meet its fruition.

Table of Contents

List of Abbreviations

ACA	additional central assistance
BFA	balancing factor amount
CDC	Commune Development Committee
CDD	centrally directed discipline
CDF	Countrywide Development Fund
CF	Calamity Fund
CHCA	Comprehensive Health Care Agreement
COA	Commission on Audit
CODEF	cost of devolved functions
CSF	Commune/Sangkat Fund
CSO	Civil Society Organization
DAK	*Dana Alokasi Khusus* (Special Allocation Fund)
DAU	*Dana Alokasi Umum* (General Allocation Fund)
DECS	Department of Education, Culture and Sports
DILG	Department of Interior and Local Government
DOH	Department of Health
DOLA	Department of Local Administration
DPWH	Department of Public Works and Highways
EFC	Eleventh Finance Commission
FA	formula amount
FC	Finance Commission
GCS	general category states
GSDP	gross state domestic product
GRP	gross regional product
HIS	high-income states
INPRES	*Instruksi Presiden* (Grants by Presidential Instruction)
IRA	Internal Revenue Allotment
LDF	Local Development Fund
LGC	Local Government Code
LGEF	Local Government Empowerment Fund
LGU	local government unit
LIS	low-income states
LPP	Local Planning Process
LSA	lump-sum amount
MBD	market-based discipline
MDF	Municipal Development Fund
MMDA	Metropolitan Manila Development Authority

MOEF	Ministry of Economy and Finance
MOI	Ministry of Interior
MTPDP	Medium-Term Philippine Development Plan
NALGU	National Assistance to Local Governments
NCSC	National Committee to Support the Communes
NFC	National Finance Commission
ODA	Official Development Assistance
PSDP	Public Sector Development Program
RTS	representative tax system
SCS	special category states
SDF	standard distance formula
SDO	*Subsidi Daerah Otonom* (Regional Autonomy Subsidy)
SFC	State Finance Commission
SFRF	States Fiscal Reform Facility
SRA	Social Reform Agenda
STA	Specific Tax Allotment
TFC	Tenth Finance Commission

List of Charts

Others

1

The Role and Challenges of Intergovernmental Fiscal Transfers in Asia

Yun-Hwan Kim, Asian Development Bank, and Paul Smoke, New York University

A. Introduction

Intergovernmental fiscal transfers are an important tool of public sector finance in both industrialized and developing countries for three principal reasons. First, central governments have advantages over subnational governments in raising revenue from many types of particularly productive sources, while subnational governments have advantages in providing many types of public services. This reality invariably results in a mismatch between the costs of expenditures that subnational governments are expected to undertake and the resources locally available to them.

Second, there are often substantial disparities in revenue-raising capacity across decentralized levels of government. If subnational governments were left to rely exclusively on their own resources, wealthier jurisdictions would be able to spend more on public services than lower-income jurisdictions. Such a situation has not only equity implications but efficiency implications as well. If decentralized governments are responsible for infrastructure and services that are essential production inputs, areas with lower resource levels may be unable to support local economic development.

Third, resources from the central level can be used to ensure that basic national priorities will be met in all subnational jurisdictions. Typical priority sectors include health and education, but often extend to roads, water, and other services. Providing these services may promote both efficiency (if externalities are involved) and equity, and also support poverty reduction efforts.

Asian Development Bank (ADB), like other international development agencies, has been focusing more attention on supporting the reform of local government finance in recent years. This has occurred as part of a broader paradigm shift in which the public sector is being decentralized and subnational governments have growing resource requirements. The decentralization trend is based on a belief that the participation of a variety of key local stakeholders, including subnational governments and local communities, is critical to realize development and poverty reduction goals. There has also been a growing recognition of the need for broader partnerships among the various levels of the public sector, the private sector, civil society, and international development agencies in promoting more equitable and sustainable development.

The developing Asia and Pacific region as a whole has achieved unprecedented sustained growth and development in the past three decades, with many countries rebounding from the serious economic crisis in 1997. Nevertheless, almost two-thirds of the world's poor live in this region. The vast majority live in the People's Republic of China and India, but poverty incidence remains high throughout the region, especially in low-income countries. In South Asia, poverty rates declined moderately during the 1990s, but the actual numbers of poor have increased. The Asia and Pacific region is thus central to the fight against global poverty, to which ADB is firmly committed.

ADB believes that the countries of the region need to address the challenges of equitable growth in a systematic manner.[1] Building and upgrading physical and social infrastructure are considered a primary condition for robust sustained growth. Large investments are required in social services, such as education and health, and in other basic services, such as water, sanitation, and shelter, especially in the poorer countries. Ensuring the environmental sustainability of growth in the region's resource-based economies is also seen as essential for development and poverty reduction. In addition, promoting the participation of all stakeholders in decision making and giving them equitable access to assets and opportunities are expected to help maximize the benefits of growth and make development more broad based. A key dimension of this approach involves strengthening capacity at subnational levels, including provinces, states, municipalities, and local communities, where stakeholders in development live and where development and poverty reduction occur. In this context, intergovernmental transfers play a critical role in providing resources, alleviating resource disparities, and creating incentives for improved performance by decentralized governments.

Against this broader background of reform, this volume examines the achievements and challenges of intergovernmental fiscal transfers in Asia. In addition to providing a broad overview of the theory and international practice of intergovernmental transfers, five case studies of selected ADB developing

---

[1] For more information on Asian Development Bank's approach to development, see ADB (1995), ADB (1999) and ADB (2000).

member countries are presented. Most of the cases focus on larger countries, including India, Indonesia, Pakistan, and the Philippines, but one smaller country with an emerging local government system, Cambodia, is also included. The chapters on India, Pakistan and the Philippines were commissioned specifically for an ADB study,[2] while the papers on Cambodia and Indonesia were added to provide a broader set of comparative cases.

The rest of this introductory chapter has four sections. First, we consider in more detail why there has been a growing international interest in reforming intergovernmental fiscal transfers in recent years. Second, we review the role of international development agencies, particularly Asian Development Bank, in supporting decentralization, including the reform of intergovernmental fiscal transfers. Third, we summarize some key trends and challenges involved in improving the design of intergovernmental transfer programs, drawing on material from the Asian cases included here. Finally, we briefly outline the contents of the rest of this volume.

B. The Growing Interest in Intergovernmental Transfers

International interest in developing efficient and equitable intergovernmental transfers has been growing in recent years for a number of interrelated reasons. First, many countries faced with deteriorating or uncertain economic conditions have been under major pressure to improve the overall fiscal performance of the public sector, including subnational governments.[3] Second, as noted above, decentralization has become a widespread international trend. As central governments carve out stronger roles for subnational governments, national leaders need to make certain that adequate resources are placed at the disposal of local communities.[4] Third, inequality has risen dramatically in many countries-both industrialized and developing-in recent years. Even countries with impressive growth have not carried the poorest elements of society with their rise, and poverty generally increased in the countries where growth has been weak.[5] Each of these factors, which are briefly discussed in turn, has raised the stakes for improving the design and maximizing the potential benefits of intergovernmental transfers.

---

[2] The papers were discussed at a workshop on "Intergovernmental Fiscal Transfers for Equitable In-country Growth" held at the National Institute of Public Finance and Policy in New Delhi on September 5–6, 2001.

[3] World Bank (1996b).

[4] World Bank (1999).

[5] World Bank (2000).

1. Improving the Fiscal Performance of Subnational Governments

General economic and fiscal difficulties have been forcing central governments of developing countries to improve public resource management. The financing of adequate public services, which is widely recognized as critical to support economic growth and basic equity goals, has been a particularly great challenge for developing countries.[6] In many cases, performance has been especially inadequate at subnational levels, which tend to be heavily subsidized through intergovernmental transfers that lack transparency in their allocation and are fragmented across multiple programs governed by complex and sometimes conflicting rules.[7] Loan financing is sometimes available for development expenditures, but it is not common in most developing countries. Where subnational borrowing occurs, often in the form of loans from multilateral development banks re-lent by central agencies to lower levels, it is heavily and nontransparently subsidized, and local repayment is often highly inadequate.[8]

Particularly at the subnational levels, substantial dependence on grants and subsidized loans developed from the 1960s through the 1980s, when international donor funds for infrastructure development and service delivery were abundant and the governments of many developing countries faced less internal or external pressure for accountability and good fiscal performance than they do now. During this period, many donors and governments believed that subsidization would improve equity in service provision and help reduce poverty.

Over time, intergovernmental fiscal arrangements came to be seen as unsustainable for a number of reasons.[9] First, subnational government subsidies, particularly if poorly targeted, place heavy fiscal burdens on central governments. Second, excessive subsidization undermines incentives for subnational governments to recover costs, potentially resulting in overconsumption. Finally, there is increasing evidence that the poverty alleviation effects of subsidized services are exaggerated; in fact, subsidization as commonly practiced often primarily benefits higher income residents. Faced with these realities and structural adjustment pressures, many countries have undertaken major reforms of intergovernmental fiscal mechanisms.

---

[6] World Bank (1993).

[7] Schroeder (1988); Bahl and Linn (1992), Ch. 13; Dillinger (1994); Bahl and Linn (1994); Shah (1994); Ter-Minassian (1997); Bird and Vaillancourt (1998); Smoke (1999); Bahl (2000); Smoke (2001).

[8] Dillinger (1994); Ferguson (1993); Smoke (1999); Petersen (2000); Peterson (2000).

[9] Bahl and Linn (1992); Smoke (1994); Ter-Minassian (1997); Bird and Vaillancourt (1998); Smoke (2001).

2. The Reemergence of Decentralization

Two emerging realities collectively generated a growing interest in developing or reviving local government.[10] First, although there had been periods of strong economic performance in the developing world, particularly East Asia, during the past few decades until the economic crisis of 1997, many countries had faced a variety of serious economic and fiscal challenges. Many countries had responded not only with the above-mentioned fiscal management reform, but also with efforts to off-load responsibilities to subnational governments, either purely to reduce national budget outlays or because subnational governments were seen as underutilized and possibly having untapped revenue potential.

Second, changing political climates also encouraged the development of subnational governments in developing countries. As people became more educated, better informed about international trends through improved communications, and more aware of the problems of central bureaucracies, they desired to bring the control of government functions closer to themselves. Many countries had moved towards greater democracy as military regimes and dictatorships were forced to relinquish power and institute political reforms that increasingly included decentralization.[11] Along with decentralization, stakeholder participation considerably broadened in many countries.

3. The Subnational Role in Poverty Reduction and Local Economic Development

With uneven development and poverty on the rise in many developing countries and the inadequate performance of many nationally managed programs on local economic development and poverty alleviation, some countries are turning to subnational governments to carry a greater burden in this important public function. Although redistribution is considered primarily a central government responsibility, there is growing recognition that subnational governments can play a role in intrajurisdictional redistribution and in implementing national policies.

In this regard, it is important to emphasize that subnational governments can target the "neediest" members of their communities better than national agencies can only if the less-well-off residents have a political voice or the local community at-large sees a value in assisting them. Under such circumstances, transfers from the center to support poverty alleviation can be very productive. More generally, there has been an increasing attention in recent

---

[10] World Bank (1999), Chapter 5.
[11] Huntington (1991); Diamond (1997); Manor (1998).

years on the role of subnational governments in promoting local economic development, and the possible advantages they might have over the central government for some types of support activities.[12]

C. The Role of International Development Agencies and ADB

International development agencies have increasingly supported for more than a decade the new focus on a greater fiscal role for local governments. The *1988–89 World Development Report* devotes an entire chapter to local government, and an influential World Bank report from the early 1980s states that an effective public sector in a modern developing country "depends on the ability of the central government to harness the resources of lower levels of government".[13] The *1999–2000 World Development Report* on "Entering the 21st Century" places considerable emphasis on decentralization and urban development. Likewise, the *2000–2001 World Development Report* on "Attacking Poverty" suggests that decentralization can bring service agencies closer to poor communities and enhance people's control of basic services.

Moreover, many of the major multilateral donors, including ADB, Inter-American Development Bank (IDB), World Bank, and United Nations Development Program (UNDP), and bilaterals, such as British Department for International Development (DFID), German *Gesellshaft fur Technische Zusammenarbeit* (GTZ), and United States Agency for International Development (USAID), are increasingly assisting efforts to decentralize and strengthen subnational governments in a broad variety of ways.[14] ADB's broad position on these issues was already outlined above, but a brief discussion of the cases included in this volume would highlight the need for such support and illustrate some of the types of projects and programs being undertaken by ADB.

In India, for example, states have considerable autonomy and play a crucial role in the delivery of social services (particularly public health, family welfare, social security, education, housing, and urban development) and the

---

[12] There is a substantial and diverse literature that focuses on the benefits of decentralization and its role in development. See, for example: Hicks (1961); Rondinelli (1982); Cheema and Rondinelli (1983); Cochrane (1983); Rondinelli (1983); Evans (1987); Lewis (1991); Gaile (1992); Dillinger (1994); Smoke (1994); Estache and Sinha (1995); Manor (1998); Cohen and Peterson (1999); World Bank (1999); Blair (2000); Smoke (2001).

[13] Cochrane (1983).

[14] World Bank (1991); United Nations Development Program (1992); World Bank (1996a); United Nations Development Program (1997); Litvack, Ahmad and Bird (1998); Asian Development Bank (1999); United Nations Capital Development Fund (1999); World Bank (1999); Asian Development Bank (2000).

provision of infrastructure (particularly power, irrigation, flood control, and transport). The states are also responsible for executing federal government policies and programs, including those for alleviating poverty. While economic reforms introduced since 1991 have contributed substantively to enhanced efficiency, competition, and the potential for higher economic growth, the initiatives have been concentrated almost exclusively at the national level, with the pace and depth of reform generally lagging at the state level. This is among the most urgent challenges that India needs to address.

The states' public finances have come under severe pressure in recent years, contributing to the increasing deficit in the current account, the compression of capital outlays, and the worsening consolidated fiscal deficit. Moreover, states are increasingly facing the possibility of a domestic debt trap, with new loans needed to service outstanding debt. Without strong measures at the state level, especially with regard to improved fiscal performance and sectoral policy reforms, the effectiveness of central government reforms in promoting sustainable development will be limited.

In accordance with ADB's current strategy, much of its program assistance to India over the medium term is planned to support state-level operations. Gujarat was the first state chosen for ADB's state-level operations, followed by Madhya Pradesh and Kerala. ADB support includes assisting in reforms in budgeting and tax administration, intergovernmental fiscal relations, public enterprise restructuring, private sector participation, and subnational government capacity building.

In Pakistan, similar types of changes and challenges are occurring. ADB now assists all provinces (Northwest Frontier Province, Balochistan, Punjab and Sindh) in various ways. Several studies on intergovernmental fiscal relationships have been undertaken in recent years. Provincial-level public sector expenditure and financial management reviews are being conducted in line with the national government's ongoing efforts to decentralize administrative authority and to devolve certain powers and responsibilities to the subnational level.

In Indonesia, the central government is accelerating a newly instituted process of decentralization and local government reform as part of its economic recovery measures. These efforts are intended to help improve the responsiveness and efficiency of basic services at the local level, stimulate development, and alleviate poverty. ADB has been supporting the country's policy with a number of programs, including the community and local government support sector development program. The specific objectives of the program are to (i) help restore economic activity and reduce poverty; (ii) support ongoing decentralization efforts; (iii) increase the capacity of local governments to implement local public works; (iv) improve the level and sustainability of basic public services; (v) empower villages and civil society to participate more fully in local development; and (vi) improve transparency, governance, monitoring, and accounting procedures at the local level.

In the Philippines where the decentralization program is rather advanced, ADB has placed an emphasis on supporting local development projects in particular regions rather than national-level policy development. ADB-funded municipal development projects have been undertaken in the Clark, Metropolitan Cebu and Subic Bay areas, among others. In addition, ADB is the major source of loans in the Philippines for rural infrastructure projects, and it has been supporting efforts to promote private sector participation in local government infrastructure development projects.

ADB has also been assisting Cambodia through a decentralization support program, which aims to contribute to the development of robust institutions and systems as the country's nascent decentralization program proceeds. This program also seeks to promote the development of effective mechanisms for coordinating decentralization activities among government ministries, among international agencies providing related assistance, and between the government and the international agencies.

The assistance to these developing member countries to improve decentralization and intergovernmental fiscal transfers is a recent development for ADB. Nevertheless, these efforts have already become an important part of ADB's programs to promote development and poverty reduction.

D. Challenges in Designing and Implementing Intergovernmental Transfers

The discussion above indicates that intergovernmental transfers play a critical role in the system of public finance in most developing countries for good reasons that have become even stronger in recent years. Transfers, however, are often controversial, and they can be challenging to design and implement effectively. A number of concerns are important. First, even if national officials recognize that stable sources of revenue are necessary for subnational governments to meet their increasing responsibilities, many worry about the macroeconomic implications of institutionalizing major intergovernmental transfer programs. Second, intergovernmental transfers are often intended to meet a variety of difficult, and sometimes conflicting, objectives. Choices have to be made about priorities, and different types of programs are often required to meet different objectives. Third, devising mechanisms to allocate intergovernmental transfers to meet particular objectives can be challenging. Selecting appropriate allocation criteria is difficult, and measuring them appropriately can be even more problematic. Fourth, transfers commonly suffer from political and institutional interference that compromises their ability to meet their intended objectives. Finally, the overall effect of intergovernmental transfers and other national policies related to subnational governments on broader development goals is difficult to determine. Each of these concerns is discussed briefly as they relate primarily to countries covered in this volume.

1. Macroeconomic Concerns

Historically, there has been considerable concern in many countries that macroeconomic problems can be created if too large a percentage of central resources are guaranteed to subnational governments each year. In some cases where the volume of resources being transferred to subnational governments is substantial, these fears are not unfounded. Fixed arrangements reduce central government control over the disposition of public resources, and a substantial proportion of subnational governments in many developing countries have weak capacity and may not use resources well. The potential dangers of guaranteed allocations, however, must be balanced against the value of providing subnational governments a reasonably stable revenue base and the potential microeconomic gains of decentralized service delivery.

Despite potential concerns about the loss of fiscal flexibility of central government and the performance of local governments, most of the cases have elected to institutionalize a fixed percentage of a major tax, a group of taxes, or total domestic revenues as the pool of resources to be allocated to subnational governments through intergovernmental transfers. In some cases, this percentage is very substantial and fixed by legislation. The Internal Revenue Allotment (IRA) mandated by the Local Government Code (1991) of the Philippines, for example, shares 40% of gross national internal revenues (in the third year prior to the allocation year) and accounts for 94% of total transfers. The *Dana Alokasi Umum* (DAU) in Indonesia represents a minimum of 25% of the Indonesian Government's national budget as required by Law No. 25 of 1999 on fiscal decentralization. It is the only major transfer program in Indonesia and accounts for nearly 75% of local government revenues. In Pakistan, the pool of resources devoted to the main intergovernmental transfer program is also high. It is comprised of 37.5% of most national revenues, with a few sources shared 100% on basis of origin, and it accounts for more than 60% of total transfers to subnational governments. Rather than being fixed by law, the definition of the pool can change based on the recommendations of a periodically constituted National Finance Commission.

The Indian government currently shares nearly 35% of its domestic revenues with the state governments, partly under the mandate of a constitutional amendment and partly on the basis of recommendations by a periodic Finance Commission. In Cambodia, the allocation is small (growing from less than 2% of domestic revenue in FY2002 to 5% in FY2006). Cambodia, however, only elected its first local governments in 2001. Their responsibilities are initially modest, and international agencies provide substantial additional resources to the transfer fund. There is no danger of macroeconomic problems at current levels of funding, and there is plenty of room for growth as Cambodia has one of the smallest public sectors in the world.

While the institutionalization of significant transfers increases the legitimacy, stability, and financial viability of subnational governments, problems can arise from deficiencies in the structure of the transfer systems. The contribution of state governments in India to the overall public sector deficit, for example, has been steadily growing in recent years, and this is found to be attributable in part to incentives imbedded in the national transfer programs. Transfers in the Philippines have greatly improved the overall access to revenues of subnational governments, but in a way that appears to aggravate fiscal imbalances among the various types of subnational governments. Disbursement problems and, in some cases, continued revenue shortfalls in Pakistan have induced the provinces to resort to borrowing, while there are concerns in Indonesia that local governments are actually receiving more resources from the center than they require and can manage responsibly. Most of the case studies raise concerns about the need to improve overall fiscal performance by getting levels of funding right and directing them to subnational governments through programs that create appropriate incentives for responsible behavior.

2. The Challenge of Multiple Objectives

Most countries have multiple objectives for their subnational governments, and this is often reflected in the variety of transfer programs. Unconditional grants, for example, are best for promoting autonomy and interjurisdictional resource redistribution, while conditional grants are a more efficient way of encouraging expenditures on particular types of target services. Sometimes the multiple transfer programs do not fit together well and get so complex that they create serious administrative problems.

Most of the countries considered here have more than one type of transfer program, but there is also a clear trend towards program consolidation. As most of the cases focus their analysis primarily on one or two major transfers in their respective countries, we cannot draw definitive comparative conclusions about the overall systems. But two observations can be made. First, all of the case countries appear to have been moving towards developing a substantial revenue-sharing system that places relatively limited conditions on the use of transferred resources on the recurrent side of the budget. The Finance Commission transfer for states' recurrent accounts in India, the DAU primarily for local governments (10% goes to the provinces) in Indonesia, the shared tax transfer to provinces in Pakistan, and the IRA shared by all subnational governments in the Philippines are good examples of this approach. Cambodia is a special case because, as a highly underdeveloped country only recently embarking on modest decentralization to one level of local government, resources are allocated under a single unconditional transfer system, only a portion of which may be used for recurrent expenditures.

Second, intergovernmental transfer programs on the capital side are typically smaller than recurrent transfers in the countries under consideration and are structured in many different ways. India has a major development-oriented transfer program under the National Planning Commission, but many of the resources apparently get used for recurrent expenditures, and problems have been identified with the distribution of development funds as a standardized grant/loan package. The Philippines have only a small number of capital transfers, but capital investment is somewhat stimulated by regulations requiring that 20% of the general IRA transfer be used for development expenditures and the availability of loans from a central institution, the Municipal Development Fund. Pakistan has one transfer program for general development expenditures, while the rest are variously targeted to components of a social action program, housing, water, rural development, and flood and disaster relief, among others. In Indonesia, there are currently no explicit development transfers, but this is the case largely because a decades-old (problematic) system of substantial conditional development transfers was dismantled under ongoing decentralization reforms. Some portion of the general-purpose DAU can potentially be used for development, and plans are under way to develop a system of conditional transfers to replace the old system. Cambodia's transfer program is intended primarily for development expenditures but aggregate transfers are, as noted above, quite small given the country's early stage of decentralization.

3. Allocating Resources

Appropriately defining the criteria for allocating the resources available under a particular transfer program can be very problematic. The problems are related to two basic sets of issues-identifying the main objective of a particular transfer program and defining how resources can best be allocated to meet that objective. A redistributive unconditional transfer program, like most of the major recurrent transfer programs in the case countries, might be designed simply to target poor areas, or it might be more ambitiously designed to meet a fiscal gap between defined expenditure needs and fiscal capacity. Thus, transfer designers must be careful to define what they are trying to achieve and how best to measure it.

The case countries have approached the problem of allocation of their major transfer program resources in very different ways. All of them have developed some type of formula-based allocation, ranging from very simple to relatively complex. For example, the shared tax transfer pool in Pakistan is allocated to provinces entirely on the basis of population, although a special grant is targeted to two backward provinces. Most of the countries incorporate additional variables in their revenue-sharing formulas. Cambodia includes a poverty index in its newly developed formula, and the Philippine IRA includes land area and an equal share component. Indonesia and India go to the greatest lengths in developing their formulas for the DAU and the state recurrent account transfer, both of which are designed to measure, in different and not entirely adequate ways, both expenditure needs and fiscal capacity.

These variations in approach nicely illustrate some of the important trade-offs in transfer formula design. The single-variable-based allocation of the Pakistan approach certainly meets the objectives of simplicity and transparency, but it is at best only a crude measure of expenditure need. The use of land area and an equal share component by the Philippine IRA attempts to broaden the measures of need beyond population, although some may question the choice and effects of these particular variables. The Cambodian attempt to incorporate a poverty index specifically targets some portion of the resources to the local governments with the lowest levels of development and the greatest service gaps.

Critics would argue, however, that all of these simple measures focus, probably in an inadequate way, on measuring only expenditure needs. In contrast, the Indian and Indonesian models both attempt to consider both the expenditure needs in greater detail and the ability of subnational governments to raise revenues from their own sources. These more complex formulas, however, can also be quite problematic. The Indian formula, for example, is essentially based on filling a fiscal gap defined largely on the basis of existing patterns of subnational expenditures and revenues. Public finance economists prefer an approach based on a careful definition of expenditure and revenue norms, an approach that the Indonesian formula is closest to taking; but even in this case, deficiencies are identified. A major constraint is that some of the variables that might be desirable to use are difficult to define accurately. Properly measuring service delivery costs, for example, is not an entirely straightforward exercise. Equal expenditures should not be expected to lead to equal results, and even if relevant interjurisdictional differences could be accounted for, there is the question of how to weigh the individual components of an expenditure index. In addition, even if the allocation variables can be defined properly, data availability and reliability, as noted in both the Indian and Indonesian cases, are often problematic. Depending on the severity of the problem, the use of inadequate data can call into question the results of the allocation exercise.

One of the major critiques often made of intergovernmental transfer allocation formulas is their lack of attention to ensuring that subnational revenue generation will not be undermined because transferred resources substitute for local tax effort. Most of the cases here, like many countries around the world, do not deal with this problem very well. India and particularly Indonesia try to take this into account, but the authors of the respective case studies have some criticisms of the way it is done. No tax effort variable is used in the Philippines, although the analysis of the case suggests that the IRA may have nevertheless stimulated local revenue mobilization, at least in the aggregate. Pakistan has a small matching grant for provincial resource mobilization that rewards (up to a certain limit) provincial revenue efforts in excess of their historical average growth rate. But provincial revenue yields remain rather low and appear to be shrinking. Cambodia does not explicitly use a tax effort variable, but local revenue sources have yet to be formally developed. In the interim, the allocation process does require minimum locally raised contributions prior to the disbursement of transfer allocations. How strictly this requirement will be enforced as the new transfer program is implemented remains to be seen.

4. Political and Bureaucratic Interference

The international review of the theory and practice of intergovernmental transfers presented in the next chapter suggests that many transfer systems—by design or by manipulation—have historically been allocated with a degree of subjectivity that undermines basic economic objectives. The evidence from the present cases, however, suggests that all the countries have exerted great efforts to move towards more objective-based, formula-driven transfer programs, at least with respect to the major types of transfers that are the focus of these case studies. A number of the countries, including India, Pakistan, and the Philippines, still have smaller transfer programs that are identified as having unclearly specified allocation mechanisms. But these at least appear to be rather limited relative to the total pool of transferred resources.

On the other hand, there are clear instances in which institutional and political issues arise. Perhaps most prominent among the cases are problems identified with the lack of coordination in India between the recurrent transfers managed by the Finance Commission and the (primarily) development transfers managed by the Planning Commission. In addition, not all of the resources under some transfer programs are distributed in a carefully considered way. Thirty percent of the Planning Commission transfers in India, for example, are allocated to a few special category states that comprise only about 5% of the population and have weak absorptive capacity. This heavy concentration of development expenditures also eventually generates greater claims from the special category states for Finance Commission recurrent transfers.

Various concerns arise in other cases as well. Although formula allocations and schedules are rather clear, the provinces in Pakistan often get only 75% of these allocations and they are often significantly delayed. This is partly due to national revenue shortfalls. But the fact that some provinces receive more or less than the average disbursement suggests that political and institutional concerns are also a contributing factor. In addition, some of the smaller transfer programs in Pakistan are clearly allocated primarily on the basis of political criteria, and the Philippines case cites a number of examples of pork barrel funds.

In all of the case countries, except Cambodia where regional allocations from the central budget are small, the central governments continue to play a major role in direct expenditures on subnational services. These may be considered implicit grants or grants-in-kind, and their allocation is apparently not very transparent. In both Indonesia and the Philippines, there has also been some local government resistance to amending the current general revenue transfer formulas to make the allocations more redistributive with respect to fiscal capacity. Intergovernmental transfers are inherently political, but the role of those who design and implement transfer programs is to keep politicization of the process from seriously undermining the fiscal and economic goals of transfers.

5. Overall Effects of Intergovernmental Transfer Programs

Are the major programs analyzed in the chapters meeting key development objectives? Clearly in all of the present cases, intergovernmental transfers support significant increases in local service delivery simply because they transfer substantial volumes of resources to subnational governments. How systematic this is, however, is more difficult to say in all of the cases. Different transfer programs have varying primary objectives which, in turn, are also measured in different ways. If a transfer program, for example, is intended to be redistributive, this can be defined in various ways, ranging from the simple approach of more heavily targeting poorer areas to a more complex fiscal equalization approach based on normatively defined measures of expenditure needs and fiscal capacity.

All of the present case studies, as noted above, fall short of the latter extreme, and other factors influence the final outcome. Cambodia heavily targets resources to poorer provinces through its revenue-sharing formula, but the formula is being phased in as part of a decentralization process that is beginning with some of the better-endowed areas. The supplementation of Pakistan's main provincial revenue-sharing formula (population-based) by special allocations to backward provinces has led to higher per capita expenditures in the backward provinces, but they still have enormous backlogs in access and higher costs of service provision. In the Philippines, the IRA is found to substantially increase the aggregate resources at the local level and possibly has a modest effect on development status. But it apparently worsens the fiscal imbalance across the various subnational levels of government.

India and Indonesia make more sophisticated attempts to deal with fiscal imbalances by considering expenditure needs relative to revenue capacity. But imbalances remain significant, partly because of deficiencies in the design and management of transfer programs and partly due to the offsetting effects of other activities. The abovementioned major role in capital outlays that the national government still plays in some countries, such as Pakistan and the Philippines, for example, has a substantial effect on the pattern of regional public resource distribution, apparently biasing it towards certain better-endowed areas. In all of the cases, aid from international agencies channeled from the central to subnational governments also plays a major role in resource allocation, sometimes exacerbating and sometimes offsetting the effects of national government behavior. Finally, none of the cases really speak significantly on the issue of intrajurisdictional redistribution, which is an important factor in reducing inequality and alleviating poverty.

Even if intergovernmental transfers are successful in meeting basic redistribution and service delivery goals, there is no guarantee that this will result in the more ambitious goal of stimulating more balanced regional growth. As many of the present cases are not even particularly redistributive, there is little reason to believe that their transfer programs have a major impact on regional growth disparities. The case studies do not in general pay a lot of attention to the broader regional growth issue. But the ones that do have not found substantial reductions in disparities; and in some cases, disparities have risen. A few of the cases, however, suggest that even where some genuine redistribution through transfers is achieved, there are substantial leakages from the regions. The India case, for example, even questions the value of channeling large volumes of resources to regions that may have limited capacity to absorb these resources and limited growth potential. Finally, as the next chapter argues more fully, too many factors as or more important than the distribution of public resources influence regional growth. Given this reality, policy makers should not place unduly excessive faith in the ability of intergovernmental transfers to improve interregional growth disparities.

6. Moving Forward

All of the authors make numerous suggestions to improve the intergovernmental transfer systems in the case countries. A few issues particularly stand out. First, there is a strong emphasis on understanding more fully the way the complete set of transfer programs relate to each other and to broader national policies. In the Philippines, for example, the case author notes the role of the IRA in raising subnational service levels, but raises concerns that the IRA may worsen fiscal imbalances and that these effects may be further aggravated by the strong role and regional biases of national expenditures at the subnational level. In India, the problematic effects of the separation of the Finance Commission (recurrent) and Planning Commission (development) transfers, combined with biases in national spending and external assistance at the local level, seem to exacerbate interregional disparities. Recommendations for improving the overall effects of the intergovernmental fiscal system on subnational governments are made in all cases, but the need for additional work is also generally recognized.

Second, all of the case authors recognize the need to improve allocation mechanisms in appropriate ways, both in terms of defining better formulas and developing more standardized data to use in them, without unduly complicating the transfer systems. In Pakistan, for example, this means, at least initially, including measures of backwardness into a simple formula that currently includes only population. In the case of India where the formula is much more developed, reform goals are more significant. Here the issue is to transform a gap-filling fiscal equalization mechanism to one that is more fully based on normative measures of expenditure need and fiscal capacity. The Philippines case particularly highlights the need for developing a national fiscal transfer accounts system.

Third, most of the cases emphasize the significance of international donor programs that channel resources to subnational governments, primarily on the development side of the budget, and make recommendations for improving their design and effects. Context seems to be quite important on this matter. In India, for example, the argument is made that using existing government mechanisms to channel donor resources to subnational governments is problematic. This is largely because the donor resources arrive in a form different from that when they are distributed to subnational governments, muddling the distinction between grants and loans and the objectives and incentives associated with each. In Cambodia, on the other hand, channeling most donor resources (largely grants to date) through the emerging single government transfer system is seen as a way of developing a standard system and taming donors that have historically behaved quite independently in allocating resources for subnational purposes using heavily inconsistent mechanisms.

E. The Remaining Chapters

There are six additional chapters in this volume. In Chapter 2, Larry Schroeder and Paul Smoke provide a detailed review of major conceptual principles and practical experience with intergovernmental transfers around the world. This chapter particularly highlights challenges in designing and implementing intergovernmental transfer programs, focusing in more detail on many of the issues briefly raised in the above review of the case study countries. In Chapter 3, Leonardo Romeo examines the emerging intergovernmental transfer program in Cambodia, which is being created along with a new tier of local government at the commune level as the country embarks on a process of decentralization. D. K. Srivastava reviews in Chapter 4 the recent experiences with intergovernmental fiscal transfers in India, primarily focusing on the evolution and effects of transfers from the central to the state level. This case also highlights the macroeconomic dimensions of transfer programs. In Chapter 5, Blane Lewis reviews the history of intergovernmental transfers in Indonesia, focusing particularly on a new revenue-sharing program intended to help solve some of the serious problems of the previous complex and fragmented system. This is being developed in the context of an ambitious decentralization effort that began recently. Nuzhat Ahmad and Syed Ashraf Wasti examine national to provincial fiscal transfers in Pakistan in Chapter 6, emphasizing the important role of the substantial tax-sharing program. They also examine a number of other less transparently allocated grants and implicit transfers. Finally, in Chapter 7, Joseph Capuno evaluates the intergovernmental transfer system in the Philippines, principally focusing on the IRA general revenue-sharing program, and reviewing other national to subnational and interlocal transfers. As in the India case, the Philippines case details, to a certain extent, the macroeconomic implications of the intergovernmental transfer system.

References

Asian Development Bank. 1995. *Governance: Sound Development Management*. Manila.
———. 1999. *Fighting Poverty in Asia and the Pacific: The Poverty Reduction Strategy*. Manila.
———. 2000. *Promoting Good Governance: ADB's Medium-Term Agenda and Action Plan*. Manila.
Bahl, R. 2000. Intergovernmental Fiscal Transfers in Developing Countries: Principles and Practice. *Urban and Local Government Background Series*, No. 2. Washington, DC: The World Bank.
Bahl, R. and Linn, J. 1992. *Urban Public Finance in Developing Countries*. Oxford: Oxford University Press. Ch. 13.
Bahl, R. and J. Linn. 1994. Fiscal Decentralization and Intergovernmental Transfers in Less Developed Countries. *Publius: The Journal of Federalism*: 1–19.
Bird, R. and F. Vaillancourt. 1998. *Fiscal Decentralization in Developing Countries*. Cambridge: Cambridge University Press.
Blair, H. 2000. Participation and Power at the Periphery: Democratic Local Governance in Six Countries. *World Development* Vol. 28, No. 1: 21–40.
Cochrane, G. 1983. Policies for Strengthening Local Governments in Developing Countries. World Bank Staff Working Paper No. 582. Washington, DC: The World Bank.
Cheema, G. S., and D. Rondinelli. 1983. *Decentralization and Development: Policy Implementation in Developing Countries*. Beverly Hills, CA: Sage Publishing.

Cohen, J. and S. Peterson. 1999. *Administrative Decentralization Strategies for Developing Countries*. West Hartford, CT: Kumarian Press.

Diamond, P. 1997. *Consolidating the Third Wave Democracies*. Baltimore and London: Johns Hopkins University Press.

Dillinger, W. 1994. Decentralization and Its Implications for Urban Service Delivery. *Urban Management Discussion Paper* No. 16. Washington, DC: The World Bank.

Estache, A. and S. Sinha. 1995. Does Decentralization Increase Public Infrastructure Expenditure? In *Decentralizing Infrastructure: Advantages and Limitations*, Discussion Paper No. 290, edited by Estache A. Washington, DC: The World Bank.

Evans, H. 1987. A Virtuous Cycle Model of Rural-Urban Development: Evidence from a Kenyan Small Town and its Hinterland. *Journal of Development Studies* Vol. 28, No. 4: 640–667.

Ferguson, B. 1993. The Design of Municipal Development Funds. *Review of Urban and Regional Development Studies* 5: 154–173.

Gaile, G. 1992. Improving Rural-Urban Linkages Through Small Town Market-Based Development. *Third World Planning Review* Vol. 14, No. 2: 131–148.

Hicks, U. K. 1961. *Development from Below: Local Government and Finance in the Developing Countries of the Commonwealth*. Oxford: Clarendon Press.

Huntington, S. 1991. *The Third Wave: Democratization in the Late Twentieth Century*. Norman, OK: University of Oklahoma Press.

Lewis, B. D. 1991. An Enquiry into Kenyan Small Town Development Policy. *Economic Geography* Vol. 67, No. 2: 147–153.

Litvack, J., J. Ahmad, and R. Bird. 1998. *Rethinking Decentralization at the World Bank* Washington, DC: The World Bank.

Manor, J. 1998. *The Political Economy of Democratic Decentralization*. Washington, DC: The World Bank.

Petersen, J. with J. Crihfield. 2000. Linkages between Local Governments and Financial Markets: A Tool Kit for Developing Sub-sovereign Credit Markets in Emerging Economies. *Urban and Local Government Background Series* No. 1. Washington, DC: The World Bank.

Peterson, G. 2000. Building Local Credit Institutions. *Urban and Local Government Background Series*, No. 3. Washington, DC: The World Bank.

Rondinelli, D. A. 1982. Government Decentralization in Comparative Perspective: Theory and Practice in Developing Countries. *International Review of Administrative Sciences* Vol. 47, No. 2.

———. 1983. National Investment Planning and Equity Policy in Developing Countries: The Challenges of Decentralized Administration. *Policy Sciences* Vol. 10, No. 1.

———. 1990. *Decentralizing Urban Development Programs: A Framework for Analyzing Policy*. Washington, DC: Office of Housing and Urban Programs, U.S. Agency for International Development.

Schroeder, L. 1988. Intergovernmental Grants in Developing Countries. *World Development Report Background Paper*. Washington, DC: The World Bank.

Shah, A. 1994. Reform of Intergovernmental Fiscal Relations in Developing and Emerging Market Economies. *Policy Paper* No. 23. Washington, DC: The World Bank.

Smoke, P. 1994. *Local Government Finance in Developing Countries: The Case of Kenya*. Oxford University Press.

————. 1999. Improving Infrastructure Finance in Developing Countries through Grant-Loan Linkages. *International Journal of Public Administration* Vol. 22, No. 12.

————. 2001. Fiscal Decentralization in Developing Countries: A Review of Current Concepts and Practice. Geneva: United Nations Research Institute for Social Development.

Ter-Minassian, T., ed., 1997. *Fiscal Federalism in Theory and Practice* Washington, DC: International Monetary Fund.

United Nations Capital Development Fund. 1999. *Taking Risks*. New York: United Nations Capital Development Fund.

United Nations Development Program. 1992. *The Urban Environment in Developing Countries*. New York: UNDP.

————. 1997. *Global Program on Decentralization*. New York, NY: Management Governance and Development Division, UNDP.

The World Bank. 1991. *Urban Policy and Economic Development: An Agenda for the 1990s*. Washington, DC: The World Bank.

————. 1993. *Infrastructure for Development: World Development Report, 1993–1994*. Washington, DC: The World Bank.

————. 1996a. *Urban Sector Policy Paper*. Washington, DC: The World Bank.

————. 1996b. *The State in a Changing World: World Development Report, 1996–1997*. Washington, DC: The World Bank.

————. 1999. *Entering the 21st Century: World Development Report, 1999–2000*. Washington, DC: The World Bank.

————. 2000. *Attacking Poverty: World Development Report, 2000–2001*. Washington, DC: The World Bank.

2

Intergovernmental Fiscal Transfers: Concepts, International Practice, and Policy Issues

Larry Schroeder, Syracuse University, and Paul Smoke, New York University

A. Introduction

There is a large conceptual and empirical literature on intergovernmental fiscal transfers.[1] Drawing on this work and examples from various countries, we provide in this chapter a broad overview of the theory and practice of intergovernmental transfers, with particular focus on developing countries. We begin with a review of the main objectives of intergovernmental transfers and the criteria used to evaluate them. We then consider the principal types of transfers and the mechanisms used to implement them. Given the common problem of fiscal disparities across subnational jurisdictions and the particular interest of Asian Development Bank in this topic, we also discuss the measurement of redistribution and equalization in theory and practice, one of the most difficult challenges in designing transfers. Finally, we examine the linkages between transfers and other major elements of the intergovernmental fiscal system, an important dimension of fiscal transfer design that often receives inadequate attention. We conclude with some broad lessons about designing intergovernmental transfer systems in developing countries.

---

1. Note that the terms "transfer" and "grant" are often used interchangeably. We prefer to primarily use the more general term transfer, which can refer to any resource flow from one level of government to another, including taxes shared by law. Grants are increasingly used to refer specifically to transfer instruments over which the level of government making the resource allocation has more direct discretionary control.

B. Objectives and Evaluative Criteria for Intergovernmental Transfers[2]

Even in cases where primary responsibility for local public services is devolved to subnational governments, several reasons justify some fiscal transfers to lower levels of government: (i) to equalize vertically (improve revenue adequacy); (ii) to equalize horizontally (interjurisdictional redistribution); (iii) to correct for interjurisdictional spillovers (externalities); and (iv) to correct for major administrative weaknesses and streamline bureaucracy. We consider each briefly.

Both central and local governments are generally expected to provide public services, but it is common to find that the own-source revenue-raising powers of subnational governments are not sufficient to meet the costs of providing the services they have been assigned. The resulting gap can be filled by vertical equalization—increasing local revenue-raising powers or transferring resource from higher levels. But increasing local own-source revenues can often be difficult. Allowing subnational governments to have substantial revenue-raising powers reduces central control over the total size of the public sector and raises concerns about macroeconomic stabilization. In addition, appropriate local revenue bases are commonly weak or too administratively complex for subnational governments to handle. Given these realities, transfer mechanisms are often the most suitable way to achieve vertical equalization.

Horizontal equalization is also important because there are generally wide differences in the ability of subnational governments to mobilize resources independently. If only subnational government own-source revenues were available to finance assigned local services, there would be substantial interjurisdictional differences in the quantity and quality of public services based largely on differences in resource endowments. Intergovernmental transfers can be a powerful mechanism to help equalize these differences in subnational fiscal capacity. Horizontal equalization, however, as we shall see in a subsequent section, is complex in a variety of ways.

A third rationale for transfers is that some seemingly local government services generate interjurisdictional spillovers, which are benefits (or costs) that extend beyond the borders of the locality. For example, health services provided in one jurisdiction may improve the overall health situation in neighboring communities. Local governments may be unwilling to provide an efficient level of certain services if they believe that people who reside outside of

---

2. The discussion in this section and the following one is based on the authors' experiences in many countries and discussions in Bahl and Linn (1992), Ch. 13; Schroeder (1988); Bahl and Linn (1994); Shah (1994); Bahl (2000a); Bird (2001); and Bird and Smart (2002).

the locality will enjoy many of the resulting benefits. To ensure that the locality provides a greater amount of those services, the central government may transfer resources to local governments with the condition that such resources be spent on services that generate spillovers. Doing so frees up other subnational resources that may or may not be used on the service in question.

Finally, administrative efficiency can often be improved by centralizing the management of certain taxes. A few taxes such as property taxes, as well as many types of fees, can be adequately collected locally. Local governments can also levy some taxes generally reserved by central governments—e.g., personal income taxes and most business taxes—and some do. However, such taxes are likely to be managed more efficiently through a central tax administration system than by a fragmented local system. Thus, such taxes are often collected nationally with the revenues (or some portion thereof) redistributed to local governments through a transfer system.

It is important to recognize that any intergovernmental transfer program, whether or not explicitly designed to help equalize the resource bases of subnational governments, will have redistributional implications. This is true because all transfer programs involve a flow of resources from the center to subnational governments such that, under most scenarios, some localities will be made better off relative to others. Thus, it is important, as we discuss in more detail below, to consider the full range of intergovernmental transfers in analyzing the overall redistributional effects of transfers, not just programs specifically defined as equalization or redistribution mechanisms.

The preceding discussion of objectives provides the basic rationale for the use of intergovernmental transfers. Equally important is a related set of desirable features that can be considered criteria for evaluating transfer mechanisms. These include revenue adequacy and growth; predictability, simplicity and transparency; allocative efficiency; equity (in terms of redistribution); and incentives for sound fiscal management and subnational resource mobilization. A brief elaboration of each is in order.

The objectives of revenue adequacy and growth are obviously related to the ability of a grant system to provide for legitimate local spending needs. A transfer system meets these criteria when it is designed to ensure that a subnational government has enough resources to cover its unmet revenue need, and when the transferred resources grow appropriately with needs over time. Full adequacy, of course, is elusive. Resources are limited, and all levels of government in most countries can make use of more resources than they have access to.

The desires for predictability, transparency, and simplicity are closely intertwined. Fiscal planning requires that a reasonable degree of certainty be associated with the flow and timing of resources from the center. This means that it is desirable for subnational governments to have a general idea of how much money they are likely to receive from their various sources of revenue as they begin the planning and budgeting process for the next fiscal year. This provides a solid basis on which to make future plans and minimizes the probability of large swings in resource availability, a situation that can compromise service delivery and frustrate subnational government constituents. Until recent reforms in Indonesia, for example, the volume of transfers was unpredictable because it was determined through annual negotiations in the central government budgeting process.[3] This made it difficult for subnational governments to plan and budget in a stable way from year to year. Similarly, it is important that the transfers allocated to subnational governments actually be distributed for their use and on a timely basis. In some cases such as Mexico and Nigeria, a portion of transfer allocations never make it to the jurisdictions that are supposed to receive them.

Subnational government officials and their constituents should also be able to ascertain how their share of a particular transfer was determined. Even if they are not satisfied, at least they will understand why they received a different amount than other jurisdictions. Such an understanding is facilitated by relatively simple but explicit transfer formulas, which also reduce the possibilities for capricious political manipulation of transfer allocations. In Vietnam, for example, the funds allocation criteria for an early program were not transparent, such that subnational units and their constituents had no way of knowing if they were being treated fairly. Using a formula effectively, however, requires that appropriate data are available and that local governments should not be able to manipulate the values of the factors included in the formula. In some cases, even if there is transparency, the allocation rule being used makes little sense. This was the case with transfers to *tambons* (districts) in Thailand and to communes in Cambodia (under an early donor-funded experiment), which initially received equal block grants regardless of differences in population or other measures of subnational need.[4]

The criterion of allocative efficiency includes two subobjectives. First, it requires that public services be provided at the lowest possible cost; equivalently, this means that for a particular level of spending, the highest amount of services possible is produced. Thus, transfers should encourage local governments to spend their limited resources carefully and in the most productive way possible. Second, efficiency means that resources should be allocated to services identified subnationally as the highest priorities. Unless spillovers exist, grants should not be allowed, intentionally or unintentionally, to distort how subnational governments allocate resources—among sectors, across locations,

---

3. Lewis discusses the new system of transfers in Indonesia in Chapter 5 of this volume.

4. There is a brief treatment of the Cambodia, Thailand and Vietnam cases in Smoke (1999a). Romeo discusses the new transfer system in Cambodia in Chapter 3 of this volume.

or in terms of how to combine factors of production. In the presence of jurisdictional spillovers, these guidelines need to be modified to achieve more efficient allocation of resources nationally.

The equity criterion relates directly to the issue of horizontal equalization discussed above. The criterion is complex, however, since it commonly entails a combination of not easily measured factors. Even if complete equalization of access to resources were possible and desirable, equal expenditures on the same service in two communities do not guarantee that equal levels of services would be provided. Transfer systems should ideally distribute resources across localities in a manner that accounts for differences in both expenditure needs (providing more to those with greater need where unit costs of producing public services are higher) and fiscal capacity (providing less to those with greater fiscal capacity), especially when a constitution, law, or central agency mandates certain types and/or levels of services. Transfers should specifically attempt to decrease or equalize those resource base differences. Obviously, difficult problems are associated with measuring need, and there is also no single standard for what constitutes fiscal capacity. We return to these issues in greater detail below.

Transfers can also significantly affect local financial management. Where grants are viewed as an entitlement with no strings attached, subnational governments may not attempt to use funds wisely, particularly if they are not adequately accountable to their local constituents. Furthermore, subnational governments may view transfers as substitutes for their own resource effort, seeking political gains by reducing local taxes. Finally, grants can adversely affect the willingness of local governments to maintain infrastructure if they expect grant levels to be determined on the basis of its condition. In such cases, local officials may prefer to allow capital facilities to deteriorate in expectation of a new flow of grant funds to replace the deteriorated infrastructure.

Unfortunately, the objectives briefly discussed here often conflict with each other, so that constructing a transfer system requires careful consideration of trade-offs among the various goals it may seek. For example, encouraging spending on services with external benefits can conflict with the assumption that subnational governments should best know their own public service needs and demands. Similarly, transfers intended to provide incentives to improve local resource mobilization can result in relatively greater resources transferred to localities with relatively greater fiscal capacities. We return to the issue of conflicting objectives below.

C. The Design of Intergovernmental Transfers: Types and Mechanisms

Any mechanism intended to transfer funds from one government to a set of others will entail three policy choices: (i) how to determine the total amount of resources to be distributed; (ii) how to allocate that resource pool across all eligible subnational governments; and (iii) if and how to restrict the way the transfer funds can be used. Appropriate design of a transfer system should consider each of these design features systematically. While each of these features is discussed separately below, the transfer instruments chosen, in fact, reflect all of them simultaneously.

1. Determination of the Transfer Pool

The size of the transfer pool can be determined in three basic ways. First, pools based on a predefined portion of national revenues in the current or recent fiscal year can provide an increased degree of certainty to subnational authorities that they will, in fact, receive the transfers. This approach can also ensure a growing source of revenues for subnational governments if the pool is tied to buoyant revenue sources such as income tax. The potential downside is that, by inflexibly dedicating a proportion of national revenues to subnational governments, the center will lose some control over macroeconomic fiscal policy. Whether this proves to be a problem depends on the volume of resources being committed to subnational governments relative to the overall size of the national budget and how subnational governments use the resources.

Second, aggregate transfer allocations may be linked depending on the spending plans of subnational governments. The overall level of grant financing for approved projects can be determined on the basis of the size of those projects planned for by the subnational governments. Alternatively, the allocation may be intended to provide transfers of a certain allowable amount to eligible individual recipients of particular types of programs such as social welfare. These transfer pools can either be closed- or open-ended. Closed-ended pools set aside a maximum amount of funds available for distribution, and not all the funds need to be distributed if an insufficient number of approved plans are submitted. Open-ended pools are determined on the basis of all approved spending and can potentially be unlimited. Such a design feature can be risky for a central government trying to keep its overall spending level under control and balancing a variety of competing demands for funds. This helps explain why they are much less common in developing countries.

Third, a common way of determining a transfer pool is through annual budget decisions. This approach gives the central government maximum flexibility to respond to national fiscal conditions. Such ad hoc allocations, however, can create uncertainty for subnational governments, making them vulnerable to fluctuating economies and the vagaries of political negotiation. Serious local fiscal problems can arise if subnational governments plan expenditures based on transfers received in previous years and the parliament unilaterally decides to cut transfers substantially in the current fiscal year.

2. Allocation of Funds Among Subnational Governments

A number of approaches are used to allocate the transfer pool across eligible jurisdictions. First, tax-sharing transfers return to a particular subnational government all or some portion of a central government tax collected within its geographical jurisdiction. Such transfers can be elastic in terms of their growth if the tax being shared has significant growth potential; however, they are usually counterequalizing since subnational governments with larger tax bases will derive greater amounts of transfer funds. Thus, these types of transfers are based on subnational fiscal capacity and are not good instruments for redistribution across subnational jurisdictions. In some cases such as the People's Republic of China, the bulk of subnational resources are derived from tax sharing.

Second, transfers allocated on the basis of an objectively defined formula are increasingly popular because they meet some of the key evaluative criteria outlined above. Specifically, they are transparent for the recipient governments and can give the granting government considerable latitude in determining which of the main objectives discussed in the previous section are to be emphasized. One limitation of formula-based transfers commonly faced in developing countries is the lack of timely and adequate data required to implement the allocation formula. In addition, there is sometimes a tendency to try to meet too many objectives with a single transfer program, and so many indicators are added to the formula that its overall effects are not clear, as in the case of Ethiopia.

Third, cost-sharing transfers reimburse subnational governments for expenditures on particular priority activities that are deemed worthy of subsidization. Such grants can be either total- or partial-cost sharing (matching). The former reimburses the subnational jurisdiction for the full costs associated with allowable services, while the latter requires a jurisdiction to contribute some minimum portion of total costs from their own resources, effectively subsidizing the price of the activity. If such subsidization is not clearly justified, e.g., to correct for an interjurisdictional spillover or to meet some equity goal, the budgets of recipient governments can be distorted in undesirable ways.

Finally, some transfer allocation mechanisms depend on ad hoc decisions of the granting authority in determining how much of the transfer pool each jurisdiction receives. Such mechanisms may create great uncertainty on the part of transfer recipients since they do not know how their grant will be allocated or how much they will receive. They also open the door to arbitrary, subjective, nontransparent allocations that may work against broader public sector goals. Some major federal systems, such as Argentina, use a fair degree of nontransparent criteria in their transfer programs.

3. Degree of Subnational Spending Autonomy and the Transfer Instrument

A final policy choice in transfer design concerns the degree of autonomy enjoyed by recipient subnational government jurisdictions in using the funds from a transfer instrument. Greater subnational autonomy also means that the central government has less control over how the funds are spent. A number of mechanisms are commonly used.

First, general-purpose allocations give a subnational government full autonomy over the use of transferred funds (within the legal limits of decentralized functional responsibilities). A recipient jurisdiction can allocate the money for whatever purpose it desires and for either labor or nonlabor inputs. Such transfers are closest to the spirit of full devolution of spending powers advocated by proponents of decentralization. Many countries, including the Asian cases considered in this volume as well as Kenya, Mexico, and South Africa, among others, have at least some general-purpose allocations in intergovernmental transfer programs.

Second, sectorally limited block allocations permit the recipient government to choose how funds are to be used, but only within a particular sector. These transfers are particularly relevant where the government determines that significant benefits external to the spending locality are associated with particular activities such as health. Similarly, a capital development grant can be structured to allow the subnational jurisdiction the choice to use the funds in constructing new roads, health centers, or school buildings, but not allow these funds to be used for constructing a new city hall.

Finally, specific-purpose transfers can be highly restrictive in how the funds are spent. Restrictions may apply to choices between labor and nonlabor inputs and/or for particular spending plans. Thus, a capital development project grant may have to be spent according to the provisions of the project plans submitted by the local council and approved by a central ministry. Similarly, spending of a grant intended to pay teachers' salaries is restricted to exactly that purpose.

This discussion suggests a theoretical total of 36 different combinations of transfer programs (3 methods of determining the transfer pool × 4 types of allocation mechanism × 3 levels of restriction on funding use). Since transfer systems commonly consist of several different types of grants, the full combination is essentially limitless. However, only a relatively limited number of these combinations are typically considered and used. Table 1 illustrates various possibilities that are usually considered feasible.[5] Eight different combina-

---

5. Table 1 is adapted from an approach originally provided in Bahl and Linn (1992).

tions of methods of determining transfer/grant pools and methods of allocating that pool among eligible local units are shown. We also identify the types of spending restrictions that are feasible in each case.

TABLE 1
Alternative Forms of Intergovernmental Transfer Programs

Allocation of Transfer Pool Among Subnational Governments	Method of Determining the Total Transfer Pool		
	Share of National Government Tax	Annual Budget Decision (Ad Hoc)	Reimbursement of Approved Spending
Origin of collection	A | General Purpose		
Formula	B | General Purpose or Sectoral Block	F | General Purpose or Sectoral Block	
Cost reimbursement (partial or total)	C | Sectoral Block or Specific Purpose	G | Sectoral Block or Specific Purpose	K | Sectoral Block or Specific Purpose
Ad Hoc (based on annual decisions by granting government)	D | General Purpose, Sectoral Block or Specific Purpose	H | General Purpose, Sectoral Block or Specific Purpose	

Source: This is an adaptation of the approach developed in Bahl and Linn (1992).

4. Choosing Among Options: Linking Transfer Instruments to Objectives

Given the numerous alternative forms of transfer instruments, it is useful to consider how these different types might relate to the objectives discussed above. Since the transfer system of most countries generally includes two or more of these mechanisms, the overall effects of the system can only be determined by evaluating all of these mechanisms relative to priority objectives.

Tax-sharing transfers (type A in Table 1) can grow if linked to elastic tax revenues; however, they tend to be counterequalizing across local governments. They can take advantage of the superior tax-administration abilities of the national government and provide a reasonably certain and continuous flow of revenues (particularly when compared with more capricious ad hoc allocation methods). Furthermore, since the subnational government is retaining a portion of the revenues collected (if subnational rather than central agencies are responsible for collection), local officials may assist national tax collectors in carrying out their duties and further improve tax-collection efficiency. Finally, tax-sharing arrangements do not require the often-challenging and contentious construction and administration of complex allocation formulas.

Formula-based transfers (types B and F) can be constructed to allow local councils to use the funds with total discretion or various formulas can be used to distribute funds intended for utilization across different sectors. The first approach gives the central government less ability to direct funds into national priority sectors than does the second. Sectorally limited, formula-based grants also allow the central government the opportunity to utilize different formulas for different sectors, e.g., to base education sector grants on the number of school-age children in an area and health sector grants on the total population of the area and/or their health characteristics.

Type B instruments link the transfer pool to a specific central government revenue source, such as income tax, as is the case in Kenya and Turkey, or to an aggregate set of certain national taxes, as is the case in Ethiopia and Mexico, or to a broad set of nearly all national taxes, as is the case in Argentina and the Philippines. Such arrangements give subnational governments greater certainty about the flow of transfers and permit improved fiscal management. Because revenue-sharing transfers decrease central government control over its financial affairs, however, type F may be preferred (at least by the granting government) so that the transfer pool decision can be made annually.

The most challenging task in formula-based transfer design is constructing the appropriate formula. Measures of relative demand for services, e.g., population, kilometers of roads, spatial area, etc., are nearly always included in transfer formulas. Also common are measures of fiscal gap, such that additional funds are provided to subnational governments with especially large differences between spending needs and local financing capacity. If not done carefully, however, this can create perverse incentives for subnational governments to overestimate their spending needs and underestimate their revenues. Sometimes there is also an attempt to measure tax effort, or how effectively subnational jurisdictions are collecting allowable taxes (relative to the size of their tax base or overall resource base).[6] These measures can create incentives for localities to mobilize their own resources rather than to use transferred funds primarily for local tax relief. The greatest practical problems in defining a transfer formula include correctly defining each term in it and obtaining adequate data for measurement.

Because cost reimbursement grants (types C, G, and K) are meant to reimburse the subnational government for all or a portion of the cost of an

---

6. Per capita local tax collection relative to per capita local income, for example, is considered a reasonable measure of such effort.

activity, they are either tied to a particular sector or to highly specific uses, regardless of the way the pool is determined. In either instance, a choice arises as to whether 100% of approved costs are to be reimbursed or if only a portion, e.g., 60%, will be financed from the grant, the remainder being the responsibility of the subnational authority. Partial cost reimbursement (a matching grant) encourages subnational governments to mobilize their own resources to meet a portion of the total costs of an activity. Requiring a local financial contribution, particularly for infrastructure projects, can also increase the perception of local ownership of a facility and can encourage continued maintenance of it. The disadvantage of partial cost reimbursement transfers is that they can bias subnational government choices of activities. A locality is more likely to use its limited funds on a subsidized activity than on one where the local council is required to fund it fully from its own resources. Thus, such grants interfere with subnational fiscal choices and can lead to locally inefficient outcomes unless there is a need to offset an externality.

Full cost reimbursement grants are also sometimes used. For example, in Indonesia all (or nearly all) subnational government employees used to be paid directly from a national government grant.[7] This practice increases the administrative costs of the transfer since, for central government financial control purposes, the center must approve the creation of all subnational government positions. It also reduces local autonomy over a fundamental set of expenditure decisions. In effect, the subnational government simply becomes the agent of the center, practically negating the potential benefits of devolution and reducing incentives for subnational resource mobilization.

Type H grants effectively give the central government full control over how much money will be available for subnational governments, while type D grants decrease this control. Both types, however, give the center control over how much each locality will get, and can even limit the spending of the funds to particular functional areas or types of spending such as labor. These are, therefore, the most centralized of all the transfer mechanisms shown in the table. They provide the lowest degree of predictability for subnational governments, limit potential gains from decentralization, and may become highly politicized. On the other hand, ad hoc transfers do give the center maximum opportunity to respond to changing and unexpected needs arising in certain localities. For this reason, some national governments reserve a portion of the transfer pool to respond to special local circumstances as they arise.

Given the various advantages and disadvantages of the different types of transfer mechanisms, the final choice in the design of a system depends on the

---

7. The new general revenue-sharing transfer system in Indonesia has a component based on salaries, but there is no longer a separate grant program for this purpose.

relative importance of the various objectives that the system is intended to achieve. This is, of course, at the heart of the policy process and the correct answers will invariably be viewed differently in different environments.

5. Other Major Issues in Transfer Design

A number of other critical issues arise in the design of transfers. First is the distinction between transfers for recurrent (routine) and capital (development) expenditure responsibilities. Recurrent expenditures are made for day-to-day administrative and operating needs, such as salaries and supplies. Development expenditures are made to construct facilities and infrastructure projects and to purchase durable equipment. In some countries, transfers for recurrent and capital expenditures are clearly separated, while in other countries a single transfer can be used for either purpose.

Thinking about how to deal with the recurrent-capital issue is important for two reasons. First, appropriate measures of recurrent and capital fiscal needs generally differ. A subnational government with adequate sources of revenue to cover basic annual operating and maintenance costs of a primary school may not have access to the resources required to construct a new, critically needed school building. Second, the decision about how to treat recurrent and capital transfers has implications for restrictions placed on the allocation and use of transfer funds. For example, a central government may wish to promote investment and cost sharing by allowing transfers to be used only for capital expenditures, thereby forcing the subnational governments to assume recurrent costs associated with service provision. In other cases, remunerating adequately trained staff may be a particular problem for subnational governments, so a transfer program may be designed to target the salaries of medical or educational personnel. Of course, targeting funds, as noted above, has both advantages and disadvantages, and it can only be controlled to a certain extent. Thus, such decisions must be made judiciously and the use of funds monitored if the central government is serious about its targets.

A second additional transfer design issue is that some countries have different types of transfers for different types of subnational governments. In countries where multiple tiers exist, programs for second-tier (provinces, states, regions, etc.) and third-tier (cities, municipalities, districts, etc.) governments are usually separate. In some cases, transfers to third-tier governments pass through the second tier, but this can be problematic if the higher tier retains the resources for its own use. In some cases, a portion of third-tier resources is shared with still lower tiers. The urban-rural distinction is often particularly important in designing differential transfers because rural governments tend to have fewer functions and sources of revenue than urban areas. More advanced approaches to measuring subnational government revenue capacity and expenditure needs discussed below capture these differences under a consolidated program. But some governments find it easier to build separate programs for urban and rural governments, or independent programs may be preferred for political reasons.

A third transfer design issue is the structure of administration. The various transfers discussed above can be administered in many ways, some of which are better than others. Although our focus is not on administration, a few key issues related to this topic are worth keeping in mind. Unrestricted and formula-driven grants are usually administered from a special unit set up in a finance, planning, or local government ministry. Although many things can be done incorrectly, the administration of these transfers is relatively straightforward. The allocation unit is given a pool of resources, determines or is given an allocation formula, and distributes resources accordingly.

Grants that involve restrictions on use are typically more problematic because they require a greater degree of information and interaction. Many restricted grant programs in developing countries are based on separate funds that are allocated on the basis of applications made by subnational governments for specific projects that meet the restrictions of the transfer program. While restricted transfer programs serve some of the useful goals outlined above, they can also generate administrative problems that must be recognized. One potential problem is that restricted grant programs are often administered by sectoral ministries. Spreading resource control across often-uncoordinated agencies, which may even be in competition with each other, complicates the tracking of the total volume of resources going to each subnational government. At one time, for example, Indonesia had eight different grant programs for funding local water supplies. Another possible concern is that different restricted sectoral transfers operated by different central government ministries often use very different access, allocation, and reporting rules. These can collectively impose an enormous administrative burden on subnational governments trying to secure resources for various local projects and activities. The ministry of finance in Uganda, for example, is currently trying to consolidate more than 20 separate sectoral transfer programs, many with different rules of access and reporting, into a smaller and less burdensome number.

The third potential administrative problem—particularly in the least developed countries that depend heavily on resources from international donor agencies—is that transfer programs may get separated from the regular administrative operations of the intergovernmental fiscal system. Particularly in very poor countries that have few intergovernmental resource flows without international aid, separate mechanisms are often set up for administering intergovernmental transfer programs because the donors do not trust the existing government system to manage the resources properly. In Cambodia, for example, a donor agency initially managed the early system of transfers to communes. There may be cases in which such an approach is temporarily justified, but without a plan for integrating the system into regular government operations, the special program may eventually do more harm than good.

In closing this section, we emphasize again that transfer systems commonly consist of a variety of different programs. Under such conditions, the desirable effects of one program may neutralize the desirable effects of another. Some countries have (e.g., India) or long had (e.g., Indonesia) a complex system of unconditional and conditional transfer systems controlled by uncoordinated (sometimes-competing) central and/or state government agencies. Because of the complex and inconsistent objectives, the aggregate effects of the transfer system are difficult to measure. This implies that all components of the entire system must be examined to ascertain its likely overall effects. Unfortunately, this is very rarely done; as a consequence, very little is generally known about the overall effects of intergovernmental transfer programs in many countries.

D. Measuring and Implementing Redistribution and Equalization

Although intergovernmental transfer systems have various objectives, equalization and redistribution are the key concerns of this paper. As indicated above, intergovernmental transfers are used to improve both vertical and horizontal differences in the abilities of governments to mobilize resources and their needs to provide public services. Although the two dimensions are generally considered separately, they are obviously related since any attempt to improve vertical equity through grants can affect horizontal equity. We now turn to a more detailed discussion of each.

1. Vertical Equalization

The issue of vertical inequities in a multitier system of governments stems primarily from the outcomes of public service responsibility and revenue assignment decisions. As discussed previously, the own-source revenues available to local governments generally fall below the spending needs associated with the public functions assigned to them.

Fiscal theory suggests a trio of economic justifications for public sector involvement in the economy. These include economic stabilization, redistribution of incomes and wealth, and allocation of goods and services to correct market failures. It is generally argued that the national or central government has an advantage in the first two of these, whereas subnational governments can provide many public services more efficiently than can a central government. This conclusion is embedded in Oates' famous decentralization theorem, which constitutes the theoretical basis for the policy of subsidiarity—responsibilities for public service should be assigned to the lowest tier of government feasible.[8] Thus, local rather than higher levels of government can often provide local roads, water supply, waste management, police and fire protection, primary education, and primary health services more efficiently. The center, however, still retains responsibility for certain services, such as national defense and postal services.[9]

There are, however, few theoretically strong justifications for decentralizing revenues to subnational governments. Some sources, such as property taxes and certain types of fees and charges, are appropriately managed at the local level, and they create some efficiency linkage between tax prices and the services that local governments provide. Many important tax revenue sources, however, such as the value-added tax, business and personal income taxes, and international trade-based taxes, are more efficiently administered by national government.[10]

These realities imply that there is likely a significant imbalance between national revenues and spending requirements and local revenues and spending needs, thus necessitating intergovernmental transfers to correct the imbalance. Implementation questions that arise when attempting to improve the balance include measuring the extent of the imbalance and choosing an appropriate transfer mechanism(s) to correct it.

2. Measuring Vertical Imbalance

Ideally, vertical imbalances are measured by comparing the revenues of a particular level of government with the costs that will be incurred if that level of government provided an appropriate quantity and quality of the public services for which it is legally responsible. The problem is that there is often no consensus on what constitutes appropriate levels of services, and measuring such levels may in any case be difficult.

One very simple indicator that purports to indicate fiscal balance is the ratio of own- source revenues to current expenditures or, equivalently, one minus the ratio (subnational resources not under subnational control / total subnational expenditures). Thus, if all local governments in a country were spending $2 million but their own-source revenues amount to only $1 million, their vertical balance indicator would be 0.50. This ratio can then be related to a comparable ratio for central (as well as state/regional governments where they exist). Such

---

8. Oates (1972).

9. Available evidence suggests that the general guidelines for service assignment among levels of government are often followed. See Bahl and Linn (1992) and Shah (1994).

10. The issues associated with assignment of revenue authority across different levels of government are reviewed in McLure (1999).

ratios were recently computed for a set of federal and unitary countries with the results generally showing that local governments were raising relatively small proportions of total expenditures from their own revenue sources.[11]

Such measures were based on the actual revenues raised and spent by different levels of government. The resulting ratio may be low because, as emphasized above, there is a substantial mismatch between the expenditures assigned to local governments and the revenue sources made available to them. However, low ratios will also result if local governments do not adequately utilize their own revenue-raising powers. In this case, it is misleading to use the low ratio to justify transfers. High ratios can also be misleading since the ratios do not indicate the degree to which the spending by a particular level of government relates to the amount of public service that ought to be provided. Thus, a local government may be raising nearly all of the revenues necessary to finance whatever services it is providing to local residents, but the quantity and quality of those services fall far short of what should be provided. This is the case in some South African municipalities where the local governments' own revenues finance nearly all of the services provided. However, large proportions of local residents are also going without any local services. Thus, vertical balance ratios close to 1.0 should not be interpreted to mean there are no vertical fiscal gaps.

Rather than observe ratios of actual own-source revenues to expenditures, the more appropriate denominator would be the amount of spending necessary to attain some minimal standard of locally assigned public services. Similarly, the numerator should reflect the potential of local governments to raise revenues from their own assigned sources rather than to rely on intergovernmental transfers. However, as detailed below, deriving accurate estimates of the required numbers is not an easy task, and it is done in relatively few countries.

3. Correcting Vertical Imbalances

National governments sometimes recognize that there is a serious mismatch between the levels of spending they expect from local governments and the revenue potential from the tax and nontax sources assigned to local jurisdictions. As suggested in Table 1, one approach used is to set aside a certain proportion of central revenues for local governments as mandated in a statute or constitution. For example, the Local Government Code of 1991 in the Philippines requires that 40% of the central government's internal revenue collections be redistributed to regional (provincial) and local governments.[12]

---

11. Ahmad and Craig (1997), pp. 74–76.
12. See Chapter 7 in this volume for a discussion of the intergovernmental system in the Philippines.

Likewise, the 1991 Constitution of Colombia requires a certain proportion of all central revenues to be shared with municipal and regional governments. The total share of central administration current revenue to be transferred was to rise during the 1990s from 36.5% to 45.5% in 2000.[13] Rather than share all central revenues, some countries designate only certain revenues, such as income taxes, to be shared. This has been the case in India, Pakistan, and Kenya, and has been proposed in Albania.[14] A potential disadvantage of this approach is that the central government may choose to raise taxes other than those that must be shared with subnational governments, possibly leading to further vertical imbalance.

The fixed-share arrangements also create potential macroeconomic instabilities since they decrease the amount of fiscal flexibility available to the central government. If contractionary fiscal policies are called for, increasing central tax rates will result in additional revenues, a portion of which will be allocated to subnational governments. Since local jurisdictions cannot be expected to have a concern for macroeconomic stability, the additional transfers will be spent, contrary to good macroeconomic policy. On the other hand, a guaranteed proportion of central revenues increase the certainty of a flow of funds from the central to subnational governments vis-à-vis annual ad hoc determination of the amount to be transferred.[15] While this can improve the vertical fiscal balance, there is still no certainty that the proportions chosen lead to a truly balanced system. Only much more detailed analysis of normative spending requirements and revenue potential at the various levels of government can resolve the issue.

As elaborated in the previous section, if vertical balance were the only criteria, type A grants constitute a reasonable sharing mechanism. However, without including some mechanism to insure that local governments continue to make an effort at raising revenues of their own, a type A grant could result in no improvement in vertical balance if a local government simply substituted the grant for local revenues. More problematic, particularly from a macroeconomic perspective, is a transfer mechanism that attempts to fill any existing gap between budgeted local spending and anticipated (or realized) own-source revenues. Such deficit grants may improve vertical balance but they encourage subnational governments to inflate expenditure needs and underestimate revenues. To overcome these incentives, some governments require local budgets

---

13. Ahmad and Baer (1997), p. 467.

14. See Chapters 4 and 6, respectively, in this volume for discussions of the intergovernmental fiscal systems in India and Pakistan.

15. Even though statutorily determined, central governments may still renege by arguing that exceptional economic circumstances make it impossible or fiscally dangerous to the nation to meet the legal provisions.

to be approved centrally. Doing so may undermine the expected advantages of fiscal decentralization and can be extremely costly and inefficient.

4. Horizontal Equalization

Although vertical equity is important, even more attention has been given to the horizontal dimension. There is little doubt that resources in most countries are not spatially distributed uniformly. All regions are not endowed with similar levels of natural resources or other economic advantages; likewise, the populations of all regions are unlikely to have identical demands for local public services.[16] Vertical and horizontal equalization efforts are not independent. Once a reasonable degree of vertical equalization is achieved, there is still the need to determine how the funds are to be distributed among subnational governments. At this point, horizontal equalization becomes the prime objective.[17]

Redistribution is a role commonly assigned to central government. The normal concern is with personal or household income distribution, such that income or wealth is transferred from wealthier to poorer individuals. Intergovernmental transfers, however, constitute a rather blunt instrument for redistribution of personal incomes and wealth. Transferring funds from high- to low-income jurisdictions does not necessarily mean that high-income households will bear the burden of the taxes used to finance the transfers that provide services consumed by low-income households. There is also no guarantee that services funded by transfers will go to the less well-off in recipient jurisdictions. The net effect of the transfer depends on the distributional incidence of both revenues and expenditures. However, central governments may still wish to equalize across subnational governments for a number of reasons, including differences in resource endowments and local public service needs across regions.

If horizontal equalization is seen as an attempt to reduce differences across governments at the same level, the gap for subnational government can be identified as

$$Fiscal\ Gap_i = Fiscal\ Needs_i - Fiscal\ Capacity_i$$

(where fiscal capacity should include other nonequalization grants transferred to subnational government i).

---

16. We use the term "region" here generically. The concepts refer to all spatial differences including differences among various towns and cities, differences between rural and urban areas, and differences across rural areas of a country.

17. Bird (2001) suggests that vertical balance can be thought of as being achieved when expenditures and revenues balance for the richest local government; all additional gap-filling is to achieve horizontal fiscal balance.

Two basic approaches are used in addressing equalization. One approach is to concentrate on the varying abilities of different regions to mobilize resources on their own and to provide relatively greater transfers to localities with lower fiscal capacities. A second approach is to include differential expenditure needs in the equalization exercise and provide relatively greater transfers to localities that have greater gaps between local spending requirements and local fiscal capacity. If all local governments are deemed to have approximately the same levels of fiscal capacity, as can occur in cases where they are provided with few local revenue-raising instruments, equalization may focus exclusively on differential spending requirements.[18]

5. Extent and Method of Financing Equalization

Regardless of whether only fiscal capacity or the difference between fiscal needs and fiscal capacity is equalized, two basic questions arise. One concerns the extent of the equalization that is desirable and the second focuses on how it is to be financed. Theory suggests that both equity and efficiency gains can be attained from equalization transfers, but the gains may be limited. If factors of production are more productive by moving from one area to another, equalization grants that discourage such mobility are inefficient. Thus, large special grants to backward areas of developing countries may be inefficient for the economy as a whole. The key question is why a region is backward. If the area is endowed with very low productivity factors of production, then trying to make the area more attractive through grants can be inefficient. On the other hand, if the low productivity stems from the fact that investment in social infrastructure has been long ignored in a region, then additional equalization grants to overcome past neglect of the area may be in order. There can also be other efficiency gains from equalization grants to backward areas. In the absence of such grants, there may be strong pressures for labor to migrate to major cities, possibly creating negative externalities—congestion, pollution, overcrowded housing, etc. Equalization grants that discourage such migration can, therefore, yield efficiency gains.

A second issue related to the achievable degree of equalization is the method used to finance the transfers. Two approaches are feasible. One is for relatively better-off subnational governments to transfer their excess revenues

---

18. A third approach is essentially to ignore horizontal inequities and instead concentrate on vertical imbalances. The idea is that mobility of labor and capital will correct for fiscal imbalances by moving to areas with relatively greater net differences between expenditure benefits and revenue burdens. This approach is essentially that taken by the federal government in the United States.

(relative to needs) to their less well-off counterparts. A second approach is for the central government to fund transfers to all subnational governments but to provide greater funds to those less well off. These have been termed, respectively, as fraternal and vertical (paternal) funding methods.[19] Fraternal methods are used in Scandinavian and some central European countries whereas the paternalistic approach is common throughout the rest of the world.

Since some subnational governments will always be relatively better off than others, funds can, at least conceptually, continue to be redistributed under the fraternal approach to equalization until fiscal gaps are totally equalized. There may, of course, be politically imposed limits. Paternal equalization will be limited by the degree to which the granting government is willing to fund the equalization effort. And, as will be made clearer in the subsequent discussion, the limits may be related to other objectives sought from the transfer in addition to fiscal equalization.

6. Equalization of Fiscal Capacity

Since resource mobilization instruments of subnational governments are commonly linked to wealth, income or consumption, interjurisdictional differences in these factors result in different abilities for subnational governments to raise revenues. That is, if tax rates are constant across localities, wealthier areas can mobilize more revenues than can poorer regions. Likewise, if local tax rates were allowed to be set locally, wealthier localities could raise equal amounts of revenue by imposing lower rates than poor regions. Such differentials can be viewed as both inefficient and inequitable.

Two approaches to fiscal capacity equalization have been advocated and are used in different places. The simpler approach focuses on a single aggregate measure of fiscal capacity. This macroeconomic approach essentially recognizes that, ultimately, the level of economic activity within the region/locality limits the ability of subnational governments to raise revenues. As such, some measure such as gross regional (local) product can be used to approximate the capacity to raise revenues. In many developing countries, subnational governments are not given autonomy to determine which taxes to levy or what tax rates to set. In these instances, the aggregate approach may be a reasonable indicator of relative fiscal capacity, and it is likely easier to implement than the alternative discussed below.

The macro approach has important limitations, even in a best-case environment. Conceptually, gross local product may not accurately reflect differential abilities of local governments to mobilize resources since the level of

---

19. Martinez-Vazquez and Boex (1999).

economic production in one locality is not necessarily equal to the income flowing to the factors that created that production. Where owners of factors of production, e.g., owners of capital, are located outside the locality, the capacity to tax those factors will be overestimated by a gross local product measure. Relying on factor income as a measure of revenue capacity will similarly yield overestimates of tax capacity if production-based taxes are employed. It is also the case that reasonably accurate measures of gross local product or local incomes are commonly not available in developing countries. In such case, the technique will be impractical. Only if reasonably current and unbiased measures are available will subnational governments view such an equalization system as being equitable.

A micro-oriented method for measuring fiscal capacity issue is generally termed the representative tax system (RTS) approach. It is particularly applicable where subnational governments are given autonomy in setting local tax rates. The method is also most relevant in federal countries where states/provinces provide local governments with different menus of revenue instruments. Among the federally organized countries that use this approach are Canada, Australia, and Germany, which are among the few countries that have a significantly equalizing transfer system.[20]

The RTS approach attempts to estimate the revenues that a local government can raise given the size of its base (for each local revenue source) and a common tax rate. Generally, the tax rates used for the computations are the average tax rates across all local governments; where central or regional government law sets rates, the statutory rate is used. Thus, interjurisdictional differences in estimated fiscal capacity arise due to differences in the observed revenue bases across localities.

Several conceptual and practical issues arise in implementing such an approach. The list of revenue sources used should be comprehensive to insure that a full measure of the capacity to mobilize resources is measured. If a local government fails to impose a tax that can be imposed legally, its local revenue potential will be greater than indicated by its current revenue flows. The list of taxes should also include the portion of all taxes that are, by statute, shared with subnational governments on a derivation basis (type A transfer in Table 1).

A second issue concerns the estimated size of the revenue base. Common definitions of the base should be used; however, this will be less of a problem where a single law governs local taxes. South Africa provides an example of where the problem can arise. Property taxes in some provinces are levied exclusively on site values whereas local governments in other provinces levy the tax on the total value of both land and improvements. In such instances, a

---

20. Shah (1994) discusses these cases in detail.

weighted average of the legal bases may be used.[21] It may, however, be difficult to obtain sufficient data for the computations since the information on value of improvements are likely to be unavailable in a site-value region.

A third issue that commonly arises in developing countries is the treatment of user charges. These can be especially important sources of revenues for subnational governments that are otherwise constrained to unproductive taxes. If such charges are used to supplement other local public services beyond those on which the charges are levied, they constitute a portion of the local revenue base. Since user charges can be particularly complex—e.g., differential connection charges across users along with quite different structures of tariffs based on both the type of user and the quantity of use—determining an average rate may be exceptionally difficult.

Given the potentially major complications involved with constructing an RTS, some countries use the tax capacity from a single base, often the local property tax, as a proxy for overall fiscal capacity. This approach may not accurately or fairly reflect differences in fiscal capacity across jurisdictions, even if the property tax is the primary local revenue source. Assessed values of the property tax may be determined locally. Seldom do local tax valuers assess properties at values that coincide exactly with those specified in the law. Furthermore, where assessment lags and property values are growing, the ratio of assessed to actual values will continue to fall. To make accurate estimates of relative taxable capacity across jurisdictions in such instances, existing tax bases must be equalized; that is, an independent body must determine the degree to which each jurisdiction's tax base underestimates (or overestimates) the legally stipulated tax base. Only then can ratios be used to determine what each jurisdiction's legal tax base could be.

The property tax base estimation issue is just one of a number of practical issues facing any agency that attempts to derive accurate estimates of fiscal capacity. As stated by Clark:

> There needs to be a professional statistics-gathering agency, which has adequate financial resources and is relatively independent of governments, charged with the responsibility for obtaining needed data broken down by province on an annual and historical basis. Such an agency should be staffed so that it can work on long-term needs as well as short-term requirements.[22]

The costs of creating and supporting such an agency are unlikely to be great in relation to the total flow of resources to local governments, and the

---

21. Clark (1997), p. 25.
22. Clark (1997), p. 27.

benefits can be substantial. However, in budget-constrained developing countries, finding the support and the expertise for such efforts can be difficult.

7. Fiscal Needs

Although equalization of fiscal capacity is a reasonable step in attempting to make the flow of public services more equitable across localities, different localities can have greater or lesser expenditure needs. By including fiscal needs with fiscal capacity, it is possible to estimate the full degree to which there are differentials in fiscal gaps across localities. The transfer system can be used to fill the gaps, at least partially. Attention to need differentials is common. Certain developed countries, including Australia and Denmark, put considerable effort in deriving estimates of such needs as a central feature of their equalization grant programs, although they also include estimates of fiscal capacity.

The objective of expenditure equalization is to empower subnational governments with the ability to provide equal public services if they put forth equivalent revenue effort. The first decision that must be made when attempting to equalize the ability to finance differential expenditure needs is determining which expenditure functions will be equalized.[23] While it is desirable to include all functional areas, the data requirements are likely to be constraining and, instead, central governments may focus on only the most critical services assigned to local governments.

A second related decision concerns whether equalization should focus exclusively on recurrent expenditures or should also include capital spending. In Australia, capital expenditure needs are not included, largely because of the difficulties in conceptualizing and measuring capital deficiencies relative to the often-diverse needs of individual subnational jurisdictions. Developing countries are likely to have significant interregional disparities in existing capital infrastructure; however, they also commonly lack good jurisdictional-level data on relative needs. In these cases, it may be preferable to rely on specific-purpose capital grants designed explicitly to target infrastructure deficiencies and also implement a system of equalization transfers that focus on recurrent expenditures.[24]

In any case, ascertaining differential recurrent expenditure needs is not easy. It is inappropriate to use actual expenditures as an indicator of needs since differences in spending can occur for a variety of reasons: (i) costs of

---

23. Rye and Searle (1997), p. 44.

24. Such a scheme is discussed by Ahmad and Craig (1997), who also consider the conceptual issues associated with determining relative infrastructure needs.

inputs are greater; (ii) it must serve a greater number of service recipients; (iii) it has a policy of providing a higher quality or quantity of services; or (iv) it uses inputs less efficiently than do other regions. Attempts to equalize spending needs should focus on only the first two; the latter two support local decisions to go beyond basic needs or reward inefficient production. Thus, an estimate must be made of the costs of providing some standard basket of public services. Even if a standard basket of public services is used to determine the equalization grant, there should be no requirement that a subnational government must allocate the funds to those services. Instead, local spending autonomy should still hold to capture expected efficiency gains from decentralized decision making.

Several broad approaches to estimating needs are possible. The most comprehensive approach is to attempt to determine the factors that are likely to relate directly to the demand or need for different services. For example, the number of school-age children who needs to be educated, the kilometers of local roads to be maintained, or the number of elderly or unemployed can be used as indicators of need for different types of local services.[25] One of the more comprehensive (and, hence, complex) formulas used for different types of municipal expenditures is found in Denmark, where 13 different criteria are used to compute expenditure needs for local public services.[26]

If generally agreed-upon factors that affect input prices or costs of providing services differ across localities but are beyond the control of local authorities, such differentials can be used to adjust the estimates. In Australia, for example, there is recognition that it is more costly to serve a highly dispersed population than a more concentrated one, and that the price of labor is generally higher in certain areas than in others.[27] In Switzerland, the expenditure requirements of cantons include a factor that recognizes the increased costs of providing public services in mountainous terrain.[28] Calibrating such cost differentials is, however, difficult. Indeed, this very comprehensive approach to horizontal equalization may be impossible for many developing countries to implement primarily because of the detailed data required.

---

25. Care must be taken when choosing such factors to avoid unintended consequences that might result from any budget allocation incentives that are built into the factors. For example, if kilometers of roads in poor condition were used as a factor, local governments would have the incentive to forego road maintenance to increase the size of their equalization grant.

26. Lotz (1997), p. 204.

27. Rye and Searle (1997), pp. 48–49. Labor cost differentials may be less relevant in developing countries where there is often a single civil service system with uniform wages paid throughout the country.

28. Dafflon (1999).

An alternative approach is to rely on the distribution of a specific grant across localities as indicative of relative needs in different areas.[29] Thus, if the ministry of education, for example, is allocating a specific purpose grant to support local education, the relative sizes of this grant can be used as an appropriate indicator of education needs. Gaining widespread agreement to such a mechanism, while necessary for the transfer to be deemed equitable and credible, may be difficult, and there may be questions about whether the ministry allocated its resources in an appropriate way. The approach does, however, significantly decrease data requirements.

An even less data-intensive approach (and perhaps most commonly used in developing countries) is to assume that population is an adequate indicator of relative needs and costs of providing local services. This leads to an equal per capita allocation across all localities, which can sometimes improve equity. In some countries these equal per capita shares are further adjusted by an indicator of backwardness or some other subjective factor that is intended to reflect differential needs (as well as local fiscal capacity). A disadvantage of such adjustments is that there may be no general agreement on what constitutes backwardness, with the resulting allocation being not much better than an ad hoc transfer. Another way to measure need is with some indicator or poverty levels. Poverty rates or indexes, for example, figure prominently in the South Africa transfer system and the one being developed in Cambodia under the new decentralization agenda.

Additional variables are sometimes added. For example, in the Philippines and Uganda, a portion of grant funds is distributed on an equal-share basis to all local governments. One rationale for this feature is that there are fixed cost requirements associated with municipal administration that do not differ substantially from locality to locality. Another need factor, which is also used in the Philippines, is the land area of the local government. This may be rationalized on the basis of cost differentials, as suggested in the Australia case above.

Fiscal needs may be used as the only determinants of equalization transfers or they may be used in conjunction with fiscal capacity measures. The latter approach, for example as used in Australia, is more appropriate, particularly where there are substantial differences in the economic and/or tax bases of subnational governments. Many developing countries rely only on need factors and ignore fiscal capacity. This approach is reasonable if local governments are not expected to raise significant resources of their own; in such instances, differences in fiscal capacity are largely irrelevant in determining a fiscal gap.

---

29. Ahmad and Craig (1997).

Thus, major practical complications are clearly involved in fiscal equalization. Both defining what a national government wants to equalize and finding an appropriate way to measure it pose significant challenges. In addition, the full set of data required to do the job properly are rarely available or easy to collect. Under these circumstances, policy makers will often have to use simpler and less than ideal approaches. Even so, a transfer system can be defined to effect at least some reduction of fiscal disparities, and the system can evolve as better information are secured over time.

8. Promoting Equitable Growth: Service Improvements

The official intergovernmental relations policies of many countries state that their transfer systems are supposed to promote equitable in-country growth, target lagging regions, help alleviate poverty in the poorest regions, and meet other similar goals. In reality, the complexity of inequality and various constraints on policy instruments make the realization of these goals a great challenge. As the discussion above indicates, it is extremely difficult to define, much less to equalize, revenue capacity and public expenditure levels across subnational jurisdictions. Even if it were possible to do this effectively, the connection between transfer policies and the desired broader outcomes are far from straightforward.

One minimalist transfer-outcome connection would be to show that the resources provided through fiscal equalization efforts were, in fact, spent on improving critical local services generally presumed to improve economic growth and income distribution. Most of the very limited studies on improvements in subnational service delivery have been conducted in the context of examining the overall impact of fiscal decentralization in general, rather than intergovernmental transfers in particular. Many alleged benefits of decentralization have been claimed in the literature, most of which relate to improvements in the level and quality of local services and revenue sources, better matching of local services to the preferences of local constituencies, and greater accountability, all of which should have some beneficial impact on economic efficiency and growth. The evidence on service delivery is actually rather limited and mixed. Some recent studies found that decentralization does increase total and subnational expenditures on public infrastructure and social services.[30] Leaving aside the issue of whether increases in spending improve services, they generally do not seem to be related directly in a significant way to increases in intergovernmental transfers. Other modest evidence suggests that,

---

30. Estache and Sinha (1995); Robalina, Picazo, and Voetburg (1999); and Freinkman and Yossifov (1999).

particularly in highly underdeveloped countries where few services are being provided at the local level, decentralization seems to lead to a genuine addition to the types and levels of services being provided to subnational government constituents, often with the help of intergovernmental transfers.[31] Studies showing a direct, positive, and significant impact of intergovernmental transfers on public spending in general or in specific key sectors are rare.[32]

The issue of whether decentralization improves the quality of public services is even more scant than the evidence on quantity. One major study develops a set of objective indicators on this question for three services traditionally provided by the public sector—roads, electricity, and water—in a large sample (minimum of 75 countries per sector) of developing countries.[33] The results are neither highly encouraging nor discouraging. The only negative impact was for one measure in the electricity sector, while there was an increase in at least one indicator in each sector. For many indicators, however, decentralization had no statistically perceptible impact. In some cases, there was evidence of a functional split, such that facilities are better provided centrally, but operation is less expensive and more effective when decentralized. Another cross-country study focusing exclusively on health care found a positive relationship between decentralization and health care outcomes.[34] Country studies are rare, but one recent case study found that public water infrastructure services provided by local authorities are generally more accessible and reliable than those provided by the center.[35]

Whether decentralization and intergovernmental transfers have genuine positive effects on service delivery is a somewhat country- and sector-specific issue. There are surely some types of local-impact, low capital-intensive services that are more likely to be efficiently decentralized, but variations in available technologies, institutional structures, local capacities, and the availability of resources will influence the desirability of decentralization of a specific function and the potential impact of intergovernmental transfers in a particular country. There is a need for much more research on the impact of fiscal decentralization, in general, and intergovernmental transfers, in particular, on public service delivery.

---

31. *Proceedings of the Technical Consultation on Decentralization* held at the FAO headquarters in Rome in December 1997.
32. See, for example, Zhou and Zhang (1998).
33. Estache and Sinha (1995).
34. Robalina, Picazo and Voetburg (1999).
35. Lewis (1998).

9. Effect of Improved Services on Economic Growth and Redistribution

Even if one could establish a linkage between intergovernmental transfers and improved public service delivery, it would be necessary to establish that the services provided by the local public sector with grant financing had a positive impact on economic growth. Some literature suggest an important impact of public expenditures, particularly infrastructure services, on economic growth, but most of it is not focused on developing countries. In addition, this literature is not linked specifically to subnational government spending or to the impact of intergovernmental transfers.[36] Very little work shows a direct relationship between services provided specifically by subnational governments and economic growth.[37] We could not find any studies that directly attribute economic growth differentials to public services provided by subnational governments and specifically financed with intergovernmental transfers. We found only one study that systematically addressed this issue, and it found that intergovernmental transfers do not appear to improve the economic performance of poor regions.[38]

A small literature focuses more generally on the broader relationship between fiscal decentralization and economic growth.[39] The majority, however, is cross-country rather than interregional within a country. The results are mixed—some show that fiscal decentralization has a positive effect; others, a negative effect on growth. The very few single country studies also show mixed results of fiscal decentralization on interregional growth disparities, again suggesting the importance of context.[40] All of these studies have methodological issues that may limit their usefulness.[41]

The impact of intergovernmental transfers on income distribution is not well studied in the developing countries. There is some modest evidence that appropriately designed transfer programs can effect meaningful interregional redistribution. But there is not a great deal of empirical research on this topic, and some of it shows that other types of transfer programs and government activities can offset redistributional transfers.[42] Some evidence also show that decentralized federal countries (of which there are few), such as Brazil, have been more successful at redistribution than more centralized federations, such

---

36. Aschauer (1989); Aschauer (1990); Munnell (1991); and Munnell (1992).

37. One example is Lewis (1998), who finds a positive impact of local roads and water infrastructure on municipal economic development in Kenya.

38. Garcia-Mila and McGuire (2001).

39. This literature is reviewed in Smoke (2001).

40. Zhang, and Zhou (1998); and Freinkman and Yossifov (1999).

41. Smoke (2001).

42. Schroeder (1988); Bahl and Linn (1992); Shah (1994); and Bahl (2000a).

as Mexico, India, and Pakistan, and this is largely attributed to tax/transfer policies and good governance.[43]

Another key distributional issue is how decentralization and intergovernmental transfers would affect the interpersonal and inter-area inequalities within local government jurisdictions. Unless there are rules about how transferred resources are to be targeted, subnational government officials are genuinely redistribution-oriented, or local democratic institutions are developed in a way that meaningfully includes the economically disadvantaged, it is unlikely that transfers will have a major impact on alleviating intrajurisdictional inequities in basic service provision. Even if they do so, it does not necessarily follow that any resulting improvements in income growth will be equitably distributed among the residents of the subnational jurisdictions benefiting from intergovernmental transfers. Much more research is needed on this topic before definitive conclusions can be drawn.

10. Concluding Thoughts on Alleviating Interregional Inequities

Intergovernmental transfer systems in decentralized or decentralizing systems can be a useful tool for improving at least some dimensions of equity across regions. Central governments are in a good position to harness resources from resource-rich areas and redistribute them to lagging regions, typically subject to political constraints. Even if transfers are distributed in a pro-poor manner, however, the direct impacts of transfers on economic growth are likely to be relatively limited for a number of reasons.

First, resources transferred to lagging regions must be spent in a way that genuinely improves equity and growth. This is by no means a given in complex political and institutional environments in which the poorest elements of society may be marginalized, central governments may be reluctant to place heavy restrictions on the use of funds, and central agencies may not have the capacity to monitor the use of funds carefully even if they do place restrictions on use. Second, we do know that some public services, including those provided by subnational governments, can have an impact on economic development, either serving directly as inputs into the production process or improving the well-being and productivity of the labor force. Public services provided by governments, however, are far from the only requirements for enhancing economic growth. Firms must have access to other needed inputs as well as to markets, and healthier and better educated people may still not have the skills to get the types of jobs that will improve their earning capacity greatly. Third, the benefits of direct redistributive intergovernmental transfers may not be

---

43. This issue is reviewed in Shah (1997).

sustained in the recipient regions. If transferred resources are used to purchase goods and services originating from more highly developed jurisdictions outside of the recipient region, at least some of the benefits of transfers will leak outside of the local economy, lowering the multiplier effect of the resources injected by the central government.

Given these realities, it is critical that policy makers do not place unduly excessive faith in the ability of intergovernmental transfers to improve interregional growth disparities. Well-structured transfers, using the basic principles and mindful of the realities outlined here, can certainly help, at least in taking the first step of improving the provision and distribution of some basic public services needed to support economic growth. But intergovernmental transfers are at best only one element of a broad program required to promote equitable in-country growth. Other key elements, depending on the context of a particular country, include the development of an appropriate regulatory framework to support private investment; the improvement of skills of the labor force, particularly disadvantaged groups; the development of capital markers and credit programs for large businesses and microenterprises; and the development of public institutions and a political system that can be made broadly accountable to the residents of the jurisdiction.

E. Intergovernmental Transfers in the Broader Fiscal System

Much of the discussion thus far has focused on the objectives, theory, and practice of intergovernmental fiscal transfers, with particular emphasis on the challenges of interregional equalization. Whatever their goals, intergovernmental transfer systems must be very well linked into the broader system of intergovernmental finance. The elements of the system include independent local taxes, fees and charges; taxes shared with higher levels of government; intergovernmental transfers; and loans from higher levels of government or commercial credit institutions.[44]

The overriding issue is whether subnational governments have access to sufficient aggregate resources from all sources to meet their responsibilities, as discussed above. This would require that some minimum level of basic services be provided to the subnational jurisdiction regardless of fiscal capacity without incurring deficits. Because such a situation is rare in developing coun-

---

44. Issues related to fiscal decentralization, local government revenues, and intergovernmental transfers in developing countries are broadly reviewed in various publications, including Bahl and Linn (1992); Dillinger (1994); Schroeder (1988); Bahl and Linn (1994); Shah (1994); Ter-Minassian (1997); Bird and Vaillancourt (1998); Bahl (2000a); de Mello (2000); Smoke (2001); and Bird and Smart (2002).

tries, a key task is to identify the principal causes of revenue deficiencies and to consider in more detail the role that transfers should play relative to subnational own-source revenues (primarily for recurrent expenditures) and loans (largely for capital expenditures). We briefly discuss recent thinking about the reform of own-source revenues and lending mechanisms and how these relate to the way analysts should think about the design of transfer programs.

1. Subnational Own-Source Revenues

Subnational governments outside of major urban areas rarely have access to substantial own sources of revenue. In a few cases such as the Philippines, subnational governments are reasonably well, although far from fully provided for in terms of local resources. In some cases such as Indonesia, very few independent sources of revenue have been available to subnational governments; generally the amounts are sufficient to cover at best a small percentage of expenditures. In other cases, numerous sources of local revenue are available to subnational governments, as in a number of states in India, but most have poor yields and are difficult to collect. In many cases, central governments have essentially full control over the local revenue bases and rates, as in Thailand and Vietnam. In virtually all cases, local revenue administration, even for potentially productive local sources of revenue, is inadequate.

Given this variety of experience, transfer systems must play different roles, from essentially funding all subnational expenditures to playing a more supplementary role, such as helping to equalize fiscal capacity or ensuring that services with spillovers are provided at an efficient level. The role of transfer systems, however, can change over time, but the evolution of transfer systems must be coordinated with other intergovernmental reforms. Countries with weak subnational own sources of revenue, for example, may initially need significant transfers. But the transfer system should be part of a broader program of reform that is trying to improve the structure and administration of existing sources, to increase the variety of sources assigned to subnational governments as appropriate, and to enhance the level of subnational autonomy in making local revenue decisions.

These various types of fiscal reforms, in turn, must be embedded in a broader program of intergovernmental reform. For example, subnational governments should not be given new sources of revenue and enhanced autonomy over them unless political reforms are improving the system to make subnational officials more responsive to their constituents and technical and administrative reforms are enhancing their capacity to perform. A key challenge for the design of transfer programs, as discussed in the previous section, is how to supplement subnational resources in places with weak fiscal capacity without undermining incentives to improve subnational resource mobilization and overall performance. As considered in detail above, this is not an easy task because of the obstacles to fairly and consistently measuring the relevant variables.

2. Subnational Government Borrowing

A substantial proportion of intergovernmental transfers in many countries is devoted to subnational capital expenditures. Subnational governments in developing countries generally have little or no direct access to capital markets or commercial lending, with the exception of a limited number of large cities in a few countries with more advanced decentralization. This occurs because of the underdevelopment of capital markets and the perception that few subnational governments are genuinely creditworthy. To the extent that subnational governments borrow, it is normally through central government credit institutions, which often subsidize interest rates and make loans for projects that are clearly not financially viable.[45] In many cases, subnational governments have no incentives to borrow because they can get resources for capital investment from the intergovernmental transfer system.

In spite of the lack of importance of subnational borrowing in most developing countries, it is important for policy makers to keep this issue in mind, as reforms to intergovernmental financial systems and subnational government capacity building may open the door to increasing local access to credit in the future. For this to occur, appropriate reforms must be made simultaneously with subnational own-source revenues, intergovernmental transfer systems, and subnational lending mechanisms. With respect to own-source revenues, the typical challenge is to concentrate reform efforts on improving yields of the most productive sources of local revenue, and to develop, as appropriate, new high-potential sources allowed under the legal and administrative framework. On the transfer side, as noted above, multiple fragmented programs should be consolidated and standardized formulas with carefully defined allocation variables developed to the extent possible. On the loan front, many countries need to adopt objective appraisal techniques, charge closer-to-market interest rates, and enforce repayment. Such reforms must often be realized through government-supported municipal development funds, as only a relatively small number of local governments in a few countries, particularly in Latin America and Eastern Europe, India, South Africa, and a few other countries, are in a position to begin to tap commercial credit and develop a municipal bond market.

The real challenge for intergovernmental fiscal reformers is to develop an appropriate spectrum of options to finance capital investment, from grants

---

45. See useful reviews in Ferguson (1993); Petersen (2000); and Peterson (2000).

and subsidized loans for poorer subnational governments and non-self-financing projects, to various types of loans and bonds for fiscally sound subnational governments and self-financing projects. As with grants, the approach that a central government takes towards enhancing subnational government access to loans depends on the fiscal context, as does the extent to which these efforts pose a danger to macroeconomic stability.[46]

Central government involvement in municipal credit institutions also creates a rarely used potential opportunity to improve the overall effectiveness of fiscal decentralization programs by creating an explicit relationship between the grant and loan systems. In most developing countries, grant and loan reforms have been independent, except to the extent that grant allocations are sometimes reduced if subnational governments fail to make loan repayments. In a few cases, grants and loans have been combined in problematic ways, but few countries have used grants and loans together in an integrated package that provides appropriate incentives.[47]

The failure to link grants and loans at the time when subnational investment decisions are being made can create conflicting signals for local fiscal behavior. Most important, subnational governments have no incentive to borrow from a development bank if they have access to grants or highly subsidized loans from other central or state agencies. If wealthy municipalities are allowed to use grants for self-financing projects, they divert scarce resources from projects with weak revenue potential and from poorer subnational governments that are unable to borrow.

---

46. In cases like Brazil or Argentina, where decentralized levels of government are relatively strong, efforts to develop direct access to capital markets make sense. As the Brazilian state debt crisis of the mid-1990s demonstrates, however, it is critical that the central government regulate municipal bond markets, develop and enforce credit limits, and stop bailing out subnational governments that default on their debt. In more typical cases where subnational government investment responsibilities are smaller and they are fiscally weak, some type of municipal development bank will generally be the correct approach. Municipal credit institutions are initially regulated or managed and substantially capitalized by central governments, either with their resources or donor loans. This approach gives central fiscal authorities considerable control over borrowing activities of subnational governments, although this power must be structured to minimize abuse. Such institutions are likely to be increasingly privatized as subnational governments develop greater creditworthiness, which will help limit the extension of nonviable loans. Serious impacts of subnational debt on the broader economy can generally be avoided if municipal credit institutions are properly structured, managed, and developed over time.

47. A few Latin American and Eastern European cases are reviewed in Peterson (2000). The Tamil Nadu (India) experience is examined in Allaudin and Rajarman (1996). The Philippine case is briefly referred to in Chapter 7 of this volume.

If grant and loan systems were properly developed and synchronized and supported by own-source revenue reforms, subnational governments making a new investment would have a greater incentive to operate more efficiently and to recover costs from service users.[48] Equity objectives will also be better served because well-off subnational governments and revenue-generating projects will rely more heavily on loans, while poorer subnational governments and important projects that cannot recover costs will be subsidized with grants. Such a system can help prevent the type of subnational government debt crisis feared by opponents of fiscal decentralization.[49]

3. Intergovernmental Transfers as Broad Policy Instruments

The preceding discussion clearly shows that intergovernmental transfers can play a much broader role than conventional wisdom suggests. The objectives outlined in previous sections—improving revenue adequacy, efficiency and equity—are extremely important, but the design of transfers cannot be separated from the design and evolution of the broader intergovernmental fiscal system. Intergovernmental transfers can be used to encourage appropriate cost sharing and resource mobilization by subnational governments. Transfers can also be structured to provide an incentive for wealthier subnational governments that can afford to borrow, at least for self-financing projects, to do so. Transfers can even be used to encourage subnational governments to adopt basic administrative reforms. A newly adopted intergovernmental transfer program in Kenya, for example, makes receipt of a percentage of formula-based allocations contingent on local government adoption of new accounting and financial management reforms.

All of these various activities can be mutually reinforcing. For this type of synergy to be successful, however, appropriate and adequately coordinated reforms and technical assistance to subnational governments will be required to improve the functioning of each of the various aspects of the intergovernmental fiscal system. In addition, a carefully planned fiscal decentralization implementation strategy has to be designed to phase in reforms in a way that improves the probability of good subnational fiscal performance.[50]

---

48. Note that what is being proposed here is quite different from the situation described in the India case in Chapter 4, where certain resources from the center are uniformly shared in fixed proportions of grants and loans that have no clear basis.

49. For more detailed discussion of grant-loan linkages, see Smoke (1999b).

50. Recent attempts to consider the strategic design and implementation of fiscal decentralization programs include Bahl (2000b) and Smoke (2000). The state fiscal reform facility in India, which is discussed in Chapter 4 of this volume, was proposed in this spirit, although it was less ambitious in practice.

F. Summary and Concluding Thoughts

Intergovernmental transfer programs serve multiple often-interrelated purposes, three of which are particularly important. First, they help cover subnational fiscal imbalances, supplementing inadequate local own-source revenues to improve the ability of subnational governments to meet their expenditure responsibilities. Second, they can be used to meet national redistributional objectives as discussed above, helping to offset fiscal capacity and fiscal gap differences among subnational governments. Third, they can be used to encourage local expenditures on particular goods and services that exhibit positive spillovers or are considered to be basic needs that should be distributed less unequally than the ability to pay for them. Most transfer systems, even in developing countries, are intended, at least officially, to meet some or all of these objectives.

Several typical issues and problems are involved in designing transfer programs. First, different types of transfers are appropriate in different circumstances. Unrestricted transfers, for example, are most appropriate for income redistribution purposes, while conditional grants are a less expensive way of encouraging expenditures on particular target services characterized by spillovers or unacceptable inequities in distribution. If designed properly, both types can help encourage local fiscal responsibility and ensure over time the provision of a basic minimum of services in all subnational governments regardless of fiscal capacity.

Second, fiscal equalization grants are often a priority, but they are very difficult to design because of technical and political complexities involved in defining an optimal distribution of income and expenditures across decentralized jurisdictions and in determining a fair way to raise and distribute revenues for redistribution. Equal resources do not guarantee equal results, and there are often inequalities within recipient jurisdictions that may not be at all alleviated by transfers. In spite of these problems, redistributive grants can generally be designed to improve the status quo, and they can often be enhanced over time as better information becomes available.

Third, intergovernmental transfers can play only a limited role in stimulating more equitable in-country growth. Even under the very best of circumstances where transfers are genuinely redistributive and spent on the types of services that are most likely to stimulate economic growth in lagging regions, a variety of other types of interventions will be required to overcome a range of additional constraints on local economic development. Transfers can serve only as one component of a broad economic development strategy.

Fourth, macroeconomic problems can be created if too large a percentage of central resources are guaranteed to subnational governments each year. The potential dangers, however, must be balanced against the value of providing subnational governments a stable revenue base and the potential microeconomic gains of decentralized service delivery. In cases where subnational governments already have a substantial legal role, how to approach this dilemma will depend on the structure of the system and the level of fiscal responsibility of lower levels of government. In countries that are in the process of decentralizing, the most likely solution is to start a fiscal decentralization effort with modest transfer programs that involve substantial central control and monitoring. The significance of transfers can be increased as subnational governments develop the capacity to deliver services and to behave in a fiscally responsible way. In all cases, some flexibility in determining the size of the transfer pool during crisis situations can give central governments the fiscal power they need to meet macroeconomic challenges.

Fifth, transfer programs may have conflicting objectives or unintended results that must be recognized. For example, restricted grants that go to wealthier areas may offset the redistributive effects of an equalizing grant. Careful research prior to transfer system design can help understand and minimize, as appropriate, such effects. Transfers may also substitute for, rather than stimulate, local tax effort, thereby failing to increase public spending as much as expected. Including a local-tax-effort variable in a transfer allocation formula can alleviate, but not eliminate, this problem. Finally, multiple transfer programs with different allocation criteria for a particular sector can confuse local officials and provide incentives for unproductive competition and problematic strategic behavior. Consolidation and simplification of transfer programs can reduce such problems.

Sixth, many transfer systems—by design or by manipulation—are allocated with a degree of subjectivity that can undermine basic economic objectives. Political realities, budget shortfalls, and bureaucratic constraints may often preclude adoption or implementation of policies required to rationalize and to streamline transfer programs, so that expectations in this regard need to be realistic. More objective and transparent distribution formulas can help move the local government system in the right direction, but intergovernmental transfers inherently have a political dimension that cannot be ignored. In addition, care must be taken that a formula does not become so complex that it is difficult to understand and apply.

Finally, intergovernmental transfer systems must be well coordinated with other aspects of the intergovernmental fiscal system. As noted above, transfers can be structured to encourage local resource mobilization. In addition, they can be structured to push wealthier subnational governments from reliance on transfers to reliance on loans for capital expenditures, thus freeing up resources for poorer subnational governments. Transfers can also be structured to help the central government enforce basic administrative reforms, such that some portion of a subnational government's allocation is not released until such reforms are undertaken at some reasonable level.

Different countries might be expected to design their intergovernmental transfer systems in rather different ways, depending on what their system looks like now and how they would like it to look like in the future. Consider, for example, the case of Cambodia, a very poor country with a highly centralized system that is beginning a relatively modest program of decentralization. Subnational governments will not be given specific mandatory responsibilities initially, only limited resources to provide subnational services that are considered important by the community and are not currently being provided by the central government.[51] This approach can make local people modestly better off and help to develop governance and capacity if adequate technical assistance is provided. Because the subnational governments will be responsible for such a small portion of public expenditures in a country with one of the lowest aggregate tax rates in the world, there is no conceivable threat to macroeconomic stability from the local public sector in this case. In addition, redistribution is not as major an issue as it is in some countries, as most of the subnational entities are extremely poor. Thus, fine-tuning measures of poverty and fiscal capacity is less critical than it might be in places where greater inequality exists. Finally, as local sources of revenue are few and the system of administration is weak, the central government has significant leverage over subnational governments. Thus, they can use transfers to help develop both fiscal and administrative capacity.

In more advanced systems where subnational governments have significant service responsibilities and inadequate sources of revenue, such as South Africa, a considerably more substantial and sophisticated system of transfers is being developed. This system includes redistributive grants designed to alleviate very substantial spatial fiscal inequalities and conditional grants designed to cover priority investment needs. In this case, subnational government revenues and local autonomy over certain taxes may be enhanced and borrowing options are being expanded at the same time that transfer programs are being reformed.[52] Under such conditions where subnational governments have significant expenditure responsibilities, proposals to increase local control over major revenue sources are under consideration, and intergovernmental transfers are significant and growing, the national treasury is justified in making

---

51. Commune Administrative Management Law (2001), Royal Government of Cambodia.

52. Smoke, Bahl, Reschovsky, Schroeder, and Solomon (2001).

serious efforts to target transfer resources carefully and to keep a watchful eye on the overall size and performance of the subnational fiscal system.

In the final analysis, it is difficult to make neatly generalizable prescriptions about the appropriate structure of an intergovernmental transfer system, which should be expected to vary across countries depending on national objectives, the extent of service and revenue functions assigned to subnational governments, the fiscal capacity of subnational governments, the extent of inequalities across subnational governments, and the specific nature of priority national objectives. Consideration of various models can help policy makers think about the advantages and disadvantages of different options for transfer design. They must remember, however, that transfers are only one mechanism for meeting important public policy goals, which will always be subject to political and institutional, as well as economic and fiscal, priorities and constraints.

References

Ahmad, E., ed. 1997. *Financing Decentralized Expenditure*. Cheltenham UK: Edward Elgar Publishing Ltd.

———— and K. Baer. 1997. Colombia. In *Fiscal Federalism in Theory and Practice*, edited by T. Ter-Minassian. Washington, DC: International Monetary Fund (IMF).

———— and J. Craig. 1997. Intergovernmental Fiscal Transfers. In *Fiscal Federalism in Theory and Practice*, edited by T. Ter-Minassian. Washington, DC: IMF.

Allaudin, K. and P.V. Rajaraman. 1996. *Urban Infrastructure Financing in India: Tamil Nadu's New Financial Intermediary*. Calcutta: Times Research Foundation.

Aschauer, D. 1989. Is Public Expenditure Productive? *Journal of Monetary Economics*, 23 (2).

————. 1990. Why is Infrastructure Important? In *Is There a Shortfall in Public Capital Investment?* Proceedings of a Conference held at Marwich Port, edited by A. Munnell. Massachusetts: Federal Reserve Bank of Boston.

Bahl, R. 1999. *Fiscal Policy in China: Taxation and Intergovernmental Fiscal Relations*. Washington, DC: The 1990 Institute.

————. 2000a. Intergovernmental Fiscal Transfers in Developing Countries: Principles and Practice. *Urban and Local Government Background Series* 2. Washington, DC: The World Bank.

————. 2000b. How to Design a Fiscal Decentralization Program. In *Local Dynamics in an Era of Globalization*, edited by S. Yusuf, W. Wu, and S. Evenett. New York: Oxford University Press.

———— and J. Linn. 1992. *Urban Public Finance in Developing Countries*. New York: Oxford University Press.

————. 1994. Fiscal Decentralization and Intergovernmental Transfers in Less Developed Countries. *Publius: The Journal of Federalism*: 1–19.

Bird, R. 1997. Intergovernmental Relations in China in International Perspective. Toronto: International Centre for Tax Studies, University of Toronto.

————. 2001. Intergovernmental Fiscal Transfers: Some Lessons from International Experience. Unpublished paper prepared for *Symposium on Intergovernmental Transfers in Asian Countries: Issues and Practices*. Tokyo, Japan: Asian Tax and Public Policy Program, Hitotsubashi University.

———— and F. Vaillancourt. 1998. *Fiscal Decentralization in Developing Countries*. Cambridge: Cambridge University Press.

———— and M. Smart. 2002. Intergovernmental Fiscal Transfers: International Lessons for Developing Countries. *World Development* 30 (6): 899–912.

Clark, D. 1997. Assessing Provincial Revenue-Raising Capacity for Transfers. In *Financing Decentralized Expenditure*, edited by E. Ahmad. Cheltenham, UK: Edward Elgar Publishing Ltd.

Dafflon, B. 1999. Fiscal Federalism in Switzerland. In *Fiscal Federalism in the European Union*, edited by A. Fossati and G. Panella. London: Routledge.

de Mello, L.R. Jr. 2000. Fiscal Decentralization and Intergovernmental Fiscal Relations: A Cross-Country Analysis. *World Development* 28 (2): 365–380.

Dillinger, W. 1994. Decentralization and Its Implications for Urban Service Delivery. *Urban Management Discussion Paper* 16. World Bank.

Estache, A. and S. Sinha. 1995 Does Decentralization Increase Public Infrastructure Expenditure? In *Decentralizing Infrastructure: Advantages and Limitations*. Discussion Paper No. 290, edited by A. Estache. Washington, DC: The World Bank.

Ferguson, B. 1993. The Design of Municipal Development Funds. *Review of Urban and Regional Development Studies* 5: 154–173.

Fossati, A. and G. Panella. 1999. *Fiscal Federalism in the European Union*. London: Routledge.

Freinkman, L. and P. Yossifov. 1999. *Decentralization in Regional Fiscal Systems: Trends and Links to Economic Performance*. Washington, DC: The World Bank.

Garcia-Mila, T. and T. McGuire. 2001. Do Interregional Transfers Improve the Economic Performance of Poor Regions? The Case of Spain. *International Tax and Public Finance* 8: 281–295.

Giugale, M. and S. Webb. 2000. *Achievements and Challenges in Fiscal Decentralization*. Washington, DC: The World Bank.

Lewis, B. 1998. The Impact of Public Infrastructure on Municipal Economic Development: Empirical Results from Kenya. *Review of Urban and Regional Development Studies* 10 (2).

Lotz, J. 1997. Denmark and Other Scandinavian Countries: Equalization and Grants. In *Financing Decentralized Expenditure*, edited by E. Ahmad. Cheltenham, UK: Edward Elgar Publishing Ltd.

Martinez-Vazquez, J. and J. Boex. 1999. *The Design of Equalization Grants: Theory and Applications*. Washington DC: The World Bank.

McLure, C. 1999. *The Tax Assignment Problem: Conceptual and Administrative Considerations in Achieving Subnational Fiscal Autonomy*. Washington, DC: The World Bank.

Munnell, A.H. 1991. How Does Pubic Infrastructure Affect Regional Economic Performance? *New England Economic Review* (September–October).

————. 1992. Infrastructure Investment and Economic Growth. *Journal of Economic Perspectives* 6 (4): 189–98.

Oates, W. 1972. *Fiscal Federalism.* New York, NY: Harcourt, Brace, Jovanovich.

Petersen, J. and J. Crihfield. 2000. Linkages between Local Governments and Financial Markets: A Tool Kit for Developing Sub-sovereign Credit Markets in Emerging Economies. *Urban and Local Government Background Series* 1. Washington, DC: The World Bank.

Peterson, G. 2000. Building Local Credit Institutions. *Urban and Local Government Background Series* 3.Washington, DC: The World Bank.

Robalina, D., Picazo, O. and Voetburg, A. 1999. *Does Fiscal Decentralization Improve Health Outcomes? Evidence from a Cross-Country Analysis.* Washington, DC: The World Bank.

Rodriguez, V. 1997. *Decentralization in Mexico: from Reforma Municipal to Solidaridad to Nuevo Federalismo.* Boulder, CO: Westview Press.

Rye, C.R. and B. Searle. 1997. Expenditure Needs: Institutions and Data. In *Financing Decentralized Expenditure,* edited by E. Ahmad. Cheltenham, UK: Edward Elgar Publishing Ltd.

Schroeder, L. 1988. Intergovernmental Grants in Developing Countries. *World Development Report Background Paper.* Washington, DC: The World Bank.

Shah, A. 1994. Reform of Intergovernmental Fiscal Relations in Developing and Emerging Market Economies. *Policy Paper* 23. Washington, DC: The World Bank.

———. 1997. Fiscal Federalism and Economic Governance: For Better or For Worse? Washington, DC: The World Bank.

Smoke, P. 1999a. Understanding Decentralization in Asia: An Overview of Key Issues and Challenges. *Regional Development Dialogue* 20 (9).

———. 1999b. Improving Infrastructure Finance Through Grant-Loan Linkages. *International Journal Public Administration* 22 (12).

———. 2000. Strategic Fiscal Decentralization in Developing Countries: Learning from Recent Innovations. In *Local Dynamics in an Era of Globalization,* edited by S. Yusuf, W. Wu, and S. Evenett. New York: Oxford University Press.

———. 2001. Fiscal Decentralization in Developing Countries: A Review of Current Concepts and Practice. Geneva: United Nations Research Institute for Social Development.

———, R. Bahl, A. Reschovsky, L. Schroeder, and D. Solomon. 2001. Furthering Local Government Fiscal Reform in South Africa: Issues, Choices and Challenges. Synthesis report prepared for the Department of Provincial and Local Government of South Africa and the U.S. Agency for International Development through Research Triangle Institute.

Ter-Minassian, T., ed. 1997. *Fiscal Federalism in Theory and Practice.* Washington, DC: International Monetary Fund.

Zhang, T. and H. Zhou. 1998. Fiscal Decentralization, Public Spending and Economic Growth in China. *Journal of Public Economics* 67.

Zhou, H. and T. Zhang. 1998. The Impact of Intergovernmental Grants on the Level and Composition of Local Government Spending. Washington, DC: The World Bank.

3

Cambodia

Leonardo G. Romeo[1]
United Nations Capital Development Fund, New York

A. Introduction

Cambodia extends over 181,035 km^2, an area about one-third the size of Thailand. With 13.5 million inhabitants, it is one of the least populated countries in Southeast Asia. The population density is relatively low, averaging 72 people/km^2 (compared with 125 in Thailand and 240 in Vietnam), but it is unevenly distributed and the more populated central provinces reach an average of 170 people/km^2. In spite of accelerating urbanization, about 80% of the population still lives in rural areas. The largest city by far is the capital, Phnom Penh, which has a population of about one million people.

Cambodia is among the poorest countries in the world. In 1999 the World Bank estimated the GDP per capita at US$260. In 1997, 36.1% of the total population lived below the poverty line.[2] The population is young (over 40% under the age of 14) and has been growing fast (at 2.7% per annum between the 1962 and 1998 censuses). High rates of growth are expected to continue in the near future due to the number of people of reproductive age. The largest sector of the Cambodian economy is agriculture (mainly rice and livestock), which accounted for about 43% of the GDP in 1998. The industrial and services sectors (20% and 37% of GDP in 1998, respectively) are steadily growing, mostly due to the recent expansion of garments manufacturing and tourism.

Cambodia is a constitutional monarchy according to the Constitution of 1993. The king appoints the prime minister and gives final approval to the choice of the cabinet members. A 1999 constitutional amendment created a

---

1. The author is Senior Technical Adviser with the United Nations Capital Development Fund (UNCDF) in New York. This chapter draws heavily on work done by the author as Senior Staff of the Institute of Public Administration at New York University in 2001 for the United Nations Office for Project Services (UNOPS). See Romeo (2001).

2. Cambodia's Poverty Profile, 1997.

bicameral parliamentary system, adding a second higher chamber—the 61-seat Senate—to the 122-seat National Assembly. The king appoints two of the Senate members, and the political parties appoint the rest in proportion to their representation in the National Assembly.

After a long period of civil war and political conflict that ended in 1998, Cambodia has enjoyed relative political stability. The national elections held in July 1998 gave the relative majority (42%) of the vote to Hun Sen of the Cambodia People's Party (CPP), and led to the formation of a coalition government including the CPP and the National United Front for an Independent, Neutral, Peaceful and Co-operative Cambodia (FUNCINPEC), which obtained 32% of the popular vote. The Sam Rainsy Party (named after its leader, a former minister of finance) represents the major opposition, with 14 % of the vote.

Administratively, Cambodia is divided into 20 provinces (*khett*) and four municipalities (*krong*). The latter include the capital city of Phnom Penh, and the towns of Sihanouk-Ville, Keb and Pailin. Provincial and municipal administrations include departments (*monti*) of national line ministries and are led by a governor (appointed by the prime minister). Below the provincial/municipal level are 171 rural districts (*srok*) and 14 urban districts (*khan*). District administrations, in which some of the provincial line departments have district offices, are led by a district chief appointed by the Ministry of Interior (MOI) upon recommendation of the provincial governor. Below the district level are 1,621 lowest-level administrative jurisdictions, including 1,510 rural communes (*khum*) and 111 urban neighborhoods (*sangkat*). They range in size from 100 to 45,000 people, averaging 8,000, which points to the problematic viability of many of them. The Government of Cambodia is only starting to address this problem, which will require extensive consolidation and interjurisdictional cooperation.

Until the commune elections held in February 2002, the administration of communes and sangkats essentially consisted of a commune chief appointed by the governor. They had limited responsibilities for local maintenance of law and order and served as a liaison between local communities and the state administration. While communes are the official units of administrative subdivision of the country, most Cambodians in rural areas still identify primarily with their villages. According to data recently issued by the MOI,[3] there are some 13,694 villages in Cambodia.

---

3. *Prakas* No. 493 PRK, 30 April 2001.

B. The First Steps of Decentralization

For the first time since the 1950s, local level elections were held in the 1,621 communes and sangkats of Cambodia in February 2002. The elections, which local and foreign observers considered generally acceptable, resulted in a landslide victory for the CPP, but also gave many members of other parties an opportunity to sit in the newly created local councils and share in the responsibility for local administration and development. These elections were the first step toward the development of an autonomous local government sector in Cambodia.

1. The Commune/Sangkat Administration Law

The Law on Commune/Sangkat Administration (the Commune Law)—approved in 2001—provides the basic legal framework for the establishment and operation of the Cambodian local councils. The law empowers the communes/sangkats with legislative and executive authority and establishes local councils (elected by a system of proportional representation) as the bodies representing their citizens. The commune functions defined by this law are broadly defined in permissive, rather than mandatory, terms and include both the provision of general administration and local development services.

With respect to local finances, the law first requires each commune to have its own financial resources, budget, and assets. Second, it gives communes the right to collect direct revenues from fiscal taxes, nonfiscal taxes, and other service charges. Third, it entitles communes to receive transfers from a share of national revenue. Fourth, it provides for Cambodia to compensate the communes when the latter perform any function on behalf of the national administration (agency functions). Fifth, it establishes the Commune/Sangkat Fund (CSF) as a primary mechanism for fiscal transfers. Sixth, it requires communes/sangkats to prepare an annual balanced budget. Seventh, it prohibits communes/sangkats from direct borrowing. Eighth, it provides for the transfer of certain government assets to the communes. Finally, it establishes a local financial management system and entrusts the Ministry of Economy and Finance (MOEF) with the responsibility to monitor and control commune finances.

The law provides a few important principles regarding the design of the CSF as a mechanism for fiscal transfers. First, it states that the level of capitalization of the fund from domestic resources should be fixed through a formula or a rate for a period of no less than three years and not more than five years. The aim is to institutionalize the capitalization of the fund into the annual national budget negotiations process and to provide a degree of predictability that will promote effective multiyear local expenditure management. However, the law stops short of mandating any particular share of national revenue to be channeled to councils. It leaves this to be determined by a subdecree. Second, the law states that the CSF should, in addition to a portion of state revenues, be allowed to accept other resources from inside and outside the country. This reflects the desire to channel grants and loans from international agencies through the CSF to the local councils. Third, the legislation stipulates that the fund's resources should be distributed to recipient councils by formula. This is meant to prevent ad hoc or arbitrary transfers, as well as to increase their predictability.

The commune law, however, does not directly provide guidance on a number of critical CSF design questions. A few of these questions are:

(i) what are the specific policy objectives of the fund and how should they be reflected in the transfer formula and other fund design features?;

(ii) how should the fund resources be managed, disbursed, and accounted for?;

(iii) should all communes, or only those fulfilling certain basic requirements, benefit from the fund or specific portions of it?;

(iv) should the access to the resources of the fund be automatic or subject to compliance with certain preconditions?; and

(v) to which type of local expenditures should the fund's resources be applied?

These and other detailed design questions were eventually to be answered by subordinate legislation, as explained below.

2. The National Committee to Support the Communes (NCSC)

Following the approval of the Commune Law, the National Committee to Support the Communes (NCSC) was established in late 2001 as an interministerial body responsible for overseeing the completion of the legal framework as well as implementing the decentralization reforms throughout the first five-year mandate of the elected councils (2002–2006). A total of five subcommittees[4] were created in the NCSC to draft regulations to implement several of the Commune Law's provisions, including the CSF.

3. The Seila Program

The context in which the system of fiscal transfers to communes was conceived, and later regulated by the NCSC, cannot be fully appreciated with-

---

4. These are planning and development, financial affairs, commune boundaries, commune powers, functions and structures, and commune councils capacity building.

out reference to the remarkable experimentation with the decentralized local development that preceded the commune elections of February 2002. Since 1996, Cambodia has been implementing the national Seila[5] program in support of subnational planning and financing of local development. By the end of its first phase (in FY2000), Seila covered 220 communes in six provinces and had mobilized over US$75 million from both the Government of Cambodia and some 11 international financing agencies. The program has now expanded its coverage to over 500 communes and is expected to reach almost all the rural communes of Cambodia by the end of its second phase (2001–2005).

Initiated before a national decentralization policy and legal framework were developed, Seila has been referred to as a decentralization experiment. Indeed, working with local Commune Development Committees (CDC) that were the forerunners of the now elected local councils, the Seila program piloted key aspects of decentralization reforms. Seila set up a decentralized financing facility, the Local Development Fund (LDF), to channel domestic and external resources to communes and support local choices in development spending. It also extended a decentralized planning procedure, the Local Planning Process (LPP), for commune-level participatory planning and investment programming. Finally, Seila developed the capacity of provincial administrations to extend technical assistance and facilitation services to communes.

The new context created by the February 2002 elections and the development of a legal and regulatory framework for decentralization prompted a realignment of Seila that can be described as a triple transition. The first transition is from the operation of the donor-managed Local Development Fund to the support of the national fiscal transfers facility, the CSF. The second transition is from the extension of the Seila-specific local planning process to the support of statutory local-level planning procedures, instruments, and institutions. The final transition is the institutionalization of the Seila-specific technical assistance and facilitation system for provincial support to and supervision of the new local authorities.

Depending on whether this transition can be made successfully with Cambodia's leadership and donors' support, Seila may provide the element that is often missing in many decentralizing countries, that is, a national program and external funding framework to support the implementation of decentralization reforms. Such mechanisms can translate decentralization policy statements and legal provisions into a system of functioning local councils that can foster local democracy and deliver development benefits to local constituencies.

---

5. In the Khmer language, Seila means "foundation stone", reflecting the local-level, grassroots approach to national development that characterizes the program.

C. Intergovernmental Fiscal Transfers: the Commune/Sangkat Fund

In February 2002, the prime minister issued a subdecree[6] stating the government's obligation (under Article 78 of the Commune Law) to regulate the establishment and the operation of the Communes/Sangkats Fund. Soon after the approval of the subdecree, the CSF began to operate and received its first contributions for the FY2002 from both domestic and external sources.

Through most of 2001, the design of the CSF was the object of intensive discussions and negotiations among the members of the finance subcommittee of the NCSC.[7] The subcommittee faced the challenging task of designing a transfer mechanism that would provide a minimum of resources to support the councils' basic functions of local administration and development management in a context in which the Commune Law defined the councils' responsibilities only in very broad terms, the management capacity of the new councils was generally low and unequal across jurisdictions, and the country was certain to remain heavily dependent on external assistance for development spending. However, given the very early stage of the decentralization process, the Cambodian CSF designers had the relative advantage of beginning from scratch, and were unencumbered by "the typical problem faced [. . . so often in other countries . . .] by reformers: how to dismantle complex, poorly funded, inefficient, unfair and often arbitrarily allocated systems of multiple transfer programs."[8]

The main features of the CSF and the issues addressed by the finance subcommittee are reviewed below. They reflect the very early stage of the decentralization process in Cambodia. They also point at the need for a comprehensive and strategic approach to fiscal decentralization reforms, one in which transparent, general-purpose transfers are but one component of a diversified local government financing system. They must also be a part of an effective system of central support and supervision of the nascent local government sector, provide incentives to build local institutional capacity, and offer a realistic channel for external financial assistance to local governments.

---

6. *Anukret* 16/ANK/BK of 25 February 2002.

7. The subcommittee was officially established only in late 2001, but most of its members had started working from the beginning of the year as a fiscal decentralization task force established in January 2001 by the ministry of finance. The task force and the subcommittee also benefited from specialist advisory services provided by UN/DESA and UNOPS respectively, under the UNDP-financed project "Local Governance and Sustainable Human Development" and the UNDP/SIDA/DFID-financed project "Partnership for Local Governance."

8. Smoke (2000).

1. Purpose of the Fund

The Commune/Sangkat Fund was set up to serve three basic purposes. The first is to provide the councils with a minimum of resources to enable them to gradually assume increasing responsibilities for local administration and development. This implies filling the gap between the costs of the local councils' responsibilities and the own-source revenues they can mobilize. However, neither mandatory responsibilities nor specific taxing powers have yet been assigned to the communes. Such assignments will likely require substantial negotiations among multiple agencies of the national administration, and this may take some time to be finalized and implemented. At the outset, it is therefore difficult to speak of vertical gaps as the main justification and actual basis for allocating transfers. On the other hand, while the devolution process may take some time to unfold, the election of the local councils has generated pressures to finance the new commune governments to some extent. Once created, the councils need to cover the cost of their operation (e.g. pay councilors' allowances and salaries of local staff and cover the cost of premises, transport, communications and sundries for the functioning of both the local council and administration). Even more important, to promote local democracy and popular participation in local affairs, the councils must show that they are relevant to the needs and concerns of their communities. Thus, the CSF designers recognized that some level of transfers was needed, even if it could not initially be determined by detailed calculation of actual fiscal gaps. Instead, the challenge was to allocate the total pool of transferable resources made available by Cambodia and donors in a way that would be fair and would maximize their productive use.

The second purpose of the fund is to correct differences in the resource mobilization potential of the local councils. No matter what type of own-source revenues the local councils may be able to assess and how efficiently they may be able to collect them, horizontal revenue gaps (imbalances between communes in the potential yield of their fiscal base) will always exist. A main objective of the fund is to correct such imbalances and equalize the fiscal capacity of the councils. Ideally, as soon as a clearer picture emerges from the NCSC regarding the devolution of local fiscal powers, an attempt should be made to estimate the potential yield of the individual communes' fiscal base. This would allow the explicit use of transfers to reduce horizontal imbalances. Meanwhile, however, a rough approximation to this objective was obtained by including an indicator of relative poverty in the allocation formula.

The third purpose of the fund is to provide incentives for the local councils to adopt good local governance practices and improve their performance. Often designers of intergovernmental fiscal relations are keen to ensure that transfers do not compromise local fiscal effort, but rather provide positive incentives to revenue generation. Pending devolution of specific resource mobilization powers, councils are required to mobilize contributions from beneficiaries of CSF-financed development activities to partially match the CSF transfers. The CSF transfers are also intended to improve the councils' expenditure performance by requiring adoption of improved planning, programming, budgeting, and accounting practices. This requires specifying conditions of access to the resources of the fund (see below) and a system of oversight of the councils' compliance with such conditions. This in turn calls for the governors and provincial offices of the MOI's Department of Local Administration (DOLA) to play a proactive role of support and supervision of the councils. The success of decentralization reforms is, in fact, predicated on the ability of provincial administrations to provide the training, technical support, and performance monitoring services that councils will require to effectively utilize the CSF resources.

2. Revenue of the CSF: Combining Domestic and External Financing

The CSF subdecree specifies that the fund account will be opened at the National Treasury to receive contributions from a share of Cambodia's recurrent domestic revenue, grants and loans made available by donor agencies and international financial institutions, and any other source.

The objective of mobilizing both domestic and external resources is a distinguishing feature of the CSF. It reflects the major role that external financing of development spending has played in recent years, and is expected to continue to play for some time in Cambodia. This reality suggests the need for a mechanism to channel external resources into the fund, but there are obstacles resulting from the preferences and practices of both donors and international financial institutions. Most donors will not support the councils' administrative expenditures, which are an important object of CSF transfers. Even for development expenditures, most donors often prefer to restrict the use of their resources to sector-specific menus of allowable investments, rather than support general-purpose transfers for local development spending. In many cases, funding agencies also insist on channeling their resources to specific areas (a subset of the newly established local councils), with risks of geographic imbalance in the distribution of resources. Finally, the channeling of external resources through the CSF may be constrained by perceived risks of liquidity problems in the National Treasury, which can disrupt the implementation of local development activities. Donors are also concerned with the extent to which existing accounting and financial reporting systems will satisfy the accountability requirements.

Overcoming the constraints to external financing of the CSF will obviously require a more open and constructive dialogue between Cambodia and its external partners than has taken place so far. This may mean going beyond the project format used to channel much current assistance and adapting the comprehensive sector-wide programming approach that is now increasingly advocated for external assistance to other sectors. Such programming will be used to support decentralization reforms and local government capacity building.

3. Management of the CSF: Establishment and Functions of the Fund Board

The CSF subdecree establishes a fund board as the upper-level management structure of the fund and specifies its responsibilities. These are (i) recommending to the Government of Cambodia the share of total current domestic revenue to be allocated to the fund; (ii) monitoring the flow of resources into the fund from external grants and loans, and establishing targets for mobilization of external resources by the Government of Cambodia; (iii) adopting the formula for distribution of the fund resources to the communes/sangkats and recommending any changes in it; (iv) adopting and annually revising a classification of communes/sangkats to allocating the components of the fund; (v) approving the annual plan of distribution of fund resources based on the above classification and formula; (vi) communicating to communes/sangkats their individual annual entitlement to fund resources and the indicative forecast of such entitlement over a three-year period; (vii) monitoring the actual transfers to the communes/sangkats against the approved annual distribution plan; and (viii) approving the annual financial statement of the fund.

The subdecree also spells out the fund board's composition. It includes a representative of the Minister of Economy and Finance (MOEF as the chair), a representative of the Minister of Interior, a representative of the Minister of Planning, a representative of the Council for Development of Cambodia, and three representatives of the elected councils to be selected by the Minister of Interior from different development level areas.

The establishment of the board was not uncontroversial within the finance subcommittee of NCSC. It was well understood that, in the operation of the fund, there would be

> . . . a need to carry out a number of tasks that cannot be settled by a decree. These include the calculation and use of the poverty index; the criteria and selection of the communes that will, year by year in the transition period, benefit from full funding; the handling of donor's money; the negotiation of the percentage of total taxes allocated to the fund; the adjustments in transfers to be made when tax receipts are higher or lower than budgeted; etc. . . .[9]

---

9. These observations were made at a workshop of the finance subcommittee in March 2001. See Prud'homme (2001).

These functions appear to justify the need for the board. However, some members of the finance subcommittee were legitimately concerned about the proliferation of nonperforming interministerial committees, which tend to dilute responsibilities and retard action rather than work as forums for real dialogue and collective decision-making. They felt that the MOEF staff, in consultation with MOI, could better perform the board's functions. Eventually it was agreed that the board should be seen not only as interministerial, but also as a venue for representatives of the elected local councils to participate in the design and monitoring of the transfers. Despite the absence of a national association of local authorities in Cambodia, the principle of such participation was accepted and the subdecree stated that, pending the establishment of a National Association of the Cambodian Commune and Sangkat Councils, the MOI would be responsible for organizing the election of the councils' representatives on the board.

In the discussion on the fund board, the issue of whether the functions of the proposed board might be assumed by the NCSC was also raised. The majority eventually favored a board independent from the NCSC. It was argued that:

> The NCSC will have many things to do and might neglect the important tasks to be performed by the Board. The NCSC has a limited life, whereas the Board will be permanent. The NCSC will be largely political, when many of the tasks of the Board have basic technical dimensions (albeit with political implications). The NCSC will largely be captured by MOI, when the tasks of the Board are largely economic and financial.[10]

Nevertheless, the issue of the relationship between the NCSC and the board could not be completely avoided: it was clearly necessary for the two bodies to make consistent and mutually supportive decisions. Eventually, the subdecree defined the relationship between the CSF board and the NCSC, by stating that, given the legal mandate of the NCSC, the board must report and make recommendations regularly to the committee on the operation of the fund. Any regulations or guidelines relative to the operation of the fund have to be submitted to the NCSC for approval.

The CSF subdecree also assigns to the MOEF the responsibility to set up a technical secretariat of the fund board, which is responsible for facilitating and recording the discussions and deliberations of the fund board, preparing quarterly financial and activity reports on the operations of the fund, and providing all necessary technical support to the fund board. The functions of the board's secretariat will eventually be taken over by the Department of Local

---

10. Prud'homme (2001).

Finances, which the MOEF is planning to establish to support and monitor the implementation of the fiscal decentralization reforms.

Having established the board as the fund management mechanism, the subdecree went on to give MOI responsibility for the fund's operational controls. Once the board has adopted a plan for distribution of the fund resources, including provisions applicable to different categories of communes and conditions of access, the MOI authorizes the transfers to participating communes after verifying their compliance with the conditions of access. The Minister of Interior is thus the official authorizing officer of the fund. In performing this role, the MOI remains, however, bound to the execution of the transfers plan adopted by the fund board.

Given the large number of communes and sangkats, the MOI responsibility to certify the compliance of the councils with the conditions of access to the CSF resources will be carried out through the provincial governors. In addition to their responsibility of monitoring the performance of the councils, the governors are expected to coordinate the provision of the legal and technical assistance that the councils may require. This opens the critical question of how the governors and the provincial administrations will assume these responsibilities. Cambodia is leaning towards a model in which the provincial offices of the Department of Local Administration (DOLA) of the MOI will act as primary interface between the newly established local councils and the provincial administration in consolidating and articulating the councils' demand for technical support services. At the same time, the governor will use his coordinating powers over the provincial sectoral departments to direct them (particularly planning, finance, and rural development) to supply such services to the councils. However, in Cambodia as in other decentralizing countries, the reorientation of the provincial bureaucracy toward servicing an emerging local government sector remains difficult. Only time will tell whether this model of relations between provincial administrations and local councils, which largely reflects the experience of the Seila program, will be adopted and successfully implemented in all provinces of Cambodia.

4. Contributions to the CSF

The subdecree specifies the minimum level of contribution of the Government of Cambodia to the fund over the first three years of the mandate of the newly elected councils (2002–2004). This contribution is expressed as a percentage of Cambodia's current domestic revenue, ranging from 1.2% in 2002 to 2.5% in 2004.[11] These percentages are low by international

---

11. In FY2002, 1.2% or KR20 billion (about US$5 million); in FY2003, not less

standards,[12] and have been substantially reduced from the level originally envisaged by the MOEF itself.[13] However they are meant to be "minima", as the subdecree itself states that Cambodia shall consider increasing these percentages upon request by the fund board. Strictly speaking, these percentages are legal obligations for Cambodia, since the annual budget law, an instrument of higher legal power than the subdecree, eventually sets the actual share of Cambodia's domestic income contributed to the fund. Nonetheless, the fact that Cambodia has set clear multiyear targets for domestic contributions to the CSF, and that it has actually started contributing to the CSF in FY2002 must be seen as positive indications of Cambodia's commitment to finance local councils.

In addition to the domestic contribution, the possibility of external grants and loans capitalizing the CSF is an important and innovative feature. Making this work, however, requires proactive management by the fund board, which must set annual targets for mobilization of external contributions to the fund, as well as address the additional requirements that may be attached to external financing agreements. Clearly, new partnership arrangements between donors and international financial institutions and Cambodia should be developed if some of the traditional concerns of external agencies with respect to funding regular fiscal transfers mechanisms were to be overcome. The Seila donors forum provides a practical mechanism to carry out a program approach in support of implementing decentralization reforms and strengthening the capacity of local governments. Indeed, the first practical arrangements to channel external contributions to the fund have been worked out through the Seila donors forum.[14]

The total resources of the CSF are estimated to exceed US$15 million in FY2004 if only the resources already pledged by donors supporting the national Seila program are directed to the capitalization of the CSF (Chart 1). This is a rather conservative assumption, given the current interest of other donors and international financing institutions in assisting the newly elected councils.

---

than 2.0%; and in FY2004, not less than 2.5%. Note that the Cambodian currency is the riel (KR).

12. The effect of their low level is compounded by the fact that the government's domestic revenue in Cambodia is also a rather low percentage (about 11%) of the country's GDP.

13. In March 2001, the MOEF discussed the possibility that the transfers could reach 4% of Cambodia's current domestic revenue in FY2004 and increase to 5% by the end of FY2006.

14. Resulting in an initial contribution of US$1.4 million in FY2002 by the Swedish International Development Agency (SIDA) and the British Department for International Development (DFID) through a UNDP-managed trust fund.

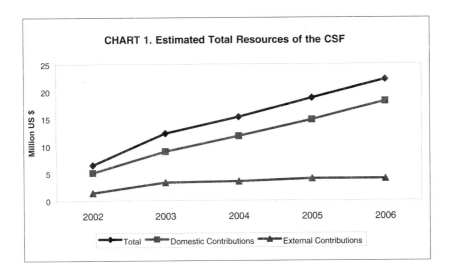

In absolute terms, this may still seem to be very little money for the new local councils. Under the current CSF financing scenario, in FY2002, all councils will receive on average US$1,500 for administrative expenditures, while about one-third of the total number of communes will receive, on average, some US$10,000 for local development expenditures.

It should be noted, however, that US$10,000 per year for development spending is comparable to what the communes have been receiving annually under the Seila program. This experience demonstrates that, beyond helping to finance a few small-scale investments of local priority, modest but regular general-purpose transfers for development spending provide the communes with a basis for a local-level participatory planning process that can be institutionalized in a commune-level public resources management cycle. This process can also be made independent from specific-purpose national and provincial programs that offer resources for local development, while providing a local strategic framework within which to access such resources.

5. Components of the Fund

The CSF subdecree specifies that the total resources of the fund should be divided into two components, a general administration component and a local development component. The former can represent no more than one-third of the total distributable resources of the fund, while the latter can be no less than two-thirds. The fund board is authorized to determine the way in which

the total fund resources are divided between these two components within these specified limits.

It must be emphasized that the constitution of the fund to support both general administration and development expenditures was controversial. During the discussions of the finance subcommittee, alternative approaches were proposed, such as limiting the fund to supporting the routine functioning of the councils while essentially leaving development financing to separate donor-funded programs. The integrated approach eventually prevailed because it was seen as consistent with the objective of attracting external donor support. The CSF offered an opportunity for the international donors and financial institutions to fund a general-purpose fiscal transfer supporting local choices in addition to financing more traditional aid-delivery mechanisms based on contractual relations between special project/program implementation units and local communities and authorities.

6. Classification of the Commune Councils

The CSF subdecree also calls for the fund board to establish a classification of the commune/sangkat councils in two categories with differential access. Category 1 includes all the communes/sangkats that the board deems capable of making effective and efficient use of the portion of fund transfers earmarked for development spending. Category 2 includes all other communes/sangkats. The fund board is expected to prepare and approve a multiyear plan for the gradual inclusion of all communes/sangkats councils in category 1. Based on this plan, the fund board will determine the number of communes/sangkats to be included in category 1 no later than October 1 of each year. The importance of this provision cannot be overemphasized. It reflects the adoption of a strategic approach to implement decentralization reforms as opposed to the politically easier but inefficient spreading of scarce development resources across all communes, regardless of their absorptive capacity.

The classification of councils in two categories is essential to ensure that a minimum but still meaningful amount of resources for development spending is allocated to those councils (category 1) that are likely to make an effective and efficient use of them. It is not easy to determine which ones fit this description, and concerns over the criteria and transparency of the classification have been legitimately raised in the finance subcommittee. Initially, however, category 1 will essentially comprise the councils participating in Seila (about one-third of the total number of communes/sangkats in FY2002), which have had, or will have, access to substantial facilitation and technical assistance services under the program. Then, over the course of 2002, the fund board will develop and adopt a detailed and time-bound plan specifying the criteria, conditions, and schedule for the progressive inclusion of all Cambodian communes/sangkats in category 1.

In addition to the classification of the communes/sangkats in two categories, the CSF subdecree partitions the fund into two components—general administration and local development. The resources of the general administration component will be accessed by all councils in categories 1 and 2, and will be shared in proportion to the number of elected commune/sangkat councilors. The recipient councils may apply these to any eligible administration or development expenditures. The resources of the local development component will be accessed only by the more advanced communes included in category 1, and will be distributed in three shares: an equal share, a share proportional to the population of the commune/sangkat, and a share proportional to a poverty index weighted by the population of the commune/sangkat. These may be applied by the recipient councils only to development expenditures. This provision raises two issues. First, how are development and administrative expenditures defined? Second, what formula should be used for allocating the CSF resources to individual communes/sangkats?

7. Classification of Eligible Expenditures

The definition of administrative and development expenditures is a key feature of the CSF design. The two categories are not entirely consistent with the traditional budgetary classification of recurrent and capital expenditures. The idea is to allow for local administration tasks and activities that directly contribute to local economic and social development. Thus, administrative funds can be used for certain capital expenditures, such as the purchase of council headquarters or vehicles. Similarly, the understanding of development expenditures as both capital and recurrent also provides the councils with the often-critical flexibility to cover the maintenance and operation costs associated with the provision of infrastructure and services, as well as the management and technical services costs associated with the preparation and implementation of investment projects.

Transfers from the CSF may be used for any expenditure (administrative or development, recurrent or capital) that is reflected in the council's approved budget and does not violate the Commune Law or any other law and regulation issued by the Government of Cambodia. Table 1 provides an illustration of their classification.

This matrix classification introduces some additional requirements in the process of local-level budgeting, as councils need to convert the general administration and local development transfers into contributions to recurrent and capital expenditures in their budgets. In the process, the councils are expected

TABLE 1
Classification of Eligible Expenditures

	Recurrent Expenditures	Capital Expenditures
Administrative Expenditures	• Allowances to councilors • Salaries of local staff and other personnel expenses • Rental of office premises • Routine repair and maintenance of administrative facilities • Utility charges • Fuel, lubricants and vehicles maintenance • Other consumables and miscellaneous	• Purchase of the council's premises • Major repair and maintenance works on administrative facilities • Furniture and office equipment for the council's or administration's facilities • Purchase of vehicles
Development Expenditures	• Personnel and other recurrent costs associated with the operation of the local infrastructure and the delivery of related services • Support of community development programs managed by local NGOs and community-based organizations, including education and information campaigns, environmental protection and natural resources management, and other programs impacting on the welfare of local population • Routine maintenance of local economic and social infrastructure	The survey, design, construction, and major repair and maintenance of: • Roads, bridges • Markets • Educational and health care facilities, community centers • Irrigation networks and structures, agricultural storage facilities • Water and power supply and • Other economic and social infrastructure

to also take into account any mandatory administrative or development expenditures that future regulations may assign to them, as well as any minimum or maximum requirements with respect to the share of CSF resources that they may use for recurrent and capital expenditures.

Table 2 summarizes illustrative general rules that commune councils will be required to follow in budgeting the CSF transfers and converting the general administration and local development transfers into allocations for recurrent and capital expenditures. The fund board is preparing detailed guidance to the councils on this reconciliation procedure.

TABLE 2
Budgetary Rules

	Rules for Budgeting the CSF Transfer Components as Contribution for	
	Recurrent Expenditures	**Capital Expenditures**
Transfer for General Administration (100%)	Minimum = MAE Maximum = 100%	Minimum = 0% Maximum = Total – MAE
Transfer for Local Development (100%)	Minimum = MDE Maximum = 20%	Minimum = 80% Maximum = Total – MDE

Note: MAE = fund's resources required to ensure the full coverage of the councils' mandatory administrative expenditures.
MDE = fund's resources required to ensure the full coverage of the councils' mandatory development expenditures.

8. CSF Allocation Formula

The CSF subdecree requires that resources transferable to individual commune/sangkat councils be determined by a formula consistent with the purpose of the fund. The general formula initially adopted by the NCSC is outlined below.

The total resources in the CSF distributable pool (T) are divided into the two components of the fund: the general administration component (T_1) and the local development component (T_2), so that $T = T_1 + T_2$ and $T_1 < \frac{1}{3} T$ and $T_2 > \frac{2}{3} T$. The resources of the general administration component (T_1) will be distributed to all communes/sangkats in proportion to the number (n_i) of councillors in their council, so that the council (i) is entitled to $T_{1i} = T_1 \cdot (n_i / \Sigma n_i)$ with $i = 1 \ldots 1,621$. The number of councilors is used here as a proxy for the council's need to support its routine operations.

The resources of the local development component (T_2) are distributed only to communes classified in category 1. The resources in this component are divided into three shares: an equal share (T_{21}), a population share (T_{22}), and a poverty share (T_{23}) so that $T_2 = T_{21} + T_{22} + T_{23}$ where $T_{21} = \alpha T_2$, $T_{22} = \beta T_2$, $T_{23} = \gamma T_2$ and α, β, γ are weights of the three shares to be determined by the CSF board such that $\alpha + \beta + \gamma = 1$ with $\gamma > 0.40$. Diagram 1 below illustrates the components and shares in which the total distributable pool (T) is decomposed.

The amount allocated to individual communes/sangkats from the equal share component is set by the CSF board as a fixed amount ($T_{21i} = K$) to be allocated equally to all participating communes/sangkats, so that $K = T_{21}/N_1$ where N_1 is the number of communes/sangkats classified in category 1. The equal share component is meant to provide a minimum of development

DIAGRAM 1
Components of the Commune/Sangkat Fund Distributable Pool

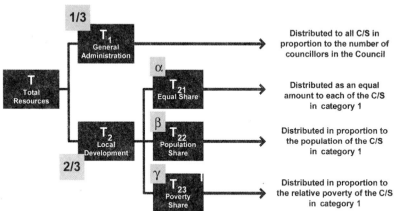

resources, irrespective of the commune/sangkat size, reflecting the indivisibility of many investment costs. This will favor smaller communes/sangkats, which will receive a higher per capita allocation.

The amount allocated from the population is proportional to the population of the commune/sangkat so that $T_{22i} = T_{22} \cdot (p_i/\Sigma\, p_i)$ where p_i is the population of the individual commune/sangkat, and Σp_i is the sum of the population of all communes/sangkats in category 1. The population share reflects the assumption that development needs generally grow with the size of the community. This portion of the transfer is neutral with respect to fiscal equalization as it distributes an equal per capita amount to all participating communes.

The amount allocated from the poverty component is proportional to the relative poverty of the commune/sangkat so that $T_{23i} = T_{23} \cdot (\pi_i p_i/\Sigma \pi_i p_i)$, where p_i is the population and π_i is an indicator of relative poverty of the individual commune/sangkat in category 1. In FY2002 the indicator of relative poverty π may be constructed as a composite index from village-level data in the commune database maintained in selected provinces (including all covered by the Seila program) by the Provincial Departments of Planning. In 2002, the commune database will have to be set up and maintained in all provinces, and/or alternative methods to allocate the poverty share of the transfers, will need to be developed by the ministry of planning and adopted by the fund board.

The full formula can be summarized as follows:

$$T_i = [T_1 \cdot (n_i/\Sigma\, n_i)] + [\alpha T_2/N_1 + \beta T_2 \cdot (p_i/\Sigma p_i) + \gamma T_2 \cdot (\pi_i p_i/\Sigma \pi_i p_i)]$$

where:

T_i = Amount transferred to commune/sangkat (i)

T_1 = Portion of the CSF earmarked to support the general administration expenditures of the C/S councils

T_2 = Portion of the CSF earmarked to support the local development expenditures of the C/S councils

n_i = Number of councilors in commune/sangkat (i)

N_1 = Number of communes/sangkats classified in category 1

p_i = Population of commune/sangkat (i)

π_i = Poverty index of commune/sangkat (i)

α = Percentage of the local development component of the CSF to be distributed as an equal share to all communes/sangkats in category 1

β = Percentage of the local development component of the CSF to be distributed in proportion to the population of the communes/sangkats in category 1

γ = Percentage of the local development component of the CSF to be distributed in proportion to the population-weighted poverty index of the communes/sangkats in category 1

Considering the difficulties involved in defining and measuring vertical and horizontal fiscal imbalances in this early stage of the process, the formula addresses such imbalances only in a rudimentary form. On the other hand, the formula does not seem to address the third objective of the CSF, which is to provide incentives for better performance of local authorities. Instead, the enhancement of the councils' performance is addressed through the establishment and administration of certain conditions of access to the CSF resources.

9. Conditions of Access

To actually receive the CSF resources to which they are entitled under the distribution formula, councils must demonstrate that they have followed a process of participatory planning, budgeting and implementation, as well as have completed all financial reports on the execution of their budget and development plan. They must also show that they have mobilized beneficiaries' contributions and other local resources to complement the transfers from the fund's local development component.

The first two conditions refer to the councils' performance on the expenditure side; that is, in their planning, programming, budgeting, implementing, monitoring, and reporting of the use of local public resources. The third condition refers to the councils' performance on the revenue side. The latter is limited to the councils' effort to mobilize counterpart funds from the direct beneficiaries of the local development activities to which CSF transfers are applied. After a minimum of specific fiscal powers are eventually devolved to the councils, this condition may be reformulated in terms of a broader fiscal effort requirement.

Clearly, the above formulation of the conditions of access is too vague to be operational. The fund board is expected to provide councils with additional operational instructions and reporting formats. Meanwhile no conditions are expected to apply to the first two of the three annual installments through which CSF resources will be transferred to communes/sangkats in FY2002. This should not pose serious problems, as the category 1 communes receiving the development component have all met most of the requirements through participation in the Seila program. The other communes/sangkats have to be brought up to this level. Once again, the keys to achieve the CSF objective of stimulating improved local level resources mobilization and management will be the development of a realistic and evolving set of performance requirements, the provision of the technical services that councils may need to assimilate and satisfy such requirements, and the effective monitoring of the councils' compliance. As much of the responsibility for these support and supervision functions will belong to the provincial governors' offices and the provincial offices of the newly created Department of Local Administrations (DOLA) of the MOI, strengthening these structures is now a priority of the Government of Cambodia and is expected to receive substantial attention from external aid agencies.

10. CSF Disbursement Procedures

The procedures for disbursement of the CSF resources reflect the constraints prevailing in Cambodia, especially the underdevelopment of a commercial bank network beyond the provincial capitals and the still embryonic character of the communes/sangkats administrations.

Communes/sangkats will hold deposit accounts at the provincial treasuries. At the request of the Minister of Interior, the National Treasury will transfer to these accounts the approved annual allocation to which the individual communes/sangkats are entitled. The annual transfers will be divided into three installments of 50%, 30% and 20%, to be made before 1 March, 1 June, and 1 September, respectively. Payments against commitments entered into by the commune/sangkat head (the *mekhun*) on behalf of the local council will be made by the commune accountant, a staff member of the Provincial Treasury, or by the manager of a petty cash reserve maintained in the commune/sangkat as authorized by the Provincial Treasury. Although these procedures will prevail in the near term, the CSF subdecree allows for the piloting of alternative arrangements under which the MOEF will authorize councils to hold their accounts in a commercial bank. Councils will then use their accountants (staff of the local administration rather than the Provincial Treasury) and internal control procedures (instead of payments controls by the treasury), subject to provincial audit. If successful, this approach can be generalized for all communes.

D. Conclusions

The commune councils created by the February 2002 elections need resources for their basic functioning as an elected body and a level of local administration, as well as for promoting local development and delivering local infrastructure and services. The latter function is critical for the new councils to become relevant to their constituents, thereby encouraging communities and individuals to invest their energies in local-level participatory governance.

Devolving own-source revenue-raising powers to the councils is the longer-term answer and the most appropriate one to foster local accountability. At some point in the future, the councils should be able to cover their operating costs through own-source revenues and to finance at least part of their local investment needs through savings on recurrent expenditures. But, at the outset of their mandate, Cambodian local councils will have to rely heavily on fiscal transfers to cover both their administration and development expenditures. And even in the long run, as worldwide experience shows, fiscal transfers are likely to remain important features of the Cambodian local finance system.

The Commune/Sangkat Fund represents the first attempt to design a mechanism for fiscal transfers in an environment characterized by very incipient decentralization reforms. This environment made the task of the CSF designers particularly challenging. The absence of legally defined service delivery responsibilities of the new councils and the lack of devolution of specific fiscal powers made it difficult to argue for any particular size of the total distributable pool of CSF resources, for developing a rational basis to correct vertical and horizontal imbalances, or for building mechanisms that would link transfers to local fiscal effort. On the other hand, starting from scratch saved the CSF designers from the complications of dismantling preexisting, and often confusing and contradicting, transfer schemes. Starting from scratch also allowed the CSF designers to better reflect on some of the specificities of the Cambodian situation in the design of the fund. Three points are worth highlighting in this respect.

First, the objectives of the fiscal transfers could not be limited to the traditional ones of correcting vertical and horizontal fiscal imbalances. It was also necessary to explicitly develop a system and incentives for local mobilization and management of local public resources. Local capacity building thus became a primary objective of the CSF, recognizing the role that transfers could play in developing and sustaining an autonomous local-level development planning, budgeting and implementation process. Local capacity is to be built by requiring that councils progressively comply with a set of good practice requirements attached to this process. As discussed above, the application of transfers to the objective of local-level capacity building raises the issue of Cambodia's capacity and willingness to invest in a provincial-level system of support and supervision to the emerging local government sector. This is perhaps the most critical constraint to the advancement of the decentralization reform process in Cambodia.

A second key feature of the CSF is to explicitly open it to external co-financing. This recognizes the role that external financing has played and is likely to continue playing for some time in Cambodia's national and local development spending. Most external mechanisms to deliver aid for local development, however, typically focus principally on the quick delivery of goods and services, limiting capacity-building efforts, if any, to enhance local capacity required to access specific external sources of funds. In this case, there is a need to open a channel for external resources to support general-purpose transfers and the related extension of institutionalized resource management practices at the local level. Developing external support for regular general-purpose fiscal transfers, however, requires that the many problems of strategy and accountability that such co-financing raises be addressed and resolved through new and more effective partnership arrangements between the Government of Cambodia and international funding agencies.

Finally, a critical feature of the CSF is its classification of communes in terms of their absorptive capacity and the establishment of a gradual and transparent process of progressive access of all communes to development spending. As difficult and politically controversial as this classification may be, it is essential as part of a strategic approach to implement decentralization reforms. In this regard, it ties the expansion of the number of communes accessing resources for local investments to the simultaneous expansion of the capacity of the provincial administrations to provide technical assistance and performance monitoring. It also ensures better use of scarce development resources by avoiding their spreading too thinly.

FY2002 is the first year of operation of the CSF. Many aspects of its design need to be tested and fine-tuned, and several additional regulations are still being drafted. An even preliminary evaluation of its capitalization, operations and impact will have to wait for some time. It will be worth waiting, however, as the CSF has the potential to become an effective mechanism for fiscal transfers and local-level capacity building in Cambodia as well as a source of lessons for other countries undertaking similar efforts. In any event, it clearly represents a first step towards the development of an efficient and equitable system of fiscal transfers in Cambodia.

References

El Mensi, Mohammed. 2001. *Commune Financial Management System, Fiscal Decentralization Background Paper 2*. Phnom Penh: UN/DESA—UNDP.

Prud'homme, Rémy. 2001. *Intergovernmental Fiscal Transfers, Fiscal Decentralization Background Paper 1*. Phnom Penh: UN/DESA—UNDP.

————. 2001. *Cambodia Mission Report*. Paris: UNDP.

Romeo, Leonardo. 2001. *Towards a Regulatory Framework for Decentralized Financing and Planning in Cambodia*. Kuala Lumpur: UNOPS—UNDP.

————. 1998. *Seila/CARERE and the Emerging Model of Decentralized Rural Development in Cambodia*. Phnom Penh: UNCDF.

————. 2000. *The Seila Program and Decentralized Planning in Cambodia*. Phnom Penh: UNOPS.

Royal Government of Cambodia. 2002. *Anukret 16/ANK/BK, Regulation of the Commune/Sangkat Fund (CSF)*. Phnom Penh.

————. 2001. *Law on the Communes/Sangkat Administration*. Phnom Penh.

Smoke, Paul. 2000. *Cambodia: Decentralized Fiscal Options and Instruments*. Phnom Penh: UN/DESA.

————. 2001. *Commune Own-Source Revenue, Fiscal Decentralization Background Paper 3*. Phnom Penh: UN/DESA—UNDP.

4

India

D.K. Srivastava[1]
National Institute of Public Finance and Policy, New Delhi

A. Introduction

The federal system in India comprises a central government, 28 states, two union territories (UTs) with legislatures, five UTs without legislatures, several autonomous regions within states, a three-tiered structure of rural local bodies, and three levels of urban local bodies. The system provides for an asymmetric constitutional treatment of the states of Jammu and Kashmir, and an asymmetric economic treatment of special category states (SCS). As per the classification of the Planning Commission, 10 states are categorized as special while the remaining states are considered general category states (GCS). Several key characteristics of the states are presented in Exhibit 1.

Critical institutions that intermediate between the central, state and local governments include the (central) Finance Commission (FC), the Planning Commission, the Interstate Council, the National Development Council, and State Finance Commissions (SFCs), one for each state. While the Planning Commission is a permanent body, the central and state level FCs are set up with a normal periodicity of five years.

Three new states—Uttaranchal, Chattisgarh, and Jharkhand—created in November 2000, were carved out from the parent states of Uttar Pradesh, Madhya

1. The study benefited from interactions with Mr. Y.H. Kim of ADB. Together with him, we had extended discussions with Dr. N.J. Kurian, Adviser (Financial Resources), Planning Commission, Mr. D. Swarup, Additional Secretary (Budget), Ministry of Finance and Mr. R.P. Sinha, Principal Adviser (State Plans), Planning Commission. At the National Institute of Public Finance and Policy, we had discussions with Dr. Ashok Lahiri, Director, Prof. Om Prakash Mathur, Principal Consultant, and Dr. Amaresh Bagchi, Emeritus Professor. At the NIPFP, I had received considerable help in the form of materials and observations on initial drafts from Mr. T.S. Rangamannar, Dr. C. Bhujanga Rao, and Ms. Ritu Bahl. Mr. R.S. Tyagi provided adept secretarial assistance. While I acknowledge and thank them for their help and support, I remain responsible for any remaining errors.

EXHIBIT 1
Introducing Indian States

States	GSDP (factor cost) PCGSDP (Nominal) Average 1994–97	GSDP (factor cost) (Rs crore) 1997–98	Population (lakhs) 1991	Literacy Rate (percent) 1991	Poverty Ratios (percent) 1993–94	Infant Mortality Rate (per 000 live births) 1991–92	Life expectancy at birth (years) 1991–95
General Category States							
Bihar	5528.7	55552	863.74	38.48	54.96	71.00	59.30
Uttar Pradesh	7702.3	129977	1391.12	41.60	40.85	85.00	56.80
Orissa	7909.0	27065	316.60	49.09	48.56	96.00	56.50
Madhya Pradesh	9589.3	70832	661.81	44.20	42.52	94.00	54.70
West Bengal	10171.0	89490	680.78	57.70	35.66	55.00	62.10
Rajasthan	10377.0	52481	440.06	38.55	27.41	85.00	59.10
Andhra Pradesh	11366.3	88387	665.08	44.09	22.19	63.00	61.80
Karnataka	12367.3	65515	449.77	56.04	33.16	53.00	62.50
Kerala	13091.3	42433	290.99	89.81	25.43	12.00	72.90
Tamil Nadu	13926.3	87394	558.59	62.66	35.03	53.00	63.30
Gujarat	16331.7	86609	413.10	61.29	24.21	62.00	61.00
Haryana	16927.3	37427	164.64	55.85	25.05	68.00	63.40
Punjab	18568.3	50358	202.82	58.51	11.77	51.00	67.20
Maharashtra	19098.0	182295	789.37	64.87	36.86	47.00	64.80
Goa	25075.7	3091	11.70	75.51	14.92	NA	NA
Special Category States							
Assam	7968.3	21336	224.14	52.89	40.86	76.00	55.70
Tripura	7983.7	2118	27.57	60.44	39.01	NA	NA
Manipur	8799.3	1809	18.37	59.89	33.78	NA	NA
Meghalaya	9823.7	2033	17.75	49.10	37.92	NA	NA
Jammu & Kashmir	10007.3	NA	77.19	NA	25.17	NA	NA
Arunachal Pradesh	10705.3	1496	8.65	41.59	39.35	NA	NA
Sikkim	11109.3	550	4.06	56.94	41.43	NA	NA
Himachal Pradesh	12153.7	6291	51.71	63.86	28.44	NA	NA
Mizoram	12378.0	995	6.90	82.27	25.66	NA	NA
Nagaland	12932.7	1914	12.10	61.65	37.92	NA	NA
All States	12075.6	1108449	8348.61	56.95	33.12	64.73	61.41
All India		1384446	8463.05	52.21	35.97	71.00	60.30

Union Territories *with Legislatures*: Delhi and Pondichery
Union Territories *without Legislatures*: Andaman and Nicober Islands, Chandigarh, Dadra and Nagar Haveli, Daman and Diu, and Lakshadweep.

New states created in Novermber 2000
Uttaranchal by dividing Uttar Pradesh into two states
Chattisgarh by dividing Madhya Pradesh
Jharkand by dividing the state of Bihar into two states

Note: PCGSDP—per capita gross state domestic product; GSDP—gross state domestic product
Figures in this table and throughout the paper are often presented in lakh or crore. Lakh represents 100,000, while crore represents 10 million (100 lakhs). The Indian currency is the rupee (Rs.)

Pradesh, and Bihar, respectively. All the three parent states are large and low-income states (LIS), and the three new states are even poorer or otherwise more disadvantaged than their parent states. The process of creating new states and demands from other regions in other states for separate statehood have gathered strength in the context of growing interregional disparities in the country. These developments have potentially major implications for public finances in India.

The focus of this chapter is the role of fiscal transfers from the center to subnational governments in ameliorating or accentuating disparities in the levels of publicly provided services and overall growth across regions and states within India. We first review the main developments in the economic and fiscal spheres in the 1990s, highlighting reforms that were initiated in the early 1990s and their implications for regional growth. We also examine the pattern of national and state economic growth and the fiscal profiles of central and state governments. The bulk of the study is devoted to an examination of the components of intergovernmental transfers for current and development purposes. We consider the various Finance and Planning Commission transfers, as well as the role of external assistance. We close with a set of recommendations for major reforms to the intergovernmental fiscal transfer system in India.

B. Economic and Fiscal Scenario in the Nineties

1. Economic Reforms: Main Features

The 1990s witnessed momentous changes in the macroeconomic scenario of India in terms of economic growth, sectoral composition of output, public finances, and the overall policy environment that influenced the macroeconomic outcomes. In particular, comprehensive economic reforms initiated in the early 1990s led to a substantial rise in the overall growth rate by the mid-1990s. Towards the close of the decade, reforms appeared to have slowed down as industrial recession seriously beset the economy for three consecutive years. The public finances of the center as well as the states have exhibited chronic imbalances in the form of large revenue and fiscal deficits.

Three events triggered economic reforms in India at the beginning of the 1990s. First, the collapse of the erstwhile USSR signaled the need to recast economic policies that had hitherto been inward-looking, centered on five-year plans, and heavily reliant on administrative mechanisms for controlling prices and outputs. Second, the transformation of GATT into WTO increased the urgency to bring reforms that would foster globalization of the economy. Third, in 1991, the foreign exchange reserves had dwindled to such low levels that reform of the exchange rate regime became urgent.

Reforms began with two massive doses of devaluation in 1991 within the span of two months. The exchange rate regime was formally changed in 1993, providing the necessary flexibility for the exchange rate to respond to market signals. Up to the mid-1990s, reforms proceeded at a fast pace with the lowering of tariff barriers, lifting of quantitative restrictions on imports, lowering of personal and corporate income taxes, reduction and rationalization of import duties, and reforms of domestic commodity taxation. The central government agreed to certain limits on borrowing from the Reserve Bank of India through ad hoc treasury bills. Bank interest rates were deregulated from October 1, 1998. Industries reserved for the public sector were limited to only six areas, including defense products, atomic energy, coal and lignite, mineral oils, railway transport, and minerals related to atomic energy. Finally, the number of items requiring industrial licensing was reduced to 15 that account for less than 15% of value added in the manufacturing sector.

The positive results of the early reforms became immediately visible. The GDP growth rate reached 5% in 1992–1993, and peaked around 7% in the mid-1990s (1994–1995 to 1996–1997). It then slumped due to an industrial recession, but still remained well above the average growth rates of the 1970s and early 1980s. The sectoral composition of output also steadily shifted towards services, which presently account for more than 50% of the GDP. A reasonable degree of control on the growth of monetary aggregates and a fall in center's monetized deficits as a proportion of the central budget and GDP have also led to an era of low inflation. The rate of inflation during 1999–2000 was about 5% compared to the previous peak of 7% in 1996–1997.

The government promised a white paper on a second generation of reforms, but this was never issued. In the latter years of the 1990s, the reform process was characterized by tardy progress in disinvestment of public sector undertakings, opening up banking and insurance sectors, full convertibility of the rupee, and reforms at the state level. Problems have arisen during this period. Nominal interest rates are high, ranging between 12–17%, and lower inflation means that real interest rates are also high. This makes the low savings rate even more worrisome than it might be if rates were lower. On the positive side, there is a reasonably healthy current account balance position, which has remained below 2% of GDP in recent years. Exports have been rising at an average rate of 11% whereas import growth was about 10% during 1999–2000. Some of the main features of the macroeconomy in the 1990s are summarized in Table 1.

2. Fiscal Scenario in the 1990s

While the growth parameters of the economy showed marked improvement during much of the 1990s, public finances have fared poorly. The decade closed with the highest-ever levels of fiscal and revenue deficits on the combined

TABLE 1
Indian Macroeconomy: Key Developments in the 1990s

	1994–1995	1995–1996	1996–1997	1997–1998	1998–1999	1999–2000
Growth Rate (% Change Over Previous Year)						
GDP (at 1993–1994 Prices)	7.0	7.3	7.5	5.0	6.8	5.9
Agriculture & Allied Services	5.0	(0.9)	9.6	(1.9)	7.2	0.8
Industry (excluding Construction)	10.4	12.8	6.8	4.9	3.7	6.4
Services (including Construction)	6.8	10.0	6.6	9.2	8.0	8.3
Implicit Price Deflator (% Change)	9.4	8.0	7.8	6.5	9.0	3.5
Sectoral Shares						
Agriculture & Allied Services	30.4	28.1	28.6	26.7	26.8	25.5
Industry (excluding Construction)	21.7	22.8	22.7	22.7	22.0	22.1
Services (including Construction)	47.9	49.1	48.7	50.6	51.2	52.3
As Percentage of GDP at Market Prices						
Gross Domestic Savings	25.0	25.5	23.3	24.7	22.3	–
Gross Domestic Capital Formation	26.1	27.2	24.6	26.2	23.4	–
Trade Balance	(2.8)	(3.2)	(3.9)	(3.8)	(3.1)	–
Current Account Balance	(1.0)	(1.7)	(1.2)	(1.4)	(1.0)	(1.5)

Note: All GDP figures pertain to new series with 1993–1994 as base year.
Source: Handbook of Statistics on Indian Economy, *Reserve Bank of India Bulletin, 1999*, Economic Survey, 1999–2000, April 2000.

account of the center and the states. Chronic and ever-growing revenue deficits were described by the Eleventh Finance Commission (EFC) as "malefic fixtures" in the public fiscal profiles. Individual states, first the fiscally weaker ones, and then, even the higher per capita income states, have successively slid into revenue deficit. These revenue deficits, embedded in unsustainable fiscal deficits, are visible manifestations of multiple and deeper deficiencies in government finances.

The magnitude of the revenue deficit on the combined account of the central and the state governments as percentage of GDP has steadily increased since 1982–1983. Throughout the period since 1987–1988, the revenue deficit has remained at more than 3% of GDP, while in three years (1990–1991, 1993–1994 and 1997–1998), it reached a level close to 4.5%. The aggregate revenue deficit of the center and the states is estimated to be 6.77% of GDP (new series) in 1999–2000, which is the highest level in India's fiscal history (Table 2).

The central budget by itself has remained in revenue deficit since 1979–1980. In 1993–1994, the central revenue deficit alone was 3.81% of GDP (new series). Since then, there was a gradual decline up to 1996–1997, but it rose again, standing at 3.81% of GDP (new series) in 1999–2000. It is estimated to

TABLE 2
Center and States: Aggregate Budgetary Balance
(% of GDP New Series)

Year	Fiscal Deficit			Revenue Deficit			Primary Deficit		
	Center	States	Combined	Center	States	Combined	Center	States	Combined
1990–91[a]	8.33	3.28	9.64	3.47	0.84	4.31	4.32	1.69	5.00
1991–92	5.89	2.93	7.17	2.64	0.81	3.45	1.58	1.19	2.19
1992–93	5.69	2.92	7.38	2.63	0.72	3.36	1.29	1.06	2.23
1990–91	7.88	3.10	9.11	3.28	0.79	4.07	4.08	1.60	4.73
1991–92	5.57	2.77	6.78	2.50	0.77	3.26	1.49	1.13	2.07
1992–93	5.38	2.76	6.98	2.49	0.68	3.18	1.22	1.00	2.11
1993–94	7.01	2.35	8.19	3.81	0.45	4.25	2.74	0.52	3.20
1994–95	5.71	2.73	7.02	3.07	0.70	3.77	1.35	0.80	1.84
1995–96	5.10	2.60	6.44	2.52	0.73	3.25	0.86	0.81	1.52
1996–97	4.90	2.79	6.40	2.40	1.34	3.73	0.53	0.91	1.26
1997–98	5.87	2.93	7.32	3.06	1.22	4.28	1.54	0.94	1.33
1998–99	6.43	4.23	8.99	3.85	2.57	6.43	2.01	2.22	3.06
1999–00[b]	5.64	4.71	9.84	3.81	2.96	6.77	0.90	2.41	2.02

Notes: [a] The first three rows refer to old series GDP, the rest to the new series, which uses a 1993–1994 base year. For the first three years, the old series was converted into new series by using a conversion factor of 1.0577, as given in the report of EFC (p. 7).

  [b] For 1999–2000, fiscal deficit and primary deficit of the center exclude the states' and UTs' share of small savings.

Source: Adapted from *Report of the Eleventh Finance Commission (EFC), June 2000, p. 7*, Government of India.

be 3.6% in 2000–2001. The states, on the other hand, after receiving the transfers from the center in the form of tax devolution and grants, remained in surplus until 1986–1987 except for some isolated years. Their aggregate revenue deficit remained below 1% of GDP until 1996–1997. By 1999–2000, their aggregate revenue deficit was estimated to be 2.96% of GDP (new series).

The time profiles of revenue deficits differ from state to state. Since 1987–1988, most of the major states have remained in revenue deficit with some sporadic exceptions.[2] Among the general category states, the last revenue surplus (for Goa) was observed in 1996–1997. Most of the special category states exhibit surplus on revenue account. This, however, is a peculiar feature of the plan transfer mechanism (discussed below) through which a large part of their capital expenditure is met by grants on revenue account under a 90:10 grant-to-loan ratio. These states are in deficit in their nonplan revenue account.

The combined fiscal deficit of the central and state governments has been

2. Andhra Pradesh was an exception for 1993–94 to 1995–96; Gujarat was in revenue surplus in 1993–94 along with Haryana and Karnataka; Rajasthan was in revenue surplus in 1990–91 and 1991–92.

substantial for many years, reaching a peak of 10.41% of GDP in 1986–1987.[3] Conscious efforts to reduce the fiscal deficit brought it down to 6.40% in 1996–1997, a gain of more than 3.20 percentage points compared to 1990–1991. Since that time, the fiscal deficit has been on the rise again. By 1999–2000, it was estimated to be 9.84% of GDP (new series), not far below its historic peak.

3. Structure of Public Finances: Key Dimensions and Causes of Deterioration

The above analysis of fiscal and revenue deficits does not tell the full story of the problems in Indian public finance. Some additional points are worth highlighting. Unless otherwise noted, the fiscal aggregates discussed here refer to old-series GDP (1980–1981 as base year).

- The tax-GDP ratio of the center and the states, which peaked at around 17% in 1986–1987 and 1987–1988, fell to about 15% in 1998–1999 (14% in relation to the new GDP series).
- The nontax revenue to GDP ratio has stagnated below 2.5% of GDP for many years. Only in the late 1980s did it reach a level of 3% of GDP.
- Interest payments as a proportion of GDP, which were a little above 2% in 1981–1982, crossed the level of 5% in 1997–1998, and have risen further since.
- Development expenditures, which were 10.40% of GDP in 1986–1987, fell by 2 percentage points in the next 10 years.
- Revenue expenditures as a percentage of GDP reached 22% in 1986–1987. They are around that level presently.
- Aggregate government expenditures in 1986–1987 were slightly above 30%, but fell to around 27% by 1998–1999 (25% with respect to new GDP series). The burden of adjustment was entirely on capital expenditures, which fell from 8.23% of GDP in 1986–1987 to 3.52% in 1998–1999.
- Pensions are becoming larger and larger relative to GDP, increasing from 0.16% in 1974–1975 to 1.34% in 1998–1999.
- Having reached a peak of 3.83% of GDP in 1986–1987, defence expenditure has steadily declined to 2.5% in recent years.
- The outstanding debt to GDP ratio rose above 65% in 1990–1991, but fell in the mid-1990s. At the end of 1999–2000, it is estimated to be back at the level of the early 1990s.

Clearly, the overall performance of government finances has been deteriorating in many respects. Three proximate reasons can be cited for the par-

---

3. The sum of center's and states' fiscal deficits exceeds the combined fiscal deficit by the extent of center's on-lending to the states.

ticularly serious crisis in government finances in the late 1990s. First, an industrial recession that had an unmitigated run for nearly three years depressed tax revenues. Second, salaries and pensions of central government employees were revised subsequent to the recommendations of the Fifth Central Pay Commission, and the consequent in-tandem revisions of salaries and pensions of state government employees pushed state budgets deep into the red. Third, the high level of nominal interest rates, itself being caused by ballooning government borrowing requirements, further deepened the crisis.

The deterioration of public finances, however, is rooted in a number of longer-term problems. Important among these is the long-term erosion of the tax-GDP ratio, which reflects undertaxation of services and agriculture, as well as inefficiencies in tax administration. The long-term history of tax revenues indicates a steady upward trend until 1987–1988. Between 1960–1961 and 1987–1988, tax revenues as a percentage of GDP (old series) increased from 8.33 to 17.10%. This ratio was still above 17% in 1989–1990. After that, it declined to 15.04% in 1993–1994, recovering marginally in the later 1990s. Tax revenues as a percentage of the new GDP series (1993–1994 base) stood at around 14% in 1999–2000. Direct taxes have picked up by about one percentage point in the 1990s, while indirect taxes have lost more than two percentage points. States' own tax revenues as percentage of GDP reached a level of 5.81% in 1991–1992, but declined in later years. States tax revenues have remained stagnant relative to GDP during the 1990s, and show a marginal decline between 1987–1988 and 1996–1997. States own tax revenues in 1999–2000 amounted to 5.15% of GDP (new series). The center's gross tax collections show a larger decline, the fall being close to 1.7 percentage points from the peak of 11.30% in 1987–1988. Tax revenue buoyancies peaked in the 1970s for both the central and state governments. Since then, decadal values indicate considerable erosion of buoyancy (Table 3).

TABLE 3
Tax Buoyancies: Combined, Center and States

	Total Tax Revenue (Combined)	Center's Gross Tax Revenue	States' Own Tax Revenue
1950–51 to 1959–60	1.38	1.38	1.39
1960–61 to 1969–70	1.16	1.15	1.17
1970–71 to 1979–80	1.30	1.27	1.35
1980–81 to 1989–90	1.14	1.15	1.12
1990–91 to 1998–99	0.96	0.91	1.04
1950–51 to 1998–99	1.17	1.17	1.19

Source: Government of India, *Report of the Eleventh Finance Commission, June 2000.*

TABLE 4
Profile of Recovery Rates
(Percent of Cost)

	Merit			Nonmerit			All
	Social	Economic	Total	Social	Economic	Total	Services
Center	2.93	1.72	1.98	12.38	11.65	11.73	10.59
States	0.60	1.63	0.92	2.15	10.75	7.35	5.58
All-India	0.74	1.66	1.10	3.54	11.17	8.98	7.21

Source: Srivastava, D.K., Tapas K. Sen and others (1997), *Government Subsidies in India*, NIPFP, New Delhi.

A second long-term cause is the indifferent performance of public sector enterprises, which claim a large amount of budgetary funds in India. Investment in these enterprises takes the form of equity as well as loans. In central public enterprises, total investment had exceeded Rs230,000 crore at the end of 1998–1999. In the states, nearly Rs75,000 crore have been invested in statutory corporations and nearly Rs42,000 crore, in government companies. Together, investment in public enterprises amounts to about Rs350,000 crore. On this investment, the rate of return generated by the state-level public enterprises is near zero, but it is difficult to provide a firm aggregate figure because these enterprises frequently fail to finalize their accounts, so that profit/loss figures are not uniformly available. The central public sector undertakings have better accounts. In 1998–1999, 127 of them made profits (83 declared dividends) while 106 made losses (dividends and interest). The return on central government investment amounted to 5.21% in 1998–1999. The profit-making enterprises are mostly in the petroleum, telecommunications, and financial sectors. Low productivity of public sector enterprises and their continued dependence on budgetary resources have been a considerable drag on the resources of the central and state governments.

A third long-term malaise is the poor cost recovery from publicly provided services. The profile of recovery rates for the center and states for both merit and nonmerit services in social and economic sectors for 1994–1995 is summarized in Table 4. Merit services are defined as services where large externalities are present and costs may be subsidized, while nonmerit services are characterized by low or no externalities and the services are akin to private goods or services. With such poor cost recovery, services have to be financed from general revenues, upsetting budgetary balance.

Finally, on the expenditure side, an intrinsic pressure evolved over time for convergence of salary structures between central and state governments, and between state and local governments. Many states gave up the practice of appointing their own Pay Commissions, and more and more salary and pension bills in the states have little relationship to their capacities to pay. The loss of the link between wages and the productivity of wage earners is potentially debilitating and has become an underlying cause for growing fiscal disequilibrium.

4. Growing Interstate Disparities

India has been suffering from regional imbalances in terms of both income (gross state domestic product, or GSDP) and the fiscal capacities of states to provide administrative, social, and economic services. Low-income states have continued to stagnate while the richer states have enjoyed very high growth rates, resulting in growing disparities in real per capita GSDP. Table 5 summarizes the pattern of growth of GSDP at 1980–1981 prices for two periods, 1980–1981 to 1989–1990 and 1990–1991 to 1997–1998. Table 6 highlights the growing differences in the levels of per capita income. The ratio of the per capita income of the highest income state (Goa) to that of the lowest income state (Bihar) was around 3.76% in 1980–1981. It has continued to increase over the years, reaching nearly 6% in 1995–1996.

Growing GSDP disparities translate into growing interstate disparities in the provision of level of public services. In spite of nearly 50 years of a system of equalizing intergovernmental transfers, per capita expenditures show wide variations. Table 7 shows the relative position of low-income states (LIS) vis-à-vis the high-income states (HIS) in general (GCS) and special category states (SCS) over the period 1994–1995 to 1996–1997. With respect to each of the three service categories (general, social, and economic), the broad pattern is that the per capita expenditure is lower in the low GSDP states. Thus, if equalization of service levels is an objective of fiscal transfers, it has not been achieved. On average, for example, the LIS spend only half as much in per capita terms as the HIS on social services, while the middle-income states spend only 73% as much. These differences translate into disparities in literacy rates, health indicators, and standards of governance.

5. Institutional Failures

The persistent deterioration of public finances in India partially results from institutional failures. In particular, there has been a failure of coordination between three important specialized institutions—the Planning Commission, the Pay Commission, and the Finance Commission. The Planning Commission operates with a temporal myopia in which its horizon is limited to finding resources for a period of five years. It develops plans that result in the creation of staff posts at the central and state levels. If these posts are continued beyond the plan period, the concerned governments must find resources to fund them. This process is repeated when a new plan is prepared. In practice, all the government

TABLE 5
Growth Rates of Per Capita GSDP (at 1980–1981 Prices)
(Percent)

State	Period		Difference (2) – (1)
	1980–81 to 1989–90	1990–91 to 1997–98	
	(1)	(2)	(3)
Low Income Group			
Bihar	2.392	0.139	(2.253)
Orissa	3.089	2.170	(0.919)
Uttar Pradesh	2.442	0.985	(1.457)
Madhya Pradesh	1.567	3.066	1.499
Rajasthan	3.352	2.638	(0.714)
Middle Income Group			
Kerala	1.756	4.324	2.568
Andhra Pradesh	1.919	5.997	4.078
Karnataka	3.325	3.902	0.577
West Bengal	2.397	4.915	2.518
Tamil Nadu	3.661	4.691	1.030
High Income Group			
Gujarat	3.015	6.834	3.819
Haryana	3.637	2.254	(1.383)
Punjab	3.435	2.826	(0.609)
Maharashtra	3.222	5.870	2.648
Goa*	3.270	3.796	0.526
Special Category States			
Assam	1.272	1.538	0.266
Meghalaya*	2.024	1.193	(0.831)
Manipur*	2.473	2.314	(0.159)
Tripura	2.366	3.975	1.609
Nagaland*	2.872	3.579	0.707
Himachal Pradesh*	2.756	2.450	(0.306)
Arunachal Pradesh	4.831	3.275	(1.556)
Sikkim*	9.008	4.723	(4.285)

Note: * Data are not available for 1997–1998. Therefore, the rates of growth have only been calculated till 1996–1997.
Source (Basic Data): Government of India, *Central Statistical Organization*.

posts exist indefinitely and a greater and greater proportion of government budgets have been devoted to salary payments. The Central Pay Commission also operates with a myopic focus on revisions of salaries and pensions of central government employees. In making its recommendations, it looks at the availability of resources at the central level. In practice, every state government also has to give the same salaries and pensions regardless of the availability of resources or the productivity of their employees. In the end, these payments are increasingly financed by borrowing, such that interest payments claim greater

TABLE 6
Real Per Capita GSDP: Growing Disparities

Year	Lowest Income State (Bihar) (Rs.)	Highest Income State (Goa) (Rs.)	All-State Average (Rs.)	Standard Deviation	Ratio of HIS to LIS GSDP	Gini Coefficient
1980–81	1061.2	3991.0	1849.4	647.3	3.761	0.0838
1981–82	1093.2	3677.9	1899.0	613.7	3.364	0.0814
1982–83	1085.2	4055.7	1934.5	668.5	3.737	0.0848
1983–84	1152.5	4037.5	2000.2	661.8	3.503	0.0824
1984–85	1220.3	4184.9	2024.2	699.9	3.429	0.0870
1985–86	1228.9	4005.1	2089.2	712.9	3.259	0.0881
1986–87	1283.8	4151.1	2129.9	737.4	3.233	0.0906
1987–88	1207.8	4494.8	2196.7	788.5	3.721	0.0928
1988–89	1322.9	5152.5	2414.2	900.5	3.895	0.0957
1989–90	1281.8	5208.3	2485.3	935.3	4.063	0.0971
1990–91	1375.7	5874.3	2596.2	1034.0	4.270	0.1015
1991–92	1295.1	5684.3	2613.8	1020.1	4.389	0.1010
1992–93	1219.8	6328.9	2743.4	1162.5	5.188	0.1099
1993–94	1238.7	6507.9	2863.0	1213.5	5.254	0.1106
1994–95	1270.9	6826.6	3008.4	1280.0	5.372	0.1122
1995–96	1232.6	7381.2	156.7	1376.1	5.988	0.1138
1996–97	1340.4	6813.4	3139.3	1330.9	5.083	0.1140

Note: The all-state average has been calculated based on 23 states (not 25) because data are not available for the two states, *viz.*, Jammu & Kashmir and Mizoram.

TABLE 7
Per Capita Current Expenditure on Services: Relativities
Between Low and High Income Group States
(Average 1996–1997 to 1998–1999)
(Percent)

	General Services excl. Int. Payment and Pensions	Interest Payment	Pension	Social Services	Economic Services	Total
General Category States (GCS)						
LIS/HIS	61.63	52.24	50.71	45.89	67.32	53.46
MIS/HIS	68.42	60.74	102.58	73.72	106.04	78.97
Special Category States (SCS)						
LIS/HIS	50.40	51.64	79.48	50.51	41.89	49.59
GCS/SCS	32.78	72.90	82.41	51.63	35.35	48.72

Note: LIS = Low Income States, MIS = Middle Income States, HIS = High Income States
Source (Basic Data): Finance accounts of various states

and greater resources of the central and the state governments. Finally, the Finance Commission looks only at the revenue side of the budgets. By following a gap-filling approach, it continues to underwrite these increases in the salary bills and growing interest payments, leaving no incentives for the states to correct their deficit spending. A process of institutional coordination among these three Commissions would force them to consider the implications of their decisions comprehensively rather than in a piecemeal manner, a point to which we return below.

6. Macroeconomic and Fiscal Prospects

Both the most recent Finance and Planning Commissions have a positive outlook for the growth of the economy in the medium term. The Finance Commission has put forward a macroeconomic scenario with an underlying GDP growth of 7–7.5% for the period from 2000–2001 to 2004–2005. Table 8 summarizes the details and compares them with the corresponding levels in 1999–2000.

TABLE 8
**Macro Scenario before and after Restructuring
Over the Period 2004–2005**

1999–2000		2000–2001 to 2004–2005
5.9	Growth Rate (% Per Annum)	7.0–7.5
3.5	Inflation Rate (% Per Annum)	5.5–5.0
(1.5)	Current Account Balance (% of GDP)	(1.5)
6.8	Revenue Deficit (% of GDP)	1.0
9.8	Fiscal Deficit (% of GDP)	6.5
14.0	Tax Revenue (% of GDP)	16.7
2.5	Non-Tax Revenue (% of GDP)*	3.2
4.2	Capital Expenditure (% of GDP)	6.6

Note: * excludes interest payment from states to center.
Source: Government of India, *Report of the Eleventh Finance Commission, June 2000.*

A growth in the range of 7–7.5% can be realized and sustained only if adequate fiscal reforms are put in place. In particular, capital expenditure, with a focus on infrastructure, has to increase substantially, and the fiscal deficit has to be contained so that the pressure on interest rates can be eased. The Finance Commission had proposed an ambitious fiscal reform program which, if successful, would bring about structural changes in the government budget designed to augment revenues, reprioritize expenditures, nearly eliminate revenue deficits, reduce fiscal deficits and debt to sustainable levels, and increase capital expenditure to levels that would sustain the stipulated growth rate in the economy.

Table 9 provides targets for expenditure side and revenue side corrections, as decomposed between the center and states. While the thrust is on expenditure compression, the composition of expenditure is also slated for restructuring in favor of priority sectors, such as elementary education, primary health care, water supply, sanitation, roads and bridges, and other infrastructure. Items that require a tight rein include salary and pensions, interest payments, and subsidies. Note that in spite of attempting to control the growth of debt, interest payments as percentage of GDP are expected to continue rising for the states because of the need to increase capital expenditure for augmenting infrastructure. In the context of the continuing revenue deficit, this will have to be financed out of borrowing.

TABLE 9
Restructuring of Public Finances: Main Features
(Percent of GDP)

	1999–2000 (1)	2004–2005 (2)	Difference (2) – (1)
Taxes			
Gross Central Taxes	8.80	10.28	1.48
State Taxes	5.29	6.43	1.14
Revenue Expenditure			
Center			
Interest Payments	4.73	4.26	(0.47)
Pensions	0.74	0.65	(0.09)
Other General Services	2.50	2.14	(0.36)
Social Services	0.36	0.29	(0.07)
Economic Services	0.36	0.29	(0.07)
States			
Interest Payments	2.30	2.55	0.25
Pensions	1.15	1.00	(0.14)
Other General Services	1.63	1.74	0.12
Social Services *of which*	5.13	5.81	0.69
Elementary Education	1.32	1.75	0.43
Primary Health	0.17	0.45	0.28
Water Supply and Sanitation	0.29	0.50	0.21
Economic Services *of which*	2.90	0.33	(0.57)
Roads and Bridges	0.22	0.60	0.38
Capital Expenditure			
Center	2.62	4.00	1.38
States	2.06	2.85	0.80

Source: Government of India, *Report of Eleventh Finance Commission, June 2000.*

C. Intergovernmental Fiscal Transfers in India: A Review

Two major institutions, the Finance Commission and the Planning Commission, oversee fiscal transfers in India. The Finance Commission looks mostly after current account needs while the Planning Commission is primarily concerned with development needs, which comprise both current and capital aspects. The expenditure accounts of governments are further divided into nonplan and plan.[4] In this section, we consider various types of transfers, but the focus is on the Finance Commission transfers, which include devolution of central taxes and grants.

Until the year 2000, sharing of central taxes was on a tax-by-tax basis. In particular, two important central taxes were shared with the states—the personal income tax and the union excise duties. Two important central taxes were not shared with the states, the corporation tax and custom duties. The 80th amendment to the Constitution (May 2000, but effective from 1996–1997) put the sharing of central taxes with the states on an entirely new level. The net proceeds of all union taxes and duties, except the central sales and consignment taxes, surcharges on central taxes and duties, and earmarked cesses, are now distributable between the center and the states.[5] The amendment is intended to serve the following main objectives:

(i)   Widen the revenue base for the states, thereby enabling them to share the aggregate buoyancy of central taxes, including the corporation tax;

(ii)   Share the burden of adjustment between the center and the states in case of any temporary revenue erosion as a result of tax reforms;

(iii) Reduce the overall volatility in the growth of shareable revenues implicit in a larger shareable base; and

(iv)   Provide an incentive for the exploitation of taxes (except central sales and consignment) mentioned in Article 269 of the Constitution by including them in the shareable pool.

The sharing of central tax revenues with the states has both a vertical dimension, the aggregate share of the states in the central taxes, and a horizontal dimension, the respective share of each state in the aggregate share of all states. We now look at each.

---

4. The Finance Commissions, with the exception of the First, Second, and Ninth, have limited their concerns to nonplan revenue (current) expenditures, although there is no constitutional ban on their dealing with the full current account expenditures.

5. The amendment is based on the alternative scheme of devolution that was recommended by the Tenth Finance Commission (TFC) in its report submitted in November 1994.

1. The Vertical Dimension

Determining the aggregate share of states in the central taxes requires a comprehensive view of (i) the expenditure needs of the center; (ii) the resources of the center; (iii) the aggregate expenditure requirements of the states; and (iv) the aggregate resources of states from their own sources. In the context of vertical devolution, the share of states and consequently that of the center is supposed to be determined in a manner that provides both sides with adequate resources subject to the overall resource constraint. Furthermore, there needs to be adequate predictability and stability in the vertical share ratio to enable both the center and the states to plan their expenditures in a longer-term perspective.

Since the transfers take place through three channels—Finance Commission, Planning Commission, and directly from the central government—these need to be considered together. Table 10 provides data on the aggregate transfers to the states through alternative channels since the First Five-Year Plan. Total transfers to states as a percentage of the center's gross revenue receipts show considerable volatility—ranging from a minimum of 23.63% to a maximum of 44.06%, standing at around 35% in recent years. Tax-sharing transfers show a steady rise up to the Fifth Plan, after which they appear to stabilize at a level a little above 21% of center's gross revenue receipts. Transfers under the Finance Commission have been in the range of 20–25% of gross central revenues since the Fifth Plan. Plan grants have been more volatile, but have settled recently in the 10–11% range. Statutory and discretionary grants have been much smaller and more unstable over the years.

2. The Horizontal Dimension

In reviewing the distribution of the aggregate share of states in central tax revenues, the approach of the Finance Commissions can be reviewed in terms of three distinct phases. Up to the Seventh Finance Commission, the distribution formulas used for determining the income tax shares were clearly distinct from those for the union excise duties. This may be considered as phase I. Since then, a process of convergence between the two sets of formulas began. The period of partial convergence from the Eighth to the Tenth Finance Commissions may be considered as phase II. Full convergence under the recent EFC may be considered as phase III. The most important factors used in the various formulas are indicated immediately below and explained in more detail subsequently.

TABLE 10
Transfers as Percent of Gross Revenue Receipts of the Center
(Percent)

Year/Plan	Share in Central Taxes	Statutory Grants	Transfers from Finance Commission	Plan Grants	Discretionary Grants	Total Grants	Total Transfers
	(1)	(2)	(3)	(4)	(5)	(6)	(7)
First Five-Year Plan	12.86	1.01	13.87	6.92	2.84	10.77	23.63
Second Five-Year Plan	14.71	4.32	19.02	11.87	1.19	17.37	32.08
Third Five-Year Plan	11.79	3.50	15.29	8.97	0.38	12.85	24.64
Three Annual Plans	14.03	5.15	19.18	9.73	0.32	15.20	29.22
Fourth Five-Year Plan	18.60	3.23	21.84	8.34	4.05	15.62	34.23
Fifth Five-Year Plan	15.94	5.32	21.26	9.31	1.15	15.79	31.73
Annual Plan	23.53	1.89	25.42	12.46	1.46	15.82	39.34
Sixth Five-Year Plan	21.19	1.83	23.02	12.74	1.51	16.08	37.27
Seventh Five-Year Plan	20.31	2.58	22.89	13.14	1.47	17.18	37.50
Annual Plan							
1990–1991	20.90	4.88	25.78	12.99	1.11	18.98	39.88
1991–1992	20.64	4.14	24.77	13.50	1.20	18.84	39.48
Period Total	**20.76**	**4.47**	**25.23**	**13.27**	**1.16**	**18.91**	**39.66**
Eighth Five-Year Plan							
1992–1993	21.67	2.19	23.86	15.53	1.10	18.82	40.49
1993–1994	22.75	1.86	24.61	18.11	1.34	21.31	44.06
1994–1995	21.43	1.47	22.90	15.21	0.61	17.29	38.72
1995–1996	21.01	3.79	24.80	10.95	0.52	15.27	36.27
1996–1997	21.73	3.31	25.04	10.57	0.48	14.35	36.08
Period Total	**21.66**	**2.66**	**24.32**	**13.52**	**0.75**	**16.93**	**38.60**
Ninth Five-Year Plan							
1997–1998	24.54	1.85	26.39	10.24	0.49	12.58	37.12
1998–1999	19.90	1.47	21.37	10.60	0.60	12.67	32.57
1999–2000	20.59	2.40	22.99	10.63	1.13	14.16	34.75
Period Total	**21.54**	**1.93**	**23.47**	**10.50**	**0.76**	**13.19**	**34.74**

Source: Government of India, *Report of the Eleventh Finance Commission, June 2000.*

a. *Phase I: Separate Criteria for Income Tax and Union Tax Duties*

Population and collection/assessment were the only two criteria used for determining the shares of the states in the income tax revenues up to the Seventh Finance Commission. The criteria for the union excise duties evolved over time, placing greater and greater emphasis on factors relating to economic backwardness and fiscal weakness of the states. Population continued to be the largest determining factor up through the Sixth Finance Commission, although its weight went down from 100 to 75%. The Seventh Finance Commission dramatically reduced its weight to 25%. For the union excise duties, the importance of population also went down with successive finance commissions while that of variously defined factors reflecting poor resource bases continued to increase. The relative weights assigned to factors by different commissions during phase I are summarized in Tables 11 and 12.

TABLE 11
Inter-*Se* Sharing of Income Tax: Phase I

Finance Commission	Percentage Weight Assigned to	
	Population	**Collection**
1, 3, 4	80	20
2	90	10
	Population	**Assessment**
5, 6, 7	90	10

Source: Reports of successive Finance Commissions, Government of India.

TABLE 12
Inter-*Se* Sharing of Union Excise Duties: Phase I

Finance Commission	Relative Weights (%)			
	Population	**Other Factors**		
1	100			
2	90	**Discretionary Adjustments** 10		
3	Major Factor (Weight Unspecified)	**Financial Weakness and Economic Backwardness** Weight Unspecified		
4	80	**Social and Economic Backwardness** 20		
5	80+16.66*	**Index of Backwardness** 3.33		
6	75	**Distance** 25		
7	25	**Inverse-Income** 25	**Poverty Ratio** 25	**Revenue Equalization** 25

Note: * Among states with per capita income below the all-state average.
Source: Reports of successive Finance Commissions, Government of India.

b. *Phase II: Towards Convergence: Eighth to Tenth Finance Commissions*

Beginning with the Eighth Finance Commission, two changes occurred. First was a move towards unifying the formulas for the distribution of the bulk of both income tax and union excise duties. Second, a portion of both the income tax and the union excise duties was kept aside for distribution among states on the basis of other criteria—collection in the case of the income tax and assessed deficits in the case of the excise duties. The unified formulas used by the Eighth, Ninth and Tenth Finance Commissions are given in Table 13. The specific criteria used in the formulas and the weights assigned to them have clearly changed during phase II, but there has been a continued emphasis on how to alleviate resource disparities among provinces. The Tenth Finance Commission (TFC) introduced certain innovations by including measures of cost disadvantage and tax effort.

TABLE 13
Inter-*Se* Sharing of Union Taxes: Phase II
Eighth, Ninth and Tenth Finance Commissions

Finance Commissions	Population	Distance	Criteria Inverse Income	Poverty Ratio	Index of Backwardness
8	25	50	25		
9(1)	25	50	12.5	12.5	
9(2)	25	50	12.5		12.5
	29.94	40.12	14.97		14.97

			Area	Index of Infrastructure	Tax Effort
10	20	60	5	5	10

Note: In the case of income tax, 90% of shareable proceeds were distributed according to criteria given in the table and the remaining 10% were to be distributed according to contribution. Similarly, the balance of the shareable amount in the case of union excise duties was to be distributed according to assessed deficits.

Source: Reports of successive Finance Commissions, Government of India.

c. *Phase III: Full Convergence: Eleventh Finance Commission*

With the 80th amendment to the Constitution, all shareable central taxes have to be treated at par, and full convergence of distributive criteria has emerged with the recommendations of the EFC.[6] The criteria followed by EFC for this

6. Apart from the two main taxes, income tax and union excise duties, two other

generalized sharing reflect various considerations. First, there is a modest allocation on the basis of population. Second, there is an effort to promote equity through use of distance, which measures how far a state is from the highest per capita income state. Third, there is an attempt to reflect cost disadvantages through the incorporation of area and an index of infrastructure deficiency. Finally, there are incentives for improved state financial performance in the form of tax effort and fiscal discipline components in the allocation formula. These measures are summarized in Table 14 and are explained in more detail below. We should point out that the population and equity components have long been the focus of the Finance Commissions, while the cost disadvantage and performance components continue and build on innovations of the TFC.

TABLE 14
Criteria and Relative Weights for Determining Inter-*Se*
Shares of States: Tenth and Eleventh Finance Commissions

Criterion	Relative Weight (Percent)	
	TFC	EFC
1. Population	20.0	10.0
2. Distance	60.0	62.5
3. Area	5.0	7.5
4. Index of Infrastructure	5.0	7.5
5. Tax Effort	10.0	5.0
6. Fiscal Discipline	–	7.5

3. Core Revenue-Sharing Criteria

In conventional devolution in India, the principle of derivation was an important guiding principle. Thus, there was an attempt to return to the states what they would have raised had the taxing power of the shareable tax remained with them. In the context of this principle, collection/assessment was given weight in the sharing of income tax. This principle was not, however, applied to the distribution of union excise duties, which was a matter of

transfers had been in use, a grant in lieu of tax on railway passenger fares and additional excise duties in lieu of sales tax on specified commodities (cotton textiles, tobacco, and sugar). Both were tax rental arrangements in the sense that the original power to levy them was vested with the state governments but was transferred to the center primarily for the sake of uniformity across states. With the amendment to the Constitution, the separate identity of these arrangements has been abolished, so only one set of shares replaced the four distinct sets used by the Tenth Finance Commission.

discretionary sharing. As indicated above, the Finance Commissions in India gradually attempted to move away from conventional devolution towards revenue sharing.

Revenue sharing seeks to bring about horizontal equity, such that the fiscal resource deficiencies across states arising out of systemic and identifiable factors, and under normative revenue effort, are evened out. Thus, revenue sharing is supposed to provide the states resources complementary to their own, so that all are enabled to provide an agreed common set of public services at comparable standards in terms of quality and quantity to all citizens, no matter which state they reside in. This approach also calls for recognition of valid cost differentials in providing services in different states. Finally, compensation for resource deficiencies can undermine efforts to improve own revenue bases. To neutralize this adverse incentive, revenue sharing needs to employ criteria that reward efforts to improve the resource bases and deliver services at minimum (efficient) costs.

In constructing a scheme of criteria-based devolution, certain features concerning the information base used for determining shares are desirable. First, the information base for reflecting capacities/needs should be broad rather than narrow, so that fiscal performance can be properly estimated. Second, the data used should be comparable across states and should have been compiled using common principles. This is why census data and income data compiled by the Central Statistical Organization (CSO) have been used with greater weight by the Finance Commissions. In the case of tax effort, data provided by the finance accounts are preferable to budget data. Finally, data should be as up-to-date as possible.

We now turn to a more detailed explanation of the individual revenue-sharing criteria. We also provide some additional details on the evolution of the Finance Commission formulas.

a. *Population Formula: Criterion Providing Equal Per Capita Transfers*

The population criterion provides equal per capita transfers to all states. A scheme of equal per capita transfers is valid if there are no resource and cost-differentials across states.[7] Since the population criterion provides equal per capita transfers, it is indifferent (or neutral) to differences in the fiscal capacities of states. It is, therefore, useful as a benchmark for considering the departures from this neutrality in other criteria. For this reason, dispensation under the population criterion is often used for purposes of comparison.

---

7. It can be shown that the (standard) distance criterion will converge to the population criterion, as the per capita incomes of the states become more and more equal.

Indicating population of a state i by N_i, where i varies from 1 to n where n is the number of states, the shares of individual states (s_i) in the population formula can be written as

$$s_i = N_i/\Sigma N_i.$$

Correspondingly, per capita shares are given by

$$s_i^* = \frac{1}{\Sigma N_i} = \text{Constant}$$

b. *Income-Based Formulas: Criteria Reflecting Fiscal Deficiency*

The income-based criteria have received the highest weights by recent Finance Commissions. Two main variations of the income-based criteria have been used. One is based on the distance of per capita income of a state from the highest per capita income state. The other is based on the inverse of per capita income of a state.[8] The difference between them is that the distance criterion measures absolute resource gaps, while the inverse income criterion measures relative gaps. Since in the context of providing services at equal standards across states it is the absolute costs gaps that are relevant, successive FCs have given more and more weight to the distance criterion.[9] The TFC dropped the inverse income criterion from the formula.

Different Commissions have defined the distance criterion with some variations. The term distance refers to the excess of the per capita income of a state or group of states (measured by per capita NSDP or GSDP, using a three-year average to even out erratic changes) of the highest per capita income over that of an individual state. If per capita income (hereafter referred to only as income) of the different states is indicated by y_i, and states are arranged in ascending order of income, y_1 refers to the per capita income of, say, Bihar, and y_{25} refers to that of Goa. In general,

$$y_i \leq y_{i+1} \leq y_n, \quad i = 1, ..., 2$$
$$n = 25$$

The distances can be defined as

$$d_i = y_n - y_i$$

---

8. See Srivastava and Aggarwal (1994) for a detailed analysis of the properties of these two criteria.

9. The inverse criterion was given a weight of 25% by the Seventh and Eighth Commissions. The Ninth Commission reduced this weight to 12.5%, and the Tenth Commission dropped it altogether.

The state shares can be determined in a number of alternative ways, which we now consider.

i. Standard Distance Formula (SDF)

In this version, the share of the ith state can be written as:

$$\text{Share of State } i = \frac{(\text{Population} \times \text{Distance}) \text{ of State } i}{\text{Sum of (Population} \times \text{Distance) for All States}}$$

In terms of symbols, this can be written as:

$$s_i = N_i \, d_i / \Sigma N_i \, d_i \qquad (i = 1, \ldots, 25)$$

Since d_i for Goa will be zero ($d_i = y_n - y_n$), its share will be zero in this standard version. The per capita shares under the formula can be obtained by dividing s_i by N_i.

$$\text{Per Capita Share Under SDF} = \frac{\text{Distance of State } i}{\text{Sum of (Population} \times \text{Distance) for All States}}$$

The distance formula provides higher per capita shares to lower income states. It is based on the principle of horizontal equity under the assumption of a normative (common) revenue effort. It can be interpreted as a fiscal capacity-equalizing formula, where fiscal capacity (y_i) is measured by the (per capita) income of a state. If each state makes a revenue effort of the same degree (θ), a state's revenue capacity is given by θy_i. The revenue capacity of the highest income state is θy_n. The difference between these revenue capacities $\theta(y_n - y_i)$ is the gap filled by the distance formula, such that the post-devolution fiscal capacities are equalized. However, this approach assumes that fiscal capacity is reflected in per capita income.

ii. Modified Distance Formula (MDF)

Some of the Finance Commissions modified the standard version of the distance formula with two considerations in mind. First, in the SDF the highest income state does not get any share, which is politically problematic. Second, because the highest income state, Goa, has a small population and high income, it was not considered representative of high-income states. These concerns were initially dealt with by measuring distances from Punjab rather than Goa, conceiving distances to both Punjab and Goa as equal to the distance between Punjab and Maharashtra. Thus, three highest income states get the same distance in the formula. The MDF provides shares according to the following dispensation:

$$s_i = \frac{N_i \, d_i^*}{\Sigma N_i \, d_i^*}$$

where $d^*_i = y_{24} - y_i$ ($i = 1, 2, 23$)

and $d^*_i = y_{24} - y_{23}$ ($i = 24, 25$)

This MDF implies a kink in the dispensation line because the per capita shares of the three states at the higher income end become equal. It also implies a higher per capita income share for a few states at the low-income end, compared to the SDF.

The EFC further modified this formula. Rather than measuring the distances from the per capita income of any single state, it defined the benchmark income from which distances are measured as the weighted average of the per capita incomes of the three highest income states—Goa, Maharashtra, and Punjab. Once the benchmark income is available (say, y^*), the distances of each state outside the highest income group are calculated as

$$d_i = y^* - y_i   i - 1, ..., 22$$

The distances of the three highest income states are fractions of the distance of Haryana, the fourth highest income state, calculated in the following way:

$$d_i = d_{22} \cdot (y_{22}/y_i)   i = 23, ..., 25$$

The shares of individual states are then given by

$$s_i = N_i d_i / \Sigma N_i d_i   i = 1, ..., 25$$

iii. Augmented Distance Formula (ADF)

Giving a positive share to the highest income state can also be realized by measuring distances from a level higher than the y_n, the highest per capita income. Let this point of reference be $y_n + z$ where z is a positive amount. In this case, the augmented distances can be written as

$$d_i = (y_n + z - y_i)$$

and shares are given by

$$s_i = \frac{N_i d_i}{\Sigma N_i d_i}   i = 1, 2, ..., 25$$

The ADF requires determination of the value of Z. The EFC used this criterion for determining shares of states in the funds used to provide grants for local bodies. The value of Z has been defined as half the standard deviation of the per capita GSDP of states.

iv. Inverse Income Formula (IIF)

As noted above, the IIF looks at relative fiscal deficiencies. If the revenue capacity on a common revenue effort is θy_n, the revenue capacity of state i is θy_i, and the relative deficiency is given by $\theta y_n / \theta_i$ $(= y_n / y_i)$, the state share under this formula is given by

$$\text{Share of State i} = \frac{(\text{Population} \times \text{Inverse of Income}) \text{ of State i}}{\text{Sum of (Population} \times \text{Inverse of Income) of All States}}$$

Correspondingly, the per capita share is given by

$$\text{Per Capita Share of State i} = \frac{\text{Inverse of Income of State i}}{\text{Sum of (Population} \times \text{Inverse of Income) of All States}}$$

As noted above, the IIF has not been used since the TFC eliminated it from the overall allocation formula.

c. *Criteria Reflecting Cost Disadvantages*

Indices relating to area and infrastructure deficits are intended to reflect cost disadvantages to state governments in providing services to their citizens. States with larger physical areas are presumed to have higher per capita service delivery costs, so they receive higher allocations. Similarly, the greater the infrastructure deficiencies of a state, the greater the costs of providing services are. A state that is relatively more deficient in infrastructure is thus given a higher share in per capita terms. In measuring infrastructure, social infrastructure (e.g., health and education) expenditure has a large revenue component.

The aggregate infrastructure index (AII) is a weighted combination of economic and social infrastructure indices.[10] In turn, the economic infrastructure index (EII) and social infrastructure index (SII) are weighted combinations of a number of subindexes. For EII, the main sectors are agriculture, communication, banking, electricity, and transportation, including roads. For SII, the main sectors are health and education. The sectoral indexes are also constructed by weighted combinations of subindexes. Given the series of infrastructure index (I_i), the shares of states may be worked out as

$$s_i = \frac{N_i(I_h - I_i)}{\Sigma N_i(I_h - I_i)}$$

where I_h is the highest index among the states, and I_i is the index value for state i. The EFC used the weighted average of I_i's of the three highest index states for

---

10. An index of infrastructure was especially constructed for the TFC by a study carried out by a team of experts (T.C.A. Anant and K.L. Krishna). A similar study updated this index for the Eleventh Finance Commission.

deriving shares of individual states in a manner similar to that used for the distance formula.

d. *Criteria for Performance/Incentives*

The criterion of tax effort used by the Tenth and Eleventh Finance Commissions rewards, in a limited way, revenue performance of the states. A state that shows higher tax revenue per unit of tax base gets a higher share in tax devolution. The TFC used a higher weight than the EFC but the latter also added a fiscal performance measure (see below).

Tax effort needs to be measured by relating tax revenues to tax potential. Measurement of tax potential (taxable capacity) usually requires an elaborate econometric exercise. Since many of the determinants of taxable capacity are not directly observable and adequate comparable data are not readily available, dummy variables and proxy measures are often used. The approach of recent Finance Commissions was to use GSDP as a proxy for the tax base of states. Using the ratio of per capita tax revenue (r) to per capita GSDP (y) as reflecting tax effort, the share of a state was defined as:

$$s_i = N_i \ w_i \ (r_i \ / \ y_i)/[\Sigma N_i w_i (\tfrac{r_i}{y_i})] \quad i = 1, ..., n$$

The weights were set as related to the inverse of income on the assumption that if two states show the same tax effort, the poorer state among the two is the more constrained, and should get a relatively higher share. Factors that constitute genuine constraints in the exploitation of the tax base can in general be used to set these weights. Such constraints could include below-average levels of development and distribution of income.

e. *Criterion Related to Improvement in Fiscal Performance*

The criterion on tax effort looks only at the tax revenues. However, to bring expenditures into the analysis, the EFC has constructed an index of fiscal discipline for use within the devolution formula. The index of improvement in fiscal performance was defined with reference to achieving improvement in revenue balance. The ratio of revenue receipts to revenue expenditure may be called z_i for the state i in the reference year. In the base year, this may be referred to as z_i^o. The corresponding ratios for the all-state average may be called Z_a and Z_o. The index of improvement in fiscal performance is given by

$$I_i = [Z_i \ / \ Z_i^o]/Z_a \ / \ Z_a^o$$

The better the performance of a state in achieving revenue balance relative to others, the higher its share in devolution. The respective shares are determined by

$$s_i = N_i I_i / \Sigma N_i I_i$$

4. General-Purpose Finance Commission Grants

Apart from revenue sharing, the main alternative channel of fiscal transfer available to the Finance Commission is grants-in-aid provided for under Article 275 of the Constitution. These are general-purpose unconditional grants. The Finance Commission determines these grants as the difference between assessed expenditures on the nonplan account of each state and the sum of projected own-source revenues and shares in central taxes. Thus, these grants are meant to fill a gap. The main issue here is whether this gap should be projected on the basis of historical trends or by an assessment of expenditures and revenues on a normative basis. It is clear that if historical basis were followed, strong adverse incentives would arise. Thus, the states would benefit if they were to maximize their histories of expenditures and minimize their histories of raising revenues. A normative basis is thus preferred.

The various Finance Commissions, with certain exceptions or qualifications, have followed only the gap-filling approach. The approach of the recent EFC was quasi-normative, such that a partial attempt was made to use normative elements in assessing both expenditures and revenues. Since these assessments were for a five-year period from 2000–2001 to 2004–2005, two sets of norms were required: one to determine base year figures (to transcend existing discrepancies and past histories) and another to define growth norms. The EFC attempted to introduce some norms for determining base year figures, such as interest payments and pensions. Most base magnitudes, however, remained largely tied to their historical path so as to avoid very large shocks to the states. Parameters affecting growth norms are summarized in Table 15. The grant allocations resulting from the assessment exercise are presented in Table 16. Because of large historical expenditures of the special category states in per capita terms, they emerge here as the largest per capita recipients of these grants.

5. Decentralization to the Third Tier

Although urban and rural local bodies have long existed in India, two constitutional amendments—the 73rd for the rural bodies and the 74th for the urban bodies—gave them a constitutional platform as institutions of self-governance. State governments were required to issue conformity legislation that clearly specifies the responsibilities of the local bodies and the resources assigned to them. A provision was made in the Constitution requiring each state government to appoint a state-level Finance Commission with a periodicity of five years. The Central Finance Commission was also required to look into the issues of the third-tier government and suggest ways and means by which the resources of the states could be augmented to strengthen the finances of their local bodies.

TABLE 15
Parameters Affecting Growth Rates of Revenues/
Expenditures Used by the Eleventh Finance Commission

	(Percent)
GDP Growth (Nominal)	13
Salary Expenditure	5
Nonsalary Expenditure	
a. Other General Services	7
b. Social Services	15
c. Economic Services	11
Interest Payments	10
Pensions	10
Identified Subsidies	0

Note: Other General Services refers to expenditure on general services excluding interest payments and pensions.
Source: Government of India, *Report of the Eleventh Finance Commission, June 2000*.

TABLE 16
Per Capita Nonplan Revenue Grants: 2000–2005
(Rupees)

State	2000–2001	2001–2002	2002–2003	2003–2004	2004–2005
General Category States (GCS)					
Uttar Pradesh	59.48	0.00	0.00	0.00	0.00
Orissa	99.49	10.03	76.10	0.00	0.00
West Bengal	212.33	128.43	63.99	0.00	0.00
Rajasthan	176.54	52.58	0.00	0.00	0.00
Punjab	119.96	0.00	0.00	0.00	0.00
Special Category States (SCS)					
Assam	41.98	0.00	0.00	0.00	0.00
Tripura	1288.97	1255.78	1225.74	1145.73	1069.79
Manipur	1391.99	1358.19	1307.99	1245.84	1192.43
Meghalaya	1372.84	1307.56	1254.25	1124.86	1007.28
Jammu & Kashmir	2107.66	2196.72	2149.33	2154.88	2150.17
Arunachal Pradesh	2028.44	1993.05	1930.35	1844.21	1843.99
Sikkim	3003.54	2943.62	2844.72	2710.75	2597.15
Himachal Pradesh	1550.86	1452.86	1341.64	1164.47	968.11
Mizoram	3348.34	3332.46	3285.77	3349.71	3139.00
Nagaland	3776.79	3844.61	3985.33	3944.33	3990.44
Average (GCS)	117.87	36.52	21.12	0.00	0.00
Average (SCS)	1034.74	1018.08	996.81	963.52	925.73

Source: Government of India, *Report of the Eleventh Finance Commission, June 2000*.

The experience following the constitutional amendments in the early 1990s has been varied. While some state governments expeditiously brought forth the conformity legislations and appointed the State Finance Commissions (SFCs), others were slow. Often, even after receiving the recommendations of the SFCs, the state governments put these under consideration for years without either accepting or rejecting them. The second set of SFCs is presently being appointed.

The process of decentralization is likely to be made more effective by the attempt of the EFC to undertake an exercise of rating the progress of decentralization in each state in a comparative framework by using a decentralization index and linking grants to reform progress. This is consistent with some recent literature [e.g., see Smoke and Lewis (1996), Lewis and Smoke (1998)], which emphasize the usefulness of performance rating of local governments as a means of improving their performance. But whether this approach will bear fruit in terms of improving decentralization in the states and of better dispensation of services at the local level remains to be seen.

6. Reforms in States: Centrally Directed vs. Market-Based Discipline

The rating scheme suggested by the EFC envisages withholding 15% of the grants recommended for the states that are assessed to be in revenue deficit. The total amount involved for five years (2000–2001 to 2001–2005) was Rs5,303.86 crore. In addition, the commission recommended an extra grant of Rs5,303.86 crore, which had been earmarked to the states according to their share in the 1971 population. The two parts of the fund, together known as the States Fiscal Reform Facility (SFRF), total Rs10,607.72 crore. Only revenue-deficit states are eligible for the first part, while all states are eligible for the second part. In both cases, the releases are to be linked to progress in reforms, including growth of tax revenue, growth of nontax revenue, ceiling on growth of salaries and allowances, interest payments, and reduction of subsidies.

In the case of tax and nontax revenues, the commission recommended that actual realization of revenues in 1999–2000 may be taken as base figure and improvements are measured against it in relation to growth rates the commission used in its main report for assessment of revenues. On the expenditure side, the commission recommended that salary expenditures be limited to a growth of 5% or the inflation rate. The growth of interest payments should be limited to 10%, while subsidies should be reduced to zero over a period of 10 years on a pro-rata basis. The progress of the reform program is to be monitored by an agency that will make recommendations on the release of funds.

These developments raise two types of questions. First is the broader issue concerning the design of suitable incentive mechanisms by which fiscal reforms may be induced and strengthened in the states. Second is the narrower question of the efficacy and implementability of the SFRF. There is hardly any dispute that fiscal reforms are urgently needed at the state level. The issue is whether the central intervention of the proposed kind is the best alternative, and whether even this will be adequate.[11]

On the narrower question of the efficacy and implementability of the SFRF, several weaknesses are evident. First, the guidelines eventually adopted are quite different from the EFC's recommendation as explained above. The actual guidelines use a single index based on the ratio of revenue deficit to revenue receipts, a very narrow measure of fiscal reform. Second, the guidelines ask states to increase tax rates annually. Other reforms, such as minimum tax rates and elimination of exemptions, are reasonable, but tax rates must stabilize and not continually increase. Third, the states do not compete against each other for better performance under the scheme. It would be easy for states to shift some expenditure to the capital side or off the budget, thereby meeting the revenue deficit reduction target without performance improvement. In fact, nothing in the SFRF is likely to include higher expenditure efficiency. Finally, the proposed formula penalizes improvement in revenue receipts, if accompanied by corresponding expenditure increase, even if spent on items like health and education.[12]

A major correction in the state's fiscal scenario can come about only if the deeper and structural causes of the growing fiscal imbalances in the states

---

11. The SFRF is, in some sense, a follow-up of an effort initiated in 1999–2000 by the MoF and the Planning Commission to link incentives to fiscal reforms at the state level. The center agreed to provide a package of advance financial assistance provided the states undertook a medium-term fiscal reform program. The reform program was to be monitored by an official committee under the chairmanship of the secretary, Planning Commission. This facility was a one-time measure and did not succeed. First, a majority of states did not agree to participate. Second, once the advance moneys were released, any pressure to pursue reforms was removed. Third, effective incentives for the medium term cannot be provided if the incentive money relates only to the first year.

12. Let i be improvement in the index defined as the ratio of revenue deficit (z) to revenue receipts (r) ($i = z/r$). Then, $di/dt: 1/r \, [dz/dt - 3/r \cdot dr/dt]$. Thus, the larger the improvement in revenue receipts (dr/dt), the lower the improvement in the index, other things being equal. This implies a penalty for better performance. And the higher the revenue receipts (r) of a state in the base year, the larger the improvement in revenue deficit required to reach the same level of improvement. Further, suppose both expenditure and revenues increase, keeping the deficit at the same level, then $dz/dt = 0$, and the improvement in the index is negative implying nonqualification $[(-z/r^2) \, (dr/dt)]$, even though the state may be on its way to reform, for example, by increasing revenue and spending it on health and education.

are identified and addressed. Many of these actually arise from central interventions, such as linkages between plan size and revenue deficits and the linkage between central and state salaries, as we shall see below.

On the more general issue of inducing fiscal discipline in the states through incentives and interventions, a distinction is often made between two approaches to reforms: one, market-based discipline (MBD), and two, centrally directed discipline (CDD) which falls in the overall category of hierarchical mechanisms, such as the SFRF. The CDD is costly to administer, compromises states' fiscal autonomy by directing them to specific courses of reforms (even if in the form of guidelines), and may fail if the amounts involved are too small or the design is faulty.

The MBD requires that a hard budget constraint be imposed on the states. This implies that the cost of borrowing is determined on the basis of the fiscal viability and risk assessment specific to that state. The market normally evaluates the states on the basis of credit ratings by rating agencies. A fiscally weak state has to pay a higher risk premium to borrow from the market. Interest rates may therefore sharply rise for a state that is fiscally slipping, immediately highlighting its developing fiscal weakness. The MBD sharply focuses on fiscally irresponsible behavior by the states and provides an impetus for pressure from citizens of the state, who do not currently get a correct picture of the management of state finances. The practice of MBD would still identify some chronically weak states where the center may have to intervene, ex-post with bail-out schemes and ex-ante with preemptive actions that prevent fiscal crises. Thus, the CDD would still have a residual role.

In India, there are obstacles to following the MBD. First, market signals are currently muted because states, weak or strong, often pay the same interest rates on various instruments. Second, small savings fund entitlements soften state budget constraints. A central government guarantee induces small savings at the current interest rates, and 80% of the small savings flow back to the state as an automatic right. The citizens of the same state would not necessarily contribute to the small savings funds if the scheme were to be entirely a state government scheme. Third, budget constraints are also softened by their ability to borrow from the provident funds of their employees and through their public sector enterprises by extending guarantees. If MBD is to be effective, a hard budget constraint must be imposed on the states, and market mechanisms for assessment of risk associated with lending to states must be developed. In addition, there is a need for the interregional allocation of central investment and management of other central policies that support balanced regional development, as well as the removal of adverse incentives in fiscal transfer mechanisms.

D. Dispensation of Development Funds

Fiscal capacities of states depend on their resource bases that, in turn, depend on the incomes and economic activities generated in their jurisdictions. Apart from other determinants of income and production, infrastructure investment plays an important role. Investment in state infrastructure is undertaken by the central and state governments, including projects financed by external assistance, and the private sector, including foreign direct investment. There is now an extensive literature that analyzes the relationship between infrastructure and economic growth. Several studies (e.g., Aschauer, 1989, and Aschauer and Munnell, 1990) find that new infrastructure investments may be potentially more productive than increases in labor or private capital. Further, better infrastructure attracts private capital to the states from the rest of the country and beyond. Since there is considerable and growing disparity across states in social and economic infrastructure, and this results in disparities in GSDP and resource bases, infrastructure investment favoring poorer states is important.

1. Trends in Capital Expenditure

A major feature of the intertemporal profile of government expenditures has been the erosion of the share of capital expenditure in total government expenditure. This feature has characterized both the central and the state budgets. In Table 17, the persistent fall of capital expenditures as a percentage of GDP since the late 1980s is highlighted.

TABLE 17
Capital Expenditure in Government Budgets
(Percent of GDP)

	1980–1981 to 1984–1985	1985–1986 to 1989–1990	1990–1991 to 1994–1995	1995–1996	1996–1997	1997–1998	1998–1999	1999–2000[a]
Center	6.13	6.78	4.61	3.43	3.29	3.61	3.72	2.78
				3.25	*3.09*	*3.41*	*3.51*	*2.62*
State	3.79	3.21	2.57	2.29	2.01	2.2	1.97	2.06
				2.17	*1.89*	*2.08*	*1.87*	*1.95*

Note: The first three columns indicate period averages. Figures in italics indicate GDP new series.
   [a] Revised estimate
Source: Government of India, *Report of the Eleventh Finance Commission, June 2000, pp. 177–178.*

The Planning Commission oversees grants meant for state development expenditures as part of an overall assistance package composed of loans and grants. The relative proportion of loans and grants is fixed but differs between general and special category states. For the general category states, assistance is 30% grant and 70% loan. For the special category states, 90% of assistance is given as grant and 10% as loan. The expenditure side of state budgets is divided into four parts: nonplan revenue expenditure, plan revenue expenditure, plan capital expenditure, and nonplan capital expenditure. The first and second components combine to give the revenue account of a state, which pertains to recurrent expenditures. Plan assistance is meant for the second and third components taken together.

In the initial stages when plan assistance was conceived in terms of an overall package, the expectation was that nearly 30% of the plan would involve recurrent expenditures and 70%, capital expenditures. The grant-to-loan ratio was set in accordance with this assumption. As states were expected to meet all capital expenditures from borrowing and surpluses on revenue account, no capital grants were envisaged for the general category states in plan assistance. The position of the special category states was different in the sense that of the 90% that they were getting as grant, 30% could be allocated for the revenue component of the plan, and the balance of 60% could be used as a capital grant. In practice, the relative claim of recurrent expenditure continues to increase generally and has become on average 60% of plan outlay in the case of general category states. Thus, borrowing finances a substantial portion of state current expenditures.

TABLE 18
Dispensation of Plan Assistance: Normal State Plan
(Percent)

States	Grants	Loans	Total
Special	27	3	30
General	21	49	70
Total	**48**	**52**	**100**

The overall dispensation of (normal) plan assistance can be summarized according to special and nonspecial category states, and according to grants and loans as indicated in Table 18. The Planning Commission allocates aggregate (normal) plan assistance among states under a set of criteria known as the Gadgil formula. The original formula has been subjected to various changes and the present version is referred to as the national development council-revised Gadgil formula. The formula works in two stages. First, 30% of total

TABLE 19 ·
Gadgil Formula: Alternative Versions
(Weight)

Criteria	Modified Gadgil Formula (1980)	NDC Revised Formula (1990)	NDC Revised Formula (1991)
A. **Special Category States (10)**	30% share of 10 States excluding North Eastern Council	30% share of 10 States including North Eastern Council	30% share of 10 States excluding North Eastern Council
B. **Nonspecial Category States (15)**			
(i) Population (1971)	60.0	55.0	60.0
(ii) Per Capita Income	20.0	25.0	25.0
Of which			
a. According to the 'deviation' method covering only the states with per capita income below the national average	20.0	20.0	20.0
b. According to the 'distance' method covering all the fifteen states	–	5.0	5.0
(iii) Performance 10.0	5.0	7.5	
Of which			
a. Tax effort 10.0	–	2.5	
b. Fiscal management	–	5.0	2.5
c. National objectives	–	–	2.5
d. Special problems	10.0	15.0	7.5
Total	100.0	100.0	100.0

Notes: 1. Fiscal management is assessed as the difference between states' own total plan resources estimated at the time of finalizing annual plans and their actual performance, considering the latest five years.
2. Under the criterion of performance in respect of certain programs of national priorities, the approved formula covers four objectives, *viz.*: (i) population control; (ii) elimination of illiteracy; (iii) on-time completion of externally aided projects; and (iv) success in land reforms.

assistance money is earmarked for the 10 special category states.[13] This is distributed among the states on the basis of their plan size and past plan expenditures, without using explicit criteria. The remaining 70% is distributed among the other states according to a weighed set of explicit criteria. These are summarized in Table 19, which also shows how the formula has changed over time. The Planning Commission does not publish the actual shares of states as is done by the Finance Commission, so transparency is not adequate.

The important elements in the distribution formula for the general category states include population, deviation of income from mean income, distance of income from highest income, and various factors reflecting fiscal discipline

---

13. Special category states were first named in the 1960s. Since then, their number has grown from 3 to 10.

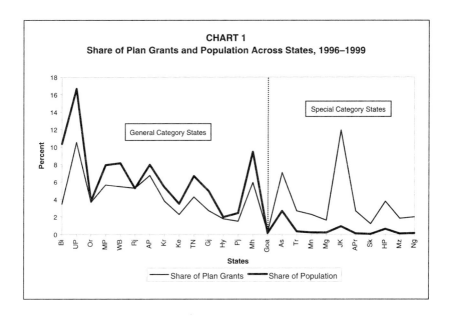

CHART 1
Share of Plan Grants and Population Across States, 1996–1999

and achievement of national objectives. Only the 1971 population is used, but shares may change as more recent data for other criteria become available. Due to the very high weight given to the population factor, which allocates equal per capita shares to all states, dispensations under the Gadgil formula are only mildly progressive.

2. Plan Assistance: Distribution of Funds

If we analyze the share of plan grants across states for the period 1996–1997 to 1998–1999, we find that more than 37% of plan grants have gone to the special category states (Table 20), which account for less than 5% of population and only 3.3% of state GSDP. For low-income general category states, such as Bihar, Uttar Pradesh, Orissa, Madhya Pradesh, West Bengal and Rajasthan, the share of plan grants amount to only about 33%, whereas they account for nearly 50% of the population and 38% of GDP (see also Chart 1). This pattern of dispensation of plan grants is both inequitable and inefficient. There is no explicit basis for earmarking 30% for special category states. This volume of funds is well beyond their absorption capacity, and there are no objective criteria for allocating it among the individual special category states.

There are also other issues with the way that plan assistance is allocated under the Gadgil formula. First, shares determined for the general category states on the basis of tax effort and fiscal discipline indexes are not scaled, implying that if a large state like Maharashtra and a small state like Goa had the same tax effort ratio, they would get the same share regardless of their size. Second, the link that used to exist between plan schemes/projects and plan assistance has been lost, leading to a severing of the relationship between costs and benefits, and a lack of effective project-based monitoring. Finally, the 30:70 grant-to-loan ratio had long become irrelevant if the 30% grant ratio were meant to cover current revenue expenditure on plans. Clearly, there is room for significant reform of the present system of plan assistance. Unless it is overhauled, the ambitious growth targets noted earlier cannot be attained.

TABLE 20
Share of Plan Grants Across States
(Percent)

State	1996–1997	1997–1998	1998–1999	Average 1996–1999
General Category States (GCS)				
Bihar	1.79	3.83	4.76	3.46
Uttar Pradesh	11.22	10.94	9.39	10.52
Orissa	3.60	3.55	3.82	3.66
Madhya Pradesh	7.29	4.82	4.83	5.65
West Bengal	5.42	4.82	6.12	5.45
Rajasthan	4.74	5.24	5.11	5.03
Andhra Pradesh	6.84	6.77	6.63	6.75
Karnataka	3.91	3.68	3.79	3.79
Kerala	2.39	2.04	2.39	2.27
Tamil Nadu	4.05	4.59	4.17	4.27
Gujarat	2.82	2.71	2.56	2.70
Haryana	1.87	1.81	1.62	1.77
Punjab	1.51	1.40	1.59	1.50
Maharashtra	7.54	5.67	4.60	5.94
Goa	0.23	0.21	0.18	0.21
GCS – Share	**65.22**	**62.08**	**61.56**	**62.95**
Special Category States (SCS)				
Assam	7.05	6.84	7.35	7.08
Tripura	2.45	2.47	3.11	2.68
Manipur	2.23	2.25	2.33	2.27
Meghalaya	1.55	1.41	1.88	1.61
Jammu & Kashmir	10.23	13.96	11.60	11.93
Arunachal Pradesh	2.62	2.60	2.79	2.67
Sikkim	1.07	1.20	1.33	1.20
Himachal Pradesh	3.92	3.56	3.85	3.78
Mizoram	1.75	1.80	1.95	1.83
Nagaland	1.90	1.84	2.23	1.99
SCS – Share	**34.77**	**37.93**	**38.42**	**37.04**

Source (Basic Data): Finance Accounts of States.

3. Finance Commission Capital Grants

Although the transfers recommended by the Finance Commission have generally been limited to the current (revenue) account of state budgets, an important exception affects capital expenditures. Plan assistance is meant for developmental expenditure in social and economic services, but there is also a need for capital investment in general services, so that the standard of services in general administration, police, jails, etc. can be improved in the backward areas. For this purpose, the Finance Commission has recommended upgrading grants that can cover related capital expenditures. Another type of Finance Commission grant meant for special problems can also cover capital expenditures. Both upgrading and special problem grants can cover general services, as well as social and economic services.

4. Finance and Planning Commissions: Dynamics of Interdependence

As noted above, the two main bodies that intermediate between the center and the states on fiscal transfers—the Finance Commission and the Planning Commission—operate in a segmented way without any means of effective coordination. Especially important in this context is the impact of the dynamic linkage between the two major streams of resource transfers.

The plan generates three major liabilities beyond the plan period: interest payments on funds borrowed for financing the plan, maintenance of assets created during the plan, and salaries of people employed in plan schemes who remain in government employment after the plan has ended. For these liabilities, state governments look to the Finance Commission for resource transfers after the plan period is over. In assessing the needs of state governments on the revenue (nonplan) account, both interest payments and committed liabilities of the state governments are taken into account by the Finance Commissions. Since the plan is linked to a program of borrowing, a larger plan is typically linked with a larger borrowing program and, therefore, leaves relatively larger future liabilities.

Interest liabilities as well as committed expenditures resulting from plan schemes of the past have been taken by the previous Finance Commissions as a first step in making an assessment of expenditure requirements. Given other things, the larger the interest and other committed liabilities, the larger is the entitlement of a state in the form of tax devolution and grants. It is implicit in this approach that larger plan outlays financed by greater borrowing create larger state-specific liabilities that generate (after five years) larger claims for Finance Commission fiscal transfers.

The fragmented methods of working out transfers by the Planning Commission and the Finance Commission thus sets up a circuit of adverse incentives.

The Finance Commission keeps looking only to the (nonplan) revenue expenditures (resulting substantially from previous actions of the planning commissions) without paying much attention to the linkage of interest payments with past fiscal deficits and accumulated debt stock. The planning commission looks only at new schemes and the scope of borrowing in the plan period without considering what future liabilities are being created and how they may be financed beyond the plan period. Projects financed by external assistance, which is transmitted to the state on the same terms and conditions as normal plan assistance, also create similar liabilities regarding interest payments and maintenance, as we shall see below.

Another concern is the way the plan assistance mechanism mixes grants and loans, two modes of resource transfers that need to be governed by entirely different sets of principles. Grants should be given in consideration of resource deficiencies and for projects with large social benefits but limited direct return, such as primary education and primary health. On the other hand, loans should be given taking into consideration the capacity of a state to absorb and service the loan, and for projects that can yield adequate returns, commensurate with the cost of the loan. By mixing the two together in an inflexible manner, the center is burdening states with debt that they cannot service, but cannot afford to forego either because they will lose the grant component.

The artificial dichotomy between plan and nonplan expenditures also induces a number of other problems. Because of the undue emphasis on taking up new schemes, uncompleted projects of the past plans and maintenance of assets acquired in the past get little attention. In effect, plan schemes as originally envisaged cannot be taken up fully because the contemplated balance from current revenues is not realized, plan finances are diverted to nonplan items, time overruns increase costs, and many schemes remain unfinished. While contributing little to output and to nontax revenues, staff appointments have already been made, and capital structure has been put in place requiring maintenance and other expenditures. While old assets degenerate rapidly due to inadequate maintenance, new assets are not ready to contribute to output because they remain incomplete, thus causing a double blow to the productivity of government expenditures.

In addition to the activities of the Finance Commission and Planning Commission, there are other channels through which resource transfers take place between the center and the states. These often provide considerable room for ad hoc behavior and have distributional implications. Among them are transfers through central plan schemes administered by states, several centrally sponsored schemes, and various departmental transfers. External assistance, which is transmitted to the states on the same terms as plan assistance, is also sustained and problematic, a point to which we now turn.

E. External Assistance: Transmission to States

External assistance to India comes from various multilateral and bilateral sources. The main multilateral sources are the International Development Association (IDA), the International Board for Reconstruction and Development (IBRD), the International Fund for Agricultural Development (IFAD), Asian Development Bank (ADB), and the Oil and Petroleum Exporting Commission (OPEC) with a combined contribution of around 60% of the total utilized external assistance in the 1990s. Considering multilateral and bilateral creditors together, six sources together contribute a significant proportion of total external assistance. These are the IDA, the IBRD, ADB, and the governments of Japan, Germany and France. Together, they account in recent years for a share exceeding 90% of total utilized external assistance in India.

1. Volume of External Assistance

Table 21 provides information on total external assistance as a percent of GDP. The figures provide the averages for the period 1982–1983 to 1998–1999 and selected subperiods. Total assistance as percent of GDP (old series) over this period has been about 1.1%. It was highest in the period 1986–1987 to 1990–1991, but it has fallen subsequently. Table 22 shows the respective shares of loans and outright grants in total assistance for the period 1980–1981 through 1998–1999. Loans have dominated external assistance, growing from around 80% of the total in 1980–1981 to around 90% in recent years. The share of outright grants in total assistance has correspondingly fallen from 19% in 1980–1981 to 9% in 1998–1999.

2. Distribution of External Assistance

The relative shares of the center and states in external assistance, and those of individual states in the all states total for the years 1990–1991 to 1998–1999 are given in Table 23. The share of the center has come down in recent years, and the share of the states has correspondingly increased. In 1998–1999, the respective share of the center and the states was 36 and 64%, essentially a reversal of the situation in 1990–1991.

The share of special category states in the state total has not been significant, having never exceeded 1%. Some assistance is passed on to a combination of states (multistate). The share of multistate assistance has exceeded 25% of the total to all states in some years. A major share of this assistance has gone to just seven states, namely, Andhra Pradesh, Gujarat, Karnataka, Maharashtra, Tamil Nadu, Uttar Pradesh, and West Bengal. With the exception of Uttar Pradesh, these states are in general the more prosperous states.

TABLE 21
Assistance as Percent of GDP: Selected Averages
(Percent)

Average	Grants	Loans	Assistance[a]	Assistance[b]
1982–83 to 1985–86	0.17	0.92	1.09	1.12
1986–87 to 1990–91	0.14	1.11	1.25	1.32
1991–92 to 1998–99	0.10	0.92	1.02	1.22
1982–83 to 1998–99	**0.13**	**0.95**	**1.08**	**1.18**
1993–94 to 1998–99[c]	**0.07**	**0.66**	**0.74**	**0.92**

Notes: [a] Pertains only to the government account.
        [b] Also includes nongovernment account.
        [c] GDP (new series) with 1993–94 as base year.
Sources: 1. Government of India, Ministry of Finance, Department of Economic Affairs, *External Assistance (Annual)*, Aid Accounts and Audit Division.
        2. Government of India, Ministry of Finance, *Economic Survey 1999–2000*, Economic Division.

TABLE 22
Loans and Grants in External Assistance: Relative Shares
(Percent)

	1980–1981	1981–1982	1982–1983	1983–1984	1984–1985	1985–1986	1986–1987	1987–1988	1988–1989	1989–1990
Loans	80.99	80.21	84.29	86.15	82.92	84.84	87.80	90.58	88.80	87.06
Grants	19.01	19.79	15.71	13.85	17.08	15.16	12.20	9.42	11.20	12.94

	1990–1991	1991–1992	1992–1993	1993–1994	1994–1995	1995–1996	1996–1997	1997–1998	1998–1999	
Loans	91.35	90.84	91.09	91.24	90.39	87.79	89.2	89.16	90.98	
Grants	8.65	9.16	8.91	8.76	9.61	12.21	10.8	10.84	9.02	

Sources (Basic Data): Government of India, Ministry of Finance, Department of Economic Affairs, *External Assistance (Annual)*, Aid Accounts and Audit Division [(see Srivastava, D.K., C. Bhujanga Rao, and T.S. Rangamannar (2000)].

This result is confirmed by other works, including a study by Kurian (1997) for the planning commission. In this study, a comparison of per capita plan outlays was made between two groups of four states each from the less-developed regions (Bihar, Orissa, Uttar Pradesh, and West Bengal) and prosperous regions (Gujarat, Karnataka, Maharashtra, and Tamil Nadu). Kurian observes that while per capita central assistance was higher during the Sixth and Seventh Plans for the poorer states, this egalitarian bias appears to have been abandoned by the center during the Eighth Plan. Since the Gadgil formula is on the whole modestly progressive, this development is explained by the role played by additional central assistance (ACA) rules that cover external resources.

TABLE 23
External Assistance: Relative Shares of States

	1990–1991	1991–1992	1992–1993	1993–1994	1994–1995	1995–1996	1996–1997	1997–1998	1998–1999
Amount (Rs Crore)									
Total (Center and States)	6123.92	10004.67	9841.16	10115.52	9529.74	8709.63	10052.07	8498.38	9924.92
Center	4236.66	6679.04	6100.14	6668.85	5697.39	4837.14	4800.07	3402.19	3569.42
All-States	1887.26	3325.63	3741.02	3446.67	3832.35	3872.49	5252.00	5096.19	6355.50
General States	1647.38	2684.89	3039.19	2718.79	2814.99	2897.95	4143.41	4031.06	5072.61
Special Category States	3.55	8.81	25.30	0.00	1.57	3.62	5.12	10.79	58.81
Share in Total (Percent)									
Center	69.18	66.76	61.99	65.93	59.79	55.54	47.75	40.03	35.96
All-States	30.82	33.24	38.01	34.07	40.21	44.46	52.25	59.97	64.04
Share in All-States (Percent)									
General States (incl. Delhi)	87.29	80.73	81.24	78.88	73.45	74.83	78.89	79.10	80.27
Special Category States	0.19	0.26	0.68	0.00	0.04	0.09	0.10	0.21	0.93
Multi-States and Others	12.52	19.00	18.08	21.12	26.51	25.07	21.01	20.69	18.80
Share of Individual States (Major Recipients) in All-States (Percent)									
Andhra Pradesh	9.03	11.08	19.01	17.08	11.90	11.83	10.04	16.34	16.19
Gujarat	12.18	8.59	11.98	3.01	1.71	2.21	7.79	3.93	4.56
Karnataka	5.85	7.73	6.47	7.65	6.77	3.26	3.62	3.40	4.75
Maharashtra	11.24	10.19	13.02	15.32	16.35	21.40	19.17	12.68	9.18
Tamil Nadu	9.33	8.72	10.30	11.55	15.78	10.64	7.82	5.99	5.07
Uttar Pradesh	24.48	23.05	10.06	12.75	5.45	7.94	11.35	10.62	7.67
West Bengal	3.42	3.44	2.42	2.12	1.90	1.44	4.59	11.00	15.06

Source: Based on Appendix XV, *External Assistance 1998–99*, Ministry of Finance, Government of India [see Srivastava, D.K., *et al.* (2000) for further details].

The Gadgil allocation principles do not apply to ACA, and it appears that the more developed states have been able to get most of this assistance. The ACA funds, however, are distributed on the same grant and loan terms as normal state plan assistance, which creates other problems that we examine below.

An analysis of the distribution of per capita external assistance among the states provides additional evidence to indicate that external assistance has generally gone disproportionately to larger states and richer states. The analysis is based on regressing per capita disbursement of external assistance (*pcextasst*: average over 1996–1997 to 1998–1999) on per capita GSDP (*pcgsdp*: comparable GSDP, average over 1994–1995 to 1996–1997 as given by EFC) and population as per 1991 census (*pop1991*). The coefficients of both the explanatory variables are positive indicating that the higher the per capita GSDP, the higher the per capita assistance. In addition, the larger the size of the state (in terms of population), the larger is the per capita assistance. The results are indicated below:

$$pcextasst = -18.284 + .0027\ pcgsdp + .0589\ pop1991$$
$$(-0.839)\ (1.755) \qquad\quad (3.122)$$

$$R^2 = 0.335 \quad n = 25$$

The estimated coefficients are significant at 10% and 1% levels respectively for *pcgsdp* and *pop1991*. Inclusion of some dummy variables that distinguish reforming states from nonreforming states might improve the explanatory power of the equation, but these distinctions could be highly subjective.

3. Sectorwise Allocation of External Assistance

The trends in the intersectoral shares of external assistance for the period 1990–1991 to 1998–1999 are shown in Table 24. The power sector has received a major share of the assistance over the period, and the share of the social sector has increased from about 4% in 1990–1991 to 25% in 1998–1999. In this period, the share of roads increased from about 1.5% to about 5%, while the water resources management share has ranged between 7% and 12%. On the other hand, the share of industry fell from 15.5% to 3.7%. The share of assistance meant for structural adjustment has also declined from about 25% in 1993–1994, to 7% by 1995–96, and becoming zero in 1998–1999. On the whole, the importance of power, social and urban development sectors has grown, while the importance of agriculture has dwindled over the years.

4. System of Additional Central Assistance

As noted above, ACA is made on the same terms as normal plan assistance. Loans are given with maturity of 20 years and at a rate of interest of

TABLE 24
Sectorwise Shares of Government Loans and Grants
from 1990–1991 to 1998–1999
(as Percent of Total Disbursement)

Sector	1990–1991	1991–1992	1992–1993	1993–1994	1994–1995	1995–1996	1996–1997	1997–1998	1998–1999
Agriculture Sector	10.90	8.13	13.25	8.12	5.64	8.33	5.81	4.06	7.10
Energy Sector-Power	34.88	29.11	25.72	28.10	35.04	29.80	33.41	31.84	26.27
Industry Sector and Finance	15.50	9.27	6.80	6.73	4.78	5.86	3.26	4.67	3.71
Infrastructure Sector-Road	1.47	2.58	2.55	3.03	4.45	5.96	4.49	6.77	5.13
Water Resources Management	8.74	8.91	7.78	8.28	7.59	6.96	9.84	11.90	11.09
Social Sector	4.25	4.36	4.99	5.87	10.16	12.78	14.74	19.28	25.25
Urban Development	4.51	4.03	4.72	4.42	4.67	6.70	5.47	4.35	1.66
Structural Adjustment	0.00	11.08	19.64	25.45	19.58	6.53	5.47	2.21	0.00
Others	19.76	22.54	14.56	9.99	8.09	17.07	17.51	14.93	19.78
Total	100.00	100.00	100.00	100.00	100.00	100.00	100.00	100.00	100.00

Source (Basic Data): Based on Appendix XIV, *External Assistance, 1998–99*, Ministry of Finance, Government of India [see, Srivastava, et al. (2000) for further details].

12.5%, with one-half of the loan carrying a grace period of five years.[14] A central issue is whether the state governments would have benefited had external assistance been passed on to them under the original terms and conditions rather than on the ACA terms. To understand this issue, it is useful to compare the aggregate grant element of external assistance under the original terms with the aggregate grant element of the ACA stream to the states.[15]

In comparing relative concessionality, appropriate interest rates for use in discounting need to be worked out. The state governments borrow from the market at interest rates somewhat higher than those for the ACA loans in most years. These actual rates of interest may be used as the relevant discount rates to reflect the opportunity cost to states if they were to borrow the same amounts domestically. However, in a federal setup, the central government borrows from a captive market and enables the state governments to also do so. The true opportunity cost of borrowing to both tiers of government would then be higher than the rates at which they had actually borrowed. To explore this further, we constructed a set of counterfactual interest rates for use as discount rates. Three considerations were taken into account. First, what would have been the interest rates if the central and the state governments were not borrowing from a captive market? Second, by what margin would the interest rates go up if an amount equal to the external loans were to be raised domestically? Third, is there a case for considering foreign capital as more productive than domestic capital? If so, extra weight needs to be given to the former while considering its replacement by the latter.

Srivastava, Rao and Rangamannar (2000) estimated patterns of net subsidization from center to states by using sets of actual as well as counterfactual rates. The counterfactual interest rates were derived as weighted averages of the mean rates at which the central and the state governments actually borrowed and the prime lending rate of the Industrial Development Bank of India, which was used as a proxy for the term-lending rate used by financial institutions for nongovernment borrowers. The weights in each case are the associated volume of medium- to long-term loans.

The magnitude of implicit subsidization or unremitted concessionality (reverse subsidization) when concessional assistance is transferred to the states under the ACA terms was derived by comparing the grant element of ACA with the grant element of external assistance measured in rupee terms. Since different assistance streams involve different concessionalities, a weighted average of these is taken to provide an estimate of the grant element of assistance

---

14. These terms are revised periodically. Notifications regarding interest rates and other terms and conditions relating to loans to state governments by the central government are usually issued in June–July each year.

15. See Srivastava, Rao and Rangamannar (2000).

loans. Further, since some assistance programs entail outright grants, the grant element of assistance is derived as a weighted average of the grant elements of loans and outright grants. If the aggregate grant elements derived as relevant weighted averages of ACA and external assistance (EA) streams are written as G(ACA) and G(EA), then G(ACA) > G(EA) indicates a situation of additional subsidization of the states by the center. In the case where G(EA) > G(ACA), there is the situation of unremitted concessionality.

The results are summarized in Table 25. A positive sign indicates subsidization of the states by the center and a negative sign indicates reverse subsidization of the center by the states. The period from 1983–1984 to 1998–1999 can be divided into two distinct subperiods.

TABLE 25
Transformation of External Assistance into Additional
Central Assistance: Net Subsidization
(Percent)

Year	Actual Discount Rates	Counterfactual Discount Rates
1983–1984	69.26	19.10
1984–1985	32.40	(4.36)
1985–1986	23.00	(4.64)
1986–1987	10.81	(2.11)
1987–1988	18.60	7.05
1988–1989	12.93	6.45
1989–1990	0.42	(8.60)
1990–1991	5.58	(3.98)
1991–1992	(8.00)	(27.15)
1992–1993	(19.00)	(28.85)
1993–1994	(18.15)	(16.98)
1994–1995	(16.66)	(21.32)
1995–1996	(20.45)	(24.16)
1996–1997	(18.12)	(23.60)
1997–1998	(17.78)	(16.75)
1998–1999	(14.32)	(15.15)

Notes: a. In these estimates, share of outright grants in external assistance to states is kept in the same proportion as for the country as a whole.
b. The grant element of ACA is the weighted sum of the respective grant elements of general and special category states.
Source: Srivastava, Rao and Rangamannar (2000).

The period prior to 1992–1993 is characterized by subsidization of the states by the center, while the later period indicates a case of unremitted concessionality. The position of reverse subsidization has emerged during the 1990s because assistance loans to the states have come predominantly from assistance streams with an extremely low interest rate in foreign currency terms and the exchange rate depreciation has gone down.[16]

5. ADB Assistance for State Projects

Although India's subscription to the capital stock of ADB is the fourth largest among the member countries, and India has long been eligible to borrow from ADB, it refrained from doing so until 1986. Between 1986 and 1994, 28 loans were approved amounting to $5159 million. ADB also provides technical assistance in the form of grants or loans or a combination of the two by making available the services of consultants or experts in various fields. By 1998–1999, a total of 45 loans amounting to $7275 million were approved, of which 21 have been closed and 24 are ongoing. ADB's lending covers transport and communication, energy, the financial sector, industry, nonfuel minerals, social and economic infrastructure, and multisector activities.

The loans from ADB are made on the basis of flexible interest rates and the interest rate changes are announced every six months. Loans from ADB also carry a commitment charge, which was rather high in the earlier part of the1990s, but has come down in recent years. It amounted to an average of 3.26% of loans utilized over the period 1990–1991 to 1998–1999. The terms and conditions of ADB loans along with some other pertinent information are given in Table 26. The grace and maturity periods are roughly the same as those of state plan assistance loans. The interest rate denominated in foreign currency terms is a little above 6% whereas the rate in domestic currency terms has ranged recently around 12.5 to 13%. The exchange rate depreciation of the US dollar in recent years has been around 6%. Since there is a 30% explicit grant in the state plan assistance, ADB loans are costlier than the state plan assistance.

6. Transmission of External Assistance to States

This discussion of the external assistance and the role of ADB indicates that the overall system of transmission of external assistance to the states is

---

16. The results are highly sensitive to the assumptions that have been made regarding aggregation, weighting, and the calculation of grant element. The loans from the IDA, Japan, Germany, and OPEC all carry interest rates in foreign currency terms ranging from 0.75 to below 2%. If an average rate of depreciation in the range of 5 to 6% is added to this, the cost of these loans comes to around 7% per annum. The component of outright grant also lowers the implicit cost of the external assistance. Two main loan streams, the IBRD and ADB, are somewhat costlier, but even their interest rates have consistently come down in the 1990s. As such, the cost of ACA (interest rate of 9% or more) has been more than the cost of external assistance.

TABLE 26
Terms and Conditions of ADB Loans and Other Relevant Information

Year	Exchange Rate (Rs Per US$)	Grace (Years)	Maturity (Years)	Interest Rate (Foreign Currency)	Interest Rate (Domestic Currency)
1986–1987	12.860	5	25	0.065	0.093
1987–1988	13.040	5	25	0.065	0.098
1988–1989	14.560	5	25	0.065	0.098
1989–1990	16.630	5	25	0.065	0.103
1990–1991	17.860	5	25	0.065	0.108
1991–1992	24.770	5	25	0.066	0.118
1992–1993	30.600	5	25	0.066	0.120
1993–1994	31.250	5	25	0.066	0.120
1994–1995	31.290	5	25	0.065	0.130
1995–1996	33.340	5	25	0.065	0.130
1996–1997	35.520	5	25	0.065	0.130
1997–1998	37.100	5	25	0.065	0.125
1998–1999	42.040	5	25	0.063	0.125

Source: Government of India, Ministry of Finance, *External Assistance (Annual)*, Aid Accounts and Audit Division, various issues.

highly problematic. In addition to the issues noted above, it should be noted that external creditors spend considerable energies in identifying states and projects to which they are willing to extend assistance. The terms and conditions of the assistance program have a clear bearing on the nature of the project. A commercial project is likely to attract a less soft assistance program. On the other hand, projects relating to education or health or other programs in the social sector are likely to attract very soft assistance packages. Mixing these up and asking for a 12.5–13% interest even in the case of social sector projects does not make sense. The existing practices of transmission of external assistance on common terms and conditions give rise to complex patterns of cross-subsidization between the center and the states, and among the states. It also undermines all the work that the external agencies do in identifying projects and areas for assistance, and the regional allocation priorities of the Gadgil formula.

F. Redesigning Fiscal Transfers in India

We conclude by bringing together the main issues discussed above. We summarize our key findings and then present recommendations on plan transfers and development expenditures, external assistance, and Finance Commission transfers.

1. Plan Transfers and Development Expenditures

We argued that the segmented treatment of transfers by the two main bodies looking after them, the Planning Commission and the Finance Commission, sets up a circuit of adverse incentives, increasing disparities and growing tensions (see Flow Chart 1). Emergence of revenue deficits in the government's budgets has resulted, to a considerable extent, from the manner of plan budgeting and financing. At the time when planning was initiated, the expectation was that the finances for the plan would primarily come from surpluses generated by the public sector. However, public sector savings turned out to be quite inadequate. The bulk of the requirements for the plans were met by borrowing from the domestic private sector or from external sources. In addition, while the focus of planning should be geared to investment expenditures, in practice, the revenue (current) expenditure emerged as the major component of plan outlay. This implies financing of current expenditures largely by borrowing.

The incentive to increase borrowing as far as possible is inherent in the design of plan transfers. To get the 30% grant component, a general category state has to take the 70% loan component. Further, the Planning Commission approves the borrowing program of the states based on the plan size. Decisions are taken with a five-year perspective, but plans create indefinite liabilities in terms of additional interest payments, salaries and pensions for which the Finance Commission has to provide resources after the plan period has ended. Because of this dynamic linkage, a comprehensive view of the transfer program, rather than the present segmented view, should be taken.

We also argue that the transfers made to the special category states via the Planning Commission and subsequently via the Finance Commission entail considerable opportunity costs and loss of development opportunities in the rest of the country. This is because under the Gadgil formula, 30% of total assistance is set aside without clear justification for distribution among special category states, whereas their share in population is only 5.3%. The actual share of plan grants from all sources for the special category states is even higher at nearly 38%. Thus, the grants being given to special category states are more than seven times their share in the national population, creating tensions with the other provinces. These massive grants, however, do not generate substantial multiplier effects within the special category states because there is considerable leakage of expenditures. And because the plan expenditure creates more recurrent needs, the special category states have become the main recipients of the general-purpose Finance Commission grants. Meanwhile, to sustain a very large plan size, these special category states have also borrowed heavily to the point where they are the most heavily indebted states in India.

The improvement of plan transfers and development expenditures requires

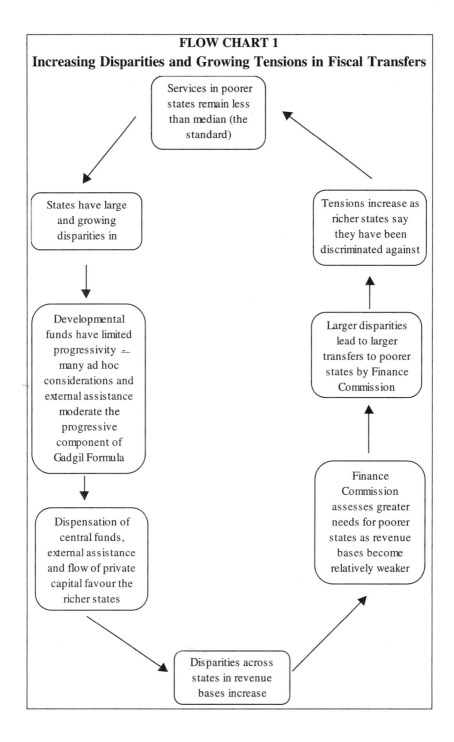

FLOW CHART 1
Increasing Disparities and Growing Tensions in Fiscal Transfers

Services in poorer states remain less than median (the standard)

States have large and growing disparities in

Developmental funds have limited progressivity — many ad hoc considerations and external assistance moderate the progressive component of Gadgil Formula

Dispensation of central funds, external assistance and flow of private capital favour the richer states

Disparities across states in revenue bases increase

Finance Commission assesses greater needs for poorer states as revenue bases become relatively weaker

Larger disparities lead to larger transfers to poorer states by Finance Commission

Tensions increase as richer states say they have been discriminated against several reforms. First, the allocation of development funds for the special cat-egory states should be reconsidered and effected by formula, taking into view their capacity to productively absorb these funds since the opportunity cost of these funds to the system is extremely high. Second, the Gadgil formula should be revised such that the determination of grants and loans is subject to separate criteria. Grants should be given according to resource deficiencies, and loans should be approved, taking into account the capacity of the states to absorb and productively utilize the loans. Third, since private capital flows, both domestic and external, are likely to favor the already prosperous states, the criteria for plan funds should more heavily favor the less prosperous states. Finally, the allocation of central expenditures has a significant impact on the profile of regional growth, and these must be recast so as to favor the poor states.

2. Reforming Transmission of External Assistance

External assistance is another major source for capital funds for the states. This comes from multilateral as well as bilateral sources. As discussed above, external assistance to states is transmitted not on the terms and conditions stipu-lated by the external creditors, but on the same terms and conditions used for plan assistance. As such, external assistance becomes a perfect substitute for plan assistance. The allocation of external assistance among states depends, however, on the selection and approval of specific projects by the multilateral and bilateral creditors. Many of the developed states that have the technical capacities to prepare the relevant project proposals are able to get a relatively larger share of total external assistance to the states. It is also important to note that a large part of external assistance is used for central government projects, the location of which also has important implications for economic activities across states.

The system of transmission of external assistance to the states in India is characterized by several deficiencies. The system gives incorrect signals re-garding the selection of projects by a state. Furthermore, external creditors are discouraged when they find that their grants or highly concessional loans, which were deemed appropriate for the concerned projects, are being converted into highly costly loans. The exchange rate movements of recent years indicate that while there clearly was a subsidization of the states by the center before 1991–1992, the situation is much closer to being that of reverse subsidization in more recent years.

The regional allocation of external assistance and the terms and condi-tions of its transfer to the states urgently require redesign. In particular, these terms and conditions should be delinked from the terms and conditions of state plan assistance. In fact, external assistance should be passed on to the states on the same terms and conditions on which they are given, grants as grants and loans as loans. The only difference should be on the interest rate of loans where the states should be given the option either to bear the full exchange risk or pay a higher interest rate to the center denominated in domestic currency terms. The difference between the original rate and this rate should be set equal to the anticipated long-term rate of depreciation of the rupee. Some additional small premium may be charged to cover the cost of administering intermediation through the central budget.

3. Finance Commission Transfers

Earlier we identified the need for harmonizing the Planning Commission and Finance Commission transfers. In addition, some reforms are required for the Finance Commission transfers. Tax revenue sharing and general purpose grants are part of the same exercise and should be considered in relation to each other. The overall objective of the fiscal transfers system should be to achieve equalization of services and progressive equalization of revenue bases supported by a system of proper incentives. Equalizing the revenue capacity of the states is a critical part of the overall equalization exercise, but the post-transfer fiscal capacities of states have remained far from equalized in the past. For this purpose, the revenue capacity of each state needs to be worked out fully on a normative basis. Norms should relate to the base year aggregates as well as the stipulated growth in these for the relevant periods. In a two-sided exercise of equalization, it is also important to look at the cost disabilities. For this purpose, a full-fledged expenditure side equalization model should be set up. Looking at the likely resources available for transfer, the benchmark for the equalization standards could be set equal to a group of states around the median income. The Finance Commission need not make any distinction between the general and the special category states. Based on a factor assessment method, interprovincial requirements could be worked out and expenditure needs should be assessed accordingly.

If the revenue-sharing criteria adequately reflect factors that determine capacity, needs and cost differentials, the revenue-sharing exercise will go a long way toward reducing interjurisdictional disparities. Even so, a residual transfer would be needed because the limited number of criteria used in revenue sharing will not capture all of the relevant considerations. Any uncovered balance of expenditures from the revenue-sharing exercise should be covered by the general-purpose grants given by the Finance Commissions.

4. Summary

A reformed system of intergovernmental transfers in India has to provide for (i) a more equitable distribution of development funds, including external assistance; (ii) a fully normative approach to Finance Commission transfers; (iii) an integrated view of plan and nonplan transfers; (iv) an integrated view of revenue sharing and grants; and (v) adequate incentives for performance. In particular, plan transfers should be made more progressive, leading to more equitable growth of revenue bases and requiring less progressivity in Finance Commission transfers, which would then also better serve efficiency objectives. Collectively, these reforms should result in reduced disparities in income levels and revenue bases, reduced disparities in the standard of services across states, fuller utilization of the growth potential of states, and improved fiscal balance at all levels of government.

References

Advisory Group. 2001. Report of the Advisory Group on *Tax Policy and Tax Administration*, Planning Commission. Government of India.

Ahluwalia, I.J. and I.M.D. Little, eds. 1998. *India's Economic Reforms and Development*. New Delhi: Oxford University Press.

Andersson, Ake E., Bjorn Harsman and John M. Quigley, eds. 1997. *Government for the Future: Unification, Fragmentation and Regionalism*. Contributions to *Economic Analysis*, 238. Amsterdam: New York and Oxford: Elsevier Science, North-Holland.

Aschauer, David A. 1989. Is Public Expenditure Productive? *Journal of Monetary Economics*, 23 (2).

———— and Munnell. 1990. Why is Infrastructure Important? in *Is There a Shortfall in Public Capital Investment? Proceedings of a Conference held at Marwich Port, Massachusetts*, edited by A.H. Munnell. Federal Reserve Bank of Boston.

Beier, Christoph and Gabriele Ferrazzi. 1998. Fiscal Decentralization in Indonesia: A Comment on Smoke and Lewis. *World Development*, 26(12): 2201–11.

Bird, Richard M. 1993. Threading the Fiscal Labyrinth: Some Issues in Fiscal Decentralization. *National Tax Journal* 46(2): 207–27.

Blejer, M.I. and T. Ter-Minassian. 1997. *Macroeconomic Dimension of Public Finance: Essays in Honour of Vito Tanzi*.

Boadway, Robin and Frank Flatters. 1982a. *Equalization in a Federal State: An Economic Analysis*. Ottawa: Economic Council of Canada.

————. 1982b. Efficiency and Equalization Payments in a Federal System of Government: A Synthesis and Extension of Recent Results. *Canadian Journal of Economics* 4.

————, Pierre Pestieau and David Wildasin. 1989. Tax Transfer Policies and the Voluntary Provision of Public Goods. *Journal of Public Economics* 39(2): 157–76.

————. 1992. *The Constitutional Division of Powers: An Economic Perspective*. Ottawa: Economic Council of Canada.

———— and M. Keen. 1996. Efficiency and Optimal Direction of Federal-State Transfers. *Internal Tax and Public Finance* 3.

Bomfim, Antulio and Anwar Shah. 1994. Macroeconomic Management and the Division of Powers in Brazil: Perspectives for the 1990s. *World Development* 22(4): 535–542.

Buchanan, James M. 1950. Federalism and Equity. *The American Economic Review* 40.

————. 1952. Federal Grants and Resource Allocation, *Journal of Political Economy* 66.

————. 1965. An Economic Theory of Clubs, *Economica* 32.

———— and R.E. Wagner. 1971. An Efficiency Basis for Federal Fiscal Equalization. In *The Analysis of Public Output*, edited by J. Margolis. Princeton: NBER.

Burki, S.J. and G. Perry, eds. *Decentralization and Accountability of Public Sector*, World Bank.

Carlsen, Fredrik. 1995. Why Is Central Regulation of Local Spending Decisions So Pervasive?: Evidence from a Case Study. *Public Budgeting and Finance* 15(1): 43–57.

Commonwealth Grants Commission. 1990. *Report on Issues in Fiscal Equalisation, Vols. I, II.* Canberra: AGPS.

Dahlby, B. 1994. The Distortionary Effect of Raising Taxes. In *Deficit Reduction, What Pain, What Gain?*, edited by W.B.P. Robson and W.M. Scarth. C.H. Howe Institute.

————. 1996. Fiscal Externalities and the Design of Intergovernmental Grants. *International Tax and Public Finance* 3.

———— and S. Wilson. 1994. Fiscal Capacity Tax Effort and Optimal Equalization Grants. *Canadian Journal of Economics* 27.

Goodspeed, Timothy J. 1998. Tax Competition, Benefit Taxes, and Fiscal Federalism. *National Tax Journal* 51(3): 579–86.

Government of India (Annual). *Finance Accounts of Union and State Government.*

————. 1994. *Report of the Tenth Finance Commission*, December, New Delhi.

————. 2000. *Economic Survey, 1999–2000*, April, New Delhi.

————. 2000. *Report of Eleventh Finance Commission*, June, New Delhi.

————. 2000. The Contribution of India, Ministry of Law, Justice and Company Affairs.

Gramlich, Edward H. 1985. Federal Fiscal Arrangements. In R. Cares and L.B. Krause, *The Australian Economy: A View from the North.* Washington, DC: The Brookings Institution.

Hayek, F.A. 1945. The Use of Knowledge in Society. *American Economic Review* 35: 519–30.

Hulten, Charles R. and Robert M. Schwab. 1997. A Fiscal Federalism Approach to Infrastructure Policy. *Regional Science and Urban Economics* 27(2): 139–59.

Keen, Michael. 1998. Vertical Tax Externalities in the Theory of Fiscal Federalism. *International Monetary Fund Staff Papers* 45(3): 454–85.

Kopits, George. 2001. Fiscal Policy Rules for India. *Economic and Political Weekly*, March 3: 749–756.

Kurian, N.J. 1997. *Emerging Regional Disparities.* Planning Commission, Government of India (mimeographed).

Levaggi, Rosella. 1991. *Fiscal Federalism and Grants-in-Aid: The Problem of Asymmetrical Information.* Aldershot, U.K., Brookfield, Vt. and Sydney: Ashgate, Avebury.

Lewis, Blane D. and Paul Smoke. 1998. Reply to Beier and Ferrazzi. *World Development* 26(12): 2213–17.

Man, Joyce Y. and Michael E. Bell. 1993. Federal Infrastructure Grants-in-Aid: An Ad Hoc Infrastructure Strategy. *Public Budgeting and Finance* 13(3): 9–22.

Mathews, Russell. 1972. Horizontal Balance in the Australian Federation: The Reduction of Inequalities. In *The Public Sector*, edited by John Dixon. Sydney: Penguin.

———. 1974. Fiscal Equalization for Local Government. *The Economic Record* 50: 131.

Mathews, Russell. 1985. Fiscal Federalism in Australia. *Conference Discussion Paper on Edward M. Gramlich's Paper*. Canberra: The Australian National University.

Munnell, A.H. 1990. How Does Pubic Infrastructure Affect Regional Economic Performance? *New England Economic Review*.

———. 1992. Infrastructure Investment and Economic Growth. *Journal of Economic Perspective* 6(4): 189–98.

Musgrave, Richard A. 1961. *Public Finance: Needs, Sources and Utilization*. Princeton: NBER .

———. 1983. Who Should Tax, Where, What? In *Tax Assignment in Federal Countries*, edited by Charles McLure, Jr. Canberra: Center for Research on Federal Financial Relations, ANU.

Myers, G.M. 1990. Optimality, Free Mobility, and Regional Authority in a Federation. *Journal of Public Economics* 43.

Niskanen, William. 1992. The Case for a New Fiscal Constitution. *Journal of Economic Perspectives* 6(2): 13–24.

Oates, Wallace. 1972. *Fiscal Federalism*. New York: Harcourt, Brace, Jovanovich.

———. 1991. *Studies in Fiscal Federalism. Economists of the Twentieth Century Series*, Aldershot, U.K. and Brookfield, VT: Elgar.

Ott, Attiat F. 1993. *Public Sector Budgets: A Comparative Study*. Aldershot, U.K.: Elgar, Distributed in the U.S. by Ashgate, Brookfield, VT.

Prud'homme, Remy. 1995. On the Dangers of Decentralization. *The World Bank Research Observer* 10: 201–220.

Qian, Yingyi and Gerard Roland. 1994. Regional Decentralization and the Soft Budget Constraint: The Case of China, Discussion Paper 1013. Center for Economic Policy Research.

——— and Barry Weingast. 1997. Federalism as Commitment to Preserving Market Incentives. *Journal of Economic Perspectives* (Fall).

——— and Gerard Roland. 1998. Federalism and the Soft Budget Constraint. AER: 1143–1162.

Reserve Bank of India. 1999. *Handbook of Statistics on Indian Economy*, Mumbai.

Sato, Motobiro. 2000. Fiscal Externalities and Efficient Transfers in a Federation. *International Tax and Public Finance* 7.

Scott, A.D. 1950. A Note on Grants in Federal Countries. *Economica* 17.

———. 1952. Federal Grants and Resource Allocation. *Journal of Political Economy* 60.

Shah, Anwar. 1991. The New Fiscal Federalism in Brazil. *World Bank Discussion Papers, No. 124*. Washington, D.C.: World Bank.

————. 1992. Dynamics of Public Infrastructure, Industrial Productivity and Profitability. *Review of Economics and Statistics* 74(1).

————. 1996. A Fiscal Need Approach to Equalization. *Canadian Public Policy* XXII(2): 99–115.

Smart, Michael. 1998. Taxation Incentives and Dead Weight Loss in a System of Intergovernmental Transfers. *Canadian Journal of Economics*: 189–206.

Smoke, Paul and Blane D. Lewis, 1986. Fiscal Decentralization in Indonesia: A New Approach to an Old Idea. *World Development* 24(8): 1281–99.

Srivastava, D.K. and Pawan K. Aggarwal. 1994. Revenue Sharing Criteria in Federal Fiscal Systems: Some Similarities and Differences. *Public Finance/Finances Publiques* 49(3).

————, Tapas K. Sen, et al. 1997. *Government Subsidies in India*. National Institute of Public Finance and Policy, New Delhi.

————, C. Bhujanga Rao and T.S. Rangamannar. 2000. *External Assistance to India, Concessionality and Transmission to States*. New Delhi: National Institute of Public Finance and Policy.

————, ed. 2000. *Fiscal Federalism in India: Contemporary Challenges*. New Delhi: Har-Anand Publications Pvt. Ltd.

Strauss, Robert P. 1990. Fiscal Federalism and the Changing Global Economy. *National Tax Journal* 43(3): 315–20.

Tanzi, Vito. 1996. *Fiscal Federalism and Decentralization: A Review of Some Efficiency and Macroeconomic Aspects*. Annual World Bank Conference on Development Economics, 1995. Washington, DC: World Bank.

Ter-Minassian, Teresa, ed. 1997. *Fiscal Federalism in Theory and Practice*. Washington, DC: International Monetary Fund.

Wildasin, David E., ed. 1997. *Fiscal Aspects of Evolving Federations*. Cambridge, New York and Melbourne: Cambridge University Press.

————. 1997. Externalities and Bailouts. *World Bank Policy Research Working Paper No. 1843*.

Wrede, Mathias. 2000. Shared Tax Sources and Public Expenditure. *International Tax and Public Finance* 7.

Zhuravskayu, Ekaterina. 2000. Incentives to Provide Local Public Goods: Fiscal Federalism, Rusian Style. *Journal of Public Economics*: 337–368.

5

Indonesia

Blane D. Lewis[1]
Research Triangle Institute, Research Triangle Park,
North Carolina, USA

A. Introduction

The Republic of Indonesia is the fourth largest country in the world with a population of over 200 million people. It is an extremely socially and culturally varied nation: there are more than 300 ethnic groups, each with its own language, customs, and form of social organization.[2] Population and attendant social, political, and economic activities are dispersed across a collection of nearly 14,000 islands, spanning more than 3,000 miles.

Indonesia is a unitary country comprising central, provincial, and local levels of government. Until recently, the regional administration of public affairs operated via a hierarchical, multitiered, and parallel system of deconcentrated central government agencies and nominally autonomous subnational units. Throughout most of its history, Indonesia's public sector has been counted among the most centralized in the world.[3]

Many observers would date Indonesia's modern administrative and fiscal decentralization program to Law No. 5 of 1974.[4] And this law did indeed provide a basis for a greater involvement of decentralized subnational governments in the provision of public services that existed until that time. Although in the early 1990s some implementing regulations were written and a pilot

---

1. The author currently serves as Senior Adviser to the Ministry of Finance (MOF) under a project financed by the United States Agency for International Development (USAID). The views expressed here are those of the author and should not be attributed to either MOF or to the USAID.

2. Guinness (1994).

3. See Smoke and Lewis (1996) for a review of the intergovernmental fiscal framework prior to decentralization and a description of earlier decentralization efforts.

4. The legal basis for decentralization existed prior to that law. See Ford (2000) for a brief review of the constitutional and other early legal underpinnings of decentralization.

program for regional autonomy was undertaken,[5] little real progress was made in operationalizing the general principles outlined in the early legislation over the succeeding 25 years.

Decentralization became more of a political imperative in the late 1990s. The impetus to move forward in a more assertive fashion derived from a special session of the Peoples Consultative Assembly (MPR) with the issuance of an important decree.[6] As a result of the MPR mandate, Indonesia has embarked upon an ambitious program of fiscal decentralization. The effort has its genesis in two laws, both promulgated in May of 1999, one on administrative matters and the other concerning fiscal and finance issues.[7] These two laws have been followed up with a large number of implementing regulations and presidential and ministerial decrees.

As a consequence of the recent legislation, the deconcentrated agencies of central government have, for the most part, been abolished[8] (although provinces continue to represent the center in certain instances) and the hierarchical relationship between autonomous provincial and local governments has been eliminated. For the first time, governors (of provinces) and mayors (of local governments) are elected by and accountable to regional parliaments.[9]

In addition, starting in FY2001, provincial and local governments assumed major new expenditure responsibilities. Substantial functions for provinces have been outlined in a recently issued government regulation.[10] Local government *(kabupaten/kota)* responsibilities, regrettably, have been only rather vaguely defined via a negative list; that is, kabupaten and kota essentially are

---

5. See Beier and Ferrazzi (1998) for a description of the pilot program, among other things.

6. MPR Decree No. XV of 1998 regarding the Implementation of Regional Autonomy: A Just Regulation: Division and Utilization of National Resources and the Balancing of Central-Regional Finances within the Unitary Republic of Indonesia.

7. See Law 22/1999 regarding Regional Administration *(Undang-Undang 22/ 1999 tentang Pemerintahan Daerah)* and Law 25/1999 regarding Financial Balance between the Center and Regional Governments *(Undang-Undang 25/99 tentang Perimbangan Keuangan antara Pemerintah Pusat dan Daerah).*

8. Deconcentrated offices may continue to operate in the regions, where relevant, for those functions that the central government retains: foreign affairs, defense, justice, monetary and fiscal affairs, and religion, among others.

9. As of this writing, there are 348 kabupaten/kota and 30 provinces in Indonesia. Kabupaten is generally translated as regency or district and kota means city.

10. See Government Regulation 25/2000 regarding Central Government Authorities and Autonomous Provincial Government Authorities *(Peraturan Pemerintah No. 25 Tahun 2000 tentang Kewenangan Pemerintah dan Kewenangan Propinsi sebagai Daerah Otonom).*

responsible for all public services that the central and provincial governments are not explicitly charged with delivering.

At the same time, the law has highlighted 11 important areas of local government service responsibility: public works, health, education and culture, agriculture, communications, industry and trade, capital investment, environment, land, cooperatives, and labor. This list makes up the so-called obligatory authorities of kabupaten/kota governments. As is clear, most of the items on this list are perhaps more analogous to sectors than they are functions per se. As such, it has been widely assumed that central and/or provincial governments must retain at least some responsibility for service delivery in the designated areas. This general approach to the assignment of local public services has generated confusion among concerned parties at both the central and regional levels. In any case, regional government expenditure responsibilities are now evidently considerable. In FY2001, for example, it was estimated that subnational governments made up around one-quarter of total public spending.[11]

Regional governments have not, unfortunately, been awarded new authority over any major tax bases. Subnational governments, as a whole, retain the right to levy essentially the same taxes and charges as before the new decentralization legislation took effect, although the distribution of tax bases across provinces and kabupaten/kota have been restructured to a certain extent. Provinces have at least some authority over taxes related to motor vehicles, change of title of motor vehicles, fuel, and ground water extraction and use (the latter being formerly under the control of kabupaten/kota). Tariffs over these taxes are set at uniform rates across the country by the central government. Local governments exercise control over taxes concerning hotels, restaurants, entertainment, advertisement, street lighting, some (class C) mineral exploitation, and parking (newly created). Kabupaten/kota control the tax rates below centrally specified ceilings.[12] Both provinces and kabupaten/kota may collect user charges and fees of various sorts.

In addition, kabupaten/kota (but not provinces) are now allowed to create their own taxes through local bylaws, if they satisfy a number of good tax criteria and central government approval.[13] As it turns out, both local

---

11. The subnational share of total public sector spending reaches nearly 35% if central government debt service payments are ignored. See Ministry of Finance (2002).

12. By law, provinces must share 30% of the motor vehicle-based taxes and 70% of the fuel and ground water taxes with kabupaten/kota. The latter must share 10% of their total own-source tax revenues with villages. See Law 34/2000 regarding Changes to Law 18/1997 regarding Regional Government Taxes and Charges *(Undang-Undang 34 Tahun 2000 tentang Perubahan atas Undang-Undang 18 Tahun 1997 tentang Pajak Daerah dan Retribusi aerah)* for the details.

13. Again, see Law 34/2000.

governments and the center have very broadly interpreted these criteria. Kabupaten/kota have set about creating new taxes in a rather aggressive fashion. Some observers have judged most of the newly created taxes to be either nuisances or economically harmful in some way.[14] Nevertheless, the central government has done little to forestall the rapid formation of these new local revenue instruments. The new local taxes notwithstanding, public revenues apparently remain heavily centralized in Indonesia. Recent estimates put the subnational government share of total national revenues at only around 4%.[15]

As part of the new decentralization initiative, the system of intergovernmental transfers has also been significantly restructured and expanded. Regional governments now gain greater access to substantial amounts of natural resource revenues than before and, in addition, receive a share of the personal income tax. Furthermore, two new and important intergovernmental grants have been created: *Dana Alokasi Umum* (DAU—General Purpose Fund) and *Dana Alokasi Khusus* (DAK—Specific Purpose Fund). These two transfers together replace the old system of *Subsidi Daerah Otonom* (SDO—Autonomous Government Subsidy) and *Instruksi Presiden* (INPRES—Presidential Instruction) grants.[16]

The basic purpose of this chapter is to review the emerging system of intergovernmental transfers in Indonesia. After the introduction, we provide a brief appraisal of transfers that existed before the country's new decentralization program began implementation. Next, we examine the current scheme of intergovernmental transfer mechanisms. As noted above, the new system comprises an array of revenue sharing and general- and specific-purpose grant instruments. In this section of the chapter, each of the various types of transfers is described and analyzed. Some of the more important emerging problems with the system are highlighted throughout. The chapter closes with a summary of the principal points and offers some policy recommendations for improving the system of intergovernmental transfers in Indonesia.

B. Intergovernmental Transfers in Indonesia before Decentralization

Prior to the implementation of the new decentralization legislation, intergovernmental transfers in Indonesia comprised a limited amount of revenue

---

14. See Ray (2001) for an inventory of such tax instruments that are trade-distorting.

15. Ministry of Finance (2002).

16. It should be mentioned that, in addition to the decentralization initiatives briefly catalogued here, the government has also structured special autonomy arrangements with the provinces of Aceh and Irian Jaya. The measures taken have awarded more responsibility and fiscal resources to the two provinces than to other places in Indonesia. These special provisions are not further discussed in this paper.

sharing as well as significant routine and development grants. Shared property taxes accounted for most of total revenue sharing, although shared forestry revenues (forestry licensing.fees and royalties) were also occasionally important over the years. Other national revenues, for example, from mining (land rents and royalties) and/or from clove and copra (cesses) were also at times shared with regional governments but not consistently and the amounts were relatively insignificant. The SDO was the basic routine-side grant for more than 30 years prior to FY2001 when it was disbanded. Development grants over the past three decades comprised a vast and, at times, bewildering array of general- and special-purpose INPRES transfers.[17]

For an illustration of the relative importance of these various transfers in regional government budgets, see Table 1 which provides aggregate data on own-source revenues, shared revenues, and grants for regional governments, in total, and for provincial and kabupaten/kota governments over the period 1995–1996 through 1999–2000. The table demonstrates the overall importance of transfers to regional government budgets. Transfers made up about 75% of total regional government revenues, on average, over the period, including just less than 60% of provincial and approximately 85% of kabupaten/kota revenues. SDO transfers were most important, in general (38% of total regional government revenues), and for both provinces (31%) and kabupaten/kota (43%), followed by INPRES (23% of total regional government revenues and 6% and 28% of provincial and kabupaten/kota revenues, respectively) and revenue sharing (13% of total subnational revenues and 12% and 14% of total revenues for provinces and kabupaten/kota).

Property taxes, the dominant form of revenue sharing until recently, underwent relatively little change in structure, administration, distribution, and use over the years since 1985. The latter is the year in which the current and principal property-related tax, PBB *(Pajak Bumi dan Bangunan)*,[18] was created and replaced the then large number of land and building taxes. Since that time, property taxes have been levied in five different sectors: rural, urban, estates, forestry, and mining. Property taxes were and continue to be administered and collected, for the most part, by central government, although local governments assist with collections in rural and urban sectors. Until just recently, the central government retained 10% of the total tax for its own use, 9% was provided to local tax offices to assist with collections, 16% was assigned to provincial governments, and 65% was distributed to local governments. Regional shares were

---

17. See Shah and Qureshi (1994) for an early and comprehensive description and discussion of intergovernmental transfers in Indonesia.

18. The other property related tax is the *Bea Perolehan Hak atas Tanah dan Bangunan* (BPHTB). The BPHTB is a tax on the transfer of title on land and buildings.

TABLE 1
Regional Government Revenues, By Source 1995–1996 through 1999–2000
(Rp Billions)

	1995–1996	Share	1996–1997	Share	1997–1998	Share	1998–1999	Share	1999–2000	Share	Ave Share
Province											
Own-Source	3,854.23	0.342	4,318.93	0.346	4,648.29	0.366	3,100.93	0.344	3,226.20	0.310	0.343
Revenue Sharing	986.54	0.088	1,189.11	0.095	1,255.54	0.099	1,882.82	0.209	1,466.25	0.141	0.121
SDO	4,145.09	0.368	4,457.03	0.357	4,605.89	0.362	1,794.42	0.199	2,264.51	0.218	0.309
INPRES	1,343.89	0.119	1,468.79	0.118	1,596.90	0.126	1,818.53	0.202	2,963.15	0.285	0.165
From Prior Year	926.24	0.082	1,046.19	0.084	605.27	0.048	413.81	0.046	489.59	0.047	0.062
Total	11,255.99	1.000	12,480.05	1.000	12,711.89	1.000	9,010.51	1.000	10,409.70	1.000	1.000
Kabupaten Kota											
Own-Source	1,531.16	0.138	1,827.35	0.142	2,076.81	0.131	2,248.63	0.109	2,354.69	0.097	0.119
Revenue Sharing	1,716.24	0.155	2,162.43	0.168	2,342.35	0.148	2,988.62	0.145	2,886.78	0.119	0.143
SDO	3,841.52	0.347	4,439.46	0.344	6,016.93	0.381	9,688.34	0.469	12,492.75	0.515	0.431
INPRES	3,636.40	0.328	4,089.01	0.317	4,873.00	0.308	5,172.78	0.251	5,964.33	0.246	0.280
From Prior Year	357.71	0.032	382.28	0.030	503.40	0.032	539.76	0.026	551.49	0.023	0.028
Total	11,083.03	1.000	12,900.53	1.000	15,812.49	1.000	20,638.13	1.000	24,250.04	1.000	1.000
All											
Own-Source	5,385.39	0.241	6,146.28	0.242	6,725.10	0.236	5,349.56	0.180	5,580.89	0.161	0.208
Revenue Sharing	2,702.78	0.121	3,351.54	0.132	3,597.89	0.126	4,871.44	0.164	4,353.03	0.126	0.134
SDO	7,986.61	0.358	8,896.49	0.351	10,622.82	0.372	11,482.76	0.387	14,757.26	0.426	0.382
INPRES	4,980.29	0.223	5,557.80	0.219	6,469.90	0.227	6,991.31	0.236	8,927.48	0.258	0.234
From Prior Year	1,283.95	0.057	1,428.47	0.056	1,108.67	0.039	953.57	0.032	1,041.08	0.030	0.041
Total	22,339.02	1.000	25,380.58	1.000	28,524.38	1.000	29,648.64	1.000	34,659.74	1.000	1.000

Note: The Indonesian currency is the rupiah (Rp).
Source: Government of Indonesia *Nota Keuangan*, various years.

and continue to be, for the most part, distributed on a derivation basis. Use of shared property taxes has been completely at the discretion of regional governments since 1985 to the present.[19]

The major concern with the property tax over the years pertains to its shared nature. While in most countries the property tax is an important local tax (arguably for good reasons related to adequacy, efficiency, fairness, and accountability), in Indonesia it has steadfastly remained under the control of central government. Proposals for decentralizing the property tax have been made and reviewed frequently over the last 15 years and the central government is now, yet again, considering partial decentralization (i.e., control over the effective tariff) of property-related taxes to local governments.

The SDO grant was also altered relatively little since its inception over 30 years ago until it was dropped in FY2001. The SDO grant was not actually a single grant but a compilation of transfers. The most important component of SDO funding was for regional government employee remuneration and it covered almost the entire amount of regional civil servant salaries and allowances, including those of primary school teachers. Other smaller components of the SDO funded various additional regional government routine expenditures, including the operations and maintenance of school buildings, and sub-kabupaten/kota (i.e. *kecamatan* and village) administrative expenditures. Central government allocation of the SDO was based, for the most part, on the number and years of experience of regional civil servants in various job classifications. Regional governments tended to take the lead on recruiting staff, although the center had responsibility for officially approving regional staffing levels, in general, and additions to such, in particular. It appears that the central government did not always make a serious attempt to discern real staffing needs, however, and regional proposals for additional staff were often approved in a pro forma manner.[20]

Many observers have found the SDO to be little more than an instrument of central control over regional governments. It is certainly clear that the grant did little to directly promote the autonomy of regional governments. At the very least, SDO operations made civil servants appear to be "free goods" to the regional governments for whom they worked. As such, the grant offered little in the way of incentives for regional expenditure efficiency.[21]

INPRES grants changed a great deal in structure and function over the last three decades until their recent demise. INPRES started out in the late 1960s

---

19. See Kelly (1993) for an early description of property taxes in Indonesia.

20. See Rohdewohld (1995) for a good description of central and regional government civil service as it existed prior to FY 2001.

21. See Davey (1989) for an early discussion of the SDO.

as a rather simple block grant but, by the late 1990s, the transfer had evolved into a fairly complicated system of general- and specific-purpose grants. While the size of general-purpose component of the system grew quite quickly during the last decade of INPRES existence, the number of specific-purpose grants also multiplied rapidly, and growth of associated funds outstripped increases in the block element. By the time INPRES grants were dissolved, there were at least 15 different specific-purpose transfers, including those for primary schools, primary health care, roads, other urban infrastructure, urban re-greening, agricultural extension, and environmental impact assessment. By FY2000, funds attendant to specific-purpose transfers were well over twice as large as those for the general-purpose grant.

Overall, most analysts seem to have concluded that the INPRES system had a relatively positive impact on regional social and economic development in Indonesia over the course of more than three decades.[22] At least the funds assisted in the development of a significant amount of regional infrastructure. These positive points notwithstanding, a number of important criticisms have been raised over the years, particularly with regard to the system's general complexity and specific lack of transparency in allocation procedures, excessive central control and attendant lack of support for regional autonomy, lack of incentives for revenue mobilization, and negative performance vis-à-vis equalization objectives, among others.[23]

At least partly as a result of the various criticisms noted above, the Indonesian system of intergovernmental transfers has now been significantly redesigned. The new structure of transfers between central and regional governments is described and examined in the next section.

C. The Current System of Intergovernmental Transfers in Indonesia

Transfers in Indonesia continue to comprise both revenue sharing and grant instruments. Revenue sharing now includes shares of property-related taxes, natural resource revenues, as well as income tax, and grants consist of a single grant mechanism each for general- and specific-purposes. Transfers, in general, remain highly significant sources of revenue for regional governments. In fact, they have grown even more important to regional budgets than they were prior to decentralization. Data for FY2001 show that all transfers together accounted for just less than 90% of total regional government revenues.

---

22. See Shah and Qureshi (1994) for a largely positive evaluation of INPRES grants.

23. Schroeder (1995) discusses some of these less positive features of the old INPRES system.

Table 2 details the relative importance of the various types of transfers, along with own-source revenues, in provincial and kabupaten/kota budgets for FY2001. As can be seen from the table, the DAU is far the most important source of revenue for regional governments, funding almost two-thirds of subnational government budgets. Revenue sharing is not unimportant, however, and it makes up more than one-fifth of regional government financial resources. Own-source revenues remain the smallest source of funds for regional governments and account for just over 10% of total regional government revenues. We now turn to an examination of revenue sharing and grant making in the new decentralized environment in Indonesia.

TABLE 2
Estimated Regional Government Revenues, FY 2001
(Rp Billions)

Source	Provinces	Percent	Kab/Kota	Percent	Total	Percent
Own-Source Revenues	6,400	34.5	4,100	5.6	10,500	11.4
Total Revenue Sharing	5,928	31.9	14,792	20.0	20,720	22.4
Property-Related Taxes	2,252	12.1	3,812	5.2	6,064	6.6
Natural Resource Revenues	2,565	13.8	9,312	12.6	11,877	12.8
Personal Income Tax	1,111	6.0	1,667	2.3	2,779	3.0
DAU	6,238	33.6	54,279	73.5	60,517	65.5
DAK	n.a	n.a	701	0.9	701	0.8
Total Transfers	12,166	65.5	69,772	94.4	81,938	88.6
Grand Total	18,566	100.0	73,872	100.0	92,438	100.0

Source: Based on Lewis (2001).

1. Revenue Sharing

As noted above, there are currently three types of revenue sharing in Indonesia. Shared sources include those for property-related taxes, natural resource revenues, and the income tax. Property-related shares comprise those for the land and buildings tax and the transfer of title on land and buildings tax. There are now eight natural resource revenue-sharing instruments: two each for forestry, mining, and fisheries along with those for oil and natural gas. The income tax shares are derived from the personal (as opposed to the business) income tax.

As demonstrated in Table 2, shared revenues account for about 22% of total regional government revenues. In general, the most important shared revenues are those derived from natural resources (13% of total regional revenues), followed by those for property taxes (7%) and then personal income taxes (3%). The relative significance of the various instruments varies across provinces and kabupaten.

Shared revenues are distributed across regional governments by various means. Table 3 lists revenue-sharing instruments along with the methods by which the shared sources are allocated across provinces and kabupaten/kota. As can be seen from the table, all shares to provinces are allocated exclusively by derivation. Shared revenues are distributed to kabupaten/kota both by derivation and, not infrequently, in equal amounts across places.

As previously indicated, property-related taxes have been shared with regional governments in Indonesia for many years now. As can be seen from the table, now all property tax revenues, including central shares are, in the event, distributed to regional governments (with the exception of 9% for collections). At least several of the natural resource revenues had already been shared with regional governments as well prior to FY2001, especially those related to forestry and mining, although sharing arrangements have been revised in many instances. The shared revenues for fisheries, oil, gas, and personal income taxes are new, however.

The main objective of revenue sharing, especially that related to newly shared revenues, is to respond to regional aspirations for increased access to and control over certain revenues. As is well known, many regions in Indonesia have long felt that they have not benefited sufficiently from the significant revenues generated in their areas and these sharing schemes constitute a real attempt to meet these demands. One problem with the attainment of this objective is that many in the regions remain unconvinced that they are getting their fair share of revenues in question. This is in part because the central government calculation of amounts of revenue to be shared is done in a less-than-transparent manner, and the regions suspect dishonest practices. Another problem concerns the timing of distribution to the regions. Although such transfers should, according to law, be made quarterly, in FY2001, the first payments on natural resource revenues were not made until July.

Revenue sharing is also intended to address fiscal imbalances between the central and regional governments. To what extent has revenue sharing been able to address such vertical imbalances? A somewhat naive, but typical, approach to the analysis of this question is to compare expenditure shares of central and subnational governments to their revenue shares before and after transfers. Before transfers, of course, subnational governments typically experience deficits. To the extent that deficits are reduced by adding transfers, then vertical imbalances are ameliorated.[24] Table 4 provides some pertinent information on vertical imbalances for Indonesia for FY2001.

As the table shows, before transfers are made, subnational governments

---

24. See Shah (1994) for a discussion of vertical imbalances and the presentation of some evidence on the same for a number of developing and developed countries.

TABLE 3
Revenue-Sharing Instruments and Distribution, Starting FY 2001

Shared Revenue	Central Share	Provincial Share	Local Share
Property Tax. (PBB: *Pajak Bumi dan Bangunan*)	10%. Distributed to kabupaten/kota: 6.5% in equal amounts across all localities and 3.5% to places based on their attainment of previous year's (urban and rural) PBB target.	16.2%. By derivation.	64.8%. By derivation (except oil and gas sectors)[a]
Property Title Transfer Tax. (BPHTB: *Bea Perolehan Hak atas Tanah dan Bangunan*)	20%. Distributed to all kabupaten and kota in equal amounts.	16%. By derivation.	64%. By derivation.
Forestry Right to Operate Levy. (IHPH: *Iuran Hak Pengusahaan Hutan*)	20%	16%. By derivation.	64%. By derivation.
Forestry Resources Commission. (PSDH: *Provisi Sumber Daya Hutan*)	20%	16%. By derivation.	32% by derivation; 32% in equal amounts across all localities within province.
Mining Sector Land Rent. PIT: *(Penerimaan Iuran Tetap)*	20%	16%. By derivation.	64%. By derivation.
Mining Sector Royalties. (PIE: *Penerimaan Iuran Eksplorasi dan Exploitasi)*	20%	16%. By derivation.	32% by derivation; 32% in equal amounts (for all places within province).
Tax Revenue on Fisheries Operations. *(Penerimaan Pungutan Pengusahaan Perikanan)*	20%	0%	80%. Equal amounts for all kabupaten and kota in country.

TABLE 3 (cont.)

Shared Revenue	Central Share	Provincial Share	Local Share
Tax Revenue on Fisheries Output. *(Penerimaan Pungutan Hasil Perikanan)*	20%	0%	80%. Equal amounts for all kabupaten and kota in country.
Oil Revenues. *(Minyak)*	85%	3%. By derivation.	6% by derivation; 6 % in equal amounts (within province).
Natural Gas Revenues. *(Gas Alam)*	70%	6%. By derivation.	12% by derivation; 12% in equal amounts (within province).
Personal Income Tax. (PPh: *Pajak Penghasilan*)	80%	8%. By taxpayer location.[b]	12%. Distribution by provincial choice.

Notes: [a] Remaining 9% of property tax revenues reserved for support of tax collections carried out by central and local governments.

[b] Taxpayer location, according to the legislation, may be employee residence, place of business activity, or employer home office location. In practice, it appears, most often, to be the latter.

Source: Government Regulation 104/2000 and Law 17/2000.

are in substantial deficit (23.4%). Vertical imbalances are less severe for provinces (deficit of 3.3%) than for kabupaten and kota (deficit of 20.1%). After the addition of shared revenues, the overall subnational deficit is narrowed to 16.8% and the deficits for provinces and kabupaten are reduced to 1.4% and 15.4%, respectively. Remaining fiscal imbalances at the subnational level are completely removed by the distribution of grants. In fact, as the table shows, subnational governments experience a surplus balance after the transfer of DAU and DAK and the central government moves to a deficit position. More will be said below about this implied overallocation of grants.

While helpful in addressing aggregate vertical fiscal imbalances, a real and well-known problem with natural resource revenue and personal income tax sharing in Indonesia is that such revenues are distributed very unevenly across regions. According to Ministry of Finance data, over 50% of the personal income tax shares, for example, are allocated to Jakarta alone. And over 75% of the total natural resource revenues shared with kabupaten/kota are distributed to just 30 places in Aceh, Riau, and Kalimantan Timur; similarly, these three places account for three quarters of the natural resource shares allocated to provinces as well.

TABLE 4
Vertical Imbalances, FY 2001
(Percentages)

	Revenue Share (1)	Expenditure Share (2)	Imbalance (1) – (2)
Own-Sources			
National	0.966	0.732	0.234
Subnational	0.034	0.268	(0.234)
Provincial	0.021	0.054	(0.033)
Kabupaten/Kota	0.013	0.214	(0.201)
Total	1.000	1.000	0.000
After Shared Revenues			
National	0.899	0.732	0.168
Subnational	0.101	0.268	(0.168)
Provincial	0.040	0.054	(0.014)
Kabupaten/Kota	0.061	0.214	(0.154)
Total	1.000	1.000	0.000
After Grants			
National	0.702	0.732	(0.030)
Subnational	0.298	0.268	0.030
Provincial	0.060	0.054	0.006
Kabupaten/Kota	0.238	0.214	0.024
Total	**1.000**	**1.000**	**0.000**

Source: Author's own calculations based on national and regional budget data.

Thus, there are severe problems regarding distributional equity of natural resource revenue and personal income tax sharing. This is typical throughout the world where such revenues are shared and a major reason many analysts argue against the idea of sharing these revenues on an origin basis. Theoretically, of course, the inequitable nature of these transfers could be mitigated, at least to a certain extent, by an equalization grant. We turn now to a discussion of Indonesia's main equalization tool, the DAU.

2. Dana Alokasi Umum (DAU)

The DAU is the most important source of revenue for regional governments. As Table 2 above shows, DAU allocations account for about two-thirds of total subnational government revenues. The DAU is especially significant for kabupaten/kota for which it makes up nearly 75% of total revenues. The transfer is not unimportant to provinces as well; DAU distributions account for around one-third of total provincial revenues.

The legislation states that the annual DAU pool of finance is to be based on a minimum 25% of total domestic revenues, where the latter is net of those amounts to be shared with regional governments via the mechanisms described above. Sharing arrangements between subnational levels of government are also governed by law and 10% and 90% of the total funds are to be distributed to provinces and kabupaten, respectively. An important goal of the DAU is to address vertical imbalances. That is, it is the intention of the DAU, together with revenues from other sources of finance, to assist provincial and kabupaten/kota governments in meeting their total respective expenditure requirements.[25]

For some evidence on questions related to the overall adequacy of DAU and other sources of finance vis-à-vis fiscal needs, consider Table 5 below. The table provides estimates of aggregate revenues available to and expenditure needs of provincial and kabupaten/kota governments for FY2001. Own-source revenue estimates are based on historical regional government budget (APBD) data (before decentralization) and shared revenues are based on FY2001 state (APBN) budgeted amounts. Regional government (routine and development) expenditure needs estimates are derived from provincial and kabupaten/kota APBDs (again, prior to FY2001) and from Kanwil and Kandep DIK (Daftar Isian Kegiatan—routine) expenditures for FY2000. Kanwils and Kandeps are the former deconcentrated offices of central level agencies, the routine operations of which were transferred to regional governments before and during FY2001.[26]

TABLE 5
Estimated Regional Government Fiscal Capacities and Expenditure Needs
FY 2001
(Rp Trillions)

Fiscal Capacity	Provinces	Kab/Kota	Total
Own-Source	6.4	4.1	10.5
Shared Revenues	5.9	14.8	20.7
DAK	n.a	0.7	0.7
DAU	6.2	54.3	60.5
Total Revenues	18.6	73.9	92.4
Expenditure Needs			
Routine, Based on FY 2000	8.4	23.2	31.6
Development, Based on FY 2000	5.5	9.4	14.9
From Kanwil and Kandep FY 2000	3.2	15.0	18.2
Total Expenditure Needs	17.1	47.6	64.7
Surplus	1.5	26.3	27.7

Source: Based on Lewis (2001).

---

25. See Ministry of Finance (2002) for a discussion of the goals of the DAU and other transfers.

26. Note that fiscal needs estimates derived from ex-Kanwil and ex-Kandep operations do not include development expenditures (Daftar Isian Proyek—DIPs). The

The above table implies that the DAU and other sources of finance, in general, appear to result in a significant funding surplus for regional governments. Given all sources of revenue, regional governments, on the whole, appear to have almost Rp28 trillion more than they require to meet their expenditure needs. The data suggest that kabupaten/kota seem to have access to substantially more funds (a surplus slightly more than Rp26 trillion) than they need to carry out their assigned duties. On the other hand, it appears that provincial level funding, while apparently still in surplus (in the amount of Rp1.5 trillion), is at least close to required levels.

In any case, the implication here is that the pool of finance available to the DAU, taking other sources of revenue as given, is too large relative to expenditure requirements. That is, arguably, the central government has, on balance, transferred too much DAU to the regions; or, alternatively, it has transferred too little in the way of expenditure responsibilities. While it may have been politically difficult to do otherwise, the economic appropriateness of making such large relative transfers to the regions, at time of rather significant pressure on the central budget, can at least be questioned.[27]

It must be emphasized that these conclusions are very tentative and more research on these questions is needed. On the fiscal capacity side, additional efforts would concentrate on developing better estimates of potential own-source revenues and would be based on a more thorough examination of the tax bases to which local governments currently have access as well as normal tax rates applied to those bases. (The estimation of other sources of subnational revenue—transfers—is rather straightforward.) Improving estimates of real expenditure requirements is more problematic. Here, needed research would be based on an examination of assigned service responsibilities of subnational levels of government and a derivation of the legitimate costs related to carrying out those responsibilities at specified standards. Such a rigorous examination is not currently possible given a lack of clarity about subnational expenditure assignments and service standards and lack of sufficient data on service delivery costs, among other things. We will return to this question of the adequacy of DAU funding below after the DAU allocation methods are described.

---

latter have not yet been decentralized to regional governments, although by law they should have been.

27. The planned central budget deficit for FY2001 was 3.7% of GDP or approximately Rp54.3 trillion. In the event the deficit appears to have been smaller, preliminary data suggest that the actual deficit amounted to just 2.3% of GDP or about Rp34.2 trillion.

3. Kabupaten/Kota DAU Allocation Methods

Provincial and kabupaten/kota DAU is allocated by formula. The methods employed to distribute DAU across kabupaten/kota in FY2002 are described and discussed next. Procedures used for the allocation of DAU to provinces are similar and briefly described later. It should be noted that DAU allocation techniques are still evolving and the distribution methods for FY2002 differ significantly from those used for FY2001, the first year of operations.[28] Where appropriate, differences in approach between the two years are noted. In addition, the appendix to this chapter examines, in tabular format, issues and outcomes related to DAU, especially regarding differences in aggregate amounts available, allocation procedures, and equalization impacts in FY2001 and 2002.

Kabupaten/kota DAU allocations may be written:

$$\text{DAU}_i = \text{LSA}_i + \text{BFA}_i + \text{FA}_i \tag{1}$$

where LSA is the lump sum amount, BFA is the balancing factor amount, and FA is the formula amount. The subscript i refers to kabupaten/kota governments. The lump-sum amount is:

$$\text{LSA}_i = \frac{0.10 \bullet \text{DAU}_T}{n} \tag{2}$$

where DAU_T refers to the total pool of finance for kabupaten/kota. In monetary terms, the lump-sum amount provided to each local government in FY2002 is Rp17.87 billion.

The balancing factor amount may be written as:

$$\text{BFA}_i = \frac{\text{Wage}_i}{\sum_i \text{Wage}_i} \bullet 0.50 \bullet \text{DAU}_T \tag{3}$$

where Wage is the estimated wage bill for kabupaten/kota civil servants for FY2002. It is perhaps useful to note that the above formulation results in the funding of 77% of each local government's civil servant wage bill this fiscal year.

Note that equations (2) and (3) taken together indicate that 60% of DAU allocations are based on the lump sum and balancing factors, so that just 40% of the DAU is allocated via the fiscal gap formula as defined below. In FY2001, lump sum and balancing factor distributions accounted for just over 80% of

---

28. See Lewis (2001) for a description and analysis of the DAU distribution mechanism for FY2001.

tota' kabupaten/kota DAU allocations. Some government officials have argued that the decrease in relative magnitude of the lump sum and balancing factor amounts this fiscal year implies an intention to phase out the use of these elements over the next couple of years.

The lump sum last year was derived simply as a residual and resulted from adjustments made to the total pool of finance for the DAU during state budget discussions with the parliament. The exact purpose of this year's lump sum is uncertain. Obviously, its significance is greater for relatively smaller places. As such, many observers have argued that the lump sum provides some, albeit limited, incentive for the creation of new (smaller) kabupaten out of established (larger) places. The extent to which the lump sum operates as such an incentive is unsure, but it is clear that the creation of new places continues in rapid fashion and strains the transfer system's ability to keep apace.

The balancing factor last fiscal year was a function of the previous year's SDO and INPRES allocations and was intended to operationalize a "hold harmless" provision. As result, in FY2001, kabupaten/kota governments were assured of a minimum 40% increase in grants compared with FY2000. The purpose behind the balancing factor this year is somewhat unclear. (Hold harmless provisions still remain but have been structured differently, as further described below). However, the fact that the BFA is based on civil servants' wages certainly suggests a different objective from the previous year. Indeed, many officials at the central and regional government level would very much like to see the balancing factor separated from the rest of the allocation mechanism with a view to creating an SDO-like transfer to fund local civil servant costs.

In equation form, the formula amount (FA) for kabupaten/kota can be written:

$$FA_i = \left(DAU_T - \sum_i LSA_i - \sum_i BFA_i \right) \cdot \frac{FG_i}{\sum_i FG_i} \tag{4}$$

where FG is the fiscal gap.

The fiscal gap is defined as the difference between expenditure needs (EN) and fiscal capacity (FC). That is:

$$FG_i = EN_i - FC_i \tag{5}$$

It is important to note that if the difference between expenditure needs and fiscal capacities is negative for a particular region, the fiscal gap, as defined in equation (5) above is set equal to zero; that is, the Indonesian system does not allow for negative grants.[29] This has significant implications vis-à-vis

---

29. In the current context, a grant would only be negative if fiscal capacity

the system's equalization performance, as discussed more fully below. The DAU formula defines expenditure needs as the product between total local government expenditure and the expenditure needs index. Expenditures are actual amounts from FY2001 local government budgets (APBD). The needs index is a function of population, area, poverty, and a cost element. Data for these variables are from the most recent years available.

More specifically, expenditure needs can be expressed in equation form as:

$$EN_i = APBDEXP_T \bullet \left(0.4 \frac{Pop_i}{\sum_i Pop_i} + 0.1 \frac{Area_i}{\sum_i Area_i} + 0.1 \frac{PovGap_i}{\sum_i PovGap_i} + 0.4 \frac{Cost_i}{\sum_i Cost_i} \right) \tag{6}$$

where $APBDEXP_T$ is total local government expenditure from the previous year, Pop is population, Area is surface area, PovGap is the so-called poverty gap, and Cost is a cost index.

The first term on the right hand side of equation (6) illustrates very clearly one of the most obvious weaknesses of the DAU allocation formula. It makes apparent that, at the aggregate level, expenditure needs are simply assumed to be equivalent to actual expenditures. The problem, of course, is that kabupaten/kota governments may not actually need what they spend. Or, they may need more. In any case, real expenditure requirements can only be derived based on a thorough examination of the true costs of discharging a clearly defined set of service responsibilities at some predetermined standard or level of quality. None of these things is known with any degree of certainty in Indonesia and so there is little choice but to opt for an approach such as the above, at least temporarily.

The needs index itself is comprised of variables that ostensibly influence the demand for and/or cost of delivering local public services. Population, for example, clearly influences the need or demand for public services—the greater the population, the greater the aggregate demand for services, all other things being equal.

Area also appears to have an indisputable influence on expenditure needs, at least for rural areas. One might plausibly argue that, all other things remaining the same, larger rural places are relatively more in need of roads, school buildings, and health centers, for example, among other services. Area is probably less relevant for urban areas, however. The fact that the DAU allocation

---

exceeded expenditure needs by an amount that was greater than the lump sum and balancing factors. The policy until now has been to guarantee DAU grants to be at least as large as lump sum and balancing factor amounts. If and when the latter two are phased out, then the stated "no negative grants" policy would take on more meaning.

procedure treats urban and rural places in a similar manner here and, in general, is of concern.

The need for including a poverty measure in determining relative local government expenditure requirements is not completely obvious. While the amount of poverty undeniably influences need for poverty-reduction programs, the level of government responsible for such efforts in Indonesia is still uncertain. It may well be that the central government has overall responsibility for poverty reduction. The impact of poverty on need for other local services, such as education, water, and roads is less than clear. While a direct relationship may exist between the extent of poverty and expenditure needs for services other than pure poverty-reduction ones, Indonesian analysts have not yet made a strong case for it.

The choice of poverty variable is also somewhat unusual. Last year, DAU designers employed the number of poor people as the poverty variable to help determine expenditure requirements. This at least makes some intuitive sense. This year the so-called poverty gap is used. The poverty gap is defined as the average proportionate distance of the poor from the poverty line across the whole population. More precisely:

$$P_1 = \frac{1}{n} \sum_{i=1}^{q} \frac{z - y_i}{z} \tag{7}$$

where P_1 is the typical notation for the poverty gap, n is total population, z is the poverty line, y_i is total expenditure of the ith person, and q is the number of people who fall below the poverty line. It is usually argued that the poverty gap measures of the depth of poverty.

No explicit reason was given for the change in formulation. Assuming that poverty is relevant in determining expenditure needs, it is hard to see how a measure of the depth of poverty would be more appropriate than the number of poor people.[30] In any case, this is clearly an area in which more research is needed.

The cost index employed in equation (6) above is intended to measure unavoidable differences in costs faced by local governments. Its derivation is based on differences in building construction costs across regions.[31] These costs

---

30. Direct poverty reduction programs in Indonesia, such as rice subsidy programs and school food programs, for example, focus on allocating benefits to people or families classified as poor; benefits are standardized and are not adjusted for the depth of poverty as defined here.

31. This may not be the most appropriate index for measuring regional variation in the cost of delivering infrastructure services. Unfortunately, there is as of yet no better alternative. The Central Statistics Bureau is currently in the process, however, of

are assumed to be positively related to expenditure requirements associated with delivering local public services. Internationally, compensation for differences in such costs (as opposed to those that might arise from local policy decisions) is often defended on equity grounds. While this may be legitimate, it must be admitted that the influence of cost differentials has been formulated in a somewhat odd manner here. Typically, a cost index is structured into an allocation formula with a view to adjusting total expenditure needs directly (i.e. multiplicatively), after accounting for other needs factors. Thus, in the current context, ignoring for a moment problems related to the use of the area and poverty gap measures as discussed above, the influence of cost differential might be structured as:

$$EN_i = \left[APBDEXP_T \bullet \left(\alpha \cdot \frac{Pop_i}{\sum_i Pop_i} + \beta \cdot \frac{Area_i}{\sum_i Area_i} + \chi \cdot \frac{PovGap_i}{\sum_i PovGap_i} \right) \right] \bullet \frac{Cost_i}{100} \quad (8)$$

where $\alpha + \beta + \chi = 1$ and all other variables are as previously defined.

In the allocation method used to actually distribute DAU, the cost index is first averaged with noncost factors and then applied to expenditure needs. There is no clear economic rationale for this.

Finally, a brief comment is warranted on the weighting of needs factors in equation (6) above. Last year, each of the four needs factors was weighted equally. Many analysts were unhappy with that weighting scheme; it was argued, in particular, as a function of an empirical analysis of regional expenditures in Indonesia, that the weight accorded population was not commensurate with its influence on expenditure needs. So, the present scheme was adopted, at least partly in response to this criticism. Whether the adjustment is sufficient on these grounds is uncertain, but based on the earlier mentioned analysis, it seems less than adequate. In the end, the true influence of various needs factors, including population, can only be ascertained by more thoroughly disaggregated sectoral and spatial analysis.

This fiscal year's operationalization of fiscal capacity constitutes perhaps the greatest improvement over last year's procedures. Fiscal capacity is now straightforwardly defined as the sum of potential own-source revenues and other transfers (somewhat reduced). In equation form:

$$FC_i = O\hat{S}R_i + SPT_i + SIT_i + 0.75 \bullet SNR_i \quad (9)$$

---

developing an index that might better measure differentials in the full range of costs associated with producing and providing subnational public services.

where SPT is shared property tax revenue, SIT is shared personal income tax revenue, and SNR is shared natural resource revenues. OŜR in equation (9) is potential local own-source tax and nontax revenue, which is derived as the predicted value based on a regression of actual own-source revenue (OSR) for the most recent year available against gross regional development product from the services sector (GRDPS). That is:

$$OSR_i = \beta_0 + \beta_1 GRDPS_i + \varepsilon_i \tag{10}$$

Potential own-source revenues are thus defined as a function of standard tax effort. The intention behind this formulation was, at least in part, to serve as an incentive to regional governments to mobilize revenues. It must be admitted, however, that regional officials do not understand well this feature. This lack of understanding detracts from possible incentive effects.

Note the natural resource revenue share coefficient limits a region's estimated fiscal capacity resulting from these transfers to 75% of the totals actually received. This unfortunate formulation resulted from the successful lobbying efforts of local government and local parliamentary associations. It is not a coincidence, of course, that the current heads of these associations are, for the most part, mayors and councillors from natural resource-rich kabupaten/kota.

Some mention might be made of missing transfers in equation (9). It is often argued that all sources of revenue should show up on the right-hand side of an equation defining fiscal capacity. And, in this regard, many analysts have argued that the DAK, for example, should be included in the definition of fiscal capacity of regional governments. The central government has asserted, however, that the DAK is reserved to fund atypical or extraordinary local expenditure needs. As such, they have explicitly rejected the inclusion of the DAK as a component of regional government fiscal capacity. On the other hand, analysts and central officials recognize that transfers made by provinces to kabupaten/kota (as mentioned above) should probably be included in the measure of the latter's fiscal capacity. Currently, however, a dearth of data prohibits such a formulation.

4. Hold Harmless Adjustments to Kabupaten/Kota DAU Allocations

Employment of the system described above generated the so-called original DAU allocations; that is, those that were presented to Parliament in the context of state budget negotiations. Parliament approved of the distribution methods, in general, but insisted, at the same time, that no local government should receive less in DAU in FY2002 than it received the previous year. This stipulation, of course, required some adjustments to the original DAU allocations.

The modifications were implemented by first comparing each place's originally derived DAU allocation to that received the previous year and noting any associated surplus or deficit. Allocations of individual surplus regions were then reduced, where the amounts subtracted were equal to each place's share of the total surplus times the aggregate deficit. This total was then distributed across deficit regions to bring each of the latter's allocations up to previous year's amounts.

Subsequently, about Rp800 billion derived from the state budget contingency fund for FY2002 was used to add some amounts back into surplus regions' depleted allocations heretofore (where additional sums were based on relative size of earlier contributions). This compensation scheme made up for part, although not all, of amounts that were earlier taken away. In the end, so-called surplus regions lost a total amount of approximately Rp2 trillion in DAU allocations due to the adjustment procedures, while deficit regions gained approximately Rp2.8 trillion. What may not be immediately obvious is that those surplus regions were, as a group, relatively less well off than deficit regions. In any case, it is now clear that the adjustment procedures related to the implementation of hold harmless condition insisted upon by Parliament were unequalizing in their impact. More will be said about this later.

5. Provincial DAU Allocations

Provincial DAU allocations were derived in basically the same manner as just presented above for kabupaten/kota except that the lump sum and balancing factor amounts were based on 20% and 30% of total provincial DAU. This resulted in a lump-sum allocation of Rp46.8 billion to each province and a funding of 31% of each province's civil servant wage bill. Overall, therefore, the fiscal gap formula was used to allocate 50% of the total provincial DAU compared to 40% for kabupaten/kota. The reasons behind the different approach employed for provincial distributions have not been clearly stated and appear to be ad hoc. Provincial distributions were also subject to parliament's hold harmless stipulations, and an adjustment procedure similar to that outlined for kabupaten/kota was used.

6. Vertical Imbalances Revisited

Having explained and operationalized the concept of the fiscal gap, we are now in a better position to undertake another approach to estimating the adequacy of the DAU pool of funds (together with other revenues) relative to aggregate expenditure needs. This method compares regional government DAU funding to the sum of regional government net fiscal requirements, where the latter are defined as the difference between expenditure needs and fiscal capacities. We use the same definitions of expenditure needs and fiscal capacities as described above except that for the latter we set the coefficient of natural resource revenue shares equal to one (assuming that the current formulation, in this regard, lacks economic merit). Given the criticisms regarding the current measures of expenditure needs noted in the earlier discussion, this procedure might best be viewed as a check of the internal consistency of government procedures in deriving the DAU pool of funds, on the one hand, and allocating those funds, on the other.

The most important difference between this technique and the method previously used is that here aggregate net requirements are "built from the ground up", as it were. In summing up these needs, regions with negative net requirements (i.e., greater fiscal capacities than expenditure needs) are first zeroed out (as they are in the determination of DAU allocations). Such a technique results in estimates of net fiscal needs that are larger than those that will be derived from a strictly aggregate examination of requirements and capacities. See Table 6 below for the output of this method using FY2002 DAU data.

TABLE 6
Net Fiscal Needs and DAU Amounts, FY 2002
(Rp Trillions)

Level of Government	Net Fiscal Needs	Share	DAU Amounts	Share
Provinces	7,285.9	0.143	6,911.4	0.100
Kabupaten/Kota	43,707.8	0.857	62,202.7	0.900
Total	50,993.7	1.000	69,114.1	1.000

Source: Author's own calculations based on MOF data.

As can be seen, total net regional fiscal needs, estimated in this manner, are just less than Rp51 trillion while actual DAU allocations are just greater than Rp69 trillion. This again suggests that the DAU is too large relative to what is needed. In addition, the information in the table implies that a more appropriate share of net domestic revenues for the DAU is around 18% rather than the current (minimum of) 25%. Also, the table suggests that provinces do not, in fact, receive enough DAU compared to what they require. And, as before, the data here imply that kabupaten/kota receive significantly more than needed. Finally, the data suggest that a more appropriate split of the DAU for provinces and kabupaten/kota might roughly be 15% and 85%, as opposed to the current distribution of 10% and 90%, given the assumptions here.

7. Equalization Performance of DAU

The goal of the DAU transfer scheme in terms of equalization, as stated in the law, is to "make even the fiscal capacities of regional governments to finance their expenditure needs." This makes clear that a proper test of the mechanism's equalization effects requires, in the first instance, the existence of good measures of regional expenditure needs and fiscal capacities. But the above examination of the DAU formula suggests that the current methods of estimating needs and capacities are at least somewhat flawed.[32]

The first approach to examining the equalization performance of the DAU ignores these complications and instead focuses on the variation in actual per capita revenues of kabupaten/kota. If DAU transfers were to equalize, it might be reasonable to expect, at a minimum, that the variation in the per capita revenues among local governments would be smaller after transfers were made than before. Table 7 below provides some information on the variation of actual revenues for FY2002.[33]

The table shows maximum and minimum per capita revenues across kabupaten/kota and the ratio between the maximum and minimum, along with the coefficient of variation (i.e., the standard deviation divided by the average) of per capita revenues. The assumption is that the smaller the ratio of maximum to minimum values and the smaller coefficient of variation of per capita revenues, the greater the equalization. The base case relates to local government own-source revenues. To these own-source revenues are added, in succession, property-related shared taxes, shared personal income taxes, shared natural resource revenues, DAU balancing factor amounts (including lump-sum amounts), DAU formula-derived amounts, and, finally, adjustments to original DAU made to operationalize the hold harmless condition.

The table shows that the variation in per capita revenues, as defined by the ratio of maximum to minimum values and the coefficient of variation, is lower after DAU allocations are made than before such transfers are added. In other words, the distribution of per capita revenues is more equal after the transfers than before. (The maximum to minimum ratio and coefficient of variation

---

32. A proper examination of equalization performance might also incorporate an analysis of direct central government expenditure in the regions. As noted above, the central government continues to make expenditures on essentially regional functions via the so-called regional DIPs. Unfortunately, there are no reliable regionally disaggregated data on such expenditures.

33. The own-source revenues here are actuals, adjusted for inflation, for the most recent year available, FY2000. Revenue-sharing figures are estimated actual amounts for FY2002. DAU amounts are actual allocations for FY2002.

of 387.0 and 2.559, respectively, before DAU transfers, declined to 45.8 and 1.030, respectively, after DAU transfers.) The general conclusion that can be drawn from this analysis, therefore, is that DAU transfers appear to be equalizing, at least under the admittedly somewhat weak standard considered here.

Furthermore, the table suggests that the formula component of the transfers is somewhat more equalizing than the balancing amount. (That is, the relevant measures decline after formula amounts are added to balancing factor distributions.) The table also shows that the hold harmless adjustments to the original DAU allocations are unequalizing under the assumptions here. The table provides other interesting results as well. It shows, for example, that the transfer of property-related taxes tends to equalize the distribution of own-source revenues and that, somewhat surprisingly, the personal income tax tends to equalize per capita revenues at the local level even further.[34] The table also demonstrates the rather extreme unequalizing nature of the natural resource transfers.

TABLE 7
Variation in Per Capita Revenues Across Local Governments
FY2002

Revenues	Max	Min	Max/Min Ratio	Coefficient of Variation
	(Rupiahs)			
Own-Source Revenues	855.3	0.3	2,835.9	2.245
+ Property-Related Transfers	918.3	10.2	90.1	1.323
+ Personal Income Tax Transfers	924.5	11.2	82.2	1.261
+ Natural Resource Revenue Transfers	4,916.4	12.7	387.0	2.559
+ DAU Balancing Factor Amounts	5,732.7	98.5	58.2	1.152
+ DAU Formula Amounts	7,108.8	160.4	44.3	0.958
+ Hold Harmless Adjustments	7,090.9	154.9	45.8	1.030

Source: Author's own calculations.

There are at least two possible criticisms of the above methodology. The first is that it has not incorporated, in an adequate way, notions of local expenditure needs and fiscal capacities (i.e., potential own-source revenues together with transfers).[35] One way to get around this is to examine the variation in the

---

34. Recall that the allocation of the shared personal income tax revenues across kabupaten/kota is carried out by the province. Unfortunately, there is, as of yet, no information on the methods employed by provinces to distribute such revenues.

35. The implicit assumptions are that per capita expenditure needs are the same

distribution of the ratio of potential revenues to expenditure needs across all local governments before and after transfers. While it may be relatively easy to plausibly estimate potential revenues, the difficulties associated with deriving a single measure of expenditure needs would seem to prohibit such an approach, at least for the time being.

The second and related concern is that the method ignores the important simultaneous relationship between expenditure needs and fiscal capacities, on the one hand, and transfers, on the other. That is, in examining the equalization performance of the DAU allocation scheme, it is useful to know how transfers vary in amount with respect to variations in expenditure needs and/or fiscal capacities. More particularly, from an equalization point of view, it might be expected that as expenditure needs rise, transfers should increase, with fiscal capacities remaining the same. And as fiscal capacities increase, it might be argued that transfers should be smaller, holding expenditure needs constant. This is perhaps a slightly stricter standard of equalization than the one employed above.

The difficulty, again, concerns estimating expenditure needs. While it may not be possible to derive a plausible single measure of expenditure needs, some of the factors that are important in determining needs, in general, are at least known. And some of these determinants were used in the current DAU methodology to estimate needs; that is, population, area, poverty, and relative cost factors, in some weighted combination, all at least conceivably help determine real requirements and therefore transfers.[36] The approach used directly below assumes that these four variables, along with urban status, help determine expenditure requirements and influence allocations. But rather than specifying exactly how they do this a priori, as the current DAU formula mechanism does, the method employed here is "let the data decide."

Defining an appropriate measure of fiscal capacity is less controversial. Fiscal capacity is defined only slightly differently from the way in which it is defined under present DAU allocation procedures. There are two minor, although conceptually important, differences. First, in the estimation of potential own-source revenues, a dummy variable to indicate urban status is added to the right-hand side of the regression equation (10) to operationalize the notion that urban own-source revenues tend to be larger than those of rural places, all other things being equal. Second, the coefficient of natural resource revenues is set

---

across all places and that own-source revenues are equivalent to potential own-source revenues. Both assumptions are obviously unrealistic.

36. The analysis holds in abeyance final judgment about the relationship between poverty and expenditure requirements. For purposes of argument, the examination here simply adopts the basic assumptions of the DAU designers; that is, that poverty is generally important in influencing expenditure needs of regional governments.

equal to one instead of 0.75 in equation (9), under the assumption that the latter specification is the result of a political deal and has no economic basis.

Transfers are posited to be a function of fiscal capacity and expenditure needs and a simple linear regression technique is used to operationalize the relationship. Both original DAU (DAUPC) and adjusted DAU (AdjDAUPC) transfer allocations are considered. In addition, the two major components of the DAU—the balancing factor (BALPC) and formula amounts (FORMPC)—are treated separately. Per capita transfers, variously defined, are regressed against per capita fiscal capacity (FISKPC); cost-index adjusted[37] population (POP•CST), area (for kabupaten only—AREA•CST•KAB, where KAB is a dummy variable for kabupaten), and poverty rate (POV•CST);[38] and a dummy variable for urban status (KOTA, set equal to 0 for kabupaten and 1 for kota). The latter variable is intended to operationalize the assumption that urban places are, de facto, charged with delivering a broader range of services than nonurban places and that therefore they have greater expenditure requirements than rural places, all other things being equal.[39] The multiplicative specification of the influence of the basic needs variables is suggested by the standard employment of a cost index, as argued above. All variables (except the dummy) are entered into the equation in logarithmic form.

The assumption here is that, for transfers to be equalizing, per capita allocations should be positively related to expenditure need variables (cost-adjusted area and poverty and urban status) and negatively related to per capita fiscal capacity. There is no a priori expectation regarding the influence of cost-adjusted population. Table 8 provides the results of the ordinary least squares regression.[40] For each of the four dependent variables, the table shows the

---

37. The costs employed here are the Rupiah costs (in thousands) per square meter of constructing a standard type of building and a standard type of fence around that building. The cost index is calculated by dividing each place's cost figure by the average for the entire sample and multiplying by 100. The current DAU allocation mechanism uses the same cost figures but the cost index was derived somewhat differently.

38. The incidence of poverty is used instead of the number of poor people or the poverty gap to operationalize poverty. This is the more straightforward approach and it also has the benefit of avoiding potential multicollinearity problems with population.

39. The problem with this dummy variable approach is that it ignores the fact that many kabupaten have significant urban populations. As such, it might be better to use a variable that denotes the percent of a local government's total population that is urban. Unfortunately, there are no up-to-date and reliable data on the proportions of kabupaten populations that are urban. This dearth of data is largely a function of statisticians' inability to keep up with the rapid creation of new local governments over the past several years.

40. The OLS technique results in no obvious problems of heteroscedasticity or autocorrelation.

estimated regression coefficients for the set of independent variables. The absolute values of the t-statistics are located in parentheses under each respective coefficient; in addition, the table notes whether the estimated coefficient is statistically different from zero at the 0.05 level. The adjusted R^2 for each regression is found along the bottom row of the table.

TABLE 8
Equalization Analysis Regression Results

Independent Variable	BALPC	FORMPC	DAUPC	Dependent Variable AdjDAUPC
Constant	8.477 *	17.294 *	9.972 *	8.297
	(34.067)	(19.302)	(36.987)	(38.357)
FISKPC	–0.030	–0.986 *	–0.165 *	0.019
	(1.625)	(14.906)	(8.303)	(1.196)
POP*CST	–0.556 *	–1.690 *	–0.755 *	–0.586
	(22.578)	(19.059)	(28.278)	(27.354)
AREA*CST*KAB	0.035 *	0.304 *	0.105 *	0.079
	(2.480)	(6.051)	(6.969)	(6.504)
POV*CST	0.040	–0.037	0.090 *	0.106
	(1.910)	(0.488)	(3.942)	(5.809)
KOTA	0.317 *	2.516 *	0.884 *	0.575
	(2.619)	(5.768)	(6.733)	(5.461)
Adjusted R^2	0.804	0.532	0.823	0.886

The table shows that per capita balancing factor transfers are significantly and positively related to (cost-adjusted) area (i.e., for kabupaten) and to urban status. Such transfers are not related to cost-adjusted poverty at the standard 0.05 level but are statistically significant at just a slightly lower level (0.056). Balancing transfers are not significantly related to per capita fiscal capacity. These results indicate that balancing factor transfers are partially equalizing with respect to expenditure needs, as defined above, but not with regard to fiscal capacity, under the assumptions employed here.

Per capita formula amounts are significantly and positively related to (cost-adjusted) area and urban status but not to (cost-adjusted) poverty. Formula-based transfers are significantly and negatively related to per capita fiscal capacity. The equalization impact of formula allocations is, therefore, again somewhat mixed with regard to expenditure needs but unambiguous with regard to fiscal capacity.

Overall, original DAU transfers perform rather well by the standards under discussion here. Per capita DAU transfers, before adjustments, are significantly and positively related to (cost adjusted) kabupaten area and poverty variables[41] as well as to urban status. In addition, per capita allocations are significantly and negatively related to fiscal capacities. These results suggest that, overall, DAU transfers are equalizing with respect to both expenditure needs and fiscal capacities.

Unfortunately, the same cannot be said for per capita adjusted DAU transfers. While per capita adjusted allocations are positively related to all expenditure needs variables, they are not significantly related to fiscal capacities. It is reasonable to conclude that adjustments related to the hold harmless stipulation insisted upon by the Indonesian parliament resulted in transfers that were less equalizing than they otherwise would have been, at least given the assumptions employed here.

As mentioned above, there are no a priori expectations regarding the significance or sign of the coefficient of the (cost-adjusted) population variable. As it turns out, population is the most important variable overall in explaining variation in per capita transfers (as judged by the values of the standardized beta coefficients—not shown in the table) and the results here are indicative of an assumption of economies of scale in the provision of services financed by transfers; that is, as population increases, per capita transfers decrease, all else remaining the same. Of course, much more detailed analysis needs to be done to confirm the existence of such economies of scale for particular services and/ or in general.

8. Dana Alokasi Khusus (DAK)

The DAK is Indonesia's new special-purpose transfer. It comprises two distinct elements. One is based on the allocation of national reforestation revenues. Forty percent of state reforestation levies on companies engaged in the sector are returned to the kabupaten of origin and are to be used exclusively for local reforestation activities. This is really nothing more than a simple revenue sharing transfer of the kind that was discussed above. Its attachment to the DAK is an artifact of the negotiations between government and parliament attendant to the ratification of Law 25 of 1999.

The second component of the DAK is the real special-purpose grant. But there will probably not be just one such DAK; most likely, there will be many,

---

41. The fact that the poverty variable is significant here may be considered somewhat of a statistical fluke as it does not appear among the statistically significant variables for either of the two components of DAU transfers (i.e., balancing and formula amounts).

one for each of the important line ministries, such as health, education, and infrastructure, among others. In any case, these DAKs are intended for use in financing expenditures on national priority infrastructure services that are outside the scope of DAU funding.

The specific focus of this particular grant component is on financing capital expenditures, although operations and maintenance can also be funded through the grant, at least for a limited period of time (three years). This element of the DAK is specified as a matching grant and government regulations insist that the region's contribution should be no less than 10% of total project expenditures. The allocation of the DAK is to be based on proposals from the regions. A recent Ministry of Finance policy paper notes that DAKs are intended to promote minimum standards and compensate for benefit/cost spillovers.[42]

Only the reforestation component of the DAK has been made operational so far. Funding related to this element of the DAK is quite limited, as shown in Table 2. The other major component of the DAK has not yet been put into effect and so it is not possible to comment on its performance vis-à-vis specific stated or more general objectives. Based on its current design, however, at least three important issues can be raised.

The first concern relates to the transfer's intended support for the attainment of minimum service standards. While the DAK hopes to promote minimum standards, somehow defined, it apparently will do so only for the construction of national priority infrastructure and possibly for limited operations and maintenance activities related to such infrastructure. The promotion of minimum standards for other sorts of (non-national priority) infrastructure investment and/or other kinds of longer-term operations and maintenance or service delivery activities will not, it appears, receive support via the DAK. This seems to be a rather uneven and inconsistent approach to the promotion of infrastructure service delivery standards.

The second and related issue concerns DAK incentives to local governments for the delivery of services with benefit spillovers. It is usually argued that subnational governments tend to underprovide (from a national point of view) services with significant interjurisdictional spillovers because they only care about benefits that accrue to their own populations. The allocation of intergovernmental transfers to regions to encourage the appropriately increased delivery of such services is one way of overcoming the potential inefficiencies. Now, the DAK apparently intends to provide incentives to regions to build infrastructure that is adequate (in size and scope) to deliver services at the nationally desired level. But such support will appear to cease after the assets have been developed (and the three-year time limit on support for operations

---

42. See Ministry of Finance (2002).

and maintenance has expired). This leaves regions without an incentive to actually deliver services at the desired level. Inefficiencies would be expected to ensue.

A final concern relates to the possible establishment of formal linkages between the DAK and loan finance for regional infrastructure development. Theory suggests that blending grants and loans in infrastructure finance might have many benefits, including supporting fiscally weak governments to borrow.[43] While the current DAK design documentation does not appear to prohibit the development of such linkages between the DAK and regional borrowing, neither does it elucidate the possibilities. This is an issue that merits increased thought and discussion.

D. Summary and Policy Recommendations

Indonesia has recently begun the implementation of a major fiscal decentralization program. As part of that effort, the system of intergovernmental transfers has undergone significant changes. Revenue sharing has been considerably expanded in scope and level, central-local transfers have been rationalized, and attendant pools of finance have been substantially increased.

The most important goals of the new system of transfers are to address regional aspirations for increased access to revenues and more control over the use of finance and to correct vertical and horizontal fiscal imbalances. There are also other objectives for the transfer system, such as supporting minimum service standards and compensating for benefit spillovers. These latter objectives are, however, linked specifically to the DAK which, as noted above, is not yet operational. It should be a priority of the government to further develop this important intergovernmental fiscal tool. In the course of doing so, the government would be wise to revisit the notion of limiting (for the most part) DAK to the support of regional capital expenditures. Keeping such restrictions would constrain the full attainment of goals related to minimum standards and benefit spillouts.

Meeting regional government aspirations and demands for more money has, in fact, been the driving force behind Indonesia's decentralization program. The regional assignment and delivery of new service responsibilities have, by comparison, been given rather short shrift. This is unfortunate and points to a major problem with fiscal decentralization in Indonesia today. The lack of clarity on service assignment hinders the appropriate assignment of revenues and constrains accountability at the regional level. The government is now developing a program to clarify regional government service assignments and to

---

43. See Smoke (1999) for a discussion of grant-loan linkages in the Indonesian context.

outline standards for service delivery. It is too early to judge the success of this important effort.

Revenue sharing has been the major instrument for central government to address regional fiscal demands. The focus on revenue sharing is a function of the historical unhappiness of many in the regions who have felt that they have not sufficiently benefited from revenues that are derived from "their land" in the first instance. Apparently, many Indonesians strongly hold the view that what is produced on or under their soil is theirs. Many officials and others in the regions remain unconvinced they are receiving adequate amounts of revenues in question.

While an expansion of revenue sharing would probably not be fiscally prudent from a macroeconomic perspective, several efforts might be undertaken to address current worries along these lines. For natural resource revenues, concerns could, at least in part, be addressed by making payments directly to the regions, instead of first collecting total revenues at the central level and then distributing them back to regions, as is the current practice. At the very least, central officials could carry out calculations of total natural resource revenues earned and shared in a more transparent manner. Distribution of the income tax will be improved by allocating it to regions based on the place of residence of the income earner rather than on location of the employer, as is apparently currently done. An even better approach to sharing the personal income tax is to restructure the transfer as a tax base sharing instrument—that is, by using a "piggyback" mechanism. In addition, the property taxes should be decentralized to regional governments. The transfer of these taxes could begin more or less immediately with devolution of tariff control but should probably eventually extend to all relevant administrative functions.[44]

Of course many would, on the contrary, advocate an outright reduction in revenue sharing from its current levels. While on paper this may seem like a good idea, it does not seem to be a real possibility, at least in the present politically charged environment. More likely, Indonesians and others will have to learn to accept the considerable downside associated with revenue sharing, as it is currently designed, at least in the near- to medium-term.

Revenue sharing and grants together have been successful in addressing vertical fiscal imbalances at the regional government level. In fact, intergovernmental transfers may have gone too far in this respect; that is, at the aggregate level, at least some evidence suggest that too much money may have been allocated to regional governments vis-à-vis their expenditure needs. Of course,

---

44. Restructuring the personal income tax sharing via piggyback methods and decentralizing the property tax are both now under discussion in the Ministry of Finance. See Ministry of Finance (2002).

more research is needed to confirm this. If true, however, this would be a particularly important problem for the central government to address head-on, especially at a time of not insignificant pressure on the state budget.

As suggested above, it is probably not politically feasible at this time to resolve this difficulty by reducing aggregate revenue sharing or DAU allocations to the regions. Another, perhaps more feasible, approach to addressing the (potential) problem of overallocation of transfers, is to devolve greater central government expenditures in the regions (i.e., regional DIPs) to the regions themselves—without decentralizing additional finance. Many central agencies have retained expenditure authority over what are now essentially local functions. The decentralization of an appropriate amount of these expenditure responsibilities to subnational governments could, theoretically at least, have the effect of bringing central and aggregate regional fiscal mismatches back into balance.

Although regional governments, in general, may have been allocated more fiscal resources than needed, this may not be true for provinces. As noted above, some evidence suggest that provinces may not have been given sufficient access to resources to meet their expenditure requirements. This again requires more study. If true, however, it suggests that the methods by which revenues are shared between provinces and kabupaten/kota and by which provincial and local DAU pools of finance are determined might need to be revisited. A modification of arrangements for distributing shared revenues and grants between levels of subnational government will not be politically uncomplicated, of course, but it may be more feasible than making outright cuts to such transfers.

It is basically the job of the DAU to correct horizontal imbalances. This task is made more difficult than it otherwise would be because of the unequalizing nature of revenue sharing, as noted above. These inequities could, to a large extent, be overcome if a system of negative grants could be implemented. Alas, such a fraternal system of transfers is probably not viable in Indonesia at present, at least as judged by reactions to initial proposals for such.

In any case, while Indonesia has made some progress in addressing equalization objectives, as demonstrated above, more could still be done, even given the constraints noted. More work needs to be done at the technical level to improve the DAU allocation formula. In the medium term, factors that better proxy expenditure requirements and fiscal capacity need to be found and employed. In the long run, expenditure requirements should be more precisely estimated for individual governments as a function of the real costs of achieving some specified standard of service delivery. In addition, fiscal capacities need to be more exactly derived as a function of size of tax bases over which local governments actually have some control. A general issue for consideration is whether urbanized and rural areas should be treated separately in estimation procedures, given their very real differences in service responsibilities, costs, and fiscal capacities. A transition plan for removing the balancing factor from the distribution formula gradually over time needs to be formally specified. The hold harmless condition, which was perhaps useful in the first year of DAU operations, should now be relaxed—its continued use directly constrains equalization goals.

In the end, of course, some horizontal imbalances are likely to remain, as they do everywhere in the world. This point notwithstanding, it would be useful for Indonesians to sort out, in more precise terms than they have so far done, the degree of fiscal inequality they are willing to tolerate. But they should not stop there. The entire process of fiscal decentralization in Indonesia would benefit greatly from increased clarity of its objectives and goals. Without a more explicit recognition of what decentralization is trying to achieve, how will Indonesians know the extent to which this important endeavor has been successful?

References

Beier, Christopher and Gabe Ferrazzi. 1998. Fiscal Decentralization in Indonesia: A Comment on Smoke and Lewis. *World Development* 26 (12): 2201–2211.

Davey, Kenneth. 1989. Central-Local Financial Relations. In *Financing Local Government in Indonesia*, edited by Nick Devas. Athens, Ohio: Ohio University Center for International Studies.

Ford, J. and Fitz, G. 2000. Inter-Governmental Fiscal Relations and State Building: The Case of Indonesia. Washington, DC: Mimeograph.

Guinness, Patrick. 1994. Local Society and Culture. In *Indonesia's New Order: The Dynamics of Socio-Economic Transformation*, edited by Hal Hill. New York: Allen and Unwin, New South Wales, Australia.

Kelly, Roy. 1993. Property Tax Reform in Indonesia: Applying a Collection-Led Implementation Strategy. *Bulletin of Indonesian Economic Studies* 29 (1): 85–104.

Lewis, Blane. 2001. The New Indonesian Equalization Transfer. *Bulletin of Indonesian Economic Studies* 37 (3): 325–43.

———— and Paul Smoke. 1998. Reply to Beier and Ferrazzi: Reconsidering Decentralization in Indonesia. *World Development* 26 (12): 2212–2230.

Ministry of Finance. 2002. Fiscal Decentralization: A Ministry of Finance Policy Agenda. Draft Paper, Directorate General for Fiscal Balance. Jakarta: Ministry of Finance.

Ray, David. 2001. Inventory of Trade-Distorting Local Regulations. Jakarta: USAID-PEG Project, Ministry of Industry and Trade.

Republic of Indonesia. 1995. Finance Note and State Budget for Fiscal Year 1995 *(Nota Keuangan dan Anggaran Pendapatan dan Belanja Tahun Anggaran)*. Jakarta.

————. 1996. Finance Note and State Budget for Fiscal Year 1996 *(Nota Keuangan dan Anggaran Pendapatan dan Belanja Tahun Anggaran 1996)*. Jakarta.

————. 1997. Finance Note and State Budget for Fiscal Year 1997 *(Nota Keuangan dan Anggaran Pendapatan dan Belanja Tahun Anggaran 1997)*. Jakarta.

————. 1998. Finance Note and State Budget for Fiscal Year 1998 *(Nota Keuangan dan Anggaran Pendapatan dan Belanja Tahun Anggaran 1998)*. Jakarta.

————. 1999. Finance Note and State Budget for Fiscal Year 1999 *(Nota Keuangan dan Anggaran Pendapatan dan Belanja Tahun Anggaran 1999).* Jakarta.

————. 1999. Law No. 22/1999 regarding Regional Administration *(Undang-Undang 22/1999 tentang Pemerintahan Daerah).* Jakarta.

————. 1999. Law No. 25/1999 regarding Financial Balance between Central and Regional Governments *(Undang-Undang No. 25/1999 tentang Perimbangan Keuangan antara Pusat dan Daerah).* Jakarta.

————. 2000. Finance Note and State Budget for Fiscal Year 2000 *(Nota Keuangan dan Anggaran Pendapatan dan Belanja Tahun Anggaran 2000).* Jakarta.

————. 2000. Government Regulation No. 25/2000 regarding Government Authorities and Autonomous Provincial Government Authorities *(Peraturan Pemerintah No. 25/2000 tentang Kewenangan Pemerintah dan Kewenangan Propinsi sebagai Daerah Otonom).* Jakarta.

————. 2000. Government Regulation No. 104/2000 regarding Balance Funds *(Peraturan Pemerintah No.104/2000 tentang Dana Perimbangan).* Jakarta.

————. 2000. Law No. 17/2000 regarding the Third Revision to Law 7/83 regarding Income Tax *(Undang-Undang 17/2000 tentang Perubahan Ketiga Atas Undang-Undang Nomor 7 Tahun/83 tentang Pajak Penghasilan).* Jakarta.

————. 2000. Law No. 34/2000 regarding the Revision to Law 18/97 regarding Regional Taxes and Charges *(Undang-Undang 34/2000 tentang Perubahan atas Undang-Undang 18/97 tentang Pajak Daerah dan Retribusi Daerah).* Jakarta.

Rohdewohld, Rainer. 1995. *Public Administration in Indonesia.* Melbourne, Australia: Graduate School of Government, Monash University.

Schroeder, Larry. 1995. Targeting Intergovernmental Transfers. Jakarta: USAID Municipal Finance Project II, Ministry of Finance.

Shah, Anwar. 1994. The Reform of Intergovernmental Fiscal Relations in Developing and Emerging Market Economies. *Policy and Research Series* 23. Washington, DC: World Bank.

Shah, Anwar and Zia Qureshi. 1994. Intergovernmental Fiscal Relations in Indonesia: Issues and Options, World Bank Discussion Paper No. 239. Washington, DC: World Bank.

Smoke, Paul. 1999. Improving Local Infrastructure Finance in Developing Countries through Grant-Loan Linkages: Ideas from Indonesia's Water Sector. *International Journal of Public Administration* 22 (11–12): 1561–1585.

———— and Blane Lewis. 1996. Fiscal Decentralization in Indonesia: A New Approach to an Old Idea. *World Development* 24 (8): 1281–1299.

Appendix: Dana Alokasi Umum, Fiscal Years 2001 and 2002

Feature	FY 2001	FY 2002
Total Pool of Funds	25% of total national revenues (net of shared amounts). Rp60.517 trillion.	25% of total national revenues (net of shared amounts). Rp69.114 trillion.
Local and Provincial Shares	90% for kabupaten/kota (Rp54.279 trillion); 10% for provinces (Rp6.238 trillion).	90% for kabupaten/kota (Rp62.203 trillion); 10% for provinces (Rp6.911 trillion).
General Allocation Mechanism	$DAU_i = LSA_i + BFA_i^{*} + FA_i$	$DAU_i = LSA_i + BFA_i + FA_i$
Lump-Sum Amount	$LSA_i = \dfrac{DAU_{T2} - \left(\sum_i BFA_i^{*} + \sum_i FA_i\right)}{n}$	$LSA_i = \dfrac{0.10 \cdot DAU_T}{n}$
Balancing Factor Amount	$BFA_i = 1.3 \cdot SDO_i + 1.1 \cdot INPRES_i$	$BFA_i = \dfrac{Wage_i}{\sum_i Wage_i} \cdot 0.50 \cdot DAU_T$
Formula Amount	$FA_i = \left(DAU_{T1} - \sum BFA_i\right) \cdot \dfrac{FG_i}{\sum_i FG_i}$	$FA_i = \left(DAU_T - \sum LSA_i - \sum BFA_i\right) \cdot \dfrac{FG_i}{\sum_i FG_i}$
Fiscal Gap Component	$FG_i = EN_i - FC_i$; allocated 20% of total DAU.	$FG_i = EN_i - FC_i$; allocated 40% of total DAU.
Expenditure Needs	$EN_i = \left(\dfrac{APBDEXP_T}{n}\right) \cdot \dfrac{1}{4} \cdot \left(\dfrac{Pop_i}{\frac{\sum Pop_i}{n}} + \dfrac{Area_i}{\frac{\sum Area_i}{n}} + \dfrac{Pov_i}{\frac{\sum Pov_i}{n}} + \dfrac{Cost_i}{100}\right)$	$EN_i = APBDEXP_T \cdot \left(0.4\dfrac{Pop_i}{\sum Pop_i} + 0.1\dfrac{Area_i}{\sum Area_i} + 0.1\dfrac{PovGap_i}{\sum PovGap_i} + 0.4\dfrac{Cost_i}{\sum Cost_i}\right)$

Fiscal Capacity	$$FC_i = \left(\frac{OSR_T + SPT_T}{n} \right) \cdot \frac{1}{3} \left(\frac{\frac{NRO_i}{GRDP_i}}{\sum_i \frac{NRO_i}{GRDP_i}} + \frac{\frac{NNRO_i}{GRDP_i}}{\sum_i \frac{NNRO_i}{GRDP_i}} + \frac{\frac{LF_i}{Pop_i}}{\sum_i \frac{LF_i}{Pop_i}} \right)$$	$FC_i = O\hat{S}R_i + SPT_i + SIT_i + 0.75 \cdot SNR_i$ where $O\hat{S}R$ is the predicted value derived from the regression: $OSR_i = \beta_0 + \beta_1 GRDPS_i + \varepsilon_i$
Provincial Allocations	$$DAU_i = 0.8 \cdot DAU_{T2} \cdot \left(\frac{SDO_i + INPRES_i}{\sum_i SDO_i + INPRES_i} \right) + 0.2 \cdot DAU_{T2} \cdot \left(\frac{FG_i}{\sum_i FG_i} \right)$$	Same as for local governments except that lump sum and balancing factor based on 20 and 30% of total provincial DAU, respectively.
Hold Harmless Condition	For local governments only. Built into balancing factor; local governments assured of at least 40% increase over previous year.	Insisted upon by Parliament. Led to "adjusted DAU" whereby both provincial and local governments assured of no less than previous year.
Use of Contingency Fund	A total of Rp2.8 trillion allocated to regional governments to cover estimated shortfalls in finance. The total includes Rp1.2 trillion for provinces and Rp1.6 for kabupaten/kota. Allocations based on proposals from the regions and made at various times during the course of the fiscal year.	A total of Rp2.1 trillion distributed to regional governments as part of DAU allocations. Distributions necessitated by Parliament's hold harmless stipulation. Total includes Rp1.2 for provinces and Rp0.81 trillion for kabupaten/kota governments.
Equalization Performance	Variation in distribution of per capita revenues smaller after DAU allocations than before. Per capita DAU allocations positively related to both expenditure needs and fiscal capacities.	Variation in distribution of per capita revenues smaller after DAU allocations than before. Per capita DAU allocations, before hold harmless adjustments, positively related to expenditure needs and negatively related to fiscal capacities. After adjustments, per capita DAU allocations positively related to expenditure needs but unrelated to fiscal capacities.

Variable Definitions

FY 2001

i	subscript denoting region
n	subscript denoting total number of regions
T	subscript denoting total of variable in question
T1	subscript denoting total value before changes to draft state budget
T2	subscript denoting total value after changes to draft state budget
DAU	DAU allocation
LSA	lump sum amount
BFA	balancing factor amount
BFA*	balancing factor amount after adjustments
FA	formula amount
SDO	routine grant, from previous fiscal year
INPRES	development grant, from previous fiscal year
FG	fiscal gap
EN	expenditure needs
FC	fiscal capacity
APBDEXP	local government expenditure
Pop	Population
Area	Area
Pov	incidence of poverty
Cost	cost index
OSR	own-source revenue
SPT	shared property taxes
NRO	product from natural resources sector
NNRO	product from non-natural resources sector
LF	labor force
GRDP	gross regional development product

See Lewis (2001) for further explanation

FY 2002

i	subscript denoting region
n	subscript denoting total number of regions
T	subscript denoting total of variable in question
DAU	DAU allocation
LSA	lump sum amount
BFA	balancing factor amount
Wage	civil service wage bill
FA	formula amount
FG	fiscal gap
EN	expenditure needs
FC	fiscal capacity
APBDEXP	local government expenditure
Pop	population
Area	area
PovGap	poverty gap
Cost	cost index
OSR	own-source revenue
SPT	shared property taxes
SIT	shared personal income tax
SNR	shared natural resource revenues
GRDPS	gross regional development product, services sector

See text for further explanation

6

Pakistan

Nuzhat Ahmad and Syed Ashraf Wasti
Applied Economic Research Center, Karachi

A. Introduction

Pakistan has a population of 133 million people. Punjab holds 57% of the population and Sindh, 23%. The two smaller provinces of North West Frontier Province (NWFP) and Baluchistan hold 15% and 5% of the population, respectively. Large income disparities exist across the four provinces. Sindh is the richest province with a per capita income of PRs2,348 which is 60% higher than the lowest per capita income of Baluchistan (PRs1,875). The province of Punjab ranks second in per capita income with PRs1,979 while NWFP has a per capita income of PRs1,418.[1]

Intergovernmental transfers are a cornerstone of the subnational government financing system in Pakistan and the focus of this chapter. We begin by describing the present intergovernmental transfer system from the federal to provincial governments. This is followed by an examination of the overall intergovernmental fiscal system, including revenue and expenditure assignments and revenue–expenditure imbalances. We then focus in more detail on the intergovernmental transfer system, considering the volume and composition of transfers, vertical and horizontal imbalances, and the equalizing role of transfers. We also review the role of implicit transfers and provide an overall evaluation of the transfer system. The final section presents a summary of results and conclusions, as well as a set of recommendations.

B. System of Intergovernmental Transfers in Pakistan

The Constitution of 1973 establishes a basic framework for the management of public finance, the division of powers, and the distribution of

---

1. These averages in incomes hide large variations in income disparities within provinces. Note that the Pakistan currency is the rupee, denoted by PRe (for 1 rupee) and PRs (for more than 1 rupee).

revenues between the federation and the provinces in Pakistan. Under the Constitution, the federation and the provinces have access to a divisible pool comprising the net proceeds of specified taxes to be shared, in addition to their exclusive sources of revenues. The federal government meets the additional requirements of the provinces through other various mechanisms, such as grants-in-aid, subsidies, subventions, emergency relief, and federalization of functions. Given the importance and complexity of revenue sharing, the Constitution provides (under Article 160) for periodically setting up a National Finance Commission (NFC) to make recommendations on the operation of the divisible pool, borrowing powers, grants-in-aid, and other such matters.

1. The National Finance Commission Awards

There have been seven different NFC awards in the country since 1951 and the eighth is under way. The revenue-sharing arrangements and the assigned share of transfers to provinces under each are presented in Table 1. The composition of the divisible pool and the proportion in which taxes are shared are shown under each award. With the exception of the 1974 award, the trend is towards an increase in transfers to the provinces, as highlighted in the bottom line of the table. The first five awards were achieved by including large provincial shares of a limited number of taxes in the divisible pool. Since 1990, there has been a change in strategy with the inclusion of new taxes in the divisible pool. Under the 1997 award that is now effective, all taxes have been included in the divisible pool, but the provincial share of individual taxes has been reduced.

The shares assigned to each of the provinces under the different awards are presented in Table 2, indicating a generally close correspondence between revenue share and population share. Table 3 highlights the evolution of the revenue-sharing formula. The principle of allocating a portion of revenues on the basis of collection was recognized in the initial awards. The sales tax revenue was distributed fully on the basis of collection from the provinces (excluding collections from Karachi seaport, which were distributed among the federated units on the basis of preassigned shares). The weight of collection was reduced to 30% in the subsequent three awards up to 1970. Revenue from other sources was distributed to the provinces according to preassigned shares, often substantially in line with population shares. In the 1970s, collection was discarded as a criterion for revenue sharing, and the preassigned share was also abandoned. Distribution has instead been based solely on population shares of the provinces (using the most recent available census).

Table 4 shows the transfers to the provinces as a percentage of GDP over time. It can be seen that these transfers generally demonstrated an increasing

TABLE 1
Revenue-Sharing Arrangements Under Various NFC Awards
(Provincial Share in Percentages)

Divisible Pool	Raisman 1951	NFC 1961–1962	NFC 1964	NFC 1970	NFC 1974	NFC 1990	NFC 1997
A. Income Tax & Corporation Tax	50	50	65	80	80	80	37.5
B. Other Direct Taxes							37.5
C. Sales Duty	50	60	65	80	80	80	37.5
D. Excise Duty							37.5
– Tea	50	60	65	80	–	–	
– Tobacco	50	60	65	80	–	80	
– Sugar	–	–	–	–	–	80	
– Betelent	50	60	65	80	–	–	
E. Export Duties							37.5
– Cotton	–	100	65	80	80	80	
– Jute	62.5	100	65	80	–	–	
F. Import Duties							37.5
G. Estate/ Succession Duties	–	100	–	100	–	–	37.5
H. Capital Value Tax on Immovable Properties	–	100	–	100	–	–	37.5
I. Petroleum Surcharge							100
J. Gas Development Surcharges							100
Total							
Div. Pool Transfers as % of Fed. Tax Revenue*	12.8	23.1	27	33.4	29.8	35.3	37.3

Source: National Finance Commission (NFC) reports.

trend until 1995–1996, after which they declined slightly. However, there has always been some variation from year to year. A more detailed analysis of the types of transfers below gives a more comprehensive picture of the importance of each component of the intergovernmental fiscal transfer system.

TABLE 2
Assigned Shares to Provinces Under NFC Awards
(Percentages)

Province	Raisman(a) 1951	NFC 1970	NFC 1974	NFC 1990	NFC 1997
Punjab	59	57	60	58	58
	(64)	(62)	(60)	(58)	(58)
Sindh	24	23	23	23	23
	(20)	(22)	(23)	(23)	(23)
NWFP	15	16	13	14	14
	(14)	(14)	(13)	(14)	(14)
Baluchistan	2	4	4	5	5
	(2)	(2)	(4)	(5)	(5)
Total	100	100	100	100	100

Source: National Finance Commission (NFC) reports. Population shares in parentheses.

TABLE 3
Revenue-Sharing Formula Under NFC Awards

AWARD		TAX	SHARING CRITERIA (Weight)
RAISMAN	1951	Sales Tax	Collection (100%)*
		Income Tax & Excise Duties	Preassigned Shares (100%)
		Export Duties	Preassigned Shares (100%)
NFC	1961–1962	Sales Tax	Collection (30%)
NFC	1964		Preassigned Share (70%)
NFC	1970	Others Taxes	Preassigned Shares (100%)
NFC	1974	All Taxes	Population (100%)
NFC	1990		
NFC	1996		

* Sales tax collections from Karachi were distributed on the basis of preassigned shares.

2. Types of Intergovernmental Transfers

Under the current NFC Award of 1997, several types of intergovernmental transfers are available to the provincial governments. Three are unconditional. First, revenue sharing on the basis of population includes revenue from a divisible pool of taxes that is shared on a 62.5:37.5 basis between the federal and provincial governments. The distribution of funds to each of the provinces is done on the basis of population shares. These revenue-sharing transfers are

TABLE 4
Transfers to the Provinces

YEAR	GDP (Current Factor Cost) (Million Rupees)	Percentage of Transfers to GDP
1985–1986	514532	6.60
1986–1987	572479	7.26
1987–1988	675389	7.60
1988–1989	769745	6.90
1989–1990	855943	6.14
1990–1991	1020600	6.19
1991–1992	1211385	7.24
1992–1993	1341629	7.04
1993–1994	1573097	7.19
1994–1995	1882071	7.06
1995–1996	2141842	6.94
1996–1997	2457381	6.23
1997–1998	2677656	5.97
1998–1999	2913514	5.79
1999–2000	3173685	6.36

Note: Transfers taken from government account documents.

the largest component of total transfers to the provinces. Second, revenue sharing by origin (straight transfers) includes revenues from royalty and development surcharge on gas, royalty on crude oil, and hydroelectricity profits. These are transferred to the provinces on a collection (origin) basis. Third, special grants to backward provinces provide Baluchistan and NWFP with grants equivalent to PRs4.1 billion and PRs3.3 billion, respectively, for a period of 5 years. This grant is adjusted in line with the annual increase in the consumer price index at a projected annual rate of 11%.

In addition to these three unconditional transfers, there are certain conditional grants from the federal to the provincial governments. The magnitude of conditional transfers, as we shall see later, is relatively low. Some of the key programs include the following:

(i) **Closed-ended matching grants for provincial resource mobilization** provide federal matching assistance at a 50% rate, up to a limit, for provincial revenue effort in excess of the historical average growth rate of 14.2%. The limits on these grants are PRs500 million each for Punjab and Sindh and PRs100 million each for NWFP and Baluchistan. The program recognizes fiscal effort only in terms of increase in tax rates, withdrawal of exemptions, imposition of new taxes, and revision of user charges rates.

(ii) **Development grants** are based on approval of provincial annual development plans of the federal government. The plan projects are designed and submitted with their cost implications to the Federal Planning Commission for approval. Ten percent (5% each) of the total amount is allocated for NWFP and Baluchistan and the remaining 90% is allocated among all of the provinces on the basis of their population.[2]

(iii) **Federal contributions under the social action program** provide matching transfers on a 75:25 basis to finance provincial development expenditures in education, health, water supply, and sanitation.

(iv) **Physical planning and housing project assistance** is used to finance federally approved provincial projects to upgrade urban infrastructure and housing. Federal assistance is given to the provinces in the form of conditional nonmatching grants.

(v) *Tameer–e–Watan* **Program** provides block fund allocations to federal legislators. In 1994–1995, PRs6 million was allocated for each member of the national assembly and PRs5 million for each senator. The funds are used for development projects of the provincial ministers of local government and rural development.

(vi) *Tameer–e–Sindh* **Program** provides federal financing on an ad hoc nonmatching basis for rural development initiatives in the province of Sindh.

(vii) **Flood and disaster relief** grants are ad hoc emergency relief allocations usually given to the provinces for repair and renovations of basic infrastructure damaged by natural disasters.

(viii) **Other federal initiatives** under line ministries fund various provincial projects, usually in the areas of social welfare, population planning, health, irrigation and drainage.

(ix) **Prime Minister's discretionary funding** allows the Prime Minister to occasionally provide on a discretionary basis provincial/local governments with funds to finance special programs.

(x) **Federal transfers to universities** support higher education. This is a provincial responsibility, but the federal government, through the University Grants Commission (UGC), has traditionally provided financing on an ad hoc basis, primarily guided by budgetary needs to cover salary expenditures.

3. Reliability of Transfers and Macroeconomic Conditions

One of the problems observed with the current NFC award is that there are large variations between projected allocations and actual disbursements.

---

2. The general practice is that the provincial governments receive development schemes from elected local bodies during the budget preparation process. Following approval from provincial planning and development division, these schemes are submitted to the federal government for approval. Given the resource position of the federal government, only selected schemes are approved, largely on a discretionary basis.

Intergovernmental Fiscal Transfers in Asia

TABLE 5
Actual Disbursements as Percentage of Total Projected Transfers
Under NFC, 1997
(Percentages)

Year	Total	Punjab	Sindh	NWFP	Baluchistan
1997–1998	79.79	76.96	97.11	52.41	125.90
1998–1999	73.71	66.99	81.66	62.73	117.23
1999–2000	74.75	66.04	89.77	59.42	119.78

Source: National Finance Commission (NFC) reports.

Table 5 presents actual shares as a percentage of total projected transfers. It can be seen that only around 75% of expected funds are typically forthcoming. NWFP is the worst, receiving limited funds of around 50–60%. Baluchistan is the only province receiving more than what it had expected. This discrepancy has resulted in a considerable shortfall of funds to most provinces, forcing them to borrow to meet their expenditure needs. It has also made planning at the provincial level more difficult.

There are a number of possible explanations for the variation between projected and disbursed funds under the latest NFC award. First, a decline in the collection of import duties due to world recession and dramatic reductions in the prices of imports has reduced the size of the divisible pool. Second, domestic recession has led to a fall in output, thereby reducing collection from income and sales taxes and subsequently limiting funds available for transfers. Third, tax concessions introduced by the Nawaz Sharif government in 1997–1998 further reduced the size of the divisible pool. Fourth, the actual inflation rate was less than the projected rate used by the NFC to adjust certain allocations. Finally, some resources may simply have been diverted.

Since funds from the divisible pool are distributed on the basis of population, any reduction in the size of the divisible pool affects larger provinces more severely. This occurred with the last NFC award when the divisible pool shrunk considerably due to world and domestic recession. The most heavily populated province of Punjab was most adversely affected.

C. The Overall Intergovernmental Fiscal System

Before proceeding with a more detailed analysis of intergovernmental transfers, we first review the overall intergovernmental fiscal system. We begin with an analysis of tax and expenditure assignments and then move on to consider revenue-expenditure imbalances in the system.

1. Tax Assignments and Composition

In most countries, assignment of taxes among different levels of government is defined in their constitutions. Two considerations are important in determining these assignments. First, there should be a match between expenditure and tax assignments so as to enable the different levels of governments to fulfill their expenditure responsibilities. Second, there may be efficiency considerations with regard to the appropriate level of government for collecting a particular tax.

Assignments of taxes between national and subnational governments in Pakistan are presented in Table 6. Significant differences in the assignments of taxes between federal and provincial governments are apparent. Customs, corporate, and natural resource taxation fall exclusively under the domain of the federal government. Property tax is the responsibility of provincial governments. A few of the bases are shared between the federal and provincial governments, but sometimes in unclearly justified ways that can create problems. These include differential treatment of portions of the same base, excessive taxation of certain bases, and increases in compliance costs.

TABLE 6
Assignment of Taxes (National and Subnational Governments in Pakistan)

FUNCTION	ASSIGNMENTS
Customs	National
Income	National/Subnational
Corporate	National
Natural Resource	National
Sales	Subnational
Excises	National/Subnational
Property	Subnational
Fees	National/Subnational
Others	National/Subnational

There is, for example, an element of sharing between levels in the personal income tax base. Provincial governments levy a professions, trade and callings tax, and income from agriculture has been subject to provincial taxation as a separate block of income while all other incomes are taxable at the federal level. This has created opportunities for tax evasion and by some accounts reduced the progressivity of the income tax system. In addition, spatial variations are a problem. Given the high tax rates levied on agricultural income in Punjab, residents are demanding a rate reduction to harmonize their treatment with that of residents in the other provinces. Similarly, capital gains on physical assets have been included in the provincial tax base while capital gains on financial assets fall in the purview of federal government. Substantial exemptions granted to the former have significantly increased the relative return and led to overinvestment in real estate.

The sales tax base is also bifurcated, as the federal government levies a sales tax on goods, whereas provincial governments levy a sales tax on services, such as electricity, hotels, entertainment, etc. This practice was adopted because the federal government did not want to transfer the full sales tax to the provincial level due to evidence of tax exporting. There was concern that, given the concentration of industry in Sindh province (over 40% of value added) and its population share of 23%, the levy of the sales tax at a provincial level would lead to a large volume of tax exporting to the three other provinces. This bifurcation, however, has created problems in introducing a neutral VAT with tax-invoicing features in the different sectors of the economy. In terms of other indirect taxes, various excises are prevalent both at the national and subnational level.

Property-related taxes are also of concern. The provincial governments levy a stamp duty on property tax, while local government taxes property transfers and the federal government levies a capital value tax on property sales. This has resulted in an increase in overall property-related tax incidence and has also increased compliance costs due to involvement of agencies from different levels of government.

The composition of taxes for the federal and provincial governments is presented in Table 7. Indirect taxes dominate the federal composition, accounting for 70–80% of federal revenue generation over the years. Within this category, customs duty and federal excises generate most of the revenues, and the income tax is the major component of direct taxes at the federal level. Stamp duties and the motor vehicle tax account for most of the provincial revenues. The agricultural income tax that was adopted recently accounts for 12% of total provincial tax revenues, and land revenue, for another 11% in recent years. Most other sources of provincial revenue are relatively small.

2. Expenditure Assignments and Composition

The literature on fiscal federalism identifies the basic principles governing the demarcation of expenditure responsibilities among different levels of government. The key determining factor is that a particular public service should be provided by that level of government which has a sufficiently large geographical jurisdiction to be able to internalize all the benefits and costs of service delivery. This enables decision making to be responsive to beneficiaries. Involvement of higher levels of government in service provision is justified where there are spatial externalities, such that provision by local government is inefficient. In addition, if the provision of services is characterized by econo-

TABLE 7
Composition of Tax Revenues (Federal and Provincial Governments)
(Percentages)

	1985–1986	1990–1991	1995–1996	1999–2000
FEDERAL GOVERNMENT				
Direct Taxes	**17.0**	**16.6**	**28.7**	**31.2**
a) Taxes on Income	16.7	15.9	27.8	29.1
b) Wealth Tax	0.2	0.5	0.5	1.2
c) Other Direct Taxes	0.1	0.2	0.4	0.9
Indirect Taxes	**83.0**	**83.4**	**71.3**	**68.8**
a) Customs	47.3	44.8	33.2	18.4
b) Sales Tax	8.7	16.6	19.0	34.2
c) Federal Excise	27.0	22.0	19.1	16.2
TOTAL FEDERAL TAX REVENUES	**100.0**	**100.0**	**100.0**	**100.0**
ALL PROVINCES				
Agricultural Income Tax	0.0	0.0	0.0	12.3
Immovable Property Tax	3.0	2.6	2.6	2.4
Tax on Transfer of Property/Registration	5.3	3.8	3.2	2.2
Land Revenue	7.0	8.8	11.5	11.3
Capital Gains Tax	6.7	0.0	0.0	0.0
Prof. Trades/Challings Tax	2.0	1.5	2.2	2.1
Provincial Excise	3.6	4.3	7.3	5.7
Stamp Duties	27.9	37.3	37.2	31.0
Motor Vehicle Tax	21.5	17.2	16.2	13.7
Entertainment Tax	8.8	3.4	1.8	1.8
Electricity Duty	7.9	15.7	10.3	7.8
Others (Opium, Education, Betterment, Cotton Fee, Hotel, Other)	6.3	5.4	7.7	9.7
TOTAL PROVINCIAL TAX REVENUES	**100.0**	**100.0**	**100.0**	**100.0**

Source: Federal and provincial governments, annual budget documents.

mies of scale or if administrative costs of central management are lower, the case for higher-level provision is stronger. Some services, such as defense, have a truly national scope and are best provided by the federal government.

The allocation of functional responsibility between national and subnational governments in Pakistan is presented in Table 8. There is general adherence to the standard principles of expenditure assignment. Services such as defense, foreign affairs, regulation of international trade, currency and banking are provided by the federal government. The role of the government in a federation like Pakistan is, of course, smaller than in a unitary state, such that the national and subnational governments share certain functions. The provision of social services, such as education, health and social welfare, is significantly decentralized.

TABLE 8
Allocation of Functions (National and Subnational Governments)

FUNCTION	ASSIGNMENTS
Defence	National
Foreign Affairs	National
International Trade	National
Currency and Banking	National
Environment	National/Subnational
Interstate Trade	National
Immigration	National/Subnational
Air and Rail	National
Industry	National
Agriculture	National/Subnational
Education	National/Subnational
Health	National/Subnational
Social Welfare	National/Subnational
Police	Subnational
Highways	National/Subnational
Power	National
Tourism	National/Subnational

The composition of expenditures for the federal and the provincial governments is presented in Table 9. The federal share in the total national expenditure ranges from about 73–75%, with provincial governments accounting for the rest. The federal government dominates the defense sector (100%) and debt servicing (90%). In most other sectors, the federal role is smaller and, in some cases, declining. The share in other social services, for example, declined from 82% in 1991 to 56% more recently. The share of the federal government in the health sector, on the other hand, gradually increased from an average of 14% (1985–1991) to around 24% more recently. This is primarily due increased federal allocations through the Social Action Program (SAP). Provincial governments have major expenditure responsibilities in education (about 87–89%), health (75–85%), community services (62–72%), and economic services (47–75%). Law and order is also a principal responsibility of provincial governments, with an expenditure share of 58–68%.

3. Imbalances in Revenues and Expenditures

Having briefly reviewed the allocation of the taxes and expenditure responsibilities to the federal and the provincial governments, we now turn to imbalances in their revenues and expenditures. In Pakistan these imbalances are such that the federal government typically has a surplus and the provincial

TABLE 9
Composition of Expenditures (Federal and Provincial Governments)
(Percentages)

YEAR	1985–1986	1986–1987	1987–1988	1988–1989	1989–1990	1990–1991	1991–1992	1992–1993	1993–1994	1994–1995	1995–1996	1996–1997	1997–1998	1998–1999	1999–2000
FEDERAL GOVERNMENT															
General Administration	64.41	65.40	61.30	57.84	58.93	57.78	62.58	59.35	60.34	60.36	48.40	52.09	51.79	48.03	48.12
Defense	100.00	100.00	100.00	100.00	100.00	100.00	100.00	100.00	100.00	100.00	100.00	100.00	100.00	100.00	100.00
Law and Order	36.41	35.61	33.61	38.06	42.25	33.15	33.95	33.10	30.30	35.90	34.48	35.19	35.20	34.20	32.26
Community Services	34.76	30.51	27.92	26.80	26.39	22.97	23.79	27.95	33.48	37.17	36.41	38.03	37.87	37.43	33.21
Health	15.14	15.33	14.86	14.88	14.49	12.89	15.96	15.23	17.66	24.64	26.08	29.20	24.77	24.13	22.96
Education	12.66	14.13	12.79	13.09	13.29	11.92	14.03	15.15	13.12	11.66	12.96	11.06	10.86	10.39	10.71
Other Social Services	79.30	82.24	82.96	83.14	83.61	80.64	61.98	61.74	64.26	67.78	65.54	65.09	60.89	59.82	55.95
Economic Services	39.08	45.87	38.10	42.55	52.68	44.75	29.02	34.55	37.35	33.64	32.36	24.19	24.91	24.80	24.37
Debt Servicing	88.50	87.79	88.63	89.10	90.01	87.16	87.68	88.32	88.91	88.55	89.08	90.12	90.60	91.21	91.70
Other	82.49	78.89	88.83	88.38	84.94	81.21	82.05	79.68	77.89	77.42	85.24	80.86	73.18	72.99	66.48
Total Expenditure	74.02	73.56	74.16	75.35	76.34	73.13	72.31	73.46	74.67	72.32	71.79	73.94	74.67	74.43	74.15
PROVINCIAL GOVERNMENTS															
General Administration	35.59	34.60	38.70	42.16	41.07	42.22	37.42	40.65	39.66	39.64	51.60	47.91	48.21	51.97	51.88
Defense	0.00	0.00	0.00	0.00	0.00	0.00	0.00	0.00	0.00	0.00	0.00	0.00	0.00	0.00	0.00
Law and Order	63.59	64.39	66.39	61.94	57.75	66.85	66.05	66.90	69.70	64.10	65.52	64.81	64.80	65.80	67.74
Community Services	65.24	69.49	72.08	73.20	73.61	77.03	76.21	72.05	66.52	62.83	63.59	61.97	62.13	62.57	66.79
Health	84.86	84.67	85.14	85.12	85.51	87.11	84.04	84.77	82.34	75.36	73.92	70.80	75.23	75.87	77.04
Education	87.34	85.87	87.21	86.91	86.71	88.08	85.97	84.85	86.88	88.34	87.04	88.94	89.14	89.61	89.29
Other Social Services	20.70	17.76	17.04	16.86	16.39	19.36	38.02	38.26	35.74	32.22	34.46	34.91	39.11	40.18	44.05
Economic Services	60.92	54.13	61.90	57.45	47.32	55.25	70.98	65.45	62.65	66.36	67.64	75.81	75.09	75.20	75.63
Debt Servicing	11.50	12.21	11.37	10.90	9.99	12.84	12.32	11.68	11.09	11.45	10.92	9.88	9.40	8.79	8.30
Other	17.51	21.11	11.17	11.62	15.06	18.79	17.95	20.32	22.11	22.58	14.76	19.14	26.82	27.01	33.52
Total Expenditure	25.98	26.44	25.84	24.65	23.66	26.87	27.69	26.54	25.33	27.68	28.21	26.06	25.33	25.57	25.85

Note: Community services include public health services, works, etc.
       Other social services include social welfare (social security), population planning, manpower and labor management, etc.
       Economic services include agriculture and food, irrigation, transport and communication, fuel, power industries, etc.
Source: Annual budget documents (federal government and provincial governments).

governments a deficit in their respective budgets. The direction of fiscal transfers is, therefore, from the federal to the provincial governments, a pattern generally observed internationally.[3]

The magnitudes of the imbalances between total revenues and total expenditures of federal and provincial governments are presented in Table 10. They indicate that the share of federal government in tax revenue has been very high (above 90%) over time. Expenditure responsibilities are also large but relatively smaller (72–74%). The share of the provincial governments in revenues is very low (5–8%), but their corresponding expenditure responsibilities are higher (26–28%). The resulting imbalance has ranged between 18% and 23% over time and represents the gap that should be ideally filled through intergovernmental transfers from the federal to the provincial governments.

TABLE 10
Imbalances Between Revenues and Expenditures
(Federal and Provincial Governments)
(Percentages)

Year	Level	Share in Revenues (1)	Share in Expenditures (2)	Imbalance (1) – (2)
1985–1986	Federal	92	74	18
	Provincial	8	26	(18)
	All	100	100	–
1990–1991	Federal	93	73	20
	Provincial	7	27	(20)
	All	100	100	–
1995–1996	Federal	95	72	23
	Provincial	5	28	(23)
	All	100	100	–
1999–2000	Federal	93	74	19
	Provincial	7	26	(19)
	All	100	100	–

Source: Percentages based on data from annual budget documents (federal government and provincial governments).

The above analysis indicates that provinces are not financially self-reliant. In further analyzing this, we can define provincial fiscal autonomy as the extent of self-financing of the provincial government expenditure (recurrent and development) by provincial own tax and nontax revenue sources. An index

---

3. For a comparison of imbalances between revenue and expenditures across countries see Pasha (2000).

of aggregate provincial autonomy is presented in Table 11 and clearly shows that provincial governments in Pakistan have only been able to finance around 12–17% of their expenditures through their own revenues.[4]

The index of provincial autonomy was also computed for each of the provinces separately. This index indicates varying levels of self-financing capabilities of the provinces. The dismal fiscal position of Baluchistan is apparent from its low capacity to finance its expenditures (3–4%), followed by around 8–12% for NWFP. However, Punjab and Sindh, the two relatively developed provinces of Pakistan, were able to meet 18% and 19% of their expenditures in 1999–2000, respectively. They must still, however, depend on the federal government to meet their remaining needs through transfers.

TABLE 11
Index of Provincial Autonomy

	Punjab	Sindh	Baluchistan	NWFP	All Provinces
1985–1986	19.3	19.6	4.3	9.5	16.3
1986–1987	18.9	17.8	4.2	8.4	15.6
1987–1988	17.5	16.3	4.5	11.6	15.2
1988–1989	19.1	16.1	4.0	11.1	15.7
1989–1990	19.0	20.6	4.4	11.6	16.8
1990–1991	19.9	18.9	4.1	10.9	16.9
1991–1992	19.5	18.0	2.8	9.7	15.6
1992–1993	17.5	13.2	3.0	8.8	13.4
1993–1994	19.3	12.4	3.2	8.5	13.9
1994–1995	14.9	13.1	3.1	8.2	12.1
1995–1996	14.3	14.6	3.1	8.3	12.3
1996–1997	16.5	16.8	3.3	10.0	14.2
1997–1998	21.1	20.2	3.2	9.1	17.2
1998–1999	18.4	22.1	3.2	10.4	16.4
1999–2000	18.1	18.9	3.7	10.5	15.7

Source: Data for computing the index were taken from various budget documents of Government of Pakistan and provincial governments.

4. The index of provincial autonomy is defined as:

$$IPA = \left\{ 1 - \left[\frac{TR + G + B}{Exp} \right] \right\} X\ 100$$

Where:
TR = Total Federal Transfers to Provinces
G   = Total Federal Grants to Provinces
B   = Total Provincial Borrowing
Exp = Provincial Total Expenditure

D. Size and Distribution of Intergovernmental Transfers

In this section, we consider the volume and distribution of the various types of intergovernmental fiscal transfers to provinces. We also consider the magnitude of vertical and horizontal imbalances and the extent to which inter-governmental transfers offset them.

1. Volume of Aggregate and Individual Types of Intergovernmental Transfers

We now turn to a review of the volume and distribution of five broad categories of intergovernmental resource flows. These are formula-based trans-fers from the divisible pool of shared taxes, straight transfers defined on the basis of collection, development and nondevelopment grants, federal loans from national own sources, and foreign loans through the federal government.

Table 12 presents some key information on the volume and importance of transfers in Pakistan. The magnitudes of real per capita transfers (measured at constant prices of 1990–1991) registered almost a fourfold increase from PRs365 in 1985–1986 to PRs1,515 by 1999–2000. The proportion of transfers as a percentage of GDP has not varied much over time, hovering between 6–7.5%. Transfers as a proportion of federal revenues ranged from 34 to 44% between the years 1985–1986 to 1999–2000. Relative to provincial own rev-enues the magnitude of transfers is enormous, indicating high financial depen-dence on the federal government. The magnitude of these transfers increased from five times that of provincial revenues in 1985–1986 to seven-and-a-half times in 1993–1994. The financing of provincial own expenditure from federal transfers peaked at 92% in 1993–1994. They averaged around 77% (during 1985–1991) and 87% (during 1991–1997), standing at 86% in 1999–2000.

The importance of the various forms of intergovernmental transfers is indicated by their share in total transfers. Table 13 presents an overall distribu-tion of intergovernmental transfers. Certain patterns are observed from this dis-tribution. The average share of divisible pool tax transfers has increased over time from 36% in 1985–1986 to 56% in 1989–1991. After rising to 78% in 1996–1997, it settled at 62% in 1999–2000. Shared transfers to provinces have increased over time mainly due to the considerable broadening of the divisible pool by including more taxes, as explained above. The same pattern is ob-served for straight transfers (origin-based) to provinces, which rose from 1 to 18% during the period from 1985–1986 and 1991–1992. Currently, they com-prise 12% of total transfers. Straight transfers assumed greater importance in the intergovernmental arrangements in Pakistan after the announcement of the NFC Award of 1991.

The increase in formula-based revenue sharing and straight transfers over

TABLE 12
Volume and Importance of Intergovernmental Transfers

YEAR	1985–1986	1986–1987	1987–1988	1988–1989	1989–1990	1990–1991	1991–1992	1992–1993	1993–1994	1994–1995	1995–1996	1996–1997	1997–1998	1998–1999	1999–2000
Per Capita Transfers (in PRs)	365	436	524	529	510	597	808	848	991	1134	1236	1241	1263	1298	1515
Transfers as % of GDP	6.60	7.26	7.60	6.90	6.14	6.19	7.24	7.04	7.19	7.06	6.94	6.23	5.97	5.79	6.36
Transfers as % of Federal Revenues	38.92	44.61	37.76	39.92	33.75	35.44	39.45	38.37	40.54	42.28	40.12	40.58	37.76	37.64	38.67
Transfers as % of Provincial Own Revenue	472.25	487.90	553.86	543.77	473.44	441.90	547.04	619.21	659.48	736.63	684.09	622.12	487.94	512.51	549.03
Transfers as % of Provincial Total Expenditure	76.98	76.08	83.96	85.17	79.52	74.49	85.47	83.08	91.84	89.11	84.28	88.46	84.13	84.15	85.95

Source: Percentages based on data from annual budget documents (federal government and provincial governments).

the years has primarily occurred at the expense of grants (development and nondevelopment). The provision of large grants (nondevelopment) to meet budget deficits was the common practice prior to 1991. The federal government has refrained from providing large provincial budgetary deficit grants (an average of 29% of the total during 1985–1991) after the increase in shared tax transfers. Greater use of formula transfers has led to more certainty in the transfer receipts for the provincial governments and provided them with some greater financial autonomy to finance and plan their expenditures. The system has also been simplified. However, the predictability is not absolute, as indicated by the large discrepancies between projected and realized NFC funds discussed above.

Table 13 further shows that development grants form a small proportion of the total transfers to the provinces, and federal loans have also assumed less importance over time. The federal government previously appeared to exercise less control over provincial government borrowing powers in the form of overdraft facilities. The Central Bank introduced stricter control in the late 1990s, and the share of loans in total resource flows to the provinces declined from 21% in 1985–1986 to 3% in 1999–2000. There has been some variation in the share over the years, but it has consistently been below 10% in recent years. In contrast, the share of foreign loans has increased as a proportion of total transfers to the provinces, 12% and 10% in 1998–1999 and 1999–2000, respectively. This has been mainly due to the greater volume of donor funds flowing through the social action program.

The distribution of the several forms of transfers from the federal to the various provincial governments is presented in Table 14. The relative importance of transfers across the various provinces indicates that in Punjab, the share of divisible pool tax transfers in overall provincial transfers has increased from 53% in 1988–1989 to around 75% in 1999–2000. The shared-transfers component was, respectively, around 58% and 51% of total transfers to Sindh and NWFP in 1999–2000. The shared transfer component is not as important for Baluchistan, and its significance has declined to 30% of total transfers for the province recently. Baluchistan and NWFP, the two backward provinces of Pakistan, have been the main beneficiaries of straight (origin-based) transfers following the NFC Award of 1991. Straight transfers are most important to Baluchistan at 31% of their total transfers in 1999–2000, mainly due to the natural resource endowment of the province.[5]

Similar to the trend with the overall transfer position, the increase in the shared and straight transfers to different provinces has been at the expense of grants, which have uniformly gone down in importance over the years. Both

---

5. The province of Baluchistan accounts for 49% of the total gas production in the country.

TABLE 13
Overall Distribution of Intergovernmental Resource Flows by Type
(Percentages)

YEAR	1985–1986	1986–1987	1987–1988	1988–1989	1989–1990	1990–1991	1991–1992	1992–1993	1993–1994	1994–1995	1995–1996	1996–1997	1997–1998	1998–1999	1999–2000
Shared Tax Transfers	36	29	29	43	56	51	55	58	62	64	71	78	66	64	62
Straight Transfers	1	1	1	2	2	2	18	18	16	15	14	11	12	11	12
Development Grants	6	5	21	18	5	10	6	5	3	6	6	1	1	2	3
Nondevelopment Grants	35	40	38	28	16	16	3	4	2	2	1	2	5	5	10
Federal Loans	21	24	10	8	21	21	15	14	14	5	1	1	7	6	3
Foreign Loans Through Federal Government	1	1	1	1	0	0	3	1	3	8	7	7	9	12	10
Total Federal Transfers	100	100	100	100	100	100	100	100	100	100	100	100	100	100	100

Source: Percentages based on data from annual budget documents (federal government and provincial governments).

TABLE 14
Distribution of Intergovernmental Resource Flows by Province
(Percentages)

YEAR	1985–1986	1986–1987	1987–1988	1988–1989	1989–1990	1990–1991	1991–1992	1992–1993	1993–1994	1994–1995	1995–1996	1996–1997	1997–1998	1998–1999	1999–2000
PUNJAB															
Shared Tax Transfers	39.0	31.8	33.4	53.4	66.2	59.0	70.0	72.1	77.0	81.9	86.8	94.4	80.6	79.9	75.5
Straight Transfers	0.0	0.0	0.0	0.0	0.0	0.2	3.0	2.1	2.3	2.3	2.5	2.2	2.3	2.0	2.5
Development Grants	6.0	3.6	21.1	15.4	2.4	8.3	3.9	4.4	0.9	4.7	4.8	0.2	0.6	1.1	2.6
Nondevelopment Grants	31.0	37.6	34.0	20.4	5.7	8.4	3.0	4.7	2.5	0.1	0.0	0.0	0.6	0.0	6.4
Federal Loans	23.5	26.6	11.2	10.4	25.4	24.0	18.5	16.2	15.5	6.5	1.4	0.6	8.0	7.5	4.9
Foreign Loans Through Federal Government	0.5	0.4	0.3	0.4	0.3	0.1	1.6	0.5	1.8	4.5	4.5	2.6	7.9	9.5	8.1
Total Federal Transfers	100.0	100.0	100.0	100.0	100.0	100.0	100.0	100.0	100.0	100.0	100.0	100.0	100.0	100.0	100.0
SINDH															
Shared Tax Transfers	34.8	27.5	28.9	37.8	56.6	50.6	53.6	61	57.3	55.5	59.7	71.7	63.9	66.9	57.5
Straight Transfers	2.5	2.1	2.2	2.0	2.4	2.8	15.2	14.9	14.5	12.4	15.9	13.4	15.7	14.6	16.1
Development Grants	8.5	6.4	19.8	22.9	8.0	14.6	11.2	3.1	6.4	10.3	9.2	1.5	2.2	2.6	2.3
Nondevelopment Grants	32.4	39.3	37.5	30.0	11.2	11.1	3.2	7.7	2.4	5.7	4.1	0.7	0.0	0.0	13.7
Federal Loans	20.6	22.8	9.4	5.0	21.6	20.6	13.6	13.1	11.1	4.2	1.0	0.4	7.0	7.1	3.8
Foreign Loans Through Federal Government	1.2	1.9	2.2	2.3	0.2	0.3	3.2	0.2	8.3	11.9	10.1	12.3	11.2	8.8	6.6
Total Federal Transfers	100.0	100.0	100.0	100.0	100.0	100.0	100.0	100.0	100.0	100.0	100.0	100.0	100.0	100.0	100.0
BALUCHISTAN															
Shared Tax Transfers	37.0	63.6	19.6	25.2	35.6	31.3	25.1	25.8	30.0	32.6	40.0	42.1	30.5	27.6	28.9
Straight Transfers	0.0	0.0	0.0	18.4	22.3	17.2	52.8	54.2	50.0	48.4	46.9	30.8	29.7	28.4	31.2
Development Grants	10.7	36.4	30.8	23.5	15.8	23.4	3.7	1.2	2.4	0.7	1.0	0.6	1.0	1.8	2.2
Nondevelopment Grants	52.3	0.0	49.6	32.9	26.3	28.1	1.3	1.0	0.9	0.1	2.9	11.4	22.6	22.0	23.3
Federal Loans	0.0	0.0	0.0	0.0	0.0	0.0	13.6	11.9	12.4	5.3	1.3	2.1	4.5	1.0	0.2
Foreign Loans Through Federal Government	0.0	0.0	0.0	0.0	0.0	0.0	3.5	5.9	4.3	12.9	7.9	13.0	11.7	19.2	14.1
Total Federal Transfers	100.0	100.0	100.0	100.0	100.0	100.0	100.0	100.0	100.0	100.0	100.0	100.0	100.0	100.0	100.0

TABLE 14 (cont.)

YEAR	1985–1986	1986–1987	1987–1988	1988–1989	1989–1990	1990–1991	1991–1992	1992–1993	1993–1994	1994–1995	1995–1996	1996–1997	1997–1998	1998–1999	1999–2000
NWFP															
Shared Tax Transfers	26.5	19.4	20.8	30.8	38.1	38.1	39.0	41.4	48.2	50.1	59.3	64.1	51.0	46.5	50.5
Straight Transfers	0.0	0.0	0.0	0.0	0.0	0.0	36.3	38.2	33.4	34.1	24.8	23.8	21.7	19.1	18.4
Development Grants	0.0	3.9	16.9	13.8	5.2	3.1	4.3	3.6	1.3	4.5	4.9	1.5	0.9	1.5	2.9
Nondevelopment Grants	50.4	53.2	52.1	45.4	36.0	36.9	2.4	1.2	1.1	0.0	0.0	0.0	12.0	11.7	12.3
Federal Loans	23.0	23.3	10.1	9.7	20.6	21.9	14.7	13.2	13.7	5.6	1.4	1.7	9.0	6.4	1.0
Foreign Loans Through Federal Government	0.1	0.2	0.1	0.3	0.1	0.0	3.3	2.4	2.3	5.7	9.6	8.9	5.4	14.8	14.9
Total Federal Transfers	100.0	100.0	100.0	100.0	100.0	100.0	100.0	100.0	100.0	100.0	100.0	100.0	100.0	100.0	100.0

Source: Based on data from annual budget documents (federal government and provincial governments).

development and nondevelopment grants constitute a very small proportion of total transfers in Punjab, 2.6% and 6.4%, respectively in 1999–2000. Development grants have been generally small in all of the provinces, with NWFP registering the highest figure at 2.9%. Nondevelopment grants were most important in Baluchistan at 23%, compared to around 12% in NWFP and 14% in Sindh.

Federal loans and foreign loans (through the center) to different provinces show a pattern similar to the overall position, with federal loans being less important than foreign loans. Due to greater availability of funds from the divisible pool of taxes and relatively stringent federal government efforts to exercise financial discipline, the share of federal loans in the total transfers has declined to generally less than 10% since 1994–1995, while foreign loans channeled to provinces through the federal government have been generally on the rise.

2. Vertical Fiscal Imbalances

The existence of revenue-expenditure imbalances was documented in the discussion of Table 10 above. Additional details on vertical fiscal imbalances presented in Table 15 indicate that this is consistently a major issue in Pakistan. These imbalances between revenue and expenditure increased from 18% in 1885–1986 to over 23% in 1995–1996. The vertical imbalance was 19% in 1999–2000.

These vertical fiscal imbalances in Pakistan are partly due to the limited and largely stagnant fiscal capacity of the provinces and substantial increases in total provincial expenditures (current and development) over time. Stagnant fiscal capacity results from overcentralization of taxing responsibility and generally weak provincial tax collection. Expenditure increases result from increased demand and slack fiscal management.

As noted above, most of the large and buoyant tax bases relating to international trade and domestic income, production and sales are reserved by the federal government, and only limited fiscal powers are available to the provincial governments. Several existing provincial taxes, such as agricultural income, urban property, services sector, vacant land, capital gains, etc., remain underdeveloped. In addition, the performance of provinces in recovering costs of service provision leaves a lot to be desired. The extent of recurrent cost recovery in economic sectors like irrigation, agriculture, highways, etc. is only about 20%. In the social sector, provincial cost recovery is only about 3%. As a whole, provincial own revenues could be substantially enhanced from their current levels.

Rauf and Rafia (1996), who documented declining fiscal effort by the provincial governments in early 1990's, found evidence of low fiscal effort (measured in terms of actual collection as percentage of potential tax capacity) of provincial governments in Pakistan. Following the announcement of 1991 NFC Award, when significantly larger federal transfers were made to the provinces, the index of fiscal effort of the two backward provinces, Baluchistan and NWFP, declined significantly. Baluchistan's effort reduced from 0.63 in 1989–1990 to 0.47 in 1991–1992, and NWFP's effort declined from 0.94 to 0.64 for the same period. The study also reported that at the time of announcement of the 1996 NFC Award, federal authorities had a perception of profligacy in the expenditures and lack of own-revenue generation effort at the provincial level. During the 1980s, provincial current expenditure increased at an average annual rate of over 17% (more than projected by NFC) while own revenue increased only at the rate of 10%. Provincial revenues also decreased from 1.2% of GDP in the 1970s to 0.6% in the mid-1990s.

Table 15 indicates that intergovernmental transfers have offset the vertical fiscal imbalances since 1992–1993, following the announcement of the 1991 NFC Award.[6] The shared tax transfer alone offsets the imbalances in the aggregate, leading to a surplus of 3%. Including straight transfers and development grants continues to improve the balance in favor of the provinces to 8%. Including other federal grants further improves the balance to 12% in favor of provincial governments in 1999–2000.

Although the extent of vertical imbalance improved in favor of provinces following receipts of intergovernmental transfers, their accounts still show borrowings from federal government. This is due to the lag in receipts of intergovernmental transfers and the timing of actual expenditures. Generally, there are procedural delays in actual disbursement of transfers due to tax auditing and accounting prerequisites of the Central Board of Revenue (CBR)/Ministry of Finance. Another reason for borrowing by provinces is the typical shortfall in federal revenue in the divisible pool of taxes compared to budgeted revenues. Normally, the provincial governments' expenditures are planned on the basis of anticipated transfers from the federation in light of the budgetary estimates. These estimates are generally revised before the end of the financial year. The timing of actual expenditure incurred and procedural delays in receipts of federal government transfers and other shortfalls in provincial revenues force pro-

---

6. These estimates of fiscal vertical imbalances are based on Shah's (1997) work on Indonesia. The method uses several indicators: (i) the share of expenditures financed through own revenues; (ii) the share of expenditures financed through own revenue plus shared taxes; and (iii) the share of expenditures financed through own revenues plus shared taxes plus unconditional grants. The analysis is done both in terms of current expenditure and total expenditures of the provincial governments. Shah found that only two of 14 countries he analyzed were able to eliminate vertical imbalances through intergovernmental fiscal arrangements.

vincial governments to resort to borrowing, usually for short durations during which they run overdrafts and may show a deficit balance in their accounts.

3. Horizontal Fiscal Imbalances

Horizontal fiscal imbalances refer to an excess of expenditures over revenues of different units of the same level of government. Revenue differences across provinces may arise due to differences in fiscal capacity or fiscal effort. Similarly, expenditure differences across provinces may be the result of differences in the unit cost of provision of public services or due to quantity and quality differentials. Baluchistan, for example, the poorest province in Pakistan, is spread over an area of 347,190 km² with a small population, which increases its per capita cost of providing certain services compared to the other provinces.

Ideally horizontal imbalances are calculated using differences in fiscal capacity and fiscal need of a sublevel of government unit. Fiscal capacity is defined as the ability of a government to raise revenues from the sources allowed to it. Fiscal capacity is measured using information on major tax bases and standard (average) tax rates. This method measures the revenue that could be raised by the sublevel government if it taxes all standard tax bases at average rates. However, it is difficult to obtain relevant data (on tax bases in particular) in Pakistan.

Similarly, fiscal need may be defined as the sum of the priority expenditure needs of a subnational government. But in the absence of a consensus regarding priority needs and given the varying degree of inter- and intraprovincial access to services and facilities, it is difficult to estimate needs and the volume of funds required to finance them. Given these data limitations, it is not possible to estimate own-revenue potential and expenditure needs of the provinces on a normative basis.

Given the lack of data, the next best option is to measure horizontal imbalance using a method applied by Pasha (2000) in a recent study of Pakistan. Horizontal imbalance is measured as the extent to which current expenditures are not covered by own revenues. This approach is similar to the analysis of provincial autonomy discussed above, but we provide additional detail in Table 16. The results indicate significant differences in fiscal capacity across provinces as measured by per capita own revenues. Sindh appears to raise the highest per capita own revenues (PRs372) almost three times more than the lowest per capita revenue province, Baluchistan (PRs121), in 1999–2000. In contrast, per capita current expenditures appear to be highest in the two backward provinces of Baluchistan (PRs2,532) and NWFP (PRs1,903). The per capita expenditure in Sindh was PRs1,841 and Punjab, PRs1,250 in 1999–2000. The higher per capita expenditure in the two backward provinces is attributed partly

TABLE 15

Intergovernmental Transfers and Vertical Imbalances

(in Percentage Shares)

	1985–1986	1986–1987	1987–1988	1988–1989	1989–1990	1990–1991	1991–1992	1992–1993	1993–1994	1994–1995	1995–1996	1996–1997	1997–1998	1998–1999	1999–2000
WITHOUT TRANSFERS															
FEDERAL GOVERNMENT															
Revenue	92.4	91.6	93.6	93.2	93.3	92.6	93.3	94.2	94.2	94.6	94.5	93.9	92.8	93.2	93.4
Federal Total Expenditure	74.0	73.6	74.2	75.3	76.3	73.1	72.3	73.5	74.7	72.3	71.8	73.9	74.7	74.4	74.1
ALL PROVINCIAL GOVERNMENTS															
Revenue	7.6	8.4	6.4	6.8	6.7	7.4	6.7	5.8	5.8	5.4	5.5	6.1	7.2	6.8	6.6
Provincial Total Expenditure	26.0	26.4	25.8	24.7	23.7	26.9	27.7	26.5	25.3	27.7	28.2	26.1	25.3	25.6	25.9
Surplus(+)/Deficit(−)															
Federal Government	18.4	18.1	19.5	17.8	17.0	19.4	21.0	20.7	19.5	22.3	22.7	19.9	18.1	18.7	19.3
All Provincial Governments	(18.4)	(18.1)	(19.5)	(17.8)	(17.0)	(19.4)	(21.0)	(20.7)	(19.5)	(22.3)	(22.7)	(19.9)	(18.1)	(18.7)	(19.3)
SHARED TAX TRANSFERS															
FEDERAL GOVERNMENT															
Revenue	79.6	79.8	83.4	77.3	75.7	75.9	73.1	73.1	70.6	68.9	67.7	64.0	69.8	70.6	71.2
Federal Total Expenditure	74.0	73.6	74.2	75.3	76.3	73.1	72.3	73.5	74.7	72.3	71.8	73.9	74.7	74.4	74.1
ALL PROVINCIAL GOVERNMENTS															
Revenue	20.4	20.2	16.6	22.7	24.3	24.1	26.9	26.9	29.4	31.1	32.3	36.0	30.2	29.4	28.8
Provincial Total Expenditure	26.0	26.4	25.8	24.7	23.7	26.9	27.7	26.5	25.3	27.7	28.2	26.1	25.3	25.6	25.9
Surplus(+)/Deficit(−)															
Federal Government	5.5	6.2	9.2	2.0	(0.6)	2.7	0.7	(0.4)	(4.1)	(3.4)	(4.1)	(9.9)	(4.9)	(3.8)	(3.0)
All Provincial Governments	(5.5)	(6.2)	(9.2)	(2.0)	0.6	(2.7)	(0.7)	0.4	4.1	3.4	4.1	9.9	4.9	3.8	3.0

SHARED TAX TRANSFERS + STRAIGHT TRANSFERS

FEDERAL GOVERNMENT															
Revenue	79.3	79.5	83.2	76.5	75.0	75.2	66.4	66.6	64.5	62.8	62.4	59.7	65.6	66.7	66.9
Federal Total Expenditure	74.0	73.6	74.2	75.3	76.3	73.1	72.3	73.5	74.7	72.3	71.8	73.9	74.7	74.4	74.1
ALL PROVINCIAL GOVERNMENTS															
Revenue	20.7	20.5	16.8	23.5	25.0	24.8	33.6	33.4	35.5	37.2	37.6	40.3	34.4	33.3	33.1
Provincial Total Expenditure	26.0	26.4	25.8	24.7	23.7	26.9	27.7	26.5	25.3	27.7	28.2	26.1	25.3	25.6	25.9
Surplus(+)/Deficit(−)															
Federal Government	5.3	6.0	9.0	1.2	1.4	2.0	(5.9)	(6.9)	(10.2)	(9.5)	(9.4)	(14.3)	(9.1)	(7.8)	(7.3)
All Provincial Governments	(5.3)	(6.0)	(9.0)	(1.2)	(1.4)	(2.0)	5.9	6.9	10.2	9.5	9.4	14.3	9.1	7.8	7.3

SHARED TAX TRANSFERS + STRAIGHT TRANSFERS + DEVELOPMENT GRANTS

FEDERAL GOVERNMENT															
Revenue	77.3	77.4	75.9	69.9	73.3	71.8	64.3	65.3	63.5	60.5	60.3	59.4	65.2	66.1	66.0
Federal Total Expenditure	74.0	73.6	74.2	75.3	76.3	73.1	72.3	73.5	74.7	72.3	71.8	73.9	74.7	74.4	74.1
ALL PROVINCIAL GOVERNMENTS															
Revenue	22.7	22.6	24.1	30.1	26.7	28.2	35.7	34.7	36.5	39.5	39.7	40.6	34.8	33.9	34.0
Provincial Total Expenditure	26.0	26.4	25.8	24.7	23.7	26.9	27.7	26.5	25.3	27.7	28.2	26.1	25.3	25.6	25.9
Surplus(+)															
Federal Government	3.3	3.9	1.7	(5.4)	(3.0)	(1.3)	(8.0)	(8.1)	(11.2)	(11.8)	(11.5)	(14.6)	(9.5)	(8.3)	(8.2)
All Provincial Governments	(3.3)	(3.9)	(1.7)	5.4	3.0	1.3	8.0	8.1	11.2	11.8	11.5	14.6	9.5	8.3	8.2

SHARED TRANSFERS + STRAIGHT TRANSFERS + TOTAL FEDERAL GRANTS

FEDERAL GOVERNMENT															
Revenue	64.4	61.0	61.9	59.2	68.7	66.6	63.3	63.8	62.7	59.9	59.8	58.9	63.5	64.4	62.0
Federal Total Expenditure	74.0	73.6	74.2	75.3	76.3	73.1	72.3	73.5	74.7	72.3	71.8	73.9	74.7	74.4	74.1
ALL PROVINCIAL GOVERNMENTS															
Revenue	35.6	39.0	38.1	40.8	31.3	33.4	36.7	36.2	37.3	40.1	40.2	41.1	36.5	35.6	38.0
Provincial Total Expenditure	26.0	26.4	25.8	24.7	23.7	26.9	27.7	26.5	25.3	27.7	28.2	26.1	25.3	25.6	25.9
Surplus(+)/Deficit(−)															
Federal Government	(9.6)	(12.6)	(12.2)	(16.1)	(7.7)	(6.5)	(9.0)	(9.7)	(11.9)	(12.4)	(12.0)	(15.1)	(11.2)	(10.1)	(12.2)
All Provincial Governments	9.6	12.6	12.2	16.1	7.7	6.5	9.0	9.7	11.9	12.4	12.0	15.1	11.2	10.1	12.2

Source: Percentages based on data from annual budget documents (federal government and provincial governments).

TABLE 16
Horizontal Fiscal Imbalances (Provinces)

	1985–1986	1986–1987	1987–1988	1988–1989	1989–1990	1990–1991	1991–1992	1992–1993	1993–1994	1994–1995	1995–1996	1996–1997	1997–1998	1998–1999	1999–2000
PER CAPITA GRP (Rupees)															
PUNJAB	4946	5374	6074	6748	7320	8865	10428	11327	13107	15418	17459	19612	20918	22278	23751
SINDH	7838	8247	9802	10891	11674	12600	14391	15453	17475	19813	21555	23973	25315	26693	28176
BALUCHISTAN	4078	4463	5161	5740	6480	8355	9882	10596	12090	14176	16691	18684	19886	21139	22501
NWFP	4630	5425	6066	6730	7374	8394	9211	9797	10829	12990	13261	14664	15416	16186	17016
CURRENT EXPENDITURE (Rupees)															
PUNJAB	313	363	418	438	425	516	594	673	748	836	1014	1067	1078	1113	1251
SINDH	340	430	461	483	534	655	749	804	955	1124	1295	1277	1436	1409	1841
BALUCHISTAN	572	707	772	791	829	956	1160	1393	1492	1633	1855	1954	2052	2081	2532
NWFP	430	523	450	465	478	708	854	951	1056	1199	1417	1510	1678	1772	1903
OWN REVENUES (Rupees)															
PUNJAB	82	95	101	105	104	137	152	150	167	153	175	201	272	243	263
SINDH	89	105	102	105	143	172	176	136	148	186	236	236	317	338	372
BALUCHISTAN	37	42	52	49	56	59	53	65	71	76	87	89	83	88	121
NWFP	56	58	74	71	82	93	119	114	113	131	146	169	169	211	222
IMBALANCE (%)															
PUNJAB	74	74	76	76	75	73	74	78	78	82	83	81	75	78	79
SINDH	74	75	78	78	73	74	76	83	84	83	82	81	78	76	80
BALUCHISTAN	94	94	93	94	93	94	95	95	95	95	95	95	96	96	95
NWFP	87	89	83	85	83	87	86	88	89	89	90	89	90	88	88
RANK															
PUNJAB	3	4	4	4	3	4	4	4	4	4	3	4	4	3	4
SINDH	4	3	3	3	4	3	3	3	3	3	4	3	3	4	3
BALUCHISTAN	1	1	1	1	1	1	1	1	1	1	1	1	1	1	1
NWFP	2	2	2	2	2	2	2	2	2	2	2	2	2	2	2

Source: Annual budget documents (federal government and provincial governments) & GRP from K. Bengali's Ph.D. dissertation.

to relatively high unit costs of provision of public services and partly to greater fixed costs of running a province covering a much smaller population.

Given the revenue and expenditure position of various provinces, the extent of horizontal imbalance is highest in the province of Baluchistan (95%). NWFP was able to finance 12% of its current expenditures through own revenues. Punjab and Sindh, which were better off, were able to finance around 20% of current expenditures through their own revenues. The distribution of horizontal imbalances was further confirmed by a rank correlation analysis of a measure of horizontal imbalances (the difference between provincial own revenues and current expenditures) relative to per capita gross regional product (GRP). The results reported in Table 17 show a rank correlation of –0.8.[7] This indicates that provinces with lower per capita incomes generally have a relatively large resource gap.

The degree of fiscal equalization achieved by the transfer system is also measured by examining rank correlation coefficients of provincial per capita GRP with per capita revenues, various provincial transfers, and (post-transfer) expenditures. Results of the analysis are presented in Table 17. The overall results suggest that, while different forms of transfers have had different relative effects at different times, fiscal decentralization has been carried to a point where per capita expenditure is generally higher in more backward areas.

TABLE 17
Rank Correlation Coefficient with Per Capita GRP

YEARS	1985–1986	1990–1991	1992–1993	1994–1995	1999–2000
Own Revenue-Expenditure Imbalances	(1.0)	(0.8)	(0.8)	(0.8)	(0.8)
Per Capita Current Expenditure	(0.8)	(0.8)	(0.8)	(0.8)	(0.8)
Per Capita Total Expenditure	(0.8)	(0.4)	(0.8)	(0.8)	(0.8)
Per Capita Own Revenues	(0.2)	1.0	1.0	1.0	0.4
Per Capita Straight Transfers	0.5	(0.2)	(0.8)	(0.8)	(0.8)
Per Capita Divisible Pool Transfers	0.4	(0.2)	(0.8)	(0.8)	(0.4)
Per Capita Total Federal Grants	(0.6)	(0.8)	0.8	0.8	(0.8)
Per Capita Federal Loans	0.4	0.2	(1.0)	(0.4)	(0.8)
Per Capita Federal Total Transfers	(0.6)	(0.8)	(0.8)	(0.8)	(0.8)
Per Capita Total Provincial Revenue	(0.8)	(0.8)	(0.8)	(0.8)	(0.8)

Source: Data for computing the coefficient was taken from various budget documents of the Government of Pakistan and provincial governments.

---

7. The coefficient of rank correlation is a measure of degree of interrelationship

It is important to mention that although the per capita expenditure is higher in two backward provinces, disparities still persist due to large backlogs in access and higher unit costs of service provision. As expected per capita own revenues have a positive correlation with per capita income. Transfers play a strong equalization role, as the magnitude of these transfers to the backward provinces is much higher as indicated by the rank correlation coefficient of up to –0.8 in recent years. Transfers have generally become more equalizing since 1992–1993. The grants are also playing a strong equalization role, as the two backward provinces, i.e., Baluchistan and NWFP, are the major beneficiaries of these grants.

E. Implicit Intergovernmental Transfers and the Role of ADB

Some of the resources that flow to provinces are not accounted for in provincial budgets. It is important to understand how these resource flows affect the overall distribution of public funds. In addition, the effects of resources provided by international agencies, such as the Asian Development Bank (ADB), are not well understood. In this section, we briefly consider these issues.

1. Implicit Intergovernmental Transfers

Having considered transfer figures reported in the budgets of the federal government and the provincial governments, we now examine transfers that are not explicit in nature. The flow of funds from these implicit transfers may be substantial and may significantly alter the equalization impact on the provinces. For the present analysis, these implicit transfers consist of the components of the federal Public Sector Development Program (PSDP).

The federal PSDP is a regular annual feature (announced with the federal budget) and prepared in line with the policy framework of the government. The PSDP document states:

---

or interdependence between ranks of two variables. It is denoted by r and can be calculated by using the following formula:

$$\rho = \left[1 - \frac{6 \sum d^2}{n(n^2 - 1)} \right]$$

where: d = difference of corresponding ranks of two variables
n = no. of paired observations

The interpretation of coefficient of rank correlation is similar to that of coefficient of correlation. Its value lies between –1 and +1. A perfect inverse relationship between ranks of two variables indicated by a value of –1 implies that the two variables are moving in opposite directions.

". . . objectives are to pursue the goal of structural and macroeconomic adjustment in order to bring stability in the economy. It aims at balanced development, wider dispersal of economic benefits amongst people at large and removing regional disparities as far as possible."

The PDSP includes development schemes of federal ministries/divisions, provincial development programs, special development programs (such as *Tameer–e–Watan* Program, *Tameer–e–Sindh* Program, Afghan Refugee Program, etc.) and nonbudgetary development programs of federal corporations. These programs are undertaken in all four provinces.

In the absence of formula-based and transparent PSDP allocations to provinces, a popular perception has developed that the politically and economically powerful and developed provinces of Punjab and Sindh are able to get greater PSDP allocations. Part of the argument is that about 45% of the PSDP goes to defense, which is allocated in favor of Punjab, such that PSDP is playing a disequalizing role. Given the overall size of the PSDP and the lack of transparency in the process of allocation across provinces, there may be major and unpredictable implications for long-term growth and regional inequalities in the country. There are also provincial fiscal implications because under the PSDP, the expenditures through completion of a funded project are included in the project costs and are the responsibility of the federal government. However, after the project is handed over, the maintenance responsibility usually shifts to the provincial governments. Thus, it is important to analyze the PSDP.

An attempt was made to examine the allocations of funds under the PSDP to different provinces with a view to determining how these funds are allocated to the relatively developed and backward provinces. The analysis was undertaken on published PSDP data of 1990–1991 and 1997–1998 to 1999–2000.[8] Various identifiable scheme/projects by sector and costs are allocated to each province. Projects with jurisdictional spillovers and without provincial breakdown costs are lumped together in one category "spillover". The spillover projects, roughly 50% of ministries/budgetary corporation program total costs, were excluded from the analysis because they cannot be allocated to specific provinces. The analysis of PSDP was also difficult in a few cases where the domestic component of cost by scheme/project was given but the foreign loan

---

8. The total size of the budgetary development program in 1999–2000 is PRs116.3 billion, which is about 18% higher than the revised budgetary program for 1998–1999. Out of the total allocation, PRs41.3 billion has been allocated to the development program of federal ministries/divisions; PRs28.8 billion for provinces, PRs3.9 billion for special areas, PRs3.6 billion for special program, and PRs38.7 billion for the federal corporations program to be financed from the budget.

or grant components were not separately identified. These were reported as overall sectoral allocations only (e.g., industry, agriculture). It was therefore not possible to allocate this foreign funding component to individual schemes. It is also important to highlight that the size of the federal nonbudgeted component of PSDP allocated to autonomous budgetary corporations is very large and has a strong bearing on regional growth and equity. Unfortunately, information on nonbudgetary allocations to these bodies was not available, so this component could not be included in the analysis.

Based on the identifiable components of the federal PSDP, the impact of implicit transfers on regional disparities was analyzed. The results are presented in Table 18, which shows per capita allocations for 1989–1990 to 1999–2000 as well as rank correlation coefficients comparing per capita PSDP with per capita gross regional product across provinces. In the years up to 1992–1993 and in 1998–1999, relatively developed provinces appeared to receive a greater PSDP allocation. In the remaining years, federal PSDP played an equalizing role, with the rank correlation coefficients ranging from –0.04 (1994–1995) to –0.69 (1996–97). Similarly, the federal corporation program from 1992–1995 and from 1998–2000 and the federal ministries program in all years except 1994–1995 and 1998–1999 also seem to have played an equalizing role. The coefficients, however, are unstable, jumping around considerably across components and years. Given this and the difficulties involved in allocating a substantial proportion of PSDP expenditures, it is inappropriate to draw any firm conclusions on their overall equalizing or disequalizing impact.

2. ADB-Funded Infrastructure Projects

Pakistan has traditionally been a large borrower from the ADB, with cumulative loans of US$9.8 billion at the end of 1999. At this time, Pakistan became the second largest borrower from ADB and the largest recipient of loans from its concessional window, Asian Development Fund (ADF). The sector distribution of cumulative lending is presented in Table 19. Agriculture and energy have been the leading recipient sectors with shares of 29% and 28%, respectively, followed by finance (14.6%), social infrastructure (11%), and transport and communications (about 8%). The small balance is lent to industry and nonfuel minerals or is multisectoral. Over time, the sectoral distribution of lending has changed to reflect development opportunities in Pakistan as well as changes in government and ADB priorities. The share of social infrastructure, for instance, rose from 27% in 1992 to 42% in 1996.

The project details of ADB lending in Pakistan are provided in Table 20 and show that ADB has undertaken varied projects in the four provinces of Pakistan. Since the 1990s, funding has substantially gone to agriculture and natural resources in Punjab, and to energy and roads in Sindh. Other areas of

TABLE 18
Public Sector Development Program (Per Capita Allocations)
(In Rupees)

YEAR	1989–1990	1990–1991	1991–1992	1992–1993	1993–1994	1994–1995	1996–1997	1997–1998	1998–1999	1999–2000
FEDERAL PUBLIC SECTOR DEVELOPMENT PROGRAM (FEDERAL MINISTRIES/DIVISIONS)										
PUNJAB	25	33	31	67	98	120	83	101	129	40
SINDH	79	86	59	152	185	250	73	169	145	130
BALUCHISTAN	263	207	189	550	577	538	477	242	201	62
NWFP	91	103	70	124	61	77	390	198	70	203
FEDERAL PUBLIC SECTOR DEVELOPMENT PROGRAM (BUDGETARY CORPORATIONS)										
PUNJAB	87	70	213	226	292	237	48	209	118	98
SINDH	230	177	356	222	124	171	69	43	98	104
BALUCHISTAN	34	120	153	573	218	115	29	40	137	205
NWFP	173	127	224	186	133	243	50	31	142	157
FEDERAL PUBLIC SECTOR DEVELOPMENT PROGRAM (OVERALL)										
PUNJAB	111	103	245	292	389	357	131	310	247	138
SINDH	309	263	414	375	309	420	142	211	243	234
BALUCHISTAN	297	327	342	1123	794	654	507	282	337	267
NWFP	265	229	294	310	194	319	440	229	213	359
COEFFICIENT OF CORRELATION WITH GRP										
Federal PSDP Ministries	(0.39)	(0.29)	(0.30)	(0.23)	(0.08)	0.03	(0.70)	(0.29)	0.51	(0.45)
Federal PSDP Budgetary Corporations	0.84	0.74	0.89	(0.25)	(0.28)	(0.22)	0.55	0.12	(0.94)	(0.51)
Federal PSDP Total	0.37	0.13	0.76	(0.24)	(0.16)	(0.04)	(0.69)	(0.15)	0.16	(0.64)

Source: Federal government Public Sector Development Program, Planning Commission, Government of Pakistan.

focus include irrigation and rural development in NWFP and gas (energy) in Baluchistan. Considering the total value of the projects and limited options available to the provinces to finance their capital projects, the role of ADB-funded projects has recently become even more significant in provincial development. An analysis of fiscal equalization should include the impact of these implicit transfers to the provinces. There is a common perception among experts that the impact of ADB-funded projects may be disequalizing. It is therefore important to analyze this matter, but sufficient disaggregated data are not available for this purpose.

TABLE 19
Cumulative ADB Lending to Pakistan (As of 31 December 1999)

Sector	No. of Loans	Amount of Loans (US$ million)	Percentage
Agriculture and Natural Resources	55	2832.6	28.9
Energy	43	2707.0	27.6
Finance	33	1427.0	14.6
Social Infrastructure	24	1078.2	11.0
Transport and Communications	11	767.0	7.8
Industry and Nonfuel Minerals	16	648.4	6.6
Multisector	3	344.0	3.5
TOTAL	**185**	**9804.2**	**100.0**

Source: Asian Development Bank.

F. Overall Evaluation of the Intergovernmental Transfer System

The intergovernmental transfer arrangements in Pakistan, which include shared taxes based on population, straight transfers based on collection origin, and various grants, have been criticized by experts for several reasons. The straight transfers component (12% of total transfer revenues) returns selected resource revenues (oil, gas excises and royalties, and hydroelectric profits) to the point of collection. These arrangements are criticized for having no particular economic justification. On the other hand, they do benefit the smaller and less wealthy provinces, but this creates some major resentment. Larger, wealthy provinces are now seeking similar resource treatment for their agricultural commodities. Some argue that revenues from straight transfers would be better utilized for equalization if they were a part of a federal general revenue pool used for financing fiscal equalization transfers to the provinces. However, given the distribution of natural resources and the current political environment, it may

TABLE 20
Project-Wise Detail of ADB Lending in Pakistan

Loan Number	Title	Date of Approval	Subsector	Approved Amount (In US$ Million)	Term	Grace Period	Interest	Provinces
0760	Tarbela Units 13&14 and 500 kV Transmission	28-Nov-85	Electric Power	118	25	5	variable	NWFP
0761	Second Telecommunications	28-Nov-85	Telecommunications	69	25	5	variable	Spillover
0772	Pat Feeder Canal Rehabilitation & Improvement	17-Dec-85	Irrigation and Rural Development	117	40	10	1	Punjab
0791	Cotton Development	30-Sep-86	Industrial Crops and Agro-industry	66	40	10	1	Spillover
0793	Karachi Urban Development	14-Oct-86	Urban Development & Housing	55	40	10	1	Sindh
0824	WAPDA Tenth Power	18-Dec-86	Electric Power	150	25	5	variable	Spillover
0837	Flood Protection Sector	25-Aug-87	Irrigation and Rural Development	115	40	10	1	Baluchistan
0874	Chashma Right Bank Irrigation (Stage II)	10-Dec-87	Irrigation & Rural Development	48	35	10	1	Punjab
0901	Khushab Salinity Control & Reclamation	22-Sep-88	Irrigation & Rural Development	53	35	10	1	Punjab
0917	Second Farm-to-Market Roads	08-Nov-88	Roads and Road Transport	106	35	10	1	Spillover
0925	KESC Fifth Power	24-Nov-88	Electric Power	100	25	4	variable	Sindh
0929	Third Pirkoh Gas Development	13-Dec-88	Natural Gas	65	20	4	variable	Punjab
0976	Swabi Salinity Control & Reclamation Project	26-Oct-89	Irrigation & Rural Development	118	35	10	1	NWFP
1004	Second Urban Development	14-Dec-89	Urban Development and Housing	66	35	10	1	Spillover
1025	Third Telecommunications	16-Aug-90	Telecommunications	115	24	4	variable	Spillover
1062	Agriculture Program	11-Dec-90	Agricultural Support Services	200	35	10	1	Spillover

Table 20 (cont.)

Loan Number	Title	Date of Approval	Subsector	Approved Amount (In US$ Million)	Term	Grace Period	Interest	Provinces
1073	WAPDA Eleventh Power	20-Dec-90	Electric Power	215	25	5	variable	Spillover
1094	Second Oil and Gas Development	22-Aug-91	Natural Gas	52	15	3	variable	Spillover
1143	WAPDA Twelfth Power	13-Dec-91	Electric Power	125	25	5	variable	Spillover
1144	WAPDA Twelfth Power	13-Dec-91	Electric Power	125	35	10	1	Spillover
1146	Chashma Right Bank Irrigation (Stage III)	17-Dec-91	Irrigation & Rural Development	185	35	10	1	Spillover
1185	Provincial Highways	05-Nov-92	Roads & Road Transport	165	35	10	1	Spillover
1209	Flood Damage Restoration	15-Dec-92	Multisector	100	35	10	1	Punjab
1260	Urban Water Supply and Sanitation	04-Nov-93	Water Supply and Sanitation	472	35	10	1	Punjab
1294	Pehur High-level Canal	22-Dec-93	Irrigation & Rural Development	128	35	10	1	NWFP
1297	Third Punjab On-Farm Management	08-Mar-94	Irrigation & Rural Development	62	35	10	1	Punjab
1301	Social Action Program (Sector)	23-Jun-94	Education	100	35	10	1	Spillover
1314	KESC Sixth Power	22-Sep-94	Electric Power	100	25	5	variable	Sindh
1315	KESC Sixth Power (Sector)	22-Sep-94	Electric Power	100	35	10	1	Sindh
1401	Rural Access Roads	09-Nov-95	Roads and Road Transport	140	35	10	1	Sindh
1413	National Drainage	12-Dec-95	Irrigation & Rural Development	140	35	10	1	Spillover
1424	Ghazi Barotha Hydropower	16-Jan-96	Electric Power	300	15	6	variable	NWFP
1493	Social Action Program II	28-Nov-96	Multisector	200	35	10	1	Spillover
1578	Second Flood Protection	13-Nov-97	Irrigation & Rural Development	100	35	10	1	Spillover

Source: Asian Development Bank.

be advisable to continue with the present system of straight transfers as they provide some resources to backward provinces.

The flow of funds through tax revenue-sharing arrangements (62% of total transfer funds) is done on basis of population. This program is to be commended for its simplicity and objectivity in transferring a large pool of resources in a predictable fashion to bridge vertical fiscal imbalances. Moreover, Shah (1997) points out that these transfers are equalizing with respect to own tax collections and also mildly redistributive with respect to provincial GDP. The program, however, does promote excessive dependence of provincial governments on federal transfers, which reduces own-source revenue collection incentives and encourages weak tax administration. As a consequence, the provincial tax bases are far from fully exploited, and further tax decentralization remains an unexplored option.

Traditionally very little attention has been given in Pakistan to fiscal capacity in addressing regional equity issues. The transfers system has lacked an explicit equalization standard against which achievements can be evaluated. Adoption of a formal fiscal capacity equalization program and allocation among provinces by an appropriate predetermined formula would set a specific standard of equalization to be achieved. This would also help to determine the total amounts of transfers in-advance, facilitating the planning of expenditures. The approach adopted by the NFC prior to the 1997 Award was purely one of gap filling where the deficits in the provincial budgets were being met. There were also no incentives in the system to reward greater revenue effort or efficiency in expenditure management.

The NFC of 1997 introduced a matching grant system. Under this system, an additional matching grant, which is equal to additional revenue mobilized from taxation reforms involving rate increases, removal of exemptions or introduction of new taxes,[9] is given to the provinces There are two contrasting views on the impact of this reform. One view is that for the first time, emphasis has been placed on incentives for better resource mobilization and an explicit premium is placed on the level of fiscal effort in the revenue sharing formula. The closed-ended nature of the program is also seen as limiting potential abuses. If considerable improvements in revenues were seen, proponents argue that the matching grants system could be expanded to include all revenues in its net.

The contrasting view is that the program of matching transfers for resource mobilization is not well conceived. It rewards provinces for higher tax effort due to changes in structure and rates of taxation but provides no incentives for

---

9. The Tenth Finance Commission in India included fiscal effort as one of the criteria for allocating revenues from the divisible pool. Ten percent of transfers have been linked to tax effort.

revenue increases due to improvements in tax collection and administration. The program also shows a lack of concern with additional burden of taxation at a time of deteriorating quality and quantity of provincial public services. The services provided by the provinces have been deteriorating over time, and additional taxation from the provinces without an accompanying increase in quality of provision may not be acceptable to the taxpayers. To be successful, rewarding general fiscal efforts as opposed to the present, more limited approach may prove to be more powerful in raising provincial revenues.

Federal-provincial specific purpose transfers in Pakistan are generally ad hoc and discretionary, and they primarily meet political rather than economic objectives. Certain transfers are intended to compensate the two fiscally disadvantaged provinces for their weak fiscal capacities but higher expenditure needs. In the absence of significant tax decentralization and a formal equalization program, these represent a pragmatic approach to dealing with expenditure need differentials. As discussed later in our recommendations, however, a distribution formula based on indicators of backwardness would be more appropriate for distributing funds to these provinces.

The deliberations of a newly constituted National Finance Commission (NFC) have commenced and the respective positions of the federation and the federation units regarding future intergovernmental revenue-sharing arrangements have become clear. The research team interviewed various representatives of the Ministry of Finance, the provincial governments of Punjab, Sindh, Baluchistan, and NWFP, experts on public finance, and media personnel. Various articles in the newspapers on the 1997 NFC Award were also consulted. First, it appears that there is a lack of federal willingness to further share tax revenues with the provinces. This stems from the current state of federal finances, with a high and rising budget deficit. The federal government has the primary responsibility for controlling the national budgetary deficit and retiring and servicing the activities in the country. Second, there exists in federal circles a perception of profligacy in expenditures and lack of own revenue generation at the provincial level, further dampening interest in providing additional resources. The federal government needs to resolve these problems by creating proper incentives for the provinces to behave as a responsible tier of government, rather than taking punitive actions, such as a substantial cut in revenue-sharing transfers.

The perspectives of the various provinces generally reflect their intent in increasing the share of resources that they receive. Sindh, for example, which accounts for 70% of the revenue from all taxes, advocates a greater weight for origin of collection in the transfer of resources. Punjab is pushing for instituting royalties on their important commodities (wheat, rice, and cotton), arguing that these, like oil, are natural resources and should be treated as such. Baluchistan, being the largest province, would like to see a distribution formula that places considerable emphasis on area. The NWFP is concerned that it is not receiving its electricity royalty as provided for in the Constitution. One point of agreement among the provinces was that the federal government has been paying little attention to the provincial concerns, and more needs to be done to meet their demands. There seemed to have been little room for negotiations in the past. The recent decision to constitute Provincial Finance Commissions is considered a step in the right direction. In the present environment and period of resource scarcity, however, there is concern that designing a system that is acceptable to all of the major players may be difficult.

G. Summary and Recommendations

In this section, we briefly summarize our main findings on the role of intergovernmental transfers in Pakistan. This is followed by a set of recommendations for reform of the transfer system.

1. Summary of Findings

The gap between the revenues and expenditures of the provincial governments has ranged between 18% and 23% over time and has been substantially filled through intergovernmental transfers. Average transfers to the provinces from the revenue-sharing divisible pool have increased over time, mainly due to a broadening of the pool by including more taxes. Federal transfers finance over 80% of the expenditures of the provincial governments, which have generally become more dependent on the center over time. Baluchistan is the most dependent province and finances only 5% of expenditures, followed by NWFP (10%), Punjab (18%), and Sindh (19%).

Shared transfers are the major component, accounting for 62% to 78% of total transfers in recent years. Straight transfers (12–15%) have assumed increased importance over time, while grants (2–13%) have been more unstable and decreased in importance. Within the grants category, the nondevelopment component has increased and the development component has decreased. Shared transfers are most important to Punjab (more than 80% of the province's total transfers in most years), but they also account for almost 50% of total transfers in Sindh and NWFP. Baluchistan and NWFP are the main beneficiaries of straight (origin-based) transfers, largely because of their endowments in the resources covered by the included revenues. Nondevelopment grants are particularly important to Baluchistan and finance substantial deficits. Federal loans have become generally less important over time due to stricter federal control, while the share of foreign loans in total transfers has increased due to donor funding through the SAP.

Shared transfers and straight transfers both play an equalizing role. Grants also mainly go to the backward provinces. There are considerable implicit transfers in the system through the PSDP that may be disequalizing, but this is not strongly established. ADB and other international institutions also provide substantial funding to Pakistan's provinces. There is a perception that these resources may be disequalizing, but adequate data are not available to support or reject this hypothesis, so that more detailed analysis is required.

2. Recommendations

Our recommendations are divided into the following broad categories: (a) improving the formula for shared taxes; (b) enhancing transparency and provincial fiscal responsibility; (c) understanding the impact of public sector development program and nonbudgetary components to autonomous bodies; (d) instituting better provincial monitoring and evaluation; (e) rationalizing taxation assignments and size of the divisible pool; (f) improving the disposition of ADB resources; (g) providing soft loans to disadvantaged provinces; and (h) conducting further study on local governments. Each is briefly discussed in turn.

a. *Improving the System for Distribution of Shared Taxes*

Backwardness and poverty should be explicitly incorporated in the allocation of shared transfers, and they should be more comprehensively measured through an index that uses multiple indicators. These may be broadly categorized as socioeconomic and demographic indicators related to income and wealth, housing, transport and communication, education, health, gender equality, etc. Some of the indicators used in the human development index, for example, would be relevant.[10] We recommend that a fixed percentage (5%) fund from the divisible pool be allocated first to the backward provinces and the remaining be disbursed on the basis of a predetermined formula. An equalizing formula similar to the one used in India could be developed, and it could be improved as better data become available. Allocations out of the equalizing fund should be made to fund a specific minimum level of basic services. More funds should be allocated to those provinces further away from the minimum required level, taking into account fiscal capacity. These allocations must also take the differences in the costs of service provision across provinces into account to achieve equalization. The funds for provision of services should be performance-based and should not reward provincial inefficiencies.

---

10. See the 1997 Human Development Report for details on the computation of the human development index (HDI).

b. *Enhancing Transparency and Provincial Fiscal Responsibility*

A number of steps could be taken to improve transparency and fiscal responsibility. First, replacement of discretionary grants with mandatory revenue-sharing transfers has the advantage of making transfers transparent and promoting greater provincial autonomy. Second, a ceiling on the provincial loans would have the effect of lowering both federal debt and the downstream debt servicing obligations of the provinces. It would also compel the provinces to generate higher revenue surpluses, either through resource mobilization or economy in current expenditure, to sustain growth in development expenditure. Finally, the federal government may promote the process of resource mobilization by the provinces through a matching grant scheme linked to a broader spectrum of provincial tax reform options than at present. If properly implemented and the federal government honors its commitments, the scheme can be a major stimulus for higher provincial fiscal effort.

c. *Documenting the Impact of the PSDP and Nonbudgetary Components*

The Public Sector Development Program (PSDP) and its components should be analyzed in greater detail to determine whether they are equalizing or disequalizing. An in-depth analysis of the flow of funds to the provinces through all PSDP activities should be undertaken. In addition to analyzing the effects of the existing PSDP and nonbudgetary items, we also recommend that the provincial components of the PSDP be increased to allow the provinces more control over development in their areas. All national budgetary bodies that spend in the provinces should ideally have provincial representation to ensure transparency in their functioning and to guard the interest of the provinces. The foreign aid component of all development activities should also be clearly identified and analyzed to determine its equalizing or disequalizing effect.

d. *Establishing Improved Monitoring and Evaluation*

When the disbursement of funds allocated through the NFC is delayed, the provinces are forced to resort to borrowing to meet their expenditure requirements. The uncertainty also causes funding from foreign-aided projects to be delayed. We recommend that an independent monitoring body be set up through legislation to ensure timely and transparent distribution of all funds, to monitor the flow of funds, and to evaluate the performance of the provinces. Donor-funded projects might also be dealt with through this body to ensure their efficient operation and timely completion.

e. *Rationalizing Tax Assignments and Size of the Divisible Pool*

The present division of certain taxing powers between the center and the provinces results in many problems; there are also issues with the sharing of the divisible pool. Taxes of local origin, such as the personal income tax and sales tax, should go the provincial governments to broaden their revenue-raising potential. The federal government may collect the taxes on behalf of the provinces and charge them collection costs, as under the present system for certain taxes. In addition, since the divisible pool for shared taxes now includes all taxes, there has been a tendency on the part of the federal government in recent years to impose certain surcharges on taxes that do not have to be included in the divisible pool. The federal government should either refrain from imposing such surcharges or the proceeds from these should also be included in the divisible pool.

f. *Improving the Use of ADB Resources*

Given concerns about the possible disequalizing effect of ADB funds, a few points are suggested to ensure that backward provinces in Pakistan get a larger share of the funds allocated for infrastructure development by ADB and that better analyses can be conducted in the future. First, ADB should use additional indicators (not only population) in its selection criteria. Indicators of backwardness and impoverishment should be incorporated with more weight given to them. Second, the funding at the moment concentrates on selected sectors (roads development, etc.) and should be more diversified. Third, ADB should lend to some projects where priority is defined by local communities rather than exclusively by the federal government. This could be done through the creation of a Municipal Development Fund with ADB seed resources to target development funds to local governments. Fourth, ADB should ensure that details of the foreign component of all projects are provided. It should provide disaggregate details of allocation shares to each of the provinces to ensure that their impact on regional inequalities is clear. Finally, ADB should consider performance criteria for specific projects before future funding.

g. *Providing Soft Loans to Disadvantaged Provinces*

Soft loans to the backward provinces can be equalizing in nature. It is recommended that the backward provinces may be provided this facility, but only for development purposes. Varying upper limits may be imposed for each of the provinces to allow the smaller provinces to borrow more to meet their needs in times of a resource crisis.

h. *Conducting Further Study on Local Governments*

We have largely limited our discussion to the fiscal relations between the federal and provincial governments. The recently announced devolution plan of the Government of Pakistan involves substantial decentralization to local governments that is unprecedented in the history of the country. According to one estimate, almost PRs90 million (equivalent to almost 3% of GDP) of expenditure will be transferred from provincial to local budgets. This will increase the total outlays of local governments to almost four times their present levels and make them almost comparable in size to the provincial governments. With the abolition of the octroi and the zila tax in 1998, whatever revenue-raising capacity existed at the local government level has been largely eroded. Given the limited scope for the reassignments of fiscal powers, it appears that transfers will increasingly be the backbone of the local government finances in the country. Some practical issues in this regard need to be reviewed immediately. First, a decision must be made about whether transfers from the federal government to the local government should be direct or routed through the provincial governments. Second, it is important to consider whether the divisible pool should include some or all provincial taxes or be extended to include NFC-mandated transfers from the federal government to the provinces. Third, the combined share of the district governments in the divisible pool must be determined. Finally, the federal government must develop a formula to allocate funds to the individual local governments. Given the lack of data and the political nature of this exercise, developing a local transfer system will undoubtedly be a great challenge.

References

Asian Development Bank. 1997. The Second-Farm-To-Market Road Project in Pakistan. Asian Development Bank.

Bahl, R. 1999. *Intergovernmental Transfers in Developing and Transition Countries: Principles and Practice.* World Bank.

Bengali, K. 1997. Regional Accounts of Pakistan. Ph.D. Dissertation.

Bennett, R. 1982. *Central Grants to Local Governments: The Political and Economic Impact of the Rate Support Grant in England and Wales.* Cambridge: Cambridge University Press.

Bird, Richard M. 1999. *Transfers and Incentives: Intergovernmental Fiscal Relations.* World Bank.

———. 2000. Intergovernmental Fiscal Relations: Universal Principles, Local Applications. *International Studies Program, Working Paper 2.* Georgia State University.

———. 2000. Intergovernmental Fiscal Relations: Universal Principles, Local

Applications. *International Studies Program Georgia State University, Andrew Young School Policy Studies, Working Paper 2.*

Bramley, G. 1990. *Equalization Grants and Local Expenditure Needs.* Hong Kong, Singapore, Sydney: Avebury, Aldershot, Brookfield.

Breton, Albert. 1987. Towards the Theory of Competitive Federalism. *European Journal of Political Economy, Special Issues* 3(1, 2): 263–328.

de Mello, R. 2000. Fiscal Decentralization and Intergovernmental Fiscal Relations: A Cross-Country Analysis. *World Development* 28(2): 365–380.

Decentralization Thematic Team. 2000. Intergovernmental Transfers/Grants Design. World Bank.

Jorge Mortinez – Vazques. L.F. Jameson Box. 1997. *A Methodological Note on the Reform of Equalization Transfers in the Russian Federation.* Georgia State University, Andrew Young, School of Policy Studies, Working Paper.

Ma, J. 1997. *Intergovernmental Fiscal Transfers: A Comparison of Nine Countries (Case Studies of the United States, Canada, United Kingdom, Australia, Germany, Japan, Korea, India and Indonesia).* Macroeconomic Management and Policy Division, Economic Development Institute, The World Bank.

Mclure, Charles, E., Martinez, V. 1998. *Intergovernmental Fiscal Relations in Vietnam.* International Studies Program. Georgia State University.

Pasha, Hafiz and Aisha Ghaus. 1995. Implication of the TOR of the New NFC. *Policy Paper* 9. Social Planning and Development Centre.

———. 1996. National Finance Commission (1995), Intergovernmental Revenue Sharing in Pakistan. *Research Report* 8. Social Planning and Development Centre.

——— and Aisha Ghaus. 1995. Dynamic Consequences of the 1991 NFC Award. *Pakistan Development Review.* Islamabad, Pakistan.

———. 2000. *Fiscal Decentralization: Lessons from the Asian Experience, Research Report.* Social Policy and Development Centre.

Rao, M. Govinda, Nirvikar Singh. 1998. *Intergovernmental Transfers: Rationale, Design and Indian Experience* (December).

Rauf, A. and Rafia Ghaus. 1996. *Fiscal Effort by Provincial Governments.* Research Report, Social Policy and Development Centre.

Roy, Jayanta. 1995. *Macroeconomic Management and Fiscal Decentralization.* Economic Development Institute, Seminar Series, World Bank.

Shah, Anwar. 1994. A Fiscal Need Approach to Equalization Transfers in a Decentralized Federation. *Policy Research Working Paper 1289.* Washington, DC: World Bank.

——— .1994. The Reform of Intergovernmental Fiscal Relations in Developing and Emerging Market Economics. *Policy and Research Series* 23. Washington, DC: World Bank.

———. 1997. *Fiscal Federalism and Macroeconomic Governance: For Better or For Worse?* Policy Research Working Paper WPS-2005. World Bank.

——— and Zia Qureshi. 1994. *Intergovernmental Fiscal Relations in Indonesia: Issues and Reform Options.* Discussion Paper No. 239. World Bank.

Smoke, Paul. 2001. *Fiscal Decentralization in Developing Countries: A Review of Current Concepts and Practice.* United Nations Research Institutes for Social Development.

Government of Pakistan. *Annual Budget Statement, Various Issues.*

————. *Central Board of Revenue Year Book 1997–98.*

————. *Annual Budget Statement, Various Issues.*

————. *White Paper on Budget, Various Issues.*

————. *Summary of Budgetary Position for Cabinet 1991–92.*

————. *Supplementary Demand (Budget), Various Issues.*

————. *Estimates of Foreign Assistance, 1994–95, 1993–94.*

————. *Demands for Grants and Appropriations, 1996–97.*

————. *State Bank of Pakistan Annual Report, Various Issues.*

————. *Explanatory Memorandum on Federal Receipts, 1995–96.*

————. *Pakistan Statistical Yearbook, Various Issues.*

————. *Federal Budget in Brief, Various Issues.*

————. *Economic Survey, 1999–2000.*

————. *Report of the National Finance Commission, 1996.*

————. *NRB Report of Devolution Plan 2000.* National Reconstructing Bureau of Pakistan.

7

Philippines
Joseph J. Capuno[1]
University of the Philippines' School of Economics, Manila

A. Introduction

The Local Government Code of 1991, which promulgated the current fiscal decentralization program in the Philippines, is under consideration for amendment. The proposed amendments involve changing the formula used to allocate the national government's internal revenues, which is the principal form of central fiscal transfer to local governments. In addition, the proposed amendments would mandate the devolution of additional expenditure functions and powers to local governments.

More importantly, perhaps, two more substantial reforms are currently being discussed in policy circles. One is the possible adoption of a fiscal equalization grant mechanism. Although various forms of intergovernmental fiscal transfers have been used in the country, none has simultaneously taken into account differences in fiscal capacities and public service needs across localities. A second important idea being discussed is the need to factor in the magnitudes and distribution of local public goods and services provided by the national government. The volume of public funds involved in the provision of these services is enormous, leading to calls for adjusting central fiscal transfers to reflect this.

These proposals to reform the intergovernmental fiscal transfer program merit greater policy attention than they have hitherto received because they reflect a far broader set of objectives than simply ensuring revenue adequacy of local governments. These include the need to ensure macroeconomic stability,

---

1. The following are gratefully acknowledged: P. Smoke, L. Schroeder, and Y.H. Kim for comments on an earlier draft; Ruby Ann Pimentel, Ronald Dofredo, Ma. Bella Salvador, and Thelma Manuel for their excellent research assistance; Rosita Santos and Jean Marie Villar for secretarial support, and the National Economic Development Agency and other national government agencies for the data.

to improve overall fiscal equity or fiscal balance, to address inefficiencies arising from interjurisdictional spillovers, to promote national objectives at the
local level, to induce greater local revenue mobilization efforts, and to encourage cooperative undertakings among local governments.

In the rest of this chapter, we broadly examine the country's overall macroeconomic performance, the government's fiscal structure and trends in regional development during the 1990s. We then review the country's present
fiscal decentralization and efforts, followed by an assessment of the size and
distribution of the various intergovernmental transfers and their impact on local
fiscal performance, overall fiscal balance and regional development. Finally,
we analyze capital grants for infrastructure investments, and we conclude with
a summary of the overall results and specific policy recommendations.

B. Macroeconomic Performance in the 1990s

The country's macroeconomic performance and its intergovernmental
fiscal transfers are closely linked. On the one hand, the country's macroeconomic performance determines both the need for and the availability of intergovernmental fiscal transfers. On the other hand, fiscal policies, which include
central fiscal transfers to local governments, affect both the demand for and the
production of goods and services. An analysis of these linkages suggests areas
where greater consistency in the design of macroeconomic policies and intergovernmental fiscal transfer policies can be attained.

The need for and the availability of central fiscal transfers to local governments are effectively determined by the country's gross national product
(GNP) performance, which varies across regions with the spatial distribution of
natural resource endowments and the mobility of capital and labor. In periods
of stagnation or recession, some form of transfers may be required to stimulate
growth and development or at least to ensure the availability of basic public
services in certain areas. However, the national government tax revenues, from
which the budget for both central fiscal transfers and other public functions is
taken, are necessarily pro-cyclical. Hence, during these periods, the national
government is financially constrained from extending full support to local governments.

The policy dilemma is no less daunting in periods of growth or prosper-
ity, when fiscal inequities may be amplified because of the differences in the
level and extent of economic activities across regions. Under this situation, a
special fiscal transfer facility may be necessary to even out such inequities. The
transfer facility would have to be carefully calibrated, however, to minimize
adverse effects on local revenue mobilization efforts and, therefore, to aggregate public sector finances.

Ultimately, the central fiscal grants impact on the country's overall economic performance as well. With the fiscal grants, local governments are able

to procure more inputs and produce more public services, thereby invigorating local economies. Unfortunately, the positive effects on GNP may be offset if the national government incurs a serious budget deficit to finance the transfers. Hence, the financing and disposition of the fiscal transfers influence overall growth and development.

1. Overall Performance

The country's overall macroeconomic performance in the 1990s shows some strength, especially during the second half of the decade, but also continued vulnerability to external shocks. The precarious performance of the economy, as well as its evolving structure, has had implications for the size, sources and the management of central fiscal transfers to local governments.

The first half of the 1990s is best characterized as stagnation (if not recession). The real per capita GNP during this period marginally improved from P27.86 thousand in 1990 to only P27.97 thousand in 1995, with the corresponding figures for 1991–1994 consistently below the 1990 level (Table 1).[2] The economy started to pick up in 1996 and 1997, but it faltered again in 1998 as a consequence of the Asian financial crisis. By 1999, the economy registered an annual growth rate of 3.02%.

Domestic output (GDP), which constitutes the bulk of the total GNP, effectively determined the pattern of the economy's overall performance during the 1990s. The net factor income from abroad (NFIA) contributes modestly to GNP, although it has the widest range of variation among the components of GNP. In terms of composition, the industrial sector has consistently surpassed the agricultural sector in relative importance, but the service sector is the biggest component of GDP.

The importance of sustained GDP growth to the overall intergovernmental fiscal transfers program was evident in the 1990s, during which the Local Government Code of 1991 was also instituted. As the major source of national government tax revenues, the country's domestic output effectively determines the pool of funds for the principal form of central fiscal transfer to local governments, called the Internal Revenue Allotment (IRA). While the fiscal decentralization program partially insulates the IRA from macroeconomic shocks, it does allow the national government to embargo part of the IRA to manage cash flow, a prerogative exercised in 1998 to mitigate the effect of the Asian financial crisis. The embargo, however, was later declared contrary to the spirit of local autonomy stipulated in the Local Government Code of 1991.

With the expected decline in tariffs and other trade levies as the Philippines complies with its World Trade Organization commitments, the central government will continue to depend heavily on domestic sources of tax revenues. Tax

---

2. The Philippine currency is the peso, denoted by P.

administration will have to be strengthened, however, given the rampant tax evasion and the high incidence of tax underreporting in the service sector. The ratio of actual to potential tax collections in the service sector, especially in the informal and self-employed formal sectors, is reportedly very low. An improved tax collection effort will perhaps enlarge the pool of funds for central fiscal transfers more than a longer list of tax sources.

TABLE 1
Gross National Product and its Composition: 1990–1999

	1990	1991	1992	1993	1994	1995	1996	1997	1998	1999
Real per capita in 1994 prices (in thousand pesos)										
GNP	27.86	26.73	26.36	26.44	27.42	27.97	29.02	30.04	29.87	30.77
GDP	28.01	26.60	25.92	25.82	26.73	27.22	27.87	28.84	28.42	29.22
Agriculture	6.14	5.58	5.66	5.58	5.88	5.89	5.75	5.44	4.93	5.15
Industry	9.66	9.05	8.51	8.44	8.70	8.73	8.94	9.27	8.90	8.88
Services	12.22	11.97	11.75	11.80	12.15	12.61	13.18	14.13	14.59	15.18
Net Factor Income from Abroad	(0.15)	0.14	0.45	0.61	0.69	0.75	1.15	1.21	1.45	1.55

	1990 –1991	1991 –1992	1992 –1993	1993 –1994	1994 –1995	1995 –1996	1996 –1997	1997 –1998	1998 –1999
Annual growth rates (%)									
GNP	(4.05)	(1.39)	0.28	3.71	2.02	3.76	3.53	(0.58)	3.02
GDP	(5.07)	(2.55)	(0.37)	3.52	1.82	2.41	3.46	(1.46)	2.83
Agriculture	(9.06)	1.34	(1.35)	5.43	0.08	(2.37)	(5.30)	(9.39)	4.45
Industry	(6.33)	(5.92)	(0.83)	3.03	0.36	2.48	3.61	(4.01)	(0.12)
Services	(2.07)	(1.82)	0.45	2.96	3.72	4.59	7.18	3.26	4.08
Net Factor Income from Abroad	(192)	219.8	37.51	11.77	9.50	52.75	5.19	20.48	6.79

Source: Philippine Statistical Yearbook (various years).

2. Structure of Public Finance

The consolidated financial position of the public sector (Table 2) reveals that the national government deficit largely determines the overall public sector deficit, which includes the Central Bank, local governments, some nonfinancial government corporations, social insurance systems, government corporations, and other government financial institutions. Local governments were doing comparatively well during the same period, consistently posting budget surpluses averaging P3.1 billion. However, the surplus was only about 11% of the average amount required to close the total public sector deficit during the period.

The combined revenues of the national and local governments have generally been increasing (Table 3), from P172.5 billion in 1990 to P609.6 billion

TABLE 2
Consolidated Public Sector Financial Position: 1990–1999
(in billion pesos)

Particulars	1990	1991	1992	1993	1994	1995	1996	1997	1998	1999
NG Surplus (Deficit)	(37.2)	(26.3)	(16.0)	(21.9)	16.3	10.2	6.3	1.6	(40.0)	(17.9)
LGU Surplus	1.7	1.3	1.2	5.9	5.0	1.9	5.7	2.8	2.7	3.2
Consolidated Public Sector Surplus (Deficit)	(51.2)	(25.9)	(26.0)	(25.9)	(8.3)	(3.5)	(7.3)	(24.1)	(73.7)	(46.7)

Note: NG is the national government; LGU is local government unit.
        Figures for 1990–1998 are actual figures. Figures for 1999 are program figures.
Source: Department of Finance.

in 1999. The combined expenditures likewise grew during the same period, from P179.6 billion to P593.7 billion. The national government accounted for at least 80% of total public revenues and expenditures during this period. The national share in total public revenues, however, progressively declined from as high as 92.9% in 1991 to 83.2% in 1999. The national share in total expenditures also declined from 90% to 80.6%. This can be attributed to the decentralization, under which some expenditure responsibilities were transferred to local governments and the local share in the national internal revenues increased significantly.

TABLE 3
Total Public Revenues and Expenditures: 1990–1999

	1990	1991	1992	1993	1994	1995	1996	1997	1998	1999
Total (in billion pesos)[a]										
Public revenues	172.5	198.5	234.8	259.3	331.0	377.5	442.9	489.6	518.0	609.6
Public expenditures	179.6	206.9	221.1	262.2	321.0	362.3	426.5	511.6	552.5	593.7
Percent Share of National Government to Total										
Public revenues	90.1	92.9	88.8	85.9	82.0	82.2	83.1	84.2	84.2	83.2
Public expenditures	90.0	88.6	88.2	84.8	82.4	81.9	82.3	81.5	81.5	80.6

Note: [a] Combined revenues (expenditures) of the national government and all local government units.
        The national government expenditures are net of debt service payments.
Source of raw data: Commission on Audit.

3. Patterns of Regional Development

With greater fiscal decentralization, local public service provision is expected to improve, leading to enhancements in local welfare and regional development. Regional development, of course, is also heavily affected by macroeconomic performance, resource endowments, and resource flows.

Figures 1 to 4 depict trends in average real per capita family income and poverty incidence (headcount index) across regions for 1988, 1991, 1994 and 1997. In the Philippines, provinces are clustered into regions that are partly drawn along sociocultural and geographic lines. Merely territorial subdivisions, most of the regions do not have regional governments. In most places, therefore, the highest subnational government is the province.

A comparison across the years reveals that Region III (Central Luzon), Region IV (Southern Tagalog), the Cordillera Autonomous Region (CAR), and the National Capital Region (NCR) or Metropolitan Manila area consistently occupy the top income slots. The NCR's economy is closely tied with the economies of Regions III and IV. The Autonomous Region of Muslim Mindanao (ARMM), Region V (Bicol), and Region VIII (Eastern Visayas) are perennially the lowest income regions. There is only minimal change in the relative income rankings of the regions over time.

The difference in the respective average real per capita family incomes of the richest region and the poorest region indicates the range of regional income inequality. It increased from P25,000 in 1994 to P40,000 in 1997. Furthermore, the increases in incomes appear to be limited to a few regions, most notably the NCR and the regions closest to it (Regions III and IV).

Poverty incidence tends to be higher in the poorer regions, although the incidence of poverty seems to have modestly improved between 1988 and 1997. The same story is also reflected in Figures 5 and 6, where regional average per capita family income and infant mortality rates are depicted. The infant mortality rate, an indicator of health status, is inversely related to income. This analysis underscores the fact that poverty incidence and its manifestations are largely a reflection of the family's command over economic resources. But a family's access to basic services, such as health, need not solely depend on their income or wealth; it is supposed to have improved under the fiscal decentralization and intergovernmental transfer programs.

4. Fiscal Prospects in the Coming Years

The macroeconomy has been threatened again recently by the political turbulence involving former President Joseph Estrada. Reportedly, the crisis has led to the withdrawal or postponement of foreign investments and to the ballooning of the national budget deficit to a historic high of P136.11 billion by the end of 2000. Business confidence, however, seems adequate, as evidenced by the relatively stable stock market and exchange rate movements. The prospects for the future critically depend on how well the present administration handles the fractious forces supporting it, neutralizes the moves of the deposed

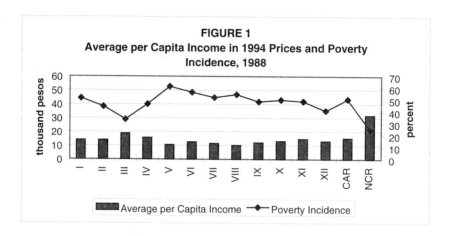

FIGURE 1
Average per Capita Income in 1994 Prices and Poverty Incidence, 1988

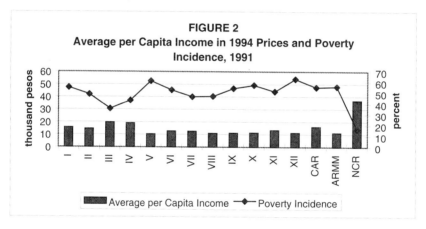

FIGURE 2
Average per Capita Income in 1994 Prices and Poverty Incidence, 1991

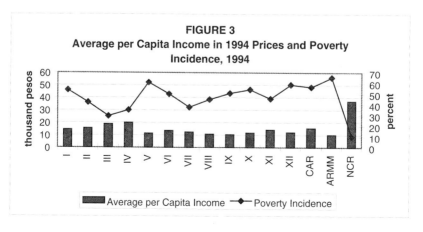

FIGURE 3
Average per Capita Income in 1994 Prices and Poverty Incidence, 1994

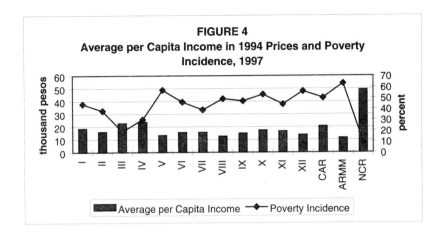

FIGURE 4
Average per Capita Income in 1994 Prices and Poverty Incidence, 1997

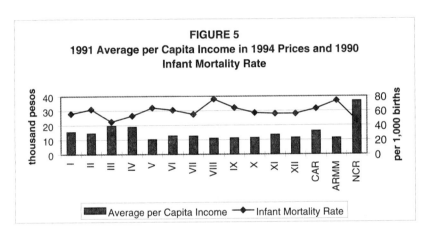

FIGURE 5
1991 Average per Capita Income in 1994 Prices and 1990 Infant Mortality Rate

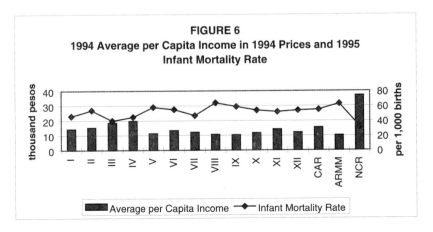

FIGURE 6
1994 Average per Capita Income in 1994 Prices and 1995 Infant Mortality Rate

President who remains popular in certain segments of population, and resolves the Mindanao problem.

The fiscal prospects for the coming years also hinge on the management of the current budget deficit, the passage of certain economic reform bills, and the improved absorption of overseas development aid. Among the more important reform bills are those concerning the banking sector, the power sector, and the revision of the Local Government Code of 1991 in the light of the country's experience under decentralization.

The administration also needs to evaluate carefully some of the assumptions of the Medium-Term Philippine Development Plan for 1998–2004, which is the blueprint of the government economic agenda. Possible domestic repercussions of the slowdown in the US and Japanese economies may necessitate reconsideration of tax revenue projections. As previous analyses have shown, tax revenue shortfalls inevitably affect central fiscal transfers. Given the linkage between GNP performance, intergovernmental fiscal transfers and regional development, ensuring consistency between macroeconomic policies and transfer policies is critical.

C. The Decentralization Program in the 1990s

One of the keys to understanding the impact of central fiscal transfers on regional growth and development in the Philippines during the last decade is the enactment of the Local Government Code (LGC) of 1991. The LGC ascribes a more expanded fiscal role to local governments and a wider scope for people's direct participation in local governance than any previous decentralization efforts (Tapales 1993, Manasan 1992 and Brillantes 1987). Thus, local governments now have a potentially more potent effect on regional growth and development.

The Philippine government basically has two levels: the national government and the local governments. The national government, through its line agencies, exercises both administrative and supervisory control over all local governments. At the lower level, the different local governments are clustered into 16 different regions, as noted above. Except in two areas, these regions are merely territorial subdivisions created to coordinate the various programs of the national agencies in contiguous local government units (LGUs).

Politically and administratively, local governments are typically organized further into three sublevels, with the provinces at the highest level, followed by cities or municipalities at the intermediate level, and the barangays (or villages) at the lowest level. Each lower-level LGU is under the administrative control of the next higher-level LGU. A number of highly urbanized cities and municipalities, especially in Metropolitan Manila, are independent of provincial governments. In fact, there is no provincial government in Metro Manila, but a special metropolitan government agency, called the Metro Manila Development Au-

TABLE 4
Number of Provinces, Cities and Municipalities in Each Region

Regions	Provinces	Cities		Municipalities		Barangays
		Component	Highly urbanized or independent	Component	Independent	
Region I	4	6	0	119	0	3265
Region II	5	1	1	91	0	2311
Region III	6	8	2	114	0	2948
Region IV	11	9	1	213	0	5615
Region V	6	4	1	109	0	3471
Region VI	6	11	2	120	0	4048
Region VII	4	9	2	121	0	3003
Region VIII	6	3	1	139	0	4390
Region IX	3	3	1	74	0	2113
Region X	4	6	1	63	0	1514
Region XI	6	4	2	61	0	1522
Region XII	3	3	2	50	0	1430
Region XIII	4	2	1	70	0	1308
ARMM	4	0	0	87	0	2139
CAR	6	0	1	76	0	1172
NCR	0	0	12	0	5	1694
Total	78	69	30	1507	5	41943

Sources: National Barangay Operations Office (Department of the Interior and Local Government, as of Dec. 31, 2000).
Bureau of Local Government Supervision (Department of the Interior and Local Government, as of Feb. 22, 2001).

thority (MMDA), was created to coordinate metro-wide services. The MMDA, however, does not have the regular powers and authority of a province over its component cities and municipalities.

Two administrative regions in the country have their own regional governments, as provided for in both the 1987 Constitution and the LGC of 1991, to address the special concerns of the indigenous people in the Cordillera and of the Moslem Filipinos. The two regional governments (Cordillera Autonomous Region and Autonomous Region of Muslim Mindanao) exercise administrative control over their component provinces, cities, municipalities and barangays. Although the two regional governments are relatively autonomous, the national government has some supervisory powers.

As shown in Table 4, there are 43,634 local governments in the country, including the two regional governments.[2] The barangays (or villages) consti-

---

3. The list does not include the newly created region of CARAGA. The provinces belonging to the CARAGA Region are Agusan del Norte, Agusan del Sur, Surigao del Norte, and Surigao del Sur. These provinces were formerly under Region X (Northern Mindanao) and Region XI (Southern Mindanao).

tute 96% of the total number of local governments, distantly followed by the municipalities with 3.5% of the total. With the recent conversion of some highly urbanized municipalities into cities (99), the latter now exceed the provinces (78) in number. Most of the highly urbanized or independent cities and all of the independent municipalities are found in the Metropolitan Manila area.

1. Main Features of the Decentralization Program

The 1987 Constitution declares that, as a matter of state policy, local autonomy shall be ensured. In particular, Section 3 of Article X of the 1987 Constitution mandates that:

> The Congress shall enact a local government code which will provide for a more responsive and accountable local government structure instituted through a system of decentralization with effective mechanisms of recall, initiative, and referendum, allocate among different local government units their powers, responsibilities, and resources, and provide for the qualifications, election, appointment and removal, term, salaries, powers and functions and duties of local officials, and all other matters relating to the organization and operation of the local units.

To fulfill this mandate, the local government code was enacted in 1991. The fiscal decentralization program has two main features. First, it is intended to promote greater local fiscal autonomy. Towards this objective, LGUs are granted higher shares in the national government revenues, bestowed broader revenue-generating powers, and allowed to enter into cooperative undertakings with the private sector or other LGUs. They are also assigned additional service delivery functions (Table 5).

The program's second main feature concerns administrative or political reforms at the local level. Designed to empower the people, these reforms include the mandatory participation of the private sector and nongovernment organizations (NGOs) in local planning and consultative bodies, such as the local health board, local school board and local development councils. The effective participation of NGOs and other civil society organizations (CSOs), especially those perceived to be critical to incumbent local political leaders, has been constrained by other factors, such as accreditation requirements imposed by the local government units. The relationship between local governments and NGOs/CSOs, however, has considerably warmed recently, resulting in various development-oriented endeavors.[3]

---

4. In the town of Irosin, Sorsogon, for example, the effective collaboration between the municipal government and local people's organizations and NGOs led to various successful livelihood projects that weaned a good part of the population away from illegal gambling activities, such as *jueteng*.

TABLE 5
Devolved Functions of National Government Agencies[a]

National Government Agency	Devolved Functions
Department of Agrarian Reform	– land and home development improvement projects
Department of Agriculture	– agriculture and fishery extension services; regulation of agricultural and fishery activity; conduct of agricultural and fishery research activity; procurement and distribution of certified seeds; purchase, expansion and conservation of breeding stocks; construction, repair and rehabilitation of water-impounding systems; support to fishermen, including purchase of fishing nets and other materials
Department of Budget and Management	– local government budget officer services
Department of Environment and Natural Resources	– forest management services; mine and geo-sciences services; environmental management services; reforestation projects; integrated social forestry projects; watershed rehabilitation projects
Department of Health	– extension of medical and health services through provincial health office, district, municipal and medicare community hospitals; purchase of drugs and medicines; implementation of primary health care programs; field health services; aid to puericulture; construction, repair, rehabilitation and renovation of provincial, district, municipal and medicare hospitals; provision for the operation of five-bed health infirmaries
Department of Public Works and Highways	– repair and maintenance of infrastructure facilities; water supply projects; communal irrigation projects
Department of Social Welfare and Development	– implementation of community-based programs for rebel-returnees; provision for the operation of a day-care center in every barangay; provision for poverty alleviation in low-income municipalities and depressed urban barangays
Department of Tourism	– domestic tourism promotion; tourism standard regulation
Department of Trade and Industry	– promotion and development of trade, industry and related institutional activities

TABLE 5 (cont.)

National Government Agency	Devolved Functions
Department of Transportation and Communication	– telecommunication services; transportation franchising and regulatory services
Cooperatives Development Authority	– promotion, development and regulation of cooperatives functions; cooperatives field operation function
Housing and Land Use Regulatory Board	– regulation of human settlement plans and programs functions
Philippine Gamefowl Commission	– regulation and supervision of cockfighting function

Note: [a] In addition, functions and locally funded projects of the Commission on Population, Fiber Industry Development Authority, National Agricultural Fishery Council, Livestock Development Council, and National Meat Inspection Commission are also devolved. Table adapted from Manasan (1997).

The LGC also provides for a system of recall whereby a local elected official (including the mayor or the governor) is removed from office if he or she loses the confidence of his or her constituents as indicated by the number of signatories to a recall petition. Theoretically, this political reform should pressure the incumbent to do well in office and fulfill his or her campaign promises, but it is subject to abuse.[4] Finally, the LGC limits an elected official to a maximum of three consecutive terms in the same position, with each term lasting for three years. While the provision is criticized for encouraging short-term planning on the part of local officials, it may also be partly credited for the emergence of young, dynamic, results-oriented local officials who may not have been elected under the old rules.[5]

At the macro level, the fiscal impact of the LGC is seen in revenue shares and expenditure obligations assigned to local governments. Under the LGC, the LGUs are entitled since 1992 to a higher share in the internal revenues of the national government, the IRA. Local governments received the IRA even before 1991, but the formula used in determining the total IRA and its allocation

---

5. Political candidates who lose an election may finance such petitions, often leading to disruption in public service provision and divisiveness among the local population, as in the cases of Kalookan City and Pasig City.

6. While many of the young crop of leaders still belong to old political clans, the provision ensures that fresh blood is periodically infused to the local political system. The Zubiris of Bukidnon, Golezes of Parañaque, and the Andayas of Camarines Sur are among the notable examples.

TABLE 6
Devolved Functions: Costs and Personnel
(Estimates as of March 1993)

National Government Agencies	Estimated Devolved Budget[a] (in million pesos)	1992 Agency Budget (in million pesos)	Share of Devolved Budget to the Total 1992 Agency Budget (%)	Number of Devolved Personnel	Number of Personnel before Devolution	Share of Devolved Personnel to Total Number of Personnel before Devolution[b] (%)
Dept of Agrarian Reform	9.4	1842.4	0.51	–		
Dept. of Agriculture	1055.6	5210.0	20.26	17673	29638	59.63
Dept. of Budget and Management	172.8	465.4	37.13	1650	3532	46.72
Dept of Environment and Natural Resources	167.7	1941.8	8.64	895	21320	4.20
Dept. of Health	3851.1	9991.4	38.54	45896	74896	61.28
Dept. of Public Works and Highways	1096.3	27109.3	4.04	–		
Dept. Social Welfare and Development	866.4	1320.7	65.60	4144	6932	59.78
Dept. of Tourism	2.8	207.7	1.35	–		
Dept. of Transportation and Communication	0.1	7563.9	0.00	–		
Philippine Gamefowl Commission	8.7	15.3	56.86	25	191	13.09
Total	1730.9	55667.9	12.99	70283	136509	51.49

Notes: [a] Based on 1992 agency budget for the full year impact of the functions/projects/activities devolved.
    [b] Only for agencies with devolved personnel.
Source: Table adapted from Manasan (1997).

among LGUs was amended under the LGC. Additionally, the LGUs receive a share in the proceeds derived from the utilization and development of the national wealth in their respective areas whether by the national government, other government agencies, or government-owned or -controlled corporations. More details on revenue sharing are provided below.

The extra expenditure burden of the LGUs under the decentralization may be indicated by the budgetary outlays in 1992 of the concerned national government agencies for the devolved functions. Among the national government functions devolved to LGUs starting in 1993 are basic health services, agricultural extension services, and social welfare services (Table 5). As can be seen from Table 6, the costs of devolved health functions constitute the bulk of the total.

2. Some Consequences of the Decentralization Program

As a consequence of the new IRA formula, the total amount of the share of local governments in the national internal revenues has been increasing steadily, from about P15.4 billion in 1992 to P42 billion in 1995. The upward trend is expected since revenue collections normally increase every year. The LGUs were also expected early on to have significant financial gains because the estimated total cost of devolved functions in 1992 was only about P7.2 billion (Table 6).

In reality, however, the incremental revenues of a number of provinces and municipalities do not match their additional expenditure obligations. This can be inferred from Table 7, which shows the respective percentage distributions of the IRA, the cost of devolved functions (CODEF) and the cost of devolved health functions (CDHF) across local government levels. The inconsistency between the IRA formula (which determines available resources) and the allocation criteria for the additional expenditure obligations (which determine resource needs) is particularly glaring in the case of provinces and cities. While both LGU levels received the same percentage shares in the IRA (23%), the share of the provinces in the CODEF was more than six times greater than the share of the cities. In terms of actual expenditure functions, most of the secondary and tertiary hospitals were devolved to provinces, while only a few city health centers (primary health care facilities) were devolved to cities.[6]

According to Loehr and Manasan (1999), however, these initial financial difficulties were eventually overcome, since the IRA has continually increased while no additional expenditure functions were devolved. In addition, the IRA allocation formula was effectively revised to account for the distribution of the cost of devolved functions. Since 1994, a part of the total cost of devolved functions is first taken out of the total IRA funds before the current formula is applied on the residual. The reserved amount is then distributed to local governments according to their actual shares in the cost of devolved functions.

TABLE 7
Percentage Distribution of the Internal Revenue Allotment and the Cost of Devolved Functions

LGU level	Internal Revenue Allotment	Cost of Devolved Functions	Cost of Devolved Health Functions
Total	100	100	100
Provinces	23	46	59
Cities	23	7	3
Municipalities	34	47	38
Barangays	20	0	0

Source: Department of Health.

7. Among the provinces with financing shortfalls during the early years of the decentralization program are Catanduanes, Surigao del Norte, Romblon, Southern Leyte, Cavite, and Bohol (Capuno 2001a).

Other financial obligations such as the so-called unfunded mandates compounded the fiscal problems of many LGUs. The unfunded mandates are the other new expenditure obligations of local governments for which they received nothing or only partial budgetary support from the national government, such as mandatory salary increases and allowances for devolved personnel.[7] Furthermore, many LGUs claimed that the devolved health facilities (hospitals and clinics) required major repairs or upgrading to be effective, thus increasing the actual budget requirements.

The magnitude and distribution of the IRA and the cost of devolved functions may account partly for the differences in local fiscal performance, and ultimately also for the variations in regional development. Figures 7 and 8 show the trend in the average IRA, revenue from local sources, and total public expenditures of provinces and cities during the period 1990–1996 (Capuno 2001b). The revenues from local sources comprise income from real property taxes, proceeds from the operation of public enterprises (such as public markets), local business taxes and other incomes. Local revenues exclude the IRA and other transfers.

The figures suggest two broad trends. First, provinces heavily rely on their IRA shares to finance expenditures, while the cities appear to be less dependent. Second, both local revenues and expenditures of the provinces and cities generally appear to be positively correlated with their respective IRA shares. This is expected for the IRA, which generally grows annually and is a major source of local finance. The apparent positive correlation between the IRA and local revenues, although less pronounced for provinces, is more surprising, considering initial fears raised about the possible substitutive effect of the increased IRA share on local revenue generation.

D. The Evolution of Intergovernmental Fiscal Transfers[8]

The various forms of intergovernmental fiscal transfers in the Philippines are administered at two levels. At the higher level are the central fiscal transfers to local governments, which may be broadly classified into revenue-sharing schemes and categorical grant schemes. The revenue-sharing schemes are intended to allocate the nationally generated tax revenues between the national government and the local governments. The principal type of revenue-sharing

---

8. These are stipulated in the Magna Carta for Health Workers (R. A. 7305), the Barangay Health Workers' Benefits and Incentives Act of 1995 (R. A. 7883) and the Technical Education and Skills Development Authority (R. A. 7796).

9. This section was co-written with Ruby Ann Pimentel.

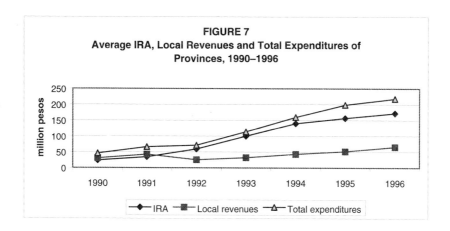

FIGURE 7
Average IRA, Local Revenues and Total Expenditures of
Provinces, 1990–1996

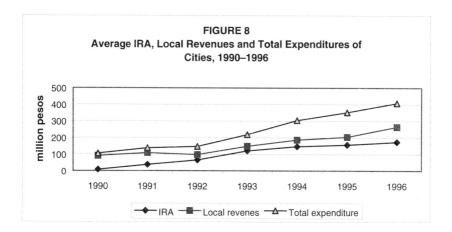

FIGURE 8
Average IRA, Local Revenues and Total Expenditures of
Cities, 1990–1996

scheme in the Philippines is the above-mentioned IRA. Other grant schemes are mostly categorical grants intended to influence the expenditure priorities of local governments or to provide for special needs.

The transfers administered at the lower level are the interlocal fiscal transfers. Although most studies have focused on central fiscal transfers, the importance of the interlocal fiscal transfers cannot be underestimated, especially now that tax revenue sharing between the province and its component cities and municipalities is strengthened under the LGC. Furthermore, greater consistency in the design of the central fiscal transfers and interlocal fiscal transfers is necessary if the various intergovernmental fiscal transfer programs are to have the desired impact on local service delivery, fiscal performance, and regional growth.

Like central transfers, the intralocal transfers may also be broadly classified into revenue-sharing schemes and grant schemes. The principal local revenue scheme is based on the real property tax collections of the different LGUs. Real property taxes are normally collected at the provincial or city levels. Exceptions to this rule are the municipalities within the Metropolitan Manila area that are not under any province. The different interlocal grants, which flow from a higher-level LGU (e.g., province) to lower-level ones (e.g., cities, municipalities, barangays), have basically the same purpose as central grants.

Both central and interlocal fiscal transfers have evolved since the 1970s, although comparatively less is known about local grants schemes that are not centrally mandated. The procedure for allocating local grants is usually determined by national directives, such as when municipal and city development plans are required to be submitted to the provincial governments to assist them in setting expenditure priorities. But provinces are generally free to decide the amount or types of grants given to their component LGUs.

1. Central Fiscal Transfers From the 1970s to the Present

Table 8 shows the major types of central fiscal transfers in recent years, while Table 9 distinguishes between the types of transfers adopted in or before 1991 and those after 1991. A few of the present central schemes are in fact continuing or modified versions of pre-1991 fiscal transfer programs, such as the IRA, the Countrywide Development Fund (CDF), and the Calamity Fund (CF).

As shown in Table 8, the IRA accounts for at least 82% of the total national allotments to local governments during the period 1995–1998. The IRA has been functioning since the 1970s, although the current IRA allocation formula is based on the LGC of 1991. New transfers introduced after 1991 include the special LGU share in the proceeds from national wealth and the Department of Education, Culture and Sports School Building Program, which are discussed in more detail below.

2. The Internal Revenue Allotment

The IRA is the share of the local governments in the internal tax revenues of the national government, which include taxes on income and other levies imposed by the Bureau of Internal Revenues (BIR). Essentially a general-purpose revenue share, the IRA is intended to augment LGU incomes.

The allocation of a certain percentage of the total internal tax revenues of the national government to local governments was originally promulgated following the passage of the Decentralization Act of 1967. Since then, the IRA system has undergone various revisions. The current formula used in the allocation of the IRA is specified in the LGC of 1991, although certain modifications have been adopted since then.

TABLE 8
Major National Government Allotments to Local Governments: 1995–1998

Allotments	1995	1996	1997	1998
(In Million pesos)				
Revenue shares				
Internal Revenue Allotment	51,925	56,594	56,592	76,941
Special Shares in National Wealth/Taxes	1,355	948	368	1,078
Categorical grants				
Municipal Development Fund	405	712	1,051	1,254
Countrywide Development Fund	1,159	1,080	903	438
Calamity Fund	440	912	344	305
Others	7,373	5,407	1,577	1,777
Total	62,657	65,653	60,835	81,793
(Percentage share to total)				
Revenue shares				
Internal Revenue Allotment	82.87	86.20	93.03	94.07
Special Shares in National Wealth/Taxes	2.16	1.44	0.60	1.32
Categorical grants				
Municipal Development Fund	0.65	1.08	1.73	1.53
Countrywide Development Fund	1.85	1.65	1.48	0.54
Calamity Fund	0.70	1.39	0.56	0.37
Others	11.77	8.24	2.59	2.17
Total	100.00	100.00	100.00	100.00

Source of raw data: COA Annual Financial Report of the National Government (various years) and General Appropriations Act (various years).

Under the LGC, the annual allocation of the internal revenues follows a three-step formula. First, the respective shares of the national government and local governments in the total internal revenues generated in the third preceding year are determined. Second, the aggregate share of the LGUs is distributed according to local government levels (i.e., provinces, cities, municipalities, and barangays). And finally, within each level, individual LGU shares are computed based on population shares, land area shares and equity considerations. Table 10 compares the formula used in the allocation of the internal revenues before and under the LGC of 1991. The current IRA formula is based more on fiscal needs, since it accounts for relative population sizes than on fiscal capacity. Existing fiscal imbalances may therefore be directly linked to weaknesses in the current IRA allocation formula.

According to the LGC, the IRA should be automatically and directly released to LGUs on a quarterly basis and within five days after the end of each quarter. The same section also states that the IRA releases "shall not be subject

TABLE 9
Major National Government Allotments to Local Governments
Before and After 1991

Allotment	Before 1991	After 1991
Revenue shares	Internal Revenue Allotment Specific Tax Allotment Local Government Revenue Stabilization Fund Budgetary Aid to Local Government Units Barangay Development Fund	Internal Revenue Allotment[a] Shares in the National Wealth Shares in Tobacco Excise Tax
Categorical grants	Calamity Fund Municipal Development Fund Countrywide Development Fund	Calamity Fund[a] Municipal Development Fund[a] Local Government Empowerment Fund Countrywide Development Fund DECS-School Building Program

Note: [a] Continuing allotment program.

to any lien or holdback that may be imposed by the national government for whatever purpose". In addition, minimal restriction is imposed on the use of the IRA resources. Under the LGC of 1991, a LGU is required to earmark 20% of its IRA for local development projects. As proof of compliance, the LGU however is only required to furnish a copy of its development plan.

In practice, however, the IRA formula has been adjusted for varied purposes, spawning a long protracted debate among national-level policy makers, local government officials, researchers and other stakeholders. The hotly debated issues include the proper interpretation of the stipulated IRA formula, the adequacy of the IRA to finance the devolved functions, and the impact of the IRA on local fiscal performance and fiscal balance. Some of these issues have been brought before the Supreme Court, although many remain unresolved.[9]

10. See papers presented during the *National Policy Workshop on Fiscal Equalization and the IRA* held on 14 June 1999 at the EDSA Shangri-La Hotel in Mandaluyong City. The workshop was jointly sponsored by the Union of Local Authorities of the Philippines, the Department of the Interior and Local Government, and the Australian Agency for International Development.

TABLE 10
Computation of the Internal Revenue Allotment before and under the Local Government Code of 1991

Allocation	Before the LGC of 1991 Local Government	Under the LGC of 1991 (under RA 7160)
A. Total LGU Share		
Funds for IRA allotment	Net general funds collected by the national government in the third year preceding the year the allotment is given*	Gross national internal revenues based on the collection in the third year preceding the year the allotment is given
Share of the IRA to total funds	Maximum of 20%	30% in the first year of the devolution; 35% in the second year of the devolution; and 40% in the third year of the devolution and thereafter
B. Share by LGU Level		
Provinces	35% of the total IRA net of the barangay share	23% of the total IRA
Cities	25% of the total IRA net of the barangay share	23% of the total IRA
Municipalities	45% of the total IRA net of the barangay share	34% of the total IRA
Barangays	10% of the total IRA	20% of the total IRA
C. Individual LGU Shares (for same level LGUs)		
Population share	70%	50%
Land area share	20%	25%
Equal sharing	10%	25%

Note: Net general funds comprise revenues collected net of special budgetary funds created by law to facilitate the planning and execution of particular activities by earmarking specific tax and nontax earnings for their use.
Sources: Lamberte et al. (1992) and Local Government Code of 1991.

3. Other Revenue Shares

Before the LGC of 1991, various laws had been adopted to increase the revenue shares of the local governments. The Republic Act 590, for example, mandated that excess income tax collections from the preceding fiscal year should be credited equally among municipalities. Provinces and cities also received a share from gross receipts, of sweepstakes, horse races and lotteries, as provided by Republic Act 1169. In 1974, LGUs also started receiving the Specific Tax Allotment (STA) or shares from specific taxes imposed by the national government on certain petroleum products, such as lubricating oils, naphtha, gasoline, bunker fuel oil and diesel fuel.[10] An umbrella fund called the National Assistance to Local Governments (NALGU) included the Specific Tax Allotment, Local Government Revenue Stabilization Fund, Barangay Development Fund and the support for local development projects.

The LGC of 1991 replaced the NALGU with the current IRA (Cuaresma 1992). Under the LGC, local governments are entitled to an "equitable share in the proceeds derived from the utilization and development of the national wealth (i.e., natural resources like land, water, forests, mineral, marine resources) within their respective areas" in addition to the IRA. This share, commonly referred to as the share in national wealth, is defined operationally in two ways, depending on whether taxes or sales receipts are generated by the national government, or by a government-owned or -controlled corporation or agency. The LGUs' share in national wealth is further divided among the LGUs where the national wealth is located (see Box 1).

It is obvious that the allocation of the funds under this transfer scheme depends on the distribution of natural resource endowments and the amount of public investments across localities. Like the IRA, therefore, these revenue shares are unlikely to correct for existing fiscal imbalances. Unlike the IRA, however, shares in national wealth comprise only a small portion of the total central transfers to local governments.

Starting in 1992, certain tobacco-producing regions also shared in revenues from excise taxes imposed on tobacco products. As provided for in Republic Act 7171 and Memorandum Order No. 61-A, provinces with an annual production volume of at least one million kilos of Virginia tobacco leaves are entitled to receive a share in tobacco excise taxes. Collectively, the beneficiary provinces are entitled to 15% of actual excise tax collections on locally manufactured Virginia-type cigarettes in the second preceding year. Each beneficiary province's share is based on the province's contribution to the total tobacco output. The province retains 30%, while 40% goes to the component municipalities and 30% to congressional districts.[11] Of the 40% that goes to the

---

11. Twenty-five percent of the STA went to the barangay infrastructure fund. The remaining 75% was divided among provinces (20%), municipalities (30%) and cities (50%). The STA was distributed to each LGU following the IRA formula in use at that time.

12. Congressional districts are electoral districts for purposes of electing members to the House of Representatives or the Lower House of Congress.

BOX 1
**Computation of the LGUs' Share in the National Wealth under the
LGC of 1991**

Section 290. *Amount of Share of Local Government Units.* Local government units shall, in addition to the internal revenue allotment, have a share of forty percent of the gross collection derived by the national government from the preceding fiscal year from mining taxes, royalties, forestry and fishery charges, and such other taxes, fees, or charges, including related surcharges, interests, or fines, and from its share in any co-production, joint venture or production sharing agreement in the utilization and development of the national wealth within their jurisdiction.

Section 291. *Share of the Local Governments from any Agency or Government-Owned and -Controlled Corporation.* Local government units shall have a share based on the preceding fiscal year from the proceeds derived by any government agency or government-owned or -controlled corporation engaged in the utilization and development of the national wealth based on the following formula, whichever will produce a higher share for the local government unit:

(a) One percent of the gross sales or receipts of the preceding calendar year; or

(b) Forty percent of the mining taxes, royalties, forestry and fishery charges and such other taxes, fees or charges, including related surcharges, interests, or fines the government agency or government-owned or -controlled corporation would have paid if it were not otherwise exempt.

Section 292. *Allocation of Shares.* The share in the preceding Section shall be distributed in the following manner:

(a) where the natural resources are located in the province:
(1) Province – Twenty percent
(2) Component City/Municipality – Forty-five percent; and
(3) Barangay – Thirty-five percent *Provided however*, that where the natural resources are located in two or more provinces, or in two or more component cities or municipalities or in two or more barangays, their respective shares shall be computed on the basis of:
(1) Population – Seventy percent; and
(2) Land area – Thirty percent.

(b) where the natural resources are located in a highly urbanized or independent component city:
(4) City – Sixty-five percent
(5) Barangay – Thirty-five percent

Provided however, that where the natural resources are located in such two (2) or more cities, the allocation of shares shall be based on the formula on population and land area as specified in paragraph (a) of this section.

component municipalities, half is distributed equally among the municipalities and the remaining half is allocated on the basis of each municipality's share in tobacco output.[12]

Like shares in the national wealth, the allocation of the local shares in tobacco excise taxes tends to favor only a few LGUs, thus further distorting fiscal imbalances in the country. Furthermore, the economic basis for singling out tobacco from the various agricultural products produced in the country is dubious. If anything, the consumption tax on tobacco products should be equally shared across LGUs since the consumption externalities are borne collectively.[13]

4. Other Central Grants

In addition to the revenue shares, local governments also receive various categorical grants from the national government. The categorical grants are intended for specific purposes, such as budgetary supplements for local personnel, funds for calamities and other contingencies, and subsidies for public works and other local infrastructure projects. Some of these grants are tied to loans, have foreign-fund components, or are targeted to the very poor or other specific LGUs. These grants are generally less transparently allocated than the IRA or other revenue-sharing schemes.

The national government administered various categorical grants before 1991.[14] Although many of them were abolished after the implementation of the LGC, the Calamity Fund (CF) and the Countrywide Development Fund (CDF) continued. Administered by the Department of the Interior and Local Government (DILG), the CF is intended for the relief and rehabilitation of areas affected by typhoons, earthquakes and other natural calamities. The fund may also be

---

13. The allotment from tobacco taxes is intended for cooperatives, livelihood, agro-industrial and industrial projects and infrastructure like farm-to-market roads.

14. An interesting aside: the fall of the Estrada Administration is linked with accusations of the (illegal) disbursement of the share in the tobacco excise tax of Ilocos Sur, as alleged by its governor, a known local gambling lord. Charges against the illegal gambling connections of former President Estrada triggered his impeachment trial and eventually the people power revolt.

15. These included the Local Government Fund, Barangay Development Fund, the Rural Improvement and Community Development Fund and a local government fund. The latter consisted of 5% of the tax collections of the Bureau Internal Revenues, over and above the 20% set aside for the then IRA, managed by the Office of the President and released as financial aid to local governments or to projects. In addition, the Rural Improvement and Community Development Fund and the Highway Special Fund were extended to LGUs as categorical grants respectively administered by the Department of the Interior and Local Government (DILG) and the Department of Public Works and Highways (DPWH).

used for the reconstruction of public works and for disaster preparation. The CDF is intended for barangay-based or community-based projects with emphasis on livelihood or income generation, sports development or physical fitness, cultural enhancement or capacity building. In addition to local government units, nongovernment organizations may also apply for subsidy under this fund facility. Often viewed as a pork-barrel fund, the CDF may only be used for projects endorsed by members of Congress, each of whom receives an annual CDF allotment.

After 1991, a new set of categorical grants was introduced to support government policy. The two most important among the new transfer schemes are the Local Government Empowerment Fund (LGEF) and the Municipal Development Fund (MDF).[15] Both fund facilities are partly financed by foreign grants and highly concessional loans from bilateral and multilateral institutions, such as the United States Agency for International Development (USAID) and the Asian Development Bank (ADB). Other categorical grants are summarized in Box 2.

Established in 1996 to support the government's social reform agenda (SRA), "the LGEF has two distinct facilities: (i) assistance to the 20 priority provinces for industrialization, livelihood, and related poverty alleviation projects; and (ii) assistance to low-income fifth and sixth class LGUs, in addition to the 20 SRA provinces, to undertake devolved activities in agriculture and water supply, sewerage and sanitation." ADB-financed rural water supply, sewerage, and sanitation project is part of the second facility. (Alonzo 1999)

The MDF, administered by the Department of Finance (DOF), consists of various Official Development Assistance (ODA) funds designed to enable the LGUs to tap foreign assistance normally granted to the national government. Unlike funds for regular central grants however, the MDF is a mixture of loan, grant and equity components. The grant component under the present MDF ranges from 50–90% of the subproject costs. The IRA and other local government assets are used as collateral for the loans. Certain eligibility requirements are imposed on the selection of grantees, on the types of projects to be financed and on the cost-sharing arrangement between the LGU-grantee and the MDF. Various livelihood and poverty alleviation projects and some of the devolved functions (like the provision of local water supply, sewerage and sanitation facilities in the poorest municipalities) receive assistance from this fund facility.[16]

---

16. The new MDF is a highly refurbished version of a grant scheme originally introduced in 1984.

17. Among the projects supported under the MDF are the Bukidnon Integrated Area Development Project (BIADP) and the Clark Area Municipal Development Project (CAMDP). With the province of Bukidnon as its direct beneficiary, the BIADP is

---

BOX 2
Summary Features of the other Central Grants to Local Governments

A. Introduced before 1991 but continued thereafter

Local Officials Insurance Premium Fund. This fund is used for the payment of the insurance premiums of local officials.

Miscellaneous Personnel Benefits Fund. This fund is used for the payment of separation and retirement benefits of employees under the streamlining program and other personnel benefits to or on behalf of national government officials and employees. Releases against the amount appropriated to cover the required national government share in the retirement benefits of devolved personnel shall be made directly to the concerned local government units.

Palarong Pambansa Fund. The amount appropriated is for the sole purpose of providing funding for the current expenditures and for the construction, repair and/or development of sites and facilities and the purchase of sports equipment necessary for the conduct of the games.

Foreign-Assisted Projects Support Fund. This fund is for the purpose of covering foreign exchange and peso requirements of foreign-assisted projects.

B. Introduced after 1991

Magna Carta for Public Health Workers. This is a temporary subsidy to local governments for the partial funding of the implementation of the Magna Carta of Public Health Workers, a law which regulates the salaries and other allowances of all health workers devolved to local governments.

Countrywide Industrialization Fund. The fund appropriated shall be used exclusively for the implementation of the countrywide industrialization projects upon prior consultation with the representative of the district concerned. Providing a maximum of P30 million in every town and P40 million in every city, the fund was intended for the establishment of manufacturing, processing and other related industries to hasten rural industrialization. Up to 10% of the total project costs can be availed as grants under this facility.

DECS-School Building Program. Under the Public Works and Highways Infrastructure Program Act of 1995 (RA 8150), "the DPWH shall, upon the request of the member(s) of Congress concerned, authorize provinces, cities, municipalities, or barangays to implement projects under the categories of local roads and other public works . . ." Included in this allowed infrastructure projects are school buildings for which the authorized LGUs may receive an appropriation from the DECS.

Poverty Alleviation Fund. For the fund requirements in accordance with the following purposes: (a) for the scholarship assistance program of the department of education, culture and sports and the state colleges and universities and colleges; (b) hiring of additional teachers to be assigned in poor municipalities; (c) additional school desks to be released through local school boards for the 4th, 5th and 6th class municipalities and cities; (d) direct assistance to farmers in depressed municipalities and barangays, including housing assistance for victims of calamities and for communal irrigation projects to be released through local government units; (e) reintegration assistance for returning undocumented overseas contract workers; (f) support of the operation of the family health nutrition welfare program of the department of health and preventive health care program of DECS; and (g) assistance program for the distressed and disadvantaged population including slum clearance and urban development program.

C. The DOH's Comprehensive Health Care Agreement (CHCA) introduced in 1994

To help finance the devolved health functions and to promote national health programs at the local level, the Department of Health (DOH) introduced the Comprehensive Health Care Agreement in 1994. Essentially a conditional matching grant scheme, the DOH commits to match every peso spent by the local government unit on nine core health programs of the DOH in their locality, provided also that the local government unit fully supports the devolved health functions. Local health projects may also be a part of the CHCA. However, the effectiveness of the CHCA is questioned because of the some problems in its design and implementation and the DOH's lack of monitoring and evaluation mechanisms to monitor local compliance [Eleria, Montalbo and Sebial 1994; Esguerra 1997].

Source: General Appropriations Act.

Clearly, the various categorical grants are intended to support local expenditure needs. However, the allocation of these grants is not as transparent as the IRA distribution, largely because they are administered by different national government agencies using various processes and criteria. Moreover, the types of local projects supported under a particular grant facility may be administered under different national line agencies. Thus, it is difficult to make a more rigorous assessment of their impact on local fiscal performance and overall fiscal balance, since many of the transfer facilities are designed poorly and not consistent with one another. The lack of transparency in the allocation of the categorical grants reinforces the perception that many of them are simply pork barrel funds. Despite the possible political opposition to the reform in these fund facilities, a more thorough accounting of their sources and beneficiaries is needed.

5. Interlocal Fiscal Transfers

Comparatively less is known about interlocal fiscal transfers, although there are both de facto and de jure mechanisms for revenue sharing and grants among local governments. The major type of local-level revenue-sharing scheme is the sharing of real property taxes. (Other local tax-sharing arrangements are summarized in Box 3). According to the LGC of 1991, a province, city, or Metropolitan Manila area municipality may levy an annual ad valorem tax on real property, such as land, building, machinery and other improvements. Provinces keep 35% of the real property tax they collect while 40% and 25%, respectively, go to the municipality and the barangay where the property is located. Cities keep 70% of what they collect and distribute 30% to their component barangays, half shared equally among all barangays and half to the barangay where the property is located. Finally, in the Metropolitan Manila Area, 35% of property tax collections accrue to the MMDA, 35% to the municipality where the property is located, and 30% to the component barangays.

Tax collection effort on real property remains low and tax underassessment is prevalent, substantially for political reasons. Moreover, there are often delays or failures in the remittance of the provincial share in the real property

---

intended to "equip the government agencies with the skills and resources to sustain economic development during and after project implementation." On the other hand", the CAMDP is "geared towards the improvements of basic infrastructure and facilities in the municipalities and cities surrounding the Clark Special Economic Zone". The localities that benefited under this fund facility are the cities of Angeles and Tarlac, and the municipalities of Bamban, Capas, Concepcion, Magalang, Mabalacat, and San Fernando.

BOX 3
Allocation of Other Local Tax Revenues under the
Local Government Code of 1991

Under Section 138 of the LGC of 1991, the province may levy and collect taxes on sand, gravel, earth and other quarry resources extracted from public lands or public waters within its territorial jurisdiction. The proceeds of such taxes will be shared among the LGUs where the resource is extracted as follows: province (30%), the component city or municipality (30%), and the barangay (40%). The maximum tax rate is 10% of the fair market value in the locality per cubic meter of ordinary stones, sand gravel, earth, and other quarry resources.

Provinces and municipalities may likewise share in the amusement tax (Section 140). "The province may levy an amusement tax to be collected from the proprietors, lessees, or operators of theaters, cinemas, concert halls, circuses, boxing stadia, and other places of amusement at a rate of not more than thirty percent of the gross receipts from admission fee . . . The proceeds from the amusement tax shall be shared equally by the province and the municipality where such amusement places are located."

The national government on the one hand and the cities, municipalities and barangays on the other hand also share in the community tax revenues (Section 164). Community taxes, which are included in the general fund of the collecting agent, are intended to finance the development of the concerned LGU. Upon payment of the tax, which is based on the person's income, a certificate is issued whose number is used for filling up public documents the person may be required to sign. Normally, the community tax is paid to the LGU where the person is residing. Revenues from this tax are minimal, however, because income is underreported of income and it is not compulsory.

The share of the national government, however, is limited to the actual cost of printing and distribution of the community tax certificates to the cities and municipalities. "The proceeds of the community tax actually and directly collected by the city or municipal treasurer shall accrue to the general fund of the city or municipality concerned. However, proceeds of the community tax collected through the barangay treasurers shall be apportioned as follows: (1) fifty percent shall accrue to the general fund of the city or municipality concerned; and (2) fifty percent shall accrue to the barangay where the tax is collected."

---

tax revenues. The need for improvements in the system of incentives and sanctions cannot be overemphasized since property tax revenues comprise the second largest source of income of most local governments and could be far more productive.

In addition to local revenue-sharing schemes, there are also some interlocal grants, although these are the least documented and studied among the different intergovernmental fiscal transfers. There are two types of pressures for such schemes. From the demand side, component cities, municipalities and barangays expect grants and other forms of assistance given the variations in their local fiscal capacities.[17] From the supply side, the province may have to adopt different mechanisms, the provision of grants and transfers included, to ensure that overall provincial expenditure responsibilities are met. In some sectors, transfers or co-financing schemes may prove to be a better alternative than direct provincial provision.

The case of the Provincial Development Council of Davao del Norte, which includes the provincial governor, the mayors of all the component municipalities, and private sector representatives, provides a good example of how provincial grants to the cities, municipalities and barangays are determined (Burton 2000). In 1999, the council assessed the unmet basic public service needs[18] in the province. Based on this assessment, nearly P27 million from the provincial funds were earmarked for local health, agricultural and cooperative, and infrastructure projects. The allocations among individual LGUs are based on local input and the development priorities of the provincial government. The process is clearly more participatory, transparent and objective than it was prior to the LGC of 1991.

One more major form of interlocal categorical grants is worth mentioning. Section 235 of the LGC provides for a Special Education Fund (SEF) at the local level. The fund comprises an additional 1% levy on the assessed value of real properties that a province, city, or Metropolitan Manila area municipality may impose for the local school boards. In the case of provinces, the total amount of the SEF is equally divided between the provincial school board and municipal school boards. The funds are intended for the operation and maintenance of public schools, construction and repair of school buildings, facilities and equipment, educational research, purchase of books and periodicals, and sports development.

The reports of the Commission on Audit (COA) show only very small and declining amounts of interlocal transfers—P14.2 million in 1995, P2.3 million in 1996, and zero in each of the three following years (1997–1999). The inadequacy of current government accounting conventions partly explains why interlocal grants appear to be smaller than they really are. Government outlays are normally classified in terms of objects of expenditures (e.g., personnel services, maintenance and other operating expenses, capital outlays), or

---

18. Under current practice, the lower-level local governments are required to develop annual development plans and budgets, which are then reviewed at the provincial level. The submitted plans often become a basis for the province's budgetary allocations for the different projects and programs in each of the component LGUs.

19. As indicated by the minimum basic needs indices. See Bautista and Juan (2000) for an introduction to the minimum basic needs approach to development planning adopted in several provinces.

sectoral or functional classifications (e.g., general public services, economic services), and very rarely by recipient units. While the recipients of cash transfers are often reported, the corresponding recipients of transfers in-kind, such as many categorical grants, are seldom indicated. Much better information is clearly needed on interlocal grants.

E. Impact on Local Fiscal Performance, Fiscal Balance, and Regional Development

Given the importance of the IRA, previous studies on intergovernmental fiscal transfers in the Philippines have focused on it. Many of these examined the mismatch between the allocation formula used for the IRA and the devolution of central government functions, which led to revenue shortfalls in a number of provinces and cities during the early years of decentralization (World Bank 1994; Capuno 2001a). Some analysts claim that the financing problem has been solved with the substantial annual increments in the IRA (Loehr and Manasan 1999). On the other hand, some studies have found that these increments may have disincentive effects on local revenue efforts (Manasan 1995, 1997). Additionally, there is the possibility that the IRA may contribute to fiscal imbalances among local government units (Capuno, Manuel and Salvador 2001). In this section we examine the impact of the IRA on local fiscal performance, fiscal balance, and regional development.

1. Overall Trends

An examination of the amounts and composition of central fiscal transfers to local governments reveals three major trends. First, the total amount of these transfers increased from about P17.41 billion in 1990 to nearly P81.8 billion in 1998, or more than four-fold over the nine-year period (Table 11). Second, the revenue-sharing components, the IRA and the shares in the proceeds of certain national taxes, constitute the bulk of total national allotments to LGUs (Table 12). In particular, the share of the IRA has steadily increased from about 63.17% in 1992 to about 94.07% in 1998. The local share in the proceeds of other national taxes, however, appears to be less than some other central grants. Third, the allocation of other types of central fiscal transfers to local governments shows greater variability than the IRA. Except for the Countrywide Development Fund and the Calamity Fund, the respective shares of other categorical grants vary widely from year to year, and some did not get appropriations in recent years.

This variability may be explained by the transient need for such funds or by the accommodationist policies of the national government. The allotment for the Magna Carta for Public Health Workers, for example, was intended as a

TABLE 11

National Government Allotments to Local Government Units, by Type of Funds: 1990–1998
(In million pesos)

Allotments	1990	1991	1992	1993	1994	1995	1996	1997	1998
IRA, Specific Tax Allotment and Local Revenue Stabilization Fund	7000	10023							
Other NALGU components	6958	37235							
Internal Revenue Allotment			18078	36734	46813	51925	56594	56594	76941
Special Shares of LGUs in the Proceeds of National Taxes					1475	1355	948	368	1078
Municipal Development Fund					413	405	712	1051	1254
Metropolitan Manila Development Authority							610	764	737
Magna Carta for Public Health Workers					662	325	164		
Countrywide Industrialization Fund					120		100		
Local Government Empowerment Fund							65	83	255
Local Officials Insurance Premium Fund		44	44	47	47	46	36		
Countrywide Development Fund	1500	2300	2480	2794	2965	1159	1080	903	438
Calamity Fund	898	1000	1400	1598	1970	440	912	344	305
UF-Municipal Development Fund							269	415	193
Miscellaneous Personnel Benefits Fund		13987	2000	1261	2747	105	127	170	273
UF-Support for Foreign-Assisted Projects						165		125	
General Fund Adjustments	253	450	500	246	197	1748	20		2
Contingent Fund	439	500	500	540	787	2	6	15	133
UF-General Funds Adjustments			650	246		6	3	4	
DECS-School Building Program						4978	3910	1	16
Special Financial Assistance to LGUs									7
Palarong Pambansa Fund	23	72	100	143					
Foreign-Assisted Projects Support Fund	343	150	2867	1614	462		91	155	155
Poverty Alleviation Fund							5	5	2
TOTAL	17413	65761	28619	45222	58658	62657	65653	60835	81793

Source: COA Annual Financial Report of the National Government (various years) and General Appropriations Act (various years).

TABLE 12
Percentage Distribution of the National Government Allotments to Local Government Units, by Type of Funds: 1990–1998

Allotments	1990	1991	1992	1993	1994	1995	1996	1997	1998
IRA, Specific Tax Allotment and Local Revenue Stabilization Fund	40.20	15.24							
Other NALGU components	39.96	56.62							
Internal Revenue Allotment			63.17	81.23	79.81	82.87	86.20	93.03	94.07
Special Shares of LGUs in the Proceeds of National Taxes					2.51	2.16	1.44	0.60	1.32
Municipal Development Fund					0.70	0.65	1.08	1.73	1.53
Metropolitan Manila Development Authority							0.93	1.26	0.90
Magna Carta for Public Health Workers					1.13	0.52	0.25		
Countrywide Industrialization Fund					0.20		0.15		
Local Government Empowerment Fund							0.10	0.14	0.31
Local Officials Insurance Premium Fund		0.07	0.15	0.10	0.08	0.07	0.06		
Countrywide Development Fund	8.61	3.50	8.67	6.18	5.05	1.85	1.65	1.48	0.54
Calamity Fund	5.16	1.52	4.89	3.53	3.36	0.70	1.39	0.56	0.37
UF-Municipal Development Fund							0.41	0.68	0.24
Miscellaneous Personnel Benefits Fund		21.27	6.99	2.79	4.68	0.17	0.19	0.28	0.33
UF-Support for Foreign-Assisted Projects						0.26		0.21	
General Fund Adjustments	1.45	0.68	1.75	0.54	0.34	2.79	0.03	0.02	0.00
Contingent Fund	2.52	0.76	1.75	1.19	1.34	0.00	0.01	0.01	0.16
UF-General Funds Adjustments			2.27	0.54		0.01	0.01		
DECS-School Building Program						7.94	5.95	0.00	0.02
Special Financial Assistance to LGUs									0.01
Palarong Pambansa Fund	0.13	0.11	0.35	0.32			0.14		0.19
Foreign-Assisted Projects Support Fund	1.97	0.23	10.02	3.57	0.79				0.01
Poverty Alleviation Fund							0.01		0.00
TOTAL	100.00	100.00	100.00	100.00	100.00	100.00	100.00	100.00	100.00

Source: COA Annual Financial Report of the National Government (various years) and General Appropriations Act (various years).

temporary budget relief for LGUs that complained of unfunded mandates heaped on them under the devolution. Partly used to support the social reform agenda, the poverty alleviation fund received allotments only in 1996 and 1998. In contrast, the CDF has more regular appropriations, perhaps because it is generally perceived to be a source of pork barrel funds. The de facto allocation formula used in the allocation of the CDF (and the DECS School Building Program) requires the approval of the local district's representative to Congress. The CF also gets a regular allotment because it is used to finance emergency operations for national disasters that occur regularly in the Philippines.

Other transfers are also variable or dwindling because they are being crowded out by the IRA. In Figure 9, the proportion of the IRA to the total national budget is shown to be rising. Starting with less than 2% of the national government budget in 1991, the IRA share sharply rose to more than 8% in 1992. The share has been above 10% since then, even in 1998 when the national government withheld the release of the 10% of the IRA as a cash management measure in the wake of the Asian financial crisis.

Thus, from the point of view of the national government, the IRA is a substantial resource outflow. From the point of view of the local governments, the IRA is the single most important form of fiscal transfers (Table 13). The respective IRAs of provinces, cities, and municipalities have grown significantly during the last decade. In 1990, the average real per capita IRAs of provinces, cities and municipalities were P47, P246, and P88, respectively. The corresponding amounts in 1998 were P210, P659, and P424. As a proportion of total local government incomes, the respective IRAs of provinces, cities, and municipalities are sizable. At the start of the 1990s, the share for all LGUs was less than 40%. By 1999, the share jumped to 80% for provinces and 76% for municipalities. Only the cities, which have comparatively vigorous economies, had relatively modest (42%) reliance on the IRA.

The heavy dependence on the IRA is no less true in the case of barangays, which are collectively entitled to 20% of the IRA as per LGC of 1991. Unlike the other LGUs, however, each barangay is assured of a minimum annual IRA share of P80,000, provided that it has at least 100 residents. Currently, the computation of the IRA of each barangay is based on population share (60%) and equal share (40%). As reported in the budget of expenditures and source of financing, the total amount of the IRAs allotted to barangays grew from P8.7 billion in 1994 to P18.04 billion in 1999. The figures represent an annual average of less than half a million pesos for each of the nearly 42,000 barangays in the country. In per capita terms, the amount represents less than P300 per year during the six-year period. Relative to higher level LGUs, these amounts thus are not significant determinants of local public service provision, but the barangays have a narrower set of expenditure functions.

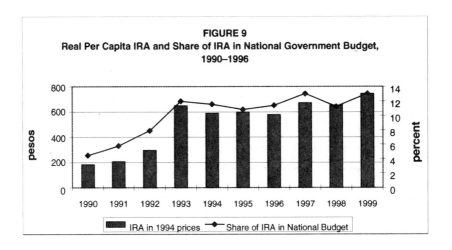

FIGURE 9
Real Per Capita IRA and Share of IRA in National Government Budget,
1990–1996

TABLE 13
The IRA of Provinces, Cities and Municipalities: 1990–1999

	1990	1991	1992	1993	1994	1995	1996	1997	1998	1999
Real Per Capita in Pesos (1994 prices)										
Provinces	47	54	78	129	168	173	163	195	186	210
Cities	246	262	387	643	705	633	611	669	595	659
Municipalities	88	109	152	241	303	321	312	363	364	424
Share in Total *LGU Income* (%)										
Provinces	38.67	40.14	61.88	74.36	74.43	74.46	75.22	75.60	77.25	80.03
Cities	32.71	35.30	48.20	53.78	51.19	45.77	41.64	42.68	42.02	42.46
Municipalities	36.91	42.22	56.85	61.34	69.40	69.03	67.82	68.27	72.59	75.79

Source of data: Commission on Audit.

2. Impact on Local Fiscal Performance

Since most local governments appear to be heavily dependent on the IRA, one of the major policy concerns raised with the implementation of the LGC is the possible negative effect of the IRA on local revenue mobilization efforts. Although some problems were reported during the early post-LGC period (1992–1994), the local revenues of provinces and cities appear to be elastic with respect to the IRA, as measured by the percentage change in local revenues over the percentage change in IRA (Table 14). Applying panel data regression techniques on individual LGU fiscal data for 1990–1996, the average "IRA elasticity" of the local revenues of provinces is estimated to be 1.374 (controlling for year-fixed effects) and 1.242 (controlling for region-fixed effects). The incomes from local sources of cities, on the other hand, are relatively less IRA elastic, with average elasticity estimates of 1.065 (controlling for year-fixed effects) and 0.929 (controlling for region-fixed effects).

During the same period, local government expenditures also appear to be elastic with respect to the IRA, although not as elastic as local revenues. In the case of provinces, the average IRA elasticity is 0.956 and 0.987, depending on whether year-fixed effects or region-fixed effects are controlled for. The corresponding estimates for the cities are 1.065 and 0.668.[19]

TABLE 14
Estimates of the Average "IRA Elasticity" of Local Revenues and Total Expenditures of Provinces and Cities (1990–1996)

LGU	Estimates of Average Elasticity	
	OLS Estimates	Panel Data Estimates[a]
A. Local Revenues		
Provinces	1.330	1.374–1.242
Cities	1.043	1.065–0.929
B. Total Expenditures		
Provinces	0.954	0.956–0.987
Cities	0.709	1.065–0.668

Note: [a] The first figure is obtained controlling for year-fixed effects, while the second figure is obtained controlling for region fixed-effects.
Source: Capuno (2001b).

A more disaggregate analysis shows the effect of the IRA on different sources of local revenues (such as real property taxes and nontax revenues) and various types of local public expenditures (general government, economic development, and capital outlays). The nontax revenues of the local government basically comprise fees and payments for the issuance of licenses and permits. Due to unavailability of more detailed data, the various expenditures items used here simply follow government accounting standards. General government services pertain to the expenditures on major local administrative offices, such as

---

20. These estimates are also adjusted for the possible effects of the change in the IRA formula, the devolution of central government functions, and the presence of national government-operated hospitals in the locality.

the executive, legislative, treasury, accounting, legal, budget, and police services. Economic development services refer to the outlays for agricultural, veterinary, engineering, and public utilities services. As in the previous exercise, individual LGU fiscal data for the years 1990–1996 are used to estimate the corresponding IRA elasticity.

TABLE 15
Estimates of the Average "IRA Elasticity" of Various Local Government
Revenues and Expenditures

Local Governments	Local Revenues		Local Public Expenditures		
	Real Property Taxes	Nontax Revenues	General Government Services	Economic Development Services	Capital Outlays
Provinces	0.585	0.355	0.839	0.940	1.24
Cities	0.364	0.187	0.720	0.804	0.201

Note: Estimates for the various revenue sources are obtained controlling for the devolution of function in 1993, adoption of the new IRA formula in 1992, presence of national hospitals in the locality and region-fixed effects. Estimates for the various expenditure services are obtained controlling for the devolution of function in 1993 and region-fixed effects.

Source: Capuno (2001c).

The results in Table 15 are generally consistent with the aggregate analysis, although the absolute amounts are lower. Both types of local government revenues appear to be positively influenced by the IRA increments, both in provinces and cities. Interestingly, tax revenues from real properties exhibit greater responsiveness to the IRA than nontax revenues. As expected, the various types of local public expenditures also show high positive responses to the increments in the IRA. More notably, the capital outlays of provinces appear to be very elastic with respect to the IRA, which is important because the IRA is largely a general-purpose block grant.

Although the previous results are highly indicative, the analysis should be extended for a more complete assessment of the IRA's impact on local fiscal performance. First, the period of analysis has to be updated since both the Asian financial crisis and the recent political turbulence in the country may have had implications for the financial performance of both the national government and local governments. Second, the investigations should also cover social services, such as health, nutrition, education, and population services. Third, the municipalities have not been investigated. A negative effect of the IRA on local revenue mobilization may be more likely in municipalities since most depend highly on their IRAs and they have narrower and relatively poorer tax bases than the provinces and cities. Finally, the impact of the other types of central fiscal transfers and intralocal fiscal transfers on local fiscal performance have yet to be determined, although this will be difficult under the current government accounting and reporting practices.

3. Impact on Fiscal Balance

In addition to their effects on local fiscal performance, intergovernmental fiscal transfers may also be assessed with respect to their impact on vertical fiscal balance, defined here as the relative real per capita revenues of the various local government levels. With such a comparison, the contribution of various forms of fiscal transfers to the differences in real per capita revenues may then be determined. Fiscal imbalance may also be measured horizontally, i.e., comparing units of the same level.

The relative impact of the IRA and, to a lesser extent, the other fiscal transfers to local governments on vertical fiscal balance may be inferred from Figure 10. In the diagram, the average total revenues and their major components are reported for provinces (P), cities (C) and municipalities (M). The averages are computed for five periods: 1990–1991 (pre-decentralization), 1992–1994 and 1995–1996 (transition periods), 1996–1997 and 1998–1999 (post-adjustment periods). The three major components of public revenues are revenues from local sources, IRA, and other external revenues. The latter includes all grants, borrowings, and interlocal government transfers.

During the last decade, there has been a general upward trend in the total revenues of provinces, cities and municipalities, although at varying rates of growth. Among the three levels of local governments, the cities have the highest average real per capita revenues, increasing from about P750 during 1990–1991 to nearly double that amount during the last two years of the decade. In contrast, the provinces have the lowest average per capita revenues throughout the last decade.

The unevenness in the average real per capita revenues across the three local government levels is mainly due to the differences in their local revenues and the apparent bias of the current IRA allocation formula for cities. The differences in local revenues may be expected given the variability in economic development and in the tax collection efficiency among local governments. In many cases, taxable economic activities are concentrated in urban areas, and cities have broader tax authorities than provinces and municipalities. In addition, the proceeds from real property taxes, sand and gravel taxes and other specific levies are shared between the provinces and municipalities, while cities have sole claim on these same levies.

Apparently, the IRA worsens the fiscal imbalances across local government levels. In each of the five sub-periods, the average real per capita IRA of

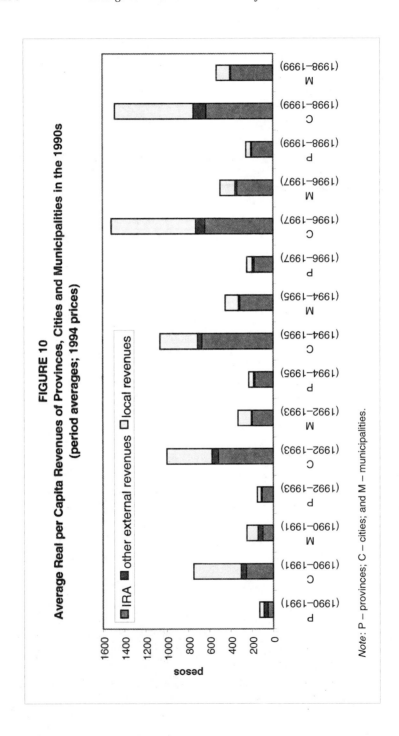

FIGURE 10

Average Real per Capita Revenues of Provinces, Cities and Municipalities in the 1990s

(period averages; 1994 prices)

Note: P – provinces; C – cities; and M – municipalities.

cities is more than twice the combined corresponding amounts for provinces and municipalities. Effectively, the IRA therefore is not sensitive to differences in the local fiscal capacities despite its seemingly equitable allocation (i.e., mandated equal shares of the provinces and cities in the total IRA).

Other external revenues appear to have minimal effects on the overall fiscal balance, which is not surprising since their contribution to total local government revenues is small. However, given the current government accounting conventions noted above, the actual amount of interlocal transfers is likely to be understated, since the expenditures of higher-level local governments are effectively in-kind transfers and their recipients are not reported. Hence, the picture of vertical fiscal balance may be different when transfers are indexed in expenditures instead of revenues.

Since the IRA is the major source of local revenue, it is necessarily also a major determinant of local public expenditures. As shown in the previous section, local government expenditures appear to be elastic with respect to the IRA. In Table 16, the average real per capita expenditures of provinces, cities and municipalities on the different types of local public services are listed for the period 1995–1999. As can be observed, city residents enjoy a huge advantage over the municipal (mostly rural) population in terms of levels of expenditure. A comparison between the average per capita spending on health services in 1999, for example, reveals that the amount spent by cities exceeds the combined outlays of provinces and municipalities. This finding is even more critical considering that many city residents also benefit from provincial health services, partly because many of the hospitals devolved to provinces are located in cities (Capuno 1997).

The relative importance of the IRA in the local budget and the effective bias of its allocation toward the cities could help explain the recent spate of conversion of many urbanized municipalities into cities under the decentralization program. Between 1992 and 1999, there were 24 newly converted cities, with many more waiting for congressional approval. Although the cities have a smaller collective share in the IRA (23%) than the municipalities (34%), their respective individual shares are bigger than the municipalities because there are about 15 municipalities to each city in the country. While the conversion of some municipalities is economically justifiable, the upsurge of conversion to cities may worsen fiscal imbalances because provinces will lose part of their revenue shares from taxes collected by the municipalities that are converted into cities. The increasing number of cities, however, may lead to lower average real per capita IRA allocations to the cities. In any case, a moratorium on the conversion of municipalities into cities or the imposition of more stringent criteria may be necessary. The impact of conversions should be examined, and fiscal imbalances should be addressed directly with adjustments in the IRA.

TABLE 16
Average Real Per Capita Expenditures of Provinces, Cities and Municipalities
by Type of Services: 1996–1999
(in 1994 pesos)

Type of Services	1995	1996	1997	1998	1999
A. General public services					
Provinces	68.70	67.02	78.13	76.97	76.68
Cities	474.87	491.08	553.14	497.33	504.02
Municipalities	232.86	231.56	268.42	266.26	281.85
B. Education services					
Provinces	12.63	10.52	17.10	15.09	12.67
Cities	143.34	161.18	193.25	196.35	174.52
Municipalities	25.99	24.59	26.02	23.22	22.17
C. Health services					
Provinces	49.97	52.52	59.34	56.95	56.52
Cities	103.18	110.98	117.72	120.02	54.29
Municipalities	42.55	45.74	55.06	54.24	118.68
D. Labor and employment services					
Provinces	0.14	0.10	0.22	0.18	0.15
Cities	2.02	1.93	2.51	0.96	0.12
Municipalities	0.06	0.03	0.11	0.08	0.39
E. Housing and community development					
Provinces	17.95	5.33	6.78	6.02	6.31
Cities	99.91	98.95	98.12	86.77	89.73
Municipalities	15.80	19.25	19.46	17.41	20.10
F. Social welfare services					
Provinces	3.36	3.82	4.91	4.22	4.21
Cities	27.18	27.86	31.08	28.84	27.69
Municipalities	12.44	12.52	14.37	14.52	15.40
G. Economic services					
Provinces	63.67	67.15	76.76	68.29	71.72
Cities	451.33	406.80	444.86	107.53	395.80
Municipalities	113.23	101.31	116.52	356.13	113.36
H. Other services					
Provinces	15.14	10.91	16.85	17.59	16.91
Cities	147.81	145.75	180.70	171.36	190.45
Municipalities	25.63	21.30	29.96	25.33	26.87

Source of raw data: Commission on Audit (COA) and *Philippine Statistical Yearbook* (various years).

4. Impact on Regional Development

The impact of the IRA on regional development is briefly evaluated in this section. We focus on the IRA because of its importance and the paucity of data on other central fiscal transfers. The United Nations Development Program (UNDP) human development index (HDI) for each of the provinces in the country is used as a measure of regional development. The HDI is a composite index of infant mortality rate (a standard measure of health status), functional literacy (a proxy for human capital), and average per capita family income (to indicate a person's command over economic resources). The Philippine Human Development Network and the UNDP have published the HDI for each of the provinces in the country for the years 1990, 1994, and 1997. The HDI is between 0 and 1, with 1 indicating the highest possible score.

The IRA has at least an indirect effect on the development indicators included in the HDI. For example, the availability of and access to primary health services, now devolved to local government units, determine the family's health status, especially in rural areas where private health services are beyond the reach of most people. In addition to the provision of health and other social services, local governments also spend on economic and infrastructure services, two factors critical to local business activities. These services then have direct effects on personal incomes in the locality.

Determining the actual impact of the IRA on the HDI poses a number of problems. First, the effect of the IRA on the HDI is not contemporaneous, since the HDI indicators do not vary widely on a year-to-year basis. Hence, a longer time series data than are currently available would be required. Second, the expenditures of the national and local governments both independently and jointly affect the HDI. National labor policies, for example, determine the minimum wage and other employment conditions. Central grants for local skill-building programs and livelihood projects enhance the local government's capability to uplift family incomes. More detailed information on other types of central fiscal transfers would help isolate their respective marginal effects on regional development.

Despite these statistical problems, we undertake a basic analysis of the possible impact of the IRA on the HDI. Given data availability, we focus on the provincial level. A simple correlation analysis between the provinces' real per capita IRAs and HDI scores is performed for 1990, 1994, and 1997. The estimated correlation coefficients are 0.02, 0.10, and 0.13, respectively, which show a positive but rather weak relationship between the IRA and HDI. This relationship is displayed in Figures 11 to 13, which show a scatter plot of the two variables for each of the three years for which data are available.

Two broad patterns may be discerned from the scatter plots. First, there has been a general improvement in HDI, since more provinces appear at the upper tail end of the HDI distribution in 1997 than in 1990. Second, the variance in the provinces' IRAs appears to have narrowed under the fiscal decentralization program, with the minimum IRA received increasing significantly after 1990. Given the way the IRA is allocated and the problems noted above, the weak relationship between contemporaneous IRA and HDI figures is expected. It is, however, interesting and worth investigating further that the general

FIGURE 11
HDI and Real Per Capita IRA of Provinces: 1990

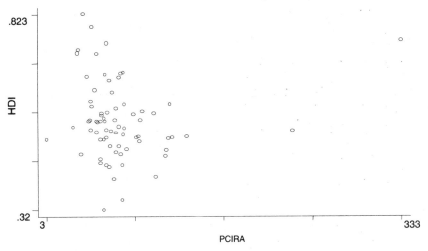

Note: PCIRA is the per capita IRA.

FIGURE 12
HDI and Real Per Capita IRA of Provinces: 1994

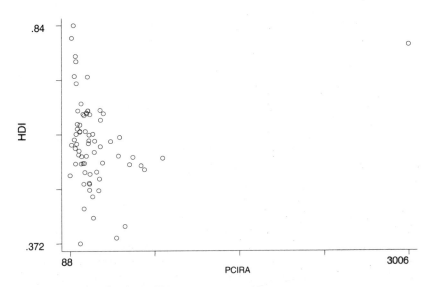

Note: PCIRA is the per capita IRA.

FIGURE 13
HDI and Real Per Capita IRA of Provinces: 1997

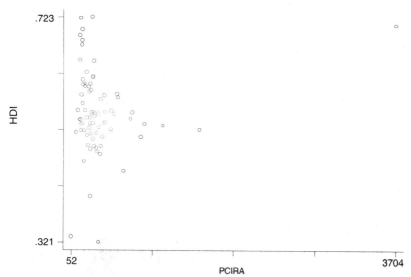

Note: PCIRA is the per capita IRA.

improvement in HDI coincided with the huge increments in the IRA under the fiscal decentralization program. Understanding this relationship more fully could help address imbalances in regional development in general and the design of a fiscal equalization grant schemes in particular.

F. Capital Outlays, Infrastructure and Capital Grants to Local Government

The Medium-Term Philippine Development Plan 1999–2004 (MTPDP) contains the blueprint of the country's infrastructure development objectives and strategies. One of the main strategies to spur infrastructure development is the increased participation of the private sector and, to a lesser extent, local government units. The relatively smaller role accorded to LGUs is due to their limited financial and technical capabilities. More importantly, local government units do not normally have the incentives to undertake infrastructure projects that encompass areas larger than their own political jurisdictions.

Nevertheless, local governments can contribute, especially in the provision of small-scale public works and other basic infrastructure. Thus, the MTPDP states that the "government will clearly establish the interfacing of national and local governments in the planning, designing, construction and operation of infrastructure". In addition, it also declares that the "coordination among agencies, LGUs, the private sector and affected communities in the formulation and implementation of infrastructure plans and projects shall be improved".

The major areas where local government participation is expected to be prominent are urban transportation, roads, irrigation, flood control and drainage, and solid waste management. The coordination of urban transportation services and traffic control is one of the principal tasks of MMDA, the agency that coordinates metropolitan-wide services in the National Capital Region. Many of the major infrastructure programs of the national government are in the NCR.

While the principal responsibility for local roads is assigned to LGUs, the MTPDP states that the national government will provide appropriate assistance to LGUs that are financially and technically constrained. This strategy is consistent with the provisions of the Agricultural and Fisheries Modernization Act, which mandates local and regional development councils to draw up plans for local roads to complement national roads, especially in improving access to priority agricultural areas and urban/industrial centers and tourism areas. A significant role in the provision of public works for irrigation, flood control and drainage, and solid waste management is also assigned to local governments as per the LGC of 1991. Correspondingly, the national government's assistance to LGUs is geared towards training and building up their capabilities in these areas.

1. Regional Allocation of Capital Outlays

The overall trend in the total capital outlays of the national government is to consistently allocate a disproportionate share to the National Capital Region. The bias for the NCR and other regional centers is a common finding of previous studies [Serafica 1998]. The major components of the total capital outlays of the national government are infrastructure spending, capital grants to local governments, and equity contributions in government corporations. As shown in Figure 14, the total capital outlays of the national government went down from P54.73 billion in 1994 to P32.81 billion in 1996, and then went up to P63.93 billion in 1998. In 1999, the total amount dropped by about P2.2 billion from the previous year's total. Although total capital outlays rose from 1994 to 1999, the share of capital outlays in the total budget of the national government decreased from about 17% in 1994 to 10.4% in 1999.

During the period 1994–1999, the annual share of the National Capital Region in the total capital outlays of the national government never went below 39% (Table 17). NCR's share in 1999 was about 62%, but this was 20 percentage points lower than its share in 1994 (80.64%). Also, the regions around Metropolitan Manila (i.e., Regions III and IV) were also consistently among

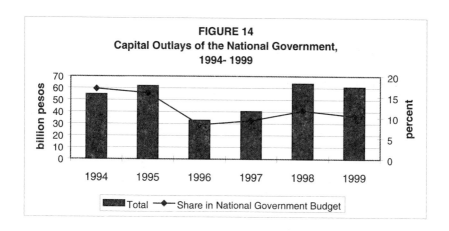

FIGURE 14
Capital Outlays of the National Government,
1994- 1999

the top recipients of the national government's capital outlays during the period.

A comparison between the regional allocations of national government with local government capital outlays will indicate whether there is complementarity in spending between the two levels of government. Between 1990 and 1997, the combined capital outlays of LGUs have increased from about P1.2 billion in 1990 to about P5.1 billion in 1997 (Table 18). Between 1994 and 1997, the capital outlays of LGUs represented less than 10% of the national government's capital outlays. It also appears that the regions with disproportionately high shares in the national total are among the regions with relatively high LGU capital outlays. The NCR and Region IV, for example, together accounted for more than 40% of the annual total capital outlays of local governments during the period 1990–1997.

To the extent that capital outlays determine infrastructure investments and, therefore, regional growth and development, the regional allocation of the national budget has implications for regional inequities. A review of the implicit criteria used in the regional allocation of the budgets of key national government agencies in 1999 suggests that infrastructure spending is not as sensitive to the poverty rate as the expenditures on health and other social services [Mercado 1999]. The poverty rate is negatively correlated with the regional budgets of the Departments of Transportation and Communication (–0.069), Agriculture (–0.132), and Health (–0.186). However, a relatively strong positive correlation is observed for the Department of Trade and Industry (0.709) and the Department of Education, Culture and Sports (0.758). Also, there is a rather weak but still a positive relationship for the Departments of Public Works and Highways (0.266) and Social Work and Development (0.216). Although no firm causal relationship between the poverty rate and the national agency's regional budgets can be inferred from these correlation results, it is worth noting that a relatively strong and positive correlation is observed prior to the fiscal decentralization program in all of the above-mentioned national government agencies. These results underscore the need for greater consistency in the regional allocation of the budgets of the different national line agencies.

2. Infrastructure and Capital Grants to Local Governments

The importance of infrastructure investments to regional growth and development in the Philippines is emphasized in a number of studies (Lamberte *et al.* 1993). Thus, one important consideration in infrastructure investment planning is to achieve consistency in the investment plans of all government agencies, including LGUs. Lack of coordination across agencies and levels of government can lead to wasteful duplications, delays, or inefficient provision of basic infrastructure.

The regional allocation of the national government's total capital outlays will determine the availability and conditions of basic infrastructure services in the countryside. The amount of capital grants to local governments will also have a strong impact on improving local welfare, especially in far-flung areas. The combined outlays of the national government for infrastructure and capital grants to local governments increased from about P53 billion in 1995 to about P64.6 billion in 1999.[20] The combined amount constitutes more than 60% of the total capital outlays in most years during the period 1995–1999. However, a comparison of the respective shares of infrastructure expenditures and capital transfers (to local governments) in the total capital outlays of the national governments reveals that, despite the decentralization program, the national government is still a major direct provider of infrastructure services. During the period 1995–1999, the share of capital transfers has not exceeded 25% of the total capital outlays, while the share of national infrastructure expenditures has not fallen below 34%.

While the national government provides certain infrastructure services for economic reasons and for expediency, the LGC of 1991 mandated a number of services to be devolved to the LGUs. Despite this mandate, however, the national government still continues to provide services to the LGUs such as education services, hospitals and other medium-scale infrastructure programs. The total amount the national government allots on local public services is

---

21. The estimates for the total capital outlays presented here are different from those contained in Tables 17 and 18. The figures reported in this section are based on the reports of the Commission on Audit, which contains the regional breakdown. The latter is based on *Budget of Expenditures and Sources of Financing* published by the Department of Budget and Management, which contains the breakdown of the total capital outlays into recipient units. Inconsistencies in government reports and the lack of detailed information make comparison across data sources difficult.

TABLE 17
Capital Outlays of the National Government, by Region: 1994–1999

Region	1994	1995	1996	1997	1998	1999
A. In million pesos						
TOTAL	54734.19	61784.28	32812.36	40383.59	63927.95	60903.20
Region I	1014.47	1505.94	1777.79	2533.00	1955.46	1251.56
Region II	917.04	987.86	1292.83	1932.00	1738.53	1468.55
Region III	1164.53	3557.97	2029.05	3514.80	3823.41	2861.60
Region IV	1657.14	2483.09	2181.10	4867.90	3655.75	4554.17
Region V	760.60	2062.89	2272.95	3014.20	3299.66	1789.15
Region VI	1045.10	1097.00	1902.89	2851.10	1554.97	1515.23
Region VII	381.94	1089.91	127.63	2317.90	1411.33	1181.34
Region VIII	585.88	927.65	1313.15	1819.20	1152.48	1340.06
Region IX	453.65	723.10	520.36	1902.80	766.77	1078.14
Region X	672.82	1231.84	1200.69	1725.80	1644.48	1127.99
Region XI	513.61	1369.43	1289.06	2286.90	1291.53	1577.98
Region XII	582.27	1023.91	601.25	2143.40	697.68	711.37
CARAGA	–	101.34	838.85	1850.90	1746.43	239.76
CAR	847.46	933.66	1228.31	2910.30	1224.25	1400.63
ARMM	0.68	960.76	50.95	90.60	25.29	1169.62
NCR	44137.02	41727.94	13085.52	52609.20	37894.93	37636.04

TABLE 17 (cont.)

Region	1994	1995	1996	1997	1998	1999
B. Percent share						
TOTAL	100.00	100.00	100.00	100.00	100.00	100.00
Region I	1.85	2.44	5.42	4.40	3.06	2.05
Region II	1.68	1.60	3.94	3.43	2.79	2.41
Region III	2.13	5.76	6.18	9.65	5.98	4.70
Region IV	3.03	4.02	6.65	8.19	5.72	7.48
Region V	1.39	3.34	6.93	5.89	5.16	2.94
Region VI	1.91	1.78	5.80	4.29	2.43	2.49
Region VII	0.70	1.76	3.74	2.58	2.21	1.94
Region VIII	1.07	1.50	4.00	2.73	1.80	2.20
Region IX	0.83	1.17	1.59	1.45	1.20	1.77
Region X	1.23	1.99	3.66	0.88	2.57	1.85
Region XI	0.94	2.22	3.93	3.28	2.02	2.59
Region XII	1.06	1.66	1.83	5.16	1.09	1.17
CARAGA	–	0.16	2.56	4.40	2.73	0.39
CAR	1.55	1.51	3.74	3.56	1.92	2.30
ARMM	0.00	1.56	0.16	0.20	0.04	1.92
NCR	80.63	67.54	39.88	39.31	59.28	61.80

Source: Commission on Audit.

TABLE 18
Capital Outlays of Local Governments, by Region: 1990–1997

Region	1990	1991	1992	1993	1994	1995	1996	1997
A. In million pesos								
TOTAL	1191.02	1901.14	2743.52	3816.72	6508.14	7004.91	6320.44	5106.48
Region I	18.70	10.09	50.82	38.22	231.39	287.49	479.54	396.01
Region II	4.56	15.87	57.63	38.38	141.24	227.61	152.13	139.01
Region III	82.98	74.15	144.88	228.59	333.64	401.52	366.86	78.42
Region IV	173.61	256.76	347.11	245.11	909.89	910.65	919.47	871.41
Region V	22.75	21.67	62.76	69.53	173.35	177.90	182.52	172.58
Region VI	31.67	72.06	150.38	166.87	422.70	510.69	431.88	355.60
Region VII	81.19	61.74	245.78	278.80	496.75	465.11	578.35	86.83
Region VIII	18.63	20.29	66.71	82.08	209.29	183.94	242.05	260.54
Region IX	25.02	30.39	130.57	242.55	312.56	387.85	188.16	165.14
Region X	20.80	48.83	147.57	319.56	519.74	590.52	479.45	74.39
Region XI	31.67	45.91	209.86	233.87	608.90	557.81	702.03	369.91
Region XII	13.28	15.58	51.99	147.84	311.08	408.65	342.20	434.07
CARAGA	–	–	–	–	–	–	–	61.29
CAR	4.65	8.97	27.48	21.42	94.77	81.44	78.74	42.30
ARMM	–	–	–	–	–	–	–	–
NCR	661.52	1218.84	1049.96	1703.90	1742.82	1813.71	1177.04	1598.98

TABLE 18 (cont.)

Region	1990	1991	1992	1993	1994	1995	1996	1997
B. Percent share								
Total	100.00	100.00	100.00	100.00	100.00	100.00	100.00	100.00
Region I	1.57	0.53	1.85	1.00	3.56	4.10	7.59	7.76
Region II	0.38	0.83	2.10	1.01	2.17	3.25	2.41	2.72
Region III	6.97	3.90	5.28	5.99	5.13	5.73	5.80	1.54
Region IV	14.58	13.51	12.65	6.42	13.98	13.00	14.55	17.06
Region V	1.91	1.14	2.29	1.82	2.66	2.54	2.89	3.38
Region VI	2.66	3.79	5.48	4.37	6.49	7.29	6.83	6.96
Region VII	6.82	3.25	8.96	7.30	7.63	6.64	9.15	1.70
Region VIII	1.56	1.07	2.43	2.15	3.2	2.63	3.83	5.10
Region IX	2.10	1.60	4.76	6.35	4.80	5.54	2.98	3.23
Region X	1.75	2.57	5.38	8.37	7.99	8.43	7.59	1.46
Region XI	2.66	2.41	7.65	6.13	9.36	7.96	11.1	7.24
Region XII	1.11	0.82	1.90	3.87	4.78	5.83	5.41	8.50
CARAGA	–	–	–	–	–	–	–	1.20
CAR	0.39	0.47	1.00	0.56	1.46	1.16	1.25	0.83
ARMM	–	–	–	–	–	–	–	–
NCR	55.54	64.11	38.27	44.64	26.78	25.89	18.62	31.31

Source: Department of Budget and Management.

substantially greater than the IRA, and the distribution of these resources seems to aggravate further the fiscal imbalances in the country (Capuno, Manuel and Salvador 2001b).

Among the major types of capital grants to local governments, two have gained relative importance in the last decade. First, under the Infrastructure Program Act of 1995, authorized LGUs may receive appropriations from the DECS for the construction of school buildings under the DECS School Building Program, which is administered by the Department of Public Works and Highways. Second, the Countrywide Development Fund is used to finance a broader scope of infrastructure projects and local livelihood programs. In 1998, the CDF went to several types of activities, including the construction, repair and maintenance of public buildings (8.1%), the purchase and repair of motor vehicles (8.9%), the construction, repair and maintenance of roads and bridges (7.3%), livelihood projects (10.6%), and health and education services (21.1%).[21]

Table 19 depicts the regional distribution of the DECS School Building Program, the Countrywide Development Fund, and the combined infrastructure outlays (both for completed and unfinished projects) of all provinces, cities and municipalities.[22] In 1999, the major infrastructure expenditures of local governments were the construction, repair and maintenance of streets and bridges (P5 billion), public buildings (P4.8 billion), educational buildings (P4.3 billion), residential buildings (P3.6 billion), water supply system (P1.6 billion), hospitals and other health buildings (P0.9 billion), and other public construction projects (P2.3 billion).

In addition to the great similarity in the types of infrastructure projects that are supported by central capital grants and local funds, available data also suggest that the two may be complementary in terms of geographical targeting. As depicted in this table, funds from the DECS School Building Program and CDF are relatively low in the NCR and Region V (Bicol), where LGU infrastructure spending is high. Conversely, the capital grants tend to be high in regions where LGU spending is low (e.g., Regions III, VI, VII, and IX). There are, however, some exceptions. In the CAR, both capital grants and local infra-

---

22. Roughly the same trend in the allocation of CDF is observed for 1996 and 1997.

23. The LGU infrastructure expenditures here are culled from *the Annual Survey of Construction Projects of Local Governments* conducted by the National Statistics Office. The respondents in this survey are the local government engineers, treasurers, planning officers and budget officers. The reported figures, which include both completed and ongoing projects for the year, are larger than the amounts reported in Table 18.

TABLE 19
**Real Per Capita Distribution of the DECS-School Building Program,
Countrywide Development Fund and LGU Infrastructure Expenditures by
Region: 1997–1999
(in 1994 pesos)**

Region	DECS		CDF		LGU	
	1998	1999	1997	1998	1998	1999
I	21.1	16.4	13.2	5.7	178.6	286.9
II	22.0	22.1	20.0	8.2	163.9	115.6
III	18.9	17.4	13.1	5.2	158.2	131.1
IV	22.8	20.1	9.4	3.5	156.4	255.0
V	22.0	22.2	11.0	5.6	80.0	88.4
VI	20.1	18.4	16.5	5.9	107.5	102.0
VII	23.0	22.6	15.2	8.6	166.1	164.6
VIII	25.3	22.7	7.7	2.6	172.8	208.8
IX	25.7	25.8	10.4	4.0	84.0	96.2
X	23.7	24.1	10.6	6.2	264.4	366.1
XI	21.0	20.7	9.7	3.0	100.8	102.1
XII	38.7	43.9	9.8	4.3	80.	64.6
CARAGA	23.5	23.8	3.9	0.8	–	–
CAR	23.2	20.9	21.7	2.7	405.7	226.3
ARMM	11.4	11.9	8.3	3.1	45.8	22.2
NCR	19.8	16.3	4.7	1.6	342.0	495.7

structure spending are relatively high. In contrast, both figures are relatively low in the ARMM.[23]

Although the available data are useful in characterizing broad trends in the allocation of capital grants, they are not sufficiently detailed for a more in-depth comparison of LGUs, for example, according to their income classes, levels of socioeconomic development, revenue potentials, etc. Thus, it is very difficult to make a definitive assessment of the overall impact of capital grants on local welfare.

3. ODA-Funded Capital Grants

With the continued vulnerability of the economy to both external and internal shocks, funds from Official Development Assistance (ODA) remain a principal source of financing of public infrastructure programs. During the last

---

24. Note that there is no reported local infrastructure outlay for the CARAGA region. However, this is likely due to accounting errors, since the provinces that now constitute the CARAGA region are still classified under their old regions.

decade, there was an effort to widen the LGUs' access to ODA funds. Recently, an ODA-funded capital-grants mechanism was restructured to direct foreign assistance to local governments.

The total amount of ODA commitments has grown from about US$4.6 billion in 1990 to about US$7.3 billion in 1998, although the total amount was highest at US$9.3 billion in 1996 (Table 20). Despite the increased amount of ODA commitments, the actual utilization of the funds has been less than 50%. This low rate is due to a number of factors, including delays arising from court-issued temporary restraining orders for public works or land conversions under the agrarian reform law and poor coordination among various national government agencies concerned.

The bulk of the ODA funds is allotted to projects with nationwide or multiregional coverage. However, the NCR, the single biggest recipient of ODA funds among the regions in the country, accounted for about 20% of the amounts availed in 1999. In contrast, the total amount committed to regions in Mindanao (total of seven regions) is only about 4% of the total. In fact, it appears that the Autonomous Region of Muslim Mindanao and the Cordillera Autonomous Region received no separate ODA allocation during most of the last decade. The apparent ODA regional biases are similar to biases in the national government's capital outlays discussed above.

Partly to increase the absorption of ODA funds, the Municipal Development Fund (MDF), originally established in 1984, was restructured to increase LGU access to foreign aid and other forms of assistance. As per the LGC of 1991, local chief executives (mayors and governors) are authorized to seek other sources of financing in the form of grants or donations from local or foreign agencies (such as ODA) without the prior clearance or approval of the national government or a higher-level local government.

To enable local governments to tap the ODA loan components, which require sovereign commitment, the MDF was reconfigured. The MDF is a revolving fund capitalized and funded by foreign assistance or grants from bilateral and multilateral sources such as the World Bank (WB), the ADB, the USAID, and the Overseas Economic Corporation Fund (OECF). Resources under the MDF are made available to local governments through the Department of Finance to bankroll local projects in accordance with agreements between bilateral/multilateral institutions and the national government.

Presently, the MDF has a total fund base of P1.1 billion, making it an important conduit for resources to LGUs. Projects financed under the MDF are mostly urban-based, although adjustments are made to accommodate more rural-based projects, such as the establishment of windows for financing livelihood and natural resource management projects of low-income local governments (Llanto 1997).

Administered by the DOF's Bureau of Local Government Finance, the

TABLE 20
Official Development Assistance to the Philippines in the 1990s
(in million US dollars)

Regions	Total Commitment on Ongoing Projects (as of the end of the period)				Total Cumulative Availment of Ongoing Projects (as of the end of the period)			
	1990	1993	1996	1998	1990	1993	1996	1998
Region I	42	49	2	2	26	43	2	2
Region II	–	–	–	–	–	–	–	–
Region III	58	353	532	579	–	23	174	330
Region IV	350	462	696	328	57	75	477	111
Region V	175	175	231	131	27	154	56	3
Region VI	23	–	–	110	23	–	–	–
Region VII	117	330	627	453	4	100	218	223
Region VIII	79	44	127	63	17	24	50	7
Region IX	–	7	7	–	–	–	7	–
Region X	3	–	40	55	3	–	2	4
Region XI	43	27	75	66	14	4	11	21
Region XII	32	39	100	176	–	9	27	43
Region XIII	–	–	–	–	–	–	–	–
ARMM	–	–	–	–	–	–	–	–
CAR	15	–	–	–	1	–	–	–
NCR	683	1125	1405	1363	163	403	539	547
Inter/multi-regional	1198	150	3391	3218	369	670	1235	1079
Nationwide	1787	2429	2060	805	520	917	1327	394
Total	4590	6538	9291	7348	1223	2422	4124	2761

Source of raw data: National Economic Development Authority.

MDF has three basic fund facilities, namely loans, grants, and a mix of loans, grants and equities (for eligible LGUs and subprojects). Under the MDF, all levels and income classes of LGUs are eligible for financing, but eligible subprojects are determined by the terms of agreement between the national government and foreign donors or lending institutions.[24]

---

25. To access loans under the MDF, the LGU is required to submit a resolution from the local sanggunian (i.e., local legislative body) authorizing the local chief executive to apply and enter into a loan agreement with the MDF-DOF. In addition, the borrowing unit must submit a project description, COA-audited financial statements for the last three years, list of elected officials and department heads, and, if available, a feasibility study and an updated socioeconomic profile of the LGU. Subprojects that are not eligible for funding under the MDF are land acquisition, payment of salaries, bonuses, taxes and fees, contingency funds for calamities, and the purchase of stocks and other nonviable investment instruments.

The loan component under the MDF is based on project requirements, although it is limited to the borrowing capacity of the local government. The interest rate charged is normally below the market rate, making it the preferred choice of many local governments. The current interest rate is 14%, which is fixed for the entire duration of the loan, which can range from three to five years. The terms of the loan normally allow a grace period of three years on principal payments for loan terms extending for five years or more. Since most LGUs have poor local tax bases, the IRA effectively becomes the only collateral for loans. The grant component of the MDF provides for 50 to 90% of a subproject's cost, depending on the type of the program, subproject and the income class of the local government. The LGU equity contribution is set to a minimum of 10% of the total project cost. The equity contribution comes from local budgetary appropriations and must be deposited in a trust fund account.

The overall impact of the MDF on regional development has yet to be established. Available records show that the total amount released under the MDF has steadily increased from about P405.2 million in 1995 to about P1,254.1 million in 1998. However, there is no available regional breakdown of the MDF allocations. A cursory review of the infrastructure projects funded under the MDF shows that both urban and rural infrastructure projects are supported, although urban seem more important. For the period 1993–2007, the total loan commitment to the various urban infrastructure projects amounts to more than US$260 million.[25]

The MDF has strong potential as a conduit of ODA funds for local development projects, but some issues have been identified. First, the MDF's policy governing board does not include representation from LGUs. Second, the MDF does not assume responsibility for technical appraisal and this slows down the project proposals. Third, there is not adequate transparency and uniformity in MDF guidelines. Fourth, there is not an adequate focus on targeting LGUs that are unable to get access to commercial credit (Alonzo 1999). Finally, the MDF

---

26. The biggest among these projects are the Local Government Finance and Development Project (LOGOFIND) and the Third Municipal Development Project (MDP 3), both financed by the World Bank. Unlike the World Bank financed projects that are intended for all LGUs in the country, the projects financed by ADB have a more limited set of beneficiaries. Among ADB-funded projects are the Clark Area Municipal Development Project (CAMDP), the Metro Cebu Development Project 3 (MDCP 3), the Subic Bay Area Municipal Development Project (SBADP) and the Philippine Regional Municipal Development Project (PRMDP). In addition, ADB is the major source of loans for rural infrastructure projects, such as the Bukidnon Integrated Area Development Project (US$30 million) and the Southern Philippines Irrigation Sector Project (US$60 million).

has been criticized as too centralized in Metropolitan Manila. This raises the transaction costs of both the MDF and the prospective local government borrowers. Perhaps for this reason, many of the MDF-funded local projects are urban-based, since local governments in remote areas are comparatively disadvantaged.

G. Summary and Policy Recommendations

1. Main Findings

Our analyses suggest several major findings. First, there was only a modest improvement in regional growth and development during the 1990s. Poverty incidence remains very high in low-income regions in the country and there has not been any significant improvement in imbalances in health status across regions during the last decade. The persistence of the gaps in regional development may be traced to the uneven growth in average family income across regions, the continued vulnerability of the economy to both external and internal shocks, and macroeconomic policies adopted before and during the period.

Second, the prospects for macroeconomic stability and growth critically depend on the ability of the new administration to contain the burgeoning budget deficit and pass crucial economic reform bills, especially those concerning the power and the banking sectors. In addition, the new administration must also enhance overall tax collection effort and explore alternative revenue sources.

Third, despite the fiscal decentralization program adopted in the 1990s, the central government remains the dominant player in the fiscal affairs of the nation. Its share in both total public revenues and total public expenditures far exceeds that of the local governments. The national government affects the trends in regional growth and development in two ways. First, macroeconomic policies and the spatial distribution of the national government's budget directly influence regional economic activities. Second, central fiscal transfers to local governments, which constitute the bulk of the total intergovernmental fiscal transfers, substantially affect local fiscal performance.

Fourth, various types of intergovernmental fiscal transfers have been adopted, but the principal types are formula-based revenue-sharing schemes between the central government and local government (IRA) and among local governments (real property tax revenues). Both from the points of view of the national and local governments, the IRA is the single most important form of transfer. Although the share of the allotment to LGUs in the total budget of the national government has significantly increased under the devolution, the increase however is still not enough to threaten overall macroeconomic stability (Loehr and Manasan 1999).

Fifth, relative to the allocation of the IRA and other tax revenues, the distribution of central and interlocal grants is less transparent. Neither the distribution formulas nor the characteristics of the recipients and the amounts they receive are well documented. The relative lack of transparency reinforces the perception that some of these grants are sources of pork barrel funds. Part of the problem also lies in current government accounting practices, which detail cash transfers but not in-kind transfers. Relatively little is known about interlocal fiscal transfers.

Sixth, the IRA generally has some positive effects on local fiscal performance and may have led to overall improvements in welfare. Both the local revenues and expenditures of the provinces and cities were found to be elastic with respect to the IRA. Increases in the IRA do not appear to have substituted for local revenue mobilization, and they have a positive impact on local economic service provision and capital outlays. The huge increments in the IRA also appear to have helped improve local health status, literacy and average family income in some areas during the last decade. However, the IRA also appear to have worsened fiscal imbalances. Neither it nor any transfer programs in the Philippines can be properly characterized as a fiscal equalization grant scheme.

Seventh, the national government appears to favor the direct provision of infrastructure over the extension of capital grants to local governments, and it continues to directly provide infrastructure services that are now officially devolved to LGUs. In addition, the distribution of the capital outlays of the national government is favorable to urban areas and traditional regional centers, particularly the Metropolitan Manila Area and its surrounding regions. Since infrastructure investment increases growth potential, the national government influences the future pattern of regional growth.

Finally, there are now various mechanisms that enable LGUs to access ODA-funded capital grants and loans, which also tend to favor urban areas. The most important is the Municipal Development Fund. Comprising ODA grants and loans, the MDF provides an alternative source of financing to LGUs. Grants under the MDF are tied to loan conditionalities and sometimes require equity contributions form LGU borrowers. For some local governments, stringent MDF requirements are difficult to meet. In addition, the centralized operations of the MDF raise the transaction costs of LGU borrowers in remote areas.

2. Policy Recommendations

Some genuine progress has been made in recent years under the Philippines' fiscal decentralization program. Given the persistent inequities and unevenness in regional growth and development and the worsening fiscal imbalances, however, we identify several policy recommendations as high priorities.

Improving consistency in the design and implementation of macroeconomic policy, fiscal policy and intergovernmental fiscal transfer programs. Various earlier studies on the history of economic development in the

Philippines consistently emphasized the disastrous consequences of certain macroeconomic policies, especially trade and industrialization policy, on regional growth and development. Given the persistent inequities in regional economic performance, these lessons should be remembered. Macroeconomic policies can greatly influence the extent of regional economic activities and local fiscal performance. Thus, macroeconomic policies must be as consistent as possible with the avowed objectives of fiscal decentralization.

A serious concern in this regard is that the national government continues to be the direct provider of many basic infrastructure services at the local level, but the regional budget allocation of key national government agencies does not seem to help reduce interregional disparities. Social service expenditures are focused on the low-income regions, but infrastructure expenditures are focused on high-income regions. How these realities affect the budget and national development goals needs more serious consideration. Furthermore, improvements in the tax collections at both the national and local levels would have major implications for the pool of resources available for intergovernmental fiscal transfers.

Enhancing consistency in the design and implementation of central fiscal transfers and interlocal fiscal transfers. The most important concern here is the extent to which central fiscal transfers promote or discourage revenue sharing among LGUs. While certain local revenue-sharing schemes are mandated, cost-sharing and other joint cooperative undertakings among local governments are seldom observed. These joint undertakings are necessary for a more efficient provision of local public services, especially where inter-jurisdictional spillovers occur and the joint use of local facilities (such as hospitals) is appropriate. Current central fiscal transfers promote efficient provision by extending a subsidy to the LGU that provides the service or maintains the facility, but this does not promote cooperation among all concerned LGUs. To achieve greater sustainability in local public service provision, the national government should facilitate cooperation rather than simply subsidize the cost of provision.

To achieve greater fiscal balance, the IRA should be adjusted to reduce the gaps in effective per capita shares of rural and urban localities or at least between provinces and cities. Interlocal transfers should also be explicitly factored into the IRA adjustments, since most provinces also provide assistance to their component cities. Moreover, the revenue-raising capabilities of the local government units should be included as an allocation criterion to encourage greater local revenue mobilization. The IRA could also be adjusted to reflect horizontal fiscal imbalances.

As the IRA allocation formula is adjusted, it should remain as simple, transparent, and predictable as the current formula. More importantly, it is necessary to build a political consensus behind the proposed changes. Toward this objective, a gradual or phased-in adjustment in the IRA that will minimize a diminution in the current shares of the LGUs is important. The adjustment, for example, may be limited to the annual increment in the total IRA share until such time that the desired level of fiscal balance is achieved. In addition, policy makers, stakeholders, and the general public must be widely informed of the real causes and consequences of the fiscal imbalances, and what the IRA adjustments will imply.

A speedy and acceptable resolution of a number of other issues concerning the IRA can help focus attention on proposed adjustments to the IRA formula. Among these are whether or not the IRA should be based on the gross or net collections of the bureau of internal revenue, whether unfunded mandates should be financed out of the IRA or with other national government funds, whether the IRA should be based on the second year instead of the third year preceding the year during which the allocations are made, and whether the required 20% allotment for local development projects overly restricts the LGUs on how to spend the IRA.

Institutionalizing a fiscal equalization grant mechanism. The proposed adjustments to the IRA at best address only the fiscal imbalances on the revenue side. A fiscal equalization grant mechanism should also be introduced to adjust for the differences in the levels and costs of public service provision and to fine-tune whatever gaps remain in local fiscal capacities. While the adjustment in the IRA would become more permanent, the fiscal equalization grant could be more flexible, an important feature given the fluctuations in local incomes.

A number of factors must be considered in the specification of the fiscal equalization grant. On the revenue side, it should factor in the effects of other central fiscal transfers on local revenue mobilization, the direct provision by the national government of local public services, and interlocal revenue-sharing schemes. On the expenditure side, the implicit transfers among LGUs must also be considered, as in the case of joint use of hospital facilities. Thus, the fiscal equalization grant could support cooperative undertakings at the local level, which would be critical to the efficient operation of certain local service network systems.

For political acceptability, the suggested adjustment in the IRA allocation formula and the fiscal equalization grant scheme should be introduced as one package intended to address imbalances in regional growth and development. To finance the fiscal equalization grant, there could be a reprogramming of certain redundant central fiscal transfers, such as the countrywide development fund. The adjustment in the IRA would likely be protracted, however, given its relative importance and long history. Thus, a pilot test of the fiscal equalization grant scheme would be necessary. The pilot should help improve the design and the implementation of the grant scheme, and serve as an advocacy mechanism for its wider acceptability. In this activity, the national government would require assistance from the donor community and other multilateral institutions.

Improving the distribution of infrastructure investments, centrally provided local public goods and services, and the access of LGUs to ODA-funded development resources. Strictly speaking, some infrastructure expenditures of the national government may not be classified as transfers. Nonetheless, they confer benefits that are limited to narrow areas, comprising perhaps a few local governments, in sectors such as education and health. These infrastructure expenditures will have an impact on the types, amounts and qualities of services available across regions as local governments adjust their own expenditure priorities. Thus, the fiscal incidence of the national government infrastructure investments can be likened to that of capital grants or other transfers and will obviously impact overall fiscal balance and, ultimately, regional development. To improve the distribution of infrastructure investments, the incidence of local capital spending must be studied carefully, starting with a proper accounting of infrastructure investments by the different levels of governments. With such information, appropriate capital financing schemes can be designed to elicit greater local capital spending.

One promising channel is the Municipal Development Fund, which has both grant and local components. To become a more effective conduit of ODA, the operation of the MDF needs to be enhanced. In particular, its operation must be simplified and decentralized to increase LGU access, especially in rural areas. In addition, it is suggested that the MDF specialize in extending assistance to low-income LGUs, which cannot access commercial credit lines. Toward this, the MDF may also open a window for small grants. While this will increase the transaction costs of the MDF, these should be weighed against the expected gains from increased beneficiaries.

Developing a national fiscal transfer accounts system. A far more complete accounting of all types of intergovernmental fiscal transfers in the country must be undertaken, with the end goal of developing a national fiscal transfer accounts system (similar to the national income accounts and the national health accounts).[26] The development of this system would serve two major purposes.

---

26. The development of a national fiscal transfer accounts system would involve the participation of key national government agencies, including NEDA, the Department of Budget and Management, the Department of Interior and Local Government, and the Department of Finance. NEDA has already undertaken some initial steps that can lead to the development of the fiscal accounts system. Once developed, the national statistical coordination board can maintain and update the accounts system.

First, it would provide a complete mapping of the different intergovernmental fiscal transfer schemes in the country. The accounts system would have all the pertinent information such as the sources, types, amounts, purposes and actual uses of the funds, as well as the characteristics of the grantor and recipients. ODA grants should also be included to have a more complete resource picture. Greater transparency and accountability in the allocation of public resources can be achieved with such a system, allowing stakeholders and policy makers to make more informed and careful decisions. In countries where most types of central fiscal transfers are jointly determined under one agency (e.g., Australia), the availability of information similar to that contained in the proposed national fiscal transfer accounts system allows for the timely, consistent and efficient adjustments in transfer schemes.

Second, policy simulations could be undertaken with the database prior to making allocation decisions to avoid unnecessary and costly mistakes, thus improving the overall efficiency, effectiveness and equity of intergovernmental fiscal transfers. If a similar system had been in place in 1991, for example, the IRA formula could have been adjusted to account for the distribution of the devolved functions. But since the relevant data were not available, the national government was forced to create adjustment funds and tinker with the IRA formula later. The database could also be used to assess the implications of suggested reforms in intergovernmental fiscal transfers schemes on local fiscal performance, local service provision, interlocal revenue- or cost-sharing arrangements, overall fiscal balance and equity, the national budget, and the macroeconomy. More importantly, the assessment could be undertaken in a more general-equilibrium type setting than is possible with partial information. Overall, creating this system would lay a solid foundation for developing intergovernmental fiscal arrangements that better support both national and local development goals.

References

Alonzo, R.P. 1999. Channeling resources to local development concerns: issues and options. In *Studies in Governance and Regulation: The Philippines*, edited by D.B. Canlas and S. Fujisaki. Tokyo: Institute of Developing Economies.

———. 1998. Local Governance and Poverty Alleviation. In *Growth, Poverty and Income Inequality in the Philippines*, edited by A.M. Balisacan and S. Fujisaki. Tokyo: Institute of Developing Economies.

Bahl, R. and B.D. Miller, eds. 1983. *Local Government Finance in the Third World: A Case Study of the Philippines*. New York: Praeger.

Balgos, C.C.A. 2001. *Investigating Local Governments. A Manual for Reporters*. Quezon City: PCIJ.

Bautista, V.A. and L.J. Juan. 2000. *An Anlysis of the Minimum Basic Needs Approach and its Potential for Assessing Governance.* Paper submitted to the Philippine Center For Policy Studies-Governance Project. Quezon City: PCPS.

Boadway, R. and F. Flatters. 1982. Efficiency and Equalization Payments in a Federal System of Government: A Synthesis and Extension of Recent Results. *Canadian Journal of Economics* 15(4): 613–633.

Brillantes, A.B. 1987. Decentralization in the Philippines: An Overview. *Philippine Journal of Public Administration* 31(2): 131–148.

Briones, L. 1983. *Philippine Public Fiscal Administration.* National Research Council of the Philippines.

Burton, E.M. 2000. *Baseline Study on the Indicators of Good Governance in Davao del Norte Province.* Paper submitted to the Philippine Center for Policy Studies-Governance Project. Quezon City: PCPS.

Capuno, J.J. 1997. *A Positive Analysis of Three Issues in the Decentralization of Health Services in the Philippines.* Unpublished Ph.D. dissertation. Quezon City: U.P. School of Economics.

————. 2001a. Policy Reform Under Decentralization: Financing of Health Services in the Philippines. *Regional Development Studies* 7 (forthcoming).

————. 2001b. *Estimating the Income Elasticity of Local Government Revenues and Expenditures Under Decentralization.* UPSE Discussion Paper No. 0102. Quezon City: U.P. School of Economics.

————. 2001c. *Further Estimates of the "IRA Elasticity" of Various Local Government Revenues and Expenditures Under Decentralization.* Quezon City: U.P. School of Economics.

————, T.C. Manuel and B.T. Salvador. 2001. *Estimating the IRA, Centrally Provided Local Public Goods Services and Other Central Fiscal Transfers.* Report submitted to NEDA. Pasig City: NEDA-RDCS.

Congress of the Philippines. 1991. *The Local Government Code of 1991.* Quezon City.

Coombs, G. 1999. *Review of the Local Government Internal Revenue Allotment Scheme in the Philippines.* Report submitted to AUSAID. Makati City.

Cuaresma, J.C. 1992. *Can Local Governments Financially Cope Up?* Mimeograph National College of Public Administration and Governance. U.P. Diliman, Quezon City.

———— and S. Ilago. 1996. *Local Fiscal Administration in the Philippines.* LGC and German Foundation for International Development.

Dahlby, B. and L.S. Wilson.1994. Fiscal Capacity, Tax Effort, and Optimal Equalization Grants. *Canadian Journal of Economics* 27(3): 657–72.

De Dios, E., ed. 1984. *An Analysis of the Philippine Economic Crisis.* Diliman, Quezon City: University of the Philippines Press.

Department of Finance. 2001. *Project Profile on Foreign-Assisted Projects under the Municipal Development Fund (MDF).* Manila.

Diokno, B.E. 1994. 1991 Decentralization Act: After the Birthing Pain—Grief or Glee? In *Political-Economic Restructuring and National Development.* Quezon City: Philippine Economic Society and the Friedrich Ebert Stiftung.

Hulten, C.H. and R.M. Schwab. 1997. A Fiscal Federalism Approach to Infrastructure Policy. *Regional Science and Urban Economics* 27: 139–159.

Human Development Network. 1994. *Philippine Human Development Report 1994.* Quezon City: Human Development Network and the United Nations Development Programme.

———. 1997. *Philippine Human Development Report 1997.* Quezon City: Human Development Network and the United Nations Development Programme.

———. 2000. *Philippine Human Development Report 2000.* Quezon City: Human Development Network and the United Nations Development Programme.

Lamberte, M., *et al.* 1993. *Decentralization and Prospects for Regional Growth.* Makati: Philippine Institute for Development Studies (PIDS).

Lim, J.Y. and K. Nozawa, eds. 1992. *Decentralization and Economic Development in the Philippines.* Tokyo: Institute of Developing Economies.

Llanto, G. 1997. *Towards Reforming the Municipal Development Fund.* GOLD Occasional Paper No. 97–02. Manila.

Loehr, W. and R. Manasan. 1999. *Fiscal Decentralization and Economic Efficiency: Measurement and Evaluation.* CAER II Discussion Paper No. 38. Cambridge, Massachussetts: Harvard Institute for International Development.

Ma, J. 1997. *Intergovernmental Fiscal Transfers in Nine Countries: Lessons for Developing Countries.* Policy Research Working Paper No. 1822. Macroeconomic Management and Policy Division. Economic Development Institute. Washington, D.C.: The World Bank.

Manasan, R.G. 1992. Fiscal Implications of the Local Government Code of 1991. *Journal of Philippine Development* 19(1): 1–58.

———. 1992. *Intergovernmental Fiscal Relations, Fiscal Federalism, and Economic Development in the Philippines.* Philippine Institute for Development Studies Working Paper Series No. 92–04. Makati City: PIDS.

———. 1994. *Breaking Away From the Fiscal Bind: Reforming the Fiscal System.* Makati City: PIDS.

———. 1995. *Revenue Mobilization in Local Government Units: The Early Years of Local Government Code Implementation.* PIDS Discussion Paper No. 95–02. Makati City: PIDS.

———. 1997. *Local Government Financing of Social Service Sectors in a Decentralized Regime: Special Focus on Provincial Governments in 1993 and 1994.* PIDS Discussion Paper No. 97–04. Makati City: PIDS.

———. 1998. *Financing and Delivery of Urban Services in the Philippines: An Overview.* PIDS Discussion Paper No. 98–37. Makati City: PIDS.

Matthews, R. 1974. Fiscal Equalization for Local Government. *The Economic Record* (September): 329–345.

Mercado, R.G. 1999. *Regional Budget Allocation: A Policy Revisit.* PIDS Discussion Paper No. 99–29. Makati City: PIDS.

Miral, Romulo Emmanuel, Jr. 2000. *An Analysis of the President's Budget for Fiscal Year 2001.* Mimeograph. Quezon City: Congressional Planning and Budget Office. House of Representatives.

National Economic Development Authority.1984. *Updated Philippine Development Plan 1984–1987.* Pasig City: NEDA.

———. 1987. *Medium-Term Philippine Development Plan 1987–1992.* Pasig City: NEDA.

————. 1993. *Medium-Term Philippine Development Plan 1993–1998.* Pasig City: NEDA.

————. 1999. *Medium-Term Philippine Development Plan 1999–2004.* Pasig City: NEDA.

————. 2000. *ODA Handbook: Guidelines on the Availment of Official Development Assistance.* Pasig City: NEDA.

Papers presented during the *National Policy Workshop on Fiscal Equalization and the IRA* on June 14, 1999 at the EDSA Shangri-la Hotel in Mandaluyong City, sponsored by the Union of Local Authorities of the Philippines, the Department of the Interior and Local Government, and the Australian Agency for Intrnational Development.

Papers presented during the *Funding Local Development Projects Conference* on May 3–5, 2000 at the Manila Midtown Hotel, Manila.

Pimentel, A., Jr. 1993. *The Local Government Code of 1991. The Key to National Development.* Mandaluyong City: Cacho Publishing House, Inc.

Premiumed II Primer. 1999. Department of Finance.

Serafica, R.B. 1998. *Beyond 2000: An Assessment of Infrastructure Policies.* PIDS Discussion Paper No. 98–07. Makati City: PIDS.

Shah, A. 1991. *Perspectives on the Design of Intergovernmental Fiscal Relations.* World Bank Policy, Research and External Affairs Working Paper Series No. 726. Washington, D.C.: The World Bank.

————. 1994. *The Reform of Intergovernmental Fiscal Relations in Developing and Emerging Market Economies.* The World Bank Policy and Research Series No. 23. Washington, D.C.: The World Bank.

Tapales, P.D. 1993. *Devolution and Empowerment: The Local Government Code of 1991 and Local Autonomy in the Philippines.* Quezon City: UP Center for Integrative and Development Studies.

Tapales, P.D. *et al.*, eds. 1998. *Local Government in the Philippines: A Book of Readings (vol. 1).* CLRG-UP NCPAG. Kadena Press, Inc.

Ter-Minassian, T. ed. 1997. *Fiscal Federalism in Theory and Practice.* Washington, D.C.: IMF.

Valdellon, I. 1998. *Strategic Planning for Locality Development: Policy Framework.* A speech delivered at the Forum-Workshop on Strategic Planning for Locality Development, Philippine Women's University on January 21, 1998.

World Bank. 1994. *Philippines Devolution and Health Services: Managing Risks and Opportunities.* Population and Human Resource Operation Division, East Asia and Pacific Region Office. Report No. 12343-PH. Washington, D.C.: The World Bank.

————. 1995. Philippines Public Expenditure Management for Sustained and Equitable Growth, Volumes I and II. Country Operations Division, East Asia and Pacific Region. Report No. 14680-PH. Washington, D.C.: The World Bank.

————. 2000. *Combating Corruption in the Philippines.* Washington, D.C.: The World Bank.

————. 2000. *Philippines. Growth with Equity: The Remaining Agenda.* Washington, D.C.: The World Bank.   ⋈